THE ṢAṬSĀHASRA SAṂHITĀ

Chapters 1-5

EDITED, TRANSLATED AND ANNOTATED

BY

J. A. SCHOTERMAN

LEIDEN
E. J. BRILL
1982

CIP-DATA

Schoterman, J.A. — The Ṣaṭsāhasra saṃhitā: chapters 1-5 / ed., transl. and annot. by J.A. Schoterman. — Leiden: Brill. — (Orientalia rheno-traiectina; vol. 27)
UDC 891.2

ISBN 90 04 06850 3

PRINTED IN THE NETHERLANDS

THE ṢAṬSĀHASRA SAṂHITĀ

ORIENTALIA RHENO-TRAIECTINA

EDIDIT

J. GONDA

VOLUMEN VICESIMUM SEPTIMUM

J. A. SCHOTERMAN

THE ṢAṬSĀHASRA SAṂHITĀ

Chapters 1-5

LEIDEN
E. J. BRILL
1982

Vis disputare? Ita. Quid est ita? Ick en weets niet.
Soo sijdy dan victus; tis een schotel beschees siet.

(from: Een schoone ende wonderlijcke prognosticatie van Sloctoors Ulenspieghels calculatie (Antwerpen, 1560))

For Bibi

CONTENTS

PART ONE

INTRODUCTION

PART TWO

ṢAṬSĀHASRA SAṂHITĀ

PREFACE

On the occasion of the publication of my doctoral thesis at the State University of Utrecht, The Netherlands, I wish to thank my supervisor, Prof. Dr. H. W. Bodewitz, who kindly took the trouble to familiarize himself profoundly with the subject and whose critical remarks and suggestions have been of great value to me. To Dr. T. Goudriaan, who acted as co-referent, I am very deeply indebted for the kind and patient way in which he followed and supported my research in the field of Hindu Tantrism. Without the never failing support of his extensive knowledge of the subject and his dedication to it the present study would have suffered from many more shortcomings. Dr. M. Witzel has been of indispensable assistance in procuring microfilms of the manuscripts from the National Archives (Kathmandu), when he was stationed in the Valley for the German-Nepal Manuscript Preservation Project. The Institute of Oriental Languages (Utrecht) has shown every possible co-operation in acquiring the microfilms and in permitting me the use of the equipment to read them.

Although Prof. Dr. J. Gonda had no direct concern with the realization of this study I consider it a matter of personal obligation to express here my feelings of sincere gratitude and admiration towards this scholar: I have always regarded it a rare privilege to have had a guru of such qualities.

Finally I whish to thank my father, because he allowed me to become an Indologist, and whose support has always been very reliable. I am proud to have such a friend.

J. A. Schoterman,
Leiden, 1981.

ABBREVIATIONS

Agni P	=	Agni Purāṇa.
ASB	=	Asiatic Society of Bengal.
AV	=	Atharva Veda.
BEFEO	=	Bulletin de l'École Française d'Extrême Orient.
BhP	=	Bhāgavata Purāṇa.
BKI	=	Bijdragen tot de Taal-, Land- en Volkenkunde.
BSOAS	=	Bulletin of the School of Oriental and African Studies.
IHQ	=	Indian Historical Quarterly.
JRAS	=	Journal of the Royal Asiatic Society.
KA	=	Kauṭilīya Arthaśāstra.
KJñN	=	Kaulajñānanirṇaya.
KmT	=	Kubjikāmata Tantra.
KnT	=	Kubjikānityāhnikatilaka.
KP	=	Kālikā Purāṇa.
KRP	=	Kulamūlaratnapañcakāvatāra.
MBh	=	Mahābhārata.
MbhT	=	Mātṛkābheda Tantra.
MNT	=	Mahānirvāṇa Tantra.
MVT	=	Mālinīvijayottara Tantra.
M.-W.	=	Sir Monier Monier-Williams' A Sanskrit-English Dictionary.
NAK	=	National Archives at Kathmandu (Nepal).
ṚgS	=	Ṛgveda Saṃhitā.
SaṃP	=	Saṃvartārthaprakāśa.
SaṃT	=	Saṃvarodaya Tantra.
ṢaṭSS	=	Ṣaṭsāhasra Saṃhitā.
ŚT	=	Śāradātilaka Tantra.
ŚT[a]	=	Śāradātilaka Tantra (ed. by Bakshi).
SVT	=	Svacchanda Tantra.
Ṭ	=	Ṭippanī.
TĀ	=	Tantrāloka.
VS	=	Vājasaneyi Saṃhitā.
ZDMG	=	Zeitschrift der Deutschen Morgenländischen Gesellschaft.

PART ONE

INTRODUCTION

INTRODUCTION

General Remarks

Of the enormous mass of Indian religious literature which is available from the Vedic period onwards, a not insignificant part is formed by a group of texts which are called Tantras or which propagate Tantric ideas. With the exception of the Sikh religion the major Indian religions have produced their own body of Tantric literature. Thus we find Hindu [1], Buddhist and Jain Tantras. Especially the Hindu and Buddhist Tantras constitute a rather voluminous body of literature. Originating from the Indian Subcontinent the Hindu and Buddhist Tantras have found their way to many Asian countries. With the expansion of Buddhism over Asia the Buddhist Tantras gained great popularity in countries such as Tibet, Mongolia (cf. Tucci & Heissig 1970: 341 ff.) and China (cf. Van Gulik 1961: Appendix I). In much the same way Hindu Tantras became widely spread in Southeast Asia (cf. Coedès 1964; Cchabra 1965), but unfortunately no tangible proof in the form of manuscripts is available. Yet from inscriptions (cf. the Sdok kak Thom inscription; Goudriaan & Gupta 1981: 21) it becomes clear that at one time Hindu Tantras were found in, for instance, Cambodia (cf. Bagchi 1926 & 1930; Sharan 1974: Index *s.v.* Tantra). Only recently the existence of part of the Vīṇāśikha Tantra, an old Śaiva Tantra, was attested for on the island of Bali (Goudriaan 1981: 477 ff.). In our times Hindu Tantras are confined to India and Nepal. Especially the latter country is important for the study of Hindu Tantrism because many of the Tantric texts were preserved in this country after the Muslim conquest of northern India.

Although especially in the last fifty years Tantra has become a subject for study by Indologists and has gained some popularity with a wider audience in Europe and abroad, Tantrism and the ideas it stands for are still insufficiently known. There are several reasons to account for this lack of knowledge. For a long period Tantric literature was ignored by Indologists as a part of their studies mainly because of the alleged depravity of its contents. In the past Tantras were often regarded as "mere manuals of mysticism, magic and superstition of the worst and most silly kind" (Monier-Williams 1877, repr. 1951: 90). Together with the fact that the kind of Sanskrit found in these texts could hardly meet *Pāṇinian* standards, Tantric literature was readily shoved aside. Due to the publications of the former Justice of the High Court at Calcutta, Sir John Woodroffe (*alias* Arthur Avalon), a true appraisal of

[1] With Hindu Tantras the Tantric texts of the Śaivas, Śāktas and Vaiṣṇavas are meant.

Tantric literature and its ideas developed with western scholars. It is quite true that Tantric Sanskrit often deviates from the rules of Classical Sanskrit, but in itself this is no reason to condemn it as bad or inferior Sanskrit. Just as Edgerton has shown that the kind of Sanskrit found in many Buddhist texts should be regarded as a separate idiom, in the same way Hindu Tantric Sanskrit might one day become accepted as a kind of Sanskrit with its own merits and pecularities. To achieve this, however, a careful study of the oldest Tantric texts is necessary, which is only possible when critical editions of these texts are available (cf. Schoterman 1979: 325 ff.). Here we encounter one of the most serious obstacles which block the way for a full appreciation of Tantric literature, i.e. the lack of critically edited texts. The majority of Tantric texts which are available in printed form suffer from a total absence of any critical standards, but at least they are edited. More often, however, we do not have at our disposal printed editions of Tantric texts. The fact that the texts are often available in the form of manuscripts only increases the inaccessibility of Tantric literature seriously. To some extent this situation is improved upon by the German-Nepal Manuscript Preservation Project which has collected on microfilm an impressive amount of Tantric manuscripts from Nepal. It can only be hoped that manuscripts from India will become available to international scholars in much the same way.

Apart from the fact that the Sanskrit as found in many Tantric texts is now slowly gaining its own place within the context of Sanskrit in general, the contents of Tantric texts are no longer regarded as sheer nonsense or as the products of deranged minds. The period that a publisher could be brought to trial because he edited a Tantra (cf. Woodroffe 1975: 44) has passed long since.

In view of the foregoing the deficient state of our knowledge of Tantrism becomes understandable. Consequently it is difficult to answer such rather basic questions as with regard to the true nature of a Tantra, its ideas, origins, antiquity etc. In recent years the study of Hindu Tantrism by western scholars has resulted in the publication of two important works: '*Recherches sur la Symbolique et l'Énergie de la Parole dans certains textes Tantriques*', which still awaits an English translation, by André Padoux (Paris, 1963; repr. 1975), and '*Hindu Tantric Literature In Sanskrit*' by Teun Goudriaan (in: Goudriaan & Gupta 1981). Especially in the second publication one finds a serious attempt to answer those questions pertaining to the contents, age etc. of Hindu Tantras, all within the limited context of our present knowledge of Hindu Tantrism. I do not think it useful to repeat here all the conclusions the author of the above study has reached. Yet it is perhaps convenient to quote the author on some problems with regard to Hindu Tantrism, which have long been the source of a general misunderstanding. Thus it is pointed out that the early development of Hindu Tantrism, especially the Śaiva component of it, "was not based upon a popular movement, but was the outgrowth of the specialistic position of an intellectual élite of religious functionaries from the upper classes, as a rule of Brahmans" (*op. cit.*, p. 9), and that "the existence of Hindu Tantras cannot as yet be proved for the period before A.D. 800, but that the origins of Tantric literature may very well lie in a considerably earlier period" (*op. cit.*, p. 22).

The School of Kubjikā

Among the numerous texts of Hindu Tantrism there exists a rather independent group of manuscripts which mainly deal with the worship and cult of the goddess Kubjikā as a manifestation of Devī. The first scholar who paid some attention to this deity and to the Tantric School to which she belongs, was H. P. Śāstri. In the two volumes of his catalogue of manuscripts from the Durbar Library (the present National Archives) at Kathmandu (Śāstri 1905 and 1915) mention is made of some twenty-five manuscripts belonging to the School of Kubjikā. Special attention is paid by Śāstri to our MS A (Śāstri's G(overnment) G(upta) MS; see p. 16), which belongs to the collection of the Royal Asiatic Society of Bengal. After Śāstri's remarks at the beginning of this century no further progress in the study of this particular Tantric School is reported, although the colophons of the various manuscripts were used to some extent to establish the early and medieval history of Nepal (cf. Regmi 1965 & 1966) because of the dates they contain.

In the early Seventies a group of scholars at the Institute of Oriental Languages (State University of Utrecht, The Netherlands) decided to prepare a critical edition of the Kubjikāmata Tantra (cf. Van Kooy 1973: 628), the oldest text of this Tantric School. In the course of research a list containing more than 250 manuscripts was compiled, all belonging to the School of Kubjikā (cf. Schoterman 1977: 932). Although our knowledge of the School of Kubjikā has increased since, it is still far from complete. Many fundamental questions remain to be answered.

The fact that all the relevant manuscripts originate from Nepal, seems to justify the assumption that the cult of Kubjikā is primarily of Nepalese origin (cf. Goudriaan & Gupta 1981: 52), although references to Kubjikā and her School are occasionally found in texts from India [2]. One does not find any

[2] There are two texts outside the body of texts belonging directly to the Kubjikā School, in which references are found to Kubjikā or the Kubjikāmata. Thus in the Agnipurāṇa there are five chapters dealing with the cult of Kubjikā (AgniP 143-147). It appears that the contents of these chapters are drawn from the ṢaṭSS and the KnT rather than from the KmT (cf. Schoterman 1980: 346). The other text is the Gorakṣa Saṃhitā which shows a close relationship to the Śrīmatottara Tantra, a text of the Kubjikā School (cf. Śāstri 1905: LXXVIII & 2; Pāṇḍeya 1976: ḍ). The manuscript of the Śrīmatottara Tantra which Śāstri describes, ends with the same lines as the 27th chapter of the Gorakṣa Saṃhitā (Śāstri 1905: 257; Gorakṣa Saṃhitā 27,240;

corroboration for this assumption in the texts themselves, however. The origin of the Kubjikāmata Tantra and the Ṣaṭsāhasra Saṃhitā, a text which is closely related to the Kubjikāmata Tantra, in historical times is set at an Indian background: the nine Nāthas who propagated the doctrine of Kubjikā in our times, are all of North Indian origin (cf. p. 37). Besides this, one region in India, namely Koṅkaṇa, seems to be of special importance for the School (cf. Schoterman 1977: 934). Are its historical origins still a mystery, the development of the School in Nepal is equally unknown. Since the oldest manuscripts of the Kubjikāmata Tantra are dated in the first half of the 12th century A.D. (MSS B&D), the existence of the School of Kubjikā is attested for the beginning of the 12th century, but may well be several centuries earlier. Despite the remark by A. Bharati that Kubjikā is still worshipped by the Bhūṭiyas of Almora and that she has many small shrines in the Nepalese and Indian *terai* (Bharati 1965: 66), I have not been able to find any confirmation for this statement. It seems that Kubjikā ceased to be worshipped sometime around the 15th or 16th century A.D. (cf. Regmi 1966: 585), although manuscripts of the School were still being copied in our century (MS C; cf. p. 19).

Despite the abundance of manuscripts relating to the Kubjikā School which is available and which suggests a rather great popularity of the cult for the period between 900-1600 A.D. in Nepal, references to Kubjikā and the Kubjikā School are very rare in contemporary literature. There are, for instance, a few quotations from the Kubjikā School in Abhinavagupta's Tantrāloka, which I have not been able to trace back in the texts so far, but on the whole contemporary sources keep silent on the Kubjikāmata. The same applies to later sources.

We are confronted then with a Tantric school which must have been rather popular at one time in view of the many manuscripts and texts still available, but which remained very independent and stood aloof from the other Tantric schools. This does not imply, however, that the fundamental concepts followed by the School of Kubjikā are completely different from those of the

---

243cd-244). The beginning of the Gorakṣa Saṃhitā probably deals with the Santānabhuvana of the ṢaṭSS (1,6-10), but unfortunately the edition of the text is not complete (cf. Gorakṣa Saṃhitā 2,26ab where *trisandhyā* (ṢaṭSS 1,8a) and *trikapāṭārgalā* (ṢaṭSS 1,8d) are mentioned). The rest of the second chapter appears to deal with the Mahāpīṭhas, and shows a close resemblance with chapter 4/5 of the ṢaṭSS (Gorakṣa Saṃhitā pp. 9 ff.). Furthermore, the *prastāra-* and *gahvara-*system (cf. Appendix I) is found in the Gorakṣasaṃhitā: *vajragahvaraṃ prastārya* (14,6c). In the 24th chapter Vajrakubjikā is discussed (24,75 ff.), who features in the 39th chapter of the ṢaṭSS (see p. 15). The initial line of the 10th chapter of the Gorakṣa Saṃhitā (10,1ab) is identical with KmT 7,1ab (= ṢaṭSS 13,1ab *yā sā deva parā yoniḥ samayā kubjinī parā*). There can be found many more instances which point to a close relationship between the Gorakṣa Saṃhitā and the texts of the Kubjikā School. A connection between the Kubjikā School and the tradition of Goraknāth was already assumed by Bharati (Bharati 1965: 66).

other Tantric schools of the period. Thus concepts as the triple or fourfold division of creation (e.g. *parāpara*; *para*, *sūkṣma*, *sthūla*; cf. 3, 103-104 Notes), the six Cakras, the four Siddhas (Khagendra, Kūrma, Meṣa, Matsyendranātha; cf. Schoterman 1977: 934) are shared by the Kubjikā School with the other Tantric schools of Kashmir Śaivism. Only further study of the relevant texts may reveal in what aspects the Kubjikā School differs from the other Tantric schools, and what its particular features are (cf. the five Cakras: 3, 32a). Although the doctrine of the Kubjikā School appears to be rather independent, this does not mean that it could escape classification within the Tantric tradition, even if the School itself may have wished to do so.

In the classification of the various Tantric schools in the six *āmnāyas*, or 'traditions' (cf. Goudriaan & Gupta 1981: 17; Gupta a.o. 1979: 41 ff.), the Kubjikāmata is alloted to the Paścimāmnāya, or Western Tradition. References to this Western Tradition, however, are conspicuous by their absence in the text of the Ṣaṭsāhasra Saṃhitā[3], although the system of classification in *āmnāyas* appears to be recognized in the text[4].

The particular *āmnāya* among which the texts of the Kubjikā School reckon themselves and which is frequently mentioned in the colophons, is the so-called Kulālikāmnāya. Since this expression is important with regard to the School of Kubjikā, it might be useful to pay some attention to it. The compound Kulālikāmnāya is usually understood as 'The Tradition of the Potters' (cf. Goudriaan & Gupta 1981: 52), which made Bharati obviously believe that Kubjikā is the tutelary deity of the 'low-caste' potters (Bharati 1965: 66). In Indian society the potter (*kulāla*) belongs to the lowest stratum, the Śūdras. This seems to justify their qualification as 'low-caste', but one should keep in mind that in a *varṇa*- dominated society the majority of the people are reckoned among the Śūdras. It appears, however, that the potters occupy a rather prominent place among these 'low-castes'. Although they are

---

[3] Although Śāstri states that there are many references to the Paścimāmnāya in our MS A of the ṢaṭSS (Śātri 1905: LXXX), I have been able to find only one such a reference in the 39th chapter of the ṢaṭSS, which appears to be lacking, however, in the manuscript of MS A which I had at my disposal. The mention of the Paścimāmnāya in the 39th chapter is made in connection with the instructions for drawing the Vajra Gahvara (cf. Appendix I): "only the followers of the Paścimāmnāya have access to the Vajra Gahvara" (MS B F.318B).

[4] Thus we find a reference to the Pūrvāmnāya in chapter 29 (MS B F.244A), while the followers of the Pūrvāmnāya are mentioned in 3,112. The Dakṣiṇāmnāya is mentioned in the 18th chapter (MS B F.168B), and the Uttarāmnāya in the 13th chapter (MS B F.104B). Besides the division in *āmnāyas* there exists a, probably older, devision according to *srotas*, 'current': Dakṣiṇa, Vāma and Siddhānta (cf. Gupta a.o. 1979: 41; Goudriaan & Gupta 1981: 16ff.). This division is also referred to in the ṢaṭSS (cf. 3,35 Notes). A division of Tantric texts which is based on geographical principles, is the division into three so-called *krāntas*, 'steps' (cf. Gupta a.o. 1979: 43ff.). Woodroffe mentions the Kubjikā Tantra as belonging to the Viṣṇukrānta, one of the three 'steps' (Woodroffe 1978: 73). this Kubjikā Tantra which especially in Bengal is very popular, has nothing to do with the Kubjikāmata Tantra (cf. Schoterman 1977: Note 6). Of this Kubjikā Tantra there appears to be a printed edition (cf. Woodroffe 1978: 75).

excluded from Vedic ritual and their product, the pot, is considered to be *asuric* (cf. Rau 1972: 13), the potters are mentioned in the Śatarudriya (VS 16, 27) together with other members of the working classes. Being the offspring of an illicit union of a Brahmin and a Vaiśya-female (Kane II-1: 78) they are regarded as *bhojyānnas*, i.e. food prepared by them could be partaken by Brahmins (Kane II-1: 122). It is quite understandable that the potters enjoyed some respect among the Śūdras. In a rural community the presence of a potter is almost indispensable because of the product he manufactures, namely a pot. Besides as the producer of this important daily utensil the potter appears to have carried out "certain ritual tasks which may date from prehistoric urn burial and have augmented to make him virtually the priest to certain lower castes" (Kosambi 1977: 21). Next to this the potter is credited with the invention of the clay-plaster in bone-setting (Kosambi 1977: 22). All this makes it clear that the potter played a significant role in the socio-religious life of an Indian village community from very early times onwards. The pot manufactured by the potter is an important daily utensil, but next to this the pot is often regarded as Devī Herself or as Her local manifestation. In many Indian villages Devī is simply represented with an earthen pot (cf. Whitehead 1921: 37 ff.; Index *s.v.*). In view of the foregoing it is understandable that the potter may have gained an important position in a Tantric context. In Tantric ritual the pot is often a central feature as a representation of the womb and by that of the Mother (cf. Przyluski 1950: 122; Neumann 1963: 132; 162) [5]. During Tantric rituals and ceremonies Devī is born again in the pot for the duration of the ritual. For this reason the pot is filled with liquor or water (cf. 3, 21-23 Notes; Devī Upaniṣad 3: *mama yonir apsv anta samudre*), and to symbolize the union of Devī with Her male consort a white thread (= *śukra*, 'semen virile') is knotted around it (cf. 3, 22d). For a supporter of Tantric concepts the potter himself is closely related to four out of the five elements which constitute human life (*mahābhūtas*): earth (*pṛthivī*), water (*āpas*), fire (*tejas*) and wind (*vāyu*).

From the foregoing the relation of the potters with one of the *āmnāyas* becomes acceptable. One might, however, raise some objections to the translation of Kulālikāmnāya with 'Tradition of the Potters'. The first member of the compound *kulālikāmnāya* is *kulālika* or *kulālikā*, most likely the latter as the suffix *-ikā* usually denotes a feminine noun (cf. Pāṇini 3, 108-111; 3, 118 where in the comm. *kaulālaka*, 'pottery', is mentioned). Thus *kulālikā* is a feminine derivation from *kulāla* which denotes a potter (cf. VS 16, 27 Uvaṭa: *kulālāḥ kumbhakārāḥ*). Consequently the expression Kulā-

[5] A very early example for the connection of the Mother-Goddess and the pot is constituted by a potsherd of a jar from the 2nd millennium B.C. (Maheśvar, Nāvdā Tolī excavations), which shows a nude female figurine with spread legs and pronounced breasts (cf. Kosambi 1977: plate 39).

likāmnāya should be understood as the 'Tradition of the Female Potters'. This may seem strange at first sight, but it were especially women who handled the potter's disc, at least its slow-turning variety (cf. Kosambi 1977: 45). Yet I do not think that the 'Tradition of the Female Potters' is what is really meant by the term Kulālikāmnāya. In my opinion the first member of the compound, Kulālikā, should be understood as a personal name for Devī. Perhaps Śāstri was of the same opinion (Śāstri 1915: 71 "Kulālikā or Kubjikā"). This assumption is corroborated by the occurrence of the name Kulālī Tantra as a synonym for Kubjikāmata Tantra (ṢaṭSS MS B F.144A = KmT 10, 33b). Therefore the term Kulālikāmnāya should be interpreted as the 'Tradition of Kulālikā'[6]. There remains the question who this Kulālikā was. We have seen that the word *kulāla* denotes a potter (see above), but this does not imply that the word literally means 'potter'. In contrast to the usual word for 'potter', namely *kuṃbhakāra*, the word *kulāla* appears not to be of Sanskrit origin and its etymology is uncertain (from *kula*, 'mouth of a jar'?). Possibly *kulāla* is a proper name also, and belongs to some non-Aryan tribe whose main occupation was the production of pottery. In this way the Kulālas are perhaps closely related to the Ambaṣṭhas, another non-Aryan tribe, who are also the offspring of a Brahmin and a Vaiśya-female (Brinkhaus 1978: 208). Like the Kulālas the Ambaṣṭhas are potters (Brinkhaus 1978: 208), and have something to do with the art of healing (cf. Manu 10, 47). It seems therefore acceptable that Kulālikā was some local goddess, probably of the Kulāla tribe, who was identified with Devī in Tantric circles — an identification which may have been facilitated by the fact that the main occupation of the Kulālas was the production of pots which are important as a representation of Devī, as we have seen. Finally it might be remarked that the term Kulālikāmnāya is used so frequently in the colophons of the chapters of the ṢaṭSS because one can easily 'recognize' in it the word *kula* (on *kula* see Goudriaan & Gupta 1981: 18 ff.).

Having dealt with the interpretation of the term Kulālikāmnāya at some length it is necessary to say a few words about the name of Kubjikā herself. As a feminine derivation of *kubja* ('bent; curved') the name Kubjikā is usually translated as the Hunchbacked Goddess (cf. Mitra 1971: 191; Bhattacharya 1974: 10). It is very doubtful, however, whether this interpretation of the name is correct. Since no images of Kubjikā seem to exist

[6] The explanation of Kulālikāmnāya as the 'Tradition of Kulālikā' is satisfying in my opinion. Yet mention should be made of another possible explanation of the expression. Besides the meaning 'potter' the word *kulāla* can also mean 'water' (cf. Kuiper 1948: 139). The feminine derivation *kulālikā* might refer to Devī in relation to the waters which are Her place of birth. Or perhaps one should supply the fem. noun *diś*, 'region of the sky'. Then *kulālikā* refers to the western region, the abode of Varuṇa, Lord of the Waters. Following this last interpretation the term Kulālikāmnāya is synonymous with Paścimāmnāya.

(Regmi 1966: 585; Sahai 1975: 205)[7], one cannot decide from iconographic sources whether Kubjikā should be visualized as a deity with a hunchbacked shape. In the Agnipurāṇa (144, 30cd-37; cf. De Mallmann 1963: 159 ff.) and in the Kubjikānityāhnikatilaka (FF. 26B ff.) we find a *dhyānaśloka* of Kubjikā (cf. Schoterman 1980: 344 ff.), but no reference is made with regard

---

[7] In his iconographical description of the images in the Dacca Museum Bhattasali seems to accept the existence of stone images of Kubjikā, whom he considers a variety of the goddess Cāmuṇḍā (cf. Bhattasali 1972: 211). He bases his identification of Kubjikā on the description of her form as found in the Agni P, and also refers to the Matsya Purāṇa. Another indication for the existence of stone images of Kubjikā comes from southern India. In the photo-archives of the 'Institut Français d'Indologie' at Pondichery there are three photographies of stone images of the goddess under the entry 'Kubjikā'. They are located at Khallikoṭe (photo Nr. 3279-11), Tirubuvai (photo Nr. 1350-7) and Halebid (photo Nr. 1595-1). Although the possibility should not be ruled out at forehand, I do not think it very probable that stone-images of Kubjikā exist. Being a goddess of a typical Tantric nature Kujbikā is in the first place an object for meditation. For that purpose the *dhyānaślokas* in the KnT and the AgniP serve. During a visit to Nepal in 1977 I was informed by a Newari acquaintance that some relative of him possessed a manuscript which contained a drawing of Kubjikā. Unfortunately, I have never been able to check this information. There seems to be a fair chance, however, that one might find drawings of Kubjikā in one of the many small manuals with directions for meditation and *pūjā*. My colleague Dr. K. R. van Kooy kindly drew my attention to an illustration in an 18th century Nepalese manuscript (Rawson 1978: plate 7), which he surmised to be a drawing of Kubjikā. The photography in Rawson's book shows two parts of the manuscript. From a rather shady photo in the catalogue for the Tantra Exhibition at Hayward Gallery (London, 1971; cf. Rawson 1971: Nr. 400) where the same manuscript was exhibited, it appears that the two parts of plate Nr. 7 should be placed one above the other (the left part on the plate comes on top of the right part). According to the legends to the drawings the following series is the result: 1) the goddess Kramakrameśvarī, 2) Kubjikeśvarī, 3) Śrīkhañjī, 4) a *maṇḍala*, 5) the deity Arghyapātreśvarī, 6) Baṭuka, Kṣetrapāla and Gaṇeśa; below each of these three a ritual vessel with rice is depicted, 7) Mahāmāyā, 8) Nircciśeśī. Only the first six drawings are of interest for the moment. It is obvious that this part of the manuscript deals with a ritual which includes Kubjikā. The ritual consists of meditation on Kramakrameśvarī, 'The Lady of the Tradition' (cf. ṢaṭSS 3,59b), Kubjikā and Śrīkhañjī who is closely related to Kubjikā (cf. Schoterman 1980: 346). Next a *maṇḍala* is drawn, in which the three deities are invited to manifest themselves; they are 'welcomed' with *arghya*-water. After this rice-offerings are presented to Baṭuka, Kṣetrapāla and Gaṇeśa (cf. KnT FF.79B ff.: *balitraya*). Our main concern lies, of course, with Kubjikā and the way she is depicted here. The illustration shows Kubjikā with one head (three eyes) and four arms. She is seated on a lion's-throne. In her two right hands she holds a rosary and the *varadā-mudrā*; in her two left hands are a book and the *abhaya-mudrā*. There is but little similarity between this drawing of Kubjikā and the two *dhyānaślokas* in the KnT and the Agni P. In these texts Kubjikā has six heads and twelve arms (KnT FF.26B ff. right hands: trident, discus, thunderbolt, elephant-goad, arrow, knife; left hands: blue lotus, club, bell, book, bow, skull-cup; Agni P 144,33d-34 right hands: trident, mirror, sword, *ratnamālā*, elephant-goad, bow; left hands: snake, skull-cup, rosary, club, conch, book). The drawing of Kubjikā has only the rosary in common with the Agni P (here left hand), and the book with both texts. Apparently the drawing of Kubjikā in this 18th century manuscript has little to do with the *dhyānaślokas* of the same goddess in the KnT and the AgniP. Before the *dhyānaśloka* of Kubjikā in the KnT we find the *dhyānaśloka* of Bhairava (KnT FF.25B ff.). Bhairava has ten arms: in the four right hands are a trident, discus, banner, *varadā-mudrā*; in the four left hands the flower of the coral-tree (*pārijāta*), rosary, book, *abhaya-mudrā*. Between the remaining right and left hands Bhairava holds the skin of a Brahmin (*brahmacarman*). The four attributes seen in the drawing of Kubjikā are found among the attributes of Bhairava. Untill other iconographic texts become available it seems that the drawing of Kubjikā constitutes a rather simplified form of a female Bhairava.

to a possible stooped form of the goddess. There is, however, one instance in the KmT and the ṢaṭSS, where it appears that the author refers to a stooped form of Kubjikā. When Devī asks Bhairava how She should imagine Herself as Kubjikā, the latter answers:

bṛhatkāyo yathā kaścit svalpe saṃcarate gṛhe |
kuñcitāṅgo viśed yasmāt tadvad eṣā maheśvarī ||
(Ms B F. 208A = KmT Ch. 16)

"Like a big man who goes around in a small house entering with a bent body, just like that is this Maheśvarī". The commentary on these lines from the ṢaṭSS explains further: *kubjikā katham | kubjo bhūtvā sarvatra praveśam āyāti | tadvat | sā sarvatra saṅkocarūpatvena vyāptiṃ karoti | tadā kubjikā*, "Why Kubjikā? Bowing down one gains access everywhere. Exactly so. Thanks to her contracted form she pervades everything. Therefore [she is called] Kubjikā". Both instances seem to point to a stooped or rather 'contracted' shape of the goddess, as is indicated by the meaning of *kubja*. Moreover, Kubjikā is referred to as *kuṭilīkṛtā*, 'bent; curved', in the above mentioned passage of the KmT.

As one might expect, the word *kubja*, which is most probably of Munda origin (cf. Kuiper 1948: 42 ff.), is etymologically 'explained'. Thus in the Saṃvartāmaṇḍalasūtravyākhyā (F.1B) the name Kubjikā is discussed and explained as a compound with the meaning 'She who is born from the earth and the waters' (sc. < *ku-ab-ja*). This Indian 'etymology' does not provide us with any factual insight into the name or the nature of the goddess, however.

It is true, however, that one should not visualize Kubjikā as some hunchbacked deity. Her name and consequently the goddess herself should rather be related with the Kuṇḍalinī Śakti, especially when she rests or sleeps in the Mūlādhāra Cakra. An indication for this assumption is found in her designation as *kuṭilīkṛtā* (see above) which points undoubtedly to the name Kuṭilāṅgī for the Kuṇḍalinī Śakti (cf. Haṭhayogapradīpikā 3,103). Moreover, when the Kuṇḍalinī Śakti rests in the Mūlādhāra Cakra, she is described as 'coiled like a sleeping serpent', or as the KmT (Ch. 2) puts it: *suptanāgendravat kuṇḍalākārarūpā*, 'her body has the shape of a circle (*kuṇḍala*) like that of a sleeping snake'. The ṢaṭSS (MS B F.230B = Ch. 28) follows this comparison and states: *kuṇḍalyākārarūpeṇa kubjinī tena sā smṛtā*, 'because she has the shape of a circle she is known as Kubjinī'. From the foregoing it becomes clear, that the goddess Kubjikā is simply another form of the Kuṇḍalinī Śakti when abiding in the Mūlādhāra Cakra, and not some hunchbacked goddess.

The Ṣaṭsāhasra Saṃhitā

The teachings or doctrine of Kubjikā, the Kubjikāmata [8], are revealed in the Kubjikāmata Tantra, the *mūla*-text of the Kubjikā School. It contains some 3.500 *ślokas* in twenty-five chapters (*paṭalas*), for which reason it is referred to twice in the Ṣaṭsāhasra Saṃhitā as *adhyuṣṭasaṃkhya sahasra*, '[containing] 3.500 [*ślokas*]' (3,41ab; MS B F.208B = Ch. 25). In the National Archives at Kathmandu there are over fifty manuscripts of the Kubjikāmata Tantra [9]. Closely related to the Kubjikāmata Tantra is the Ṣaṭsāhasra Saṃhitā which contains approximately 6.000 ślokas, as its title indicates, in fifty chapters. Of the Ṣaṭsāhasra Saṃhitā there appear to exist only three manuscripts (see below pp. 16ff.) [10], which is a rather insignificant number in comparison with the number of manuscripts of the Kubjikāmata Tantra. Moreover, one of the manuscripts of the Ṣaṭsāhasra Saṃhitā (MS C) was copied in the first half of this century when the cult of Kubikā did not exist any more. This leaves us with actually two manuscripts of the Ṣaṭsāhasra Saṃhitā, which were written in the period when Kubjikā was still worshipped.

The date of composition of the Ṣaṭsāhasra Saṃhitā is not known, but the oldest available manuscript (MS A) of the text can be dated in the 12th century A.D. (cf. Van Kooy 1977: 888). As the oldest manuscripts of the Kubjikāmata Tantra are dated in the first half of the 12th century A.D. (cf. p. 6), the oldest manuscripts of both texts do not differ much in age. Since the Ṣaṭsāhasra Saṃhitā is merely an enlarged version of the Kubjikāmata Tantra (cf. p. 13), it follows that rather soon after the compilation of the

[8] The teachings or doctrine of Kubjikā, the Kubjikāmata (on *mata* see Goudriaan & Gupta 1981: 17ff.), are usually referred to in the ṢaṭSS as the Śrīmata, 'The Sublime Doctrine'. The expression is undoubtedly a proper name because in some of the colophons of the chapters in the ṢaṭSS it is supplied with the honorific *śrī* (cf. colophon of the 2nd chapter: *śrīśrīmate*, 'in the revered Śrīmata'). Other designations as found in the ṢaṭSS are Mahāmata, Mahottara, Mahottama; connected with the name of the goddess we find Kubjikāmata, Kubjinīmata, Śrīkubjikāmata, Śrīmatkubjikāmata and Śrīmatkubjikāmatottama.

[9] In 1974 I was given the opportunity by a grant from the 'Netherlands Organization for the Advancement of Pure Research' (ZWO) to consult the catalogue of manuscripts which were microfilmed in the scope of the German-Nepal Manuscript Preservation Project, at Marburg. The manuscripts of the Kubjikāmata Tantra are found under the titles Śrīkubjikāmatatantra and Kulālikāmnāya. Since I have not read through all the manuscripts bearing these titles, it is possible that some of these manuscripts may contain other texts (cf. Note 10).

[10] The name Ṣaṭsāhasra is found twice in the catalogue (Nrs. 1-1363 & 2-219/1565). but these two manuscripts are merely commentaries on the Ṣaṭsāhasra Saṃhitā. The texts of the Ṣaṭsāhasra Saṃhitā are called Kubjikāmata and Kulālikāmnāya. For this reason it is possible that among the more than fifty manuscripts of the Kubjikāmata Tantra in the catalogue some may contain the Ṣaṭsāhasra Saṃhitā actually. It is not very probable, however, because of the number of leaves these manuscripts contain. A manuscript of the Ṣaṭsāhasra Saṃhitā requires evidently more leaves than a manuscript of the Kubjikāmata Tantra because of the difference in size between both texts. In case there are more manuscripts of the Ṣaṭsāhasra Saṃhitā in the catalogue, it most likely concerns incomplete versions of the text (cf. pp. 19; 20).

Kubjikāmata Tantra the need was felt for a more elaborate version of the text, which dealt more *in extenso* with the subject-matter of the Kubjikāmata Tantra. Perhaps the Kubjikāmata Tantra proved to be too concise, and therefore difficult to understand.

One should expect the Ṣaṭsāhasra Saṃhitā to have become the more popular version of both texts, but this is apparently not the case in view of the scarcity of its manuscripts. On the other hand, it is peculiar that there appears to be no secondary literature directly related to the Kubjikāmata Tantra[11], whereas there are at least six manuscripts containing a commentary on the Ṣaṭsāhasra Saṃhitā[12], two of which are written on palm-leaf[13]. Furthermore, the Kubjikānityāhnikatilaka which deals with the practical side of the worship (*sc.* rituals, *mantras* etc.) concurs with the Ṣaṭsāhasra Saṃhitā rather than with the Kubjikāmata Tantra (cf. Schoterman 1980: 346). The same applies to the Kubjikā-section in the Agnipurāṇa (cf. Schoterman 1980: 346). This leaves us with a text difficult to understand, but available in at least fifty manuscripts, and an easier version of the same text which gave rise to a secondary literature, but which is actually available in two manuscripts only. For this obvious inconsistency there appears to be no explanation, as far as I can see.

The close relationship between the Kubjikāmata Tantra and the Ṣaṭsāhasra Saṃhitā becomes clear from the fact that the greater part of the Kubjikāmata Tantra is found almost *verbatim* in the Ṣaṭsāhasra Saṃhitā. On an earlier occasion[14] I have pointed out the various reasons which account for the difference of some 3.000 *ślokas* between the two texts. It should suffice therefore to repeat briefly these reasons here: 1) the ṢaṭSS provides additional information elaborating in more detail on certain passages in the KmT, 2) it deals in a more elaborate way with many subjects found in the KmT, 3) it deals with subjects not found in the KmT, 4) the wide usage in the ṢaṭSS of the *prastāra-* and *gahvara-*systems in presenting the various *mantras*.

[11] It seems that there exist no commentaries on the Kubjikāmata Tantra, at least I have not been able to trace any. Śāstri, however, mentions a manuscript from a private collection, which could be a commentary on the Kubjikāmata Tantra (Śāstri 1915: 116). The title of the manuscript is Kubjikāmatalaghuṭippanī, and from its colophon it becomes clear that it contains twenty-five chapters (*iti śrīkubjikāmate laghuṭippanyāṃ pañcaviṃśatipaṭalaḥ samāptaḥ*). From the fact that it contains twenty-five chapters one could infer that it is a commentary (*ṭippanī*) on the Kubjikāmata Tantra which also contains twenty-five chapters.

[12] These manuscripts are the following: 5-4775/209; 1-1363/194; 1-30/300; 2-219/1565; 5-4776/210; 1-285/50. All from the National Archives.

[13] The two manuscripts of the commentary on the ṢaṭSS written on palm-leaf are 1-1363/194 and 1-285/50 of the NAK. Since in Nepal palm-leaf was generally replaced by paper in the 14th or 15th century (cf. Goudriaan & Gupta 1981: 22), these two manuscripts were written at least before the 15th century A.D.

[14] On the occasion of the 'XIX. Deutscher Orientalistentag' (Freiburg im Breisgau, 1975) I presented a paper on the Kubjikāmata Tantra. It was published in abridged form in 1977 (see Schoterman 1977).

The following table shows clearly the close relationship between the Kubjikāmata Tantra and the Ṣaṭsāhasra Saṃhitā (for the ṢaṭSS MS B has been used, for the KmT MS G; the titles of the chapters are those of MS B of the ṢaṭSS).

ṢaṭSS Ch.:	KmT Ch.:
1	1
2	1
3	(3)
4/5	2
6	4
7	4
8	5&6
9/10	5&6
11 Aghoryāṣṭakatrividyā	6
12	
13	7
14	8
15 Mātṛcakroddhāra	8&9
16 Ṣaḍmūrtyuddhāra	10
17	10
18 Svādhiṣṭhānākhyaliṅga	11&12
19	13&14
20	
21 Cakroddhāra	14
22 Dūtīcakranirṇaya	14
23 Mātṛcakroddhāra	15
24 Ṣaḍyoginyaḥ	15
25 Khecarīcakranirṇaya	16
26 Mitreśānasamāyoga	17
27	17&18
28 Mahantārīsaptacakravidhāna	18&19
29 Catuṣkabheda	19
30 Pañcaratnapañcakoddhāra	18
31 Dvīpāmnāyāvatāra	20
32 Dvīpāmnāyabheda	21
33 Bhairavāvalinīrāvalyoddhāra	22
34 Pīṭhakīrtana	22
35 Kālavañcana	23
36 Devyāpūjāvidhāna	23
37 Yamarājavidhāna	23

ṢaṭSS Ch.:	KmT Ch.:
38 Saṃhāraṣoḍaśabheda	24
39 Vajragahvaroddhāra	
40 Śrīpūjāvidhāna	24
41 Samayādhikāra	
42 Śrī Ādināthavaktrāvatāra	
43 Śrīmūlanāthāvatāra	
44 Śrīsiddhanāthastotrābhidhāna	
45 Ṣoḍhāhṛdayaḍāmara	
46 Śrīmātryaṣṭakabheda	
47 Śarīrotpatti Antaryajñavidhi	
48 Pavitrakavidhāna	24
49 Pañcātmasvarūpayor Bheda	25
50 Ādhyātmacaryāṇi	25

The chapters 12, 20, 39 and 41-47 find no parallel in the Kubjikāmata Tantra with regard to their contents. The 12th chapter of the Ṣaṭsāhasra Saṃhitā deals with the Dvādaśāṅga (cf. Schoterman 1977: 936); chapter 20 explains the Kulābhiṣeka; chapter 39 treats the Vajra Gahvara (cf. Appendix I), the *mantra* of Vajrakubjikā and her *maṇḍala*; the chapters 41-47 deal with a variety of subjects, most notably with the Siddhas and Nāthas who passed on the text to our times.

Ṣaṭsāhasra Saṃhitā 1-5

In the present study we have confined ourselves to the first five chapters of the Ṣaṭsāhasra Saṃhitā. It appears that the chapters 1-12 of the Ṣaṭsāhasra Saṃhitā (= KmT 1-6) constitute a kind of introduction to the rest of the text (cf. Schoterman 1977: 936; Goudriaan & Gupta 1981: 53 ff.). The chapters 6-12 agree to a high degree with the corresponding chapters in the Kubjikāmata Tantra (4-6), but present the various *mantras* in it by means of the Mālinī Gahvara (cf. Appendix I), a procedure which requires a lot of space. Thus, for instance, the Umāmāheśvaracakra, a very long *mantra* (cf. Goudriaan & Gupta 1981: 53), fills the leaves 39B up to 49A of the 7th chapter (MS B) because it is presented by means of the Mālinī Gahvara. The first two chapters of the ṢaṭSS represent a very elaborate working out of only six *ślokas* of the Kubjikāmata Tantra (1,3-8). The third chapter deals with approximately the same subject as is found in the third chapter of the KmT, but in a completely different way. The combined chapters four and five describe the visit of Mālinī / Kubjikā / Devī to several Pīṭhas all over India. The same subject is treated in the second chapter of the KmT. Many lines from the KmT are found almost literally in these combined chapters, but much more information on the subject is provided by the Ṣaṭsāhasra Saṃhitā. As such the first five chapters of the Ṣaṭsāhasra Saṃhitā constitute a fair representation of the text as a whole in comparison to the Kubjikāmata Tantra.

Besides the fact that the contents of these first five chapters are interesting, there are other grounds for selecting these chapters as the subject for the present study. The oldest manuscript of the Ṣaṭsāhasra Saṃhitā (MS A) is very incomplete: it is actually only legible up to the tenth chapter. The remaining chapters are virtually illegible, or are lacking all together. This makes it actually impossible to prepare an acceptable edition of the chapters after the tenth. As the contents of the chapters 6-10 are not of much interest in comparison with the corresponding chapters in the Kubjikāmata Tantra, the present study confines itself to the Ṣaṭsāhasra Saṃhitā 1-5.

The Manuscripts

The following three manuscripts have been used for the critical edition of the first five chapters of the Ṣaṭsāhasra Saṃhitā:

MS A Nr. G.8329 (Cat. ASB Nr. 5804); palm-leaf; FF. 239; incomplete (lacking are the leaves 49, 56, 69, 72-84, 86-104, 106-132, 134-187, 189, 190, 192-229); date; 12th century A.D.

This oldest manuscript of the ṢaṭSS was discovered by H. P. Śāstri in 1898 in the Nepalese Durbar Library, the present National Archives at Kathmandu. The manuscript was brought to Calcutta, and subsequently included in the collection of the Asiatic Society of Bengal. Śāstri dated the manuscript in the 7th century A.D., which made it one of the oldest existing Tantra manuscripts. This allegedly old age of the manuscript caused it to be used by several scholars for the purpose of proving the existence of Tantrism in the 7th century (cf. Farquhar 1920: 199 ff.; Gonda 1963: 31). Only recently (1975) it has been shown that the manuscript is of a much later date. It was probably written in the 12th century A.D. or somewhat later in the Śārada-region (Van Kooy 1977: 881-890) [15].

The manuscript shows several peculiar features which warrant a closer examination. Usually no distinctive marker such as a single or double *daṇḍa* is used to indicate the end of a line. When a single *daṇḍa* is occasionally used, the preceding line ends quite often with a vocative. In some instances the end of a line is indicated by two dots placed above each other. It resembles very strongly the sign for the *visarga*, but the two dots are written

[15] For any further information with regard to this particular manuscript of the ṢaṭSS I refer to Dr. Van Kooy's publication (Van Kooy 1977), which contains a survey of the script as well as an illustration of FF.12B; 13A of the text.

more pronouncedly. Yet, it is often difficult to decide whether the scribe intended a *visarga* or this particular sign. Noteworthy is the fact that it occurs only after a word ending in *-a*. In some instances the two dots are followed by a single *daṇḍa*.

The characteristics of the alphabet make it sometimes difficult to make a distinction between the vowels *e*, *ai*, *o* and *au* in combination with a consonant (क or के = ke; क or कै = kai; क̃ = ko; क̆̃ = kau). Furthermore there is but little difference between initial *u-* and *o-*, and between initial *ū-* and *rū-*. With regard to the consonants the characters used for the *c*, *dh*, *v/b* are often very similar in shape. The same applies to the signs of the *p*, *m*, *y* and *s*.

Apart from these pecularities which belong to the alphabet proper, the scribe has added several of his own. A common feature in many manuscripts is the use of the *anusvāra* instead of *ṅ* or *ñ*. The same we find here, but sometimes the scribe uses both at the same time (e.g. *saṃṅgha*). In the same way the *m* before a labial is sometimes written twice (e.g. *saṃmpanna*). Almost invariably instead of *ri* in combination with a consonant *ṛ* is used; thus the scribe writes *pṛya* instead of *priya*, *tṛkūṭa* for *trikūṭa*, *kṛyā* for *kriyā* etc., and even *tṛsra* instead of *tryasra*. The reverse is found twice for metrical reasons (cf. 3,18d; 91c).

On the whole the orthography of the manuscript creates a rather sloppy impression. It suggests a considerable lack of orthographic knowledge on the part of the scribe. The frequent confusion between *ś*, *ṣ* and *s*, the writing of *-ṣṭa* instead of *-ṣṭha*, *-d-* for *-dd-*, *-dh-* and *-ddh-*, *-dh-* instead of *-ddh-* or *-d-*, the confusion between *ṇ* and *n*, etc. strongly support the impression that although the scribe knew the language well enough, his capability for the correct spelling of many Sanskrit words was often very poor.

The observation that the orthographic knowledge of the scribe is poor in many instances, does not account for all the irregularities as found in the manuscript. Some of the irregularities are perhaps not based on individual mistakes. Especially with regard to the vowels, the manuscript shows several features which it shares with many other manuscripts. Thus, for instance, the change from *-o-* to *-u-* is frequently found (e.g. *huma*, *viluma*, *saṃyuga* etc.). Less frequently *-e-* becomes *-ī-* (e.g. *upīta*, *mīru*), or *-ī-* becomes *-e-* (*śrīmateya*, *dekṣā*). Such irregularities are most probably due to the manner of pronunciation of the Sanskrit language in the time of the scribe. One should keep in mind that in the time of writing of our manuscript the Sanskrit language was not used for daily conversation, but was replaced since long by all kinds of vernaculars which are very likely to have influenced the pronunciation of the Sanskrit language when it was used.

Pronunciation indeed may have influenced the written transmission of a Tantra as our MS A. In the previous pages I have deliberately used the term 'scribe' rather than 'copyist', because the latter implies that the manuscript was copied from another manuscript. It is very likely, however, that this was not the case with the present manuscript. As we will learn from the third chapter of the ṢaṭSS, it was a rule that a manuscript was not simply copied from another manuscript, but that it was written down from a recited text: while the teacher reads the text aloud, the pupil notes it down at the same time in order to procure a copy of the text for himself. In later times this procedure may have been abandoned, but it is very likely that the present manuscript is the result of writing down a recited text. This, of course, renders the task of the pupil far more difficult. The environment was probably not very quiet, since the participants in the ceremony (Yoginīs etc.) were present. Furthermore, the quality of the manuscript depends a great deal on a clear pronunciation by the teacher. Next to this one should wish to know to what degree the pupil had the liberty to correct from his own knowledge an incorrect pronunciation by his teacher, who is the personification of Śiva on earth. Thus, for instance, when the teacher distinctly said "*dekṣā*", the pupil probably had to write it down, even if he knew from his own knowledge that it should be *dīkṣā*. Consequently, for some of the irregularities the teacher is to blame and not the pupil who actually wrote down the text.

An indication for the assumption that the text was noted down from a recited text is perhaps found in the constant writing down of *śrībhairav uvāca* instead of *śrībhairava uvāca*. The final *-a* in *bhairava* was most probably not written by the pupil/scribe, because he did not hear it actually pronounced by his teacher. This disappearance of the final *-a* is only found in this instance. When it should occur within the text itself, the metre would have been seriously disturbed. In these small prose parts between the metric parts of the text, however, it does not matter, and the scribe simply wrote down what he heard from his teacher's mouth. In the same perspective should most likely be understood the frequent writing of *-nn-* instead of *-ṇ-* (e.g. *kramenna*, *trīnni*, *konna*, *raudrānni*, *kāranna* etc.). It is quite understandable that one writes *-n-* instead of *-ṇ-*, although it is not correct. Writing a double *n*, however, seems quite pointless, unless one assumes that the words were pronounced in such a way, that a scribe with insufficient orthographic knowledge wrote them down exactly as he heard them. It falls beyond the scope of the present study to deal more *in extenso* with this important aspect of the manuscript, but a separate study of this phenomenon together with a comparison of the contemporary vernaculars may prove fruitful.

MS B Nr. 5-428/52 in the National Archives (Kathmandu); Folia, 399; paper; complete.

Manuscript B contains the complete text of the Ṣaṭsāhasra Saṃhitā in fifty chapters. It has no colophon, but ends after the colophon to the 50th chapter simply with *samāptam iti*, 'Thus it is completed'. The manuscript is written in very clear *nāgarī*-characters, which makes it well legible. It is difficult to say anything definite with regard to its exact date. To judge from the microfilm the manuscript has an old appearance; perhaps 16th or 17th century?

MS C Nr. 5-4775/209 in the National Archives (Kathmandu); Folio, 121; paper complete; date, 1929 A.D..

Manuscript Nr. 5-4775/209 of the National Archives actually contains three different texts which belong to the School of Kubjikā. It contains the complete text of the Ṣaṭsāhasra Saṃhitā, the text of the 10th chapter and a text of the Ṭippanī on the ṢaṭSS. The text of the ṢaṭSS ends with a very elaborate colophon: *idaṃ tantraṃ samāptam iti* || || *1986 vaikramābde āṣādhaśuklapūrṇimāyāṃ (saura śrāvaṇa 6 gatadine niśi 11* | *10 ghaṇṭāsu lagne* [)] *śrīrājaguru hemarāja vidvadvarāṇāṃ dvitīyāpatyabhūtaṃ* ˙ *śrīkubjikāprasādarūpaṃ kanyāratnaṃ prādurbhūt* ˙ *tasminn eva dine tadīyabhāratībhavanārthaṃ pracīnadevākṣaralikhitāt 399 patrātmatāḍapatrapustakād uddhṛtya pūrṇaprasādaśarmaṇā vilikhya idaṃ pustakaṃ tatkanyāratnasya janmasamayaṃ saṃsmārayañcirāya śrīkubjikāprasādāt tadīyadīrghāyurārogyāya bhūyāt* ||. It appears then that the present manuscript was copied by a certain Pūrṇaprasādaśarman to commemorate the birth of a 'daughter like a jewel' for the Rājaguru Hemarāj. The date of copying is given as the day of the full moon in the light half of the month Āṣāḍha in the Vaikrama-year 1986, which corresponds to the period June/July of 1929-'30 A.D. Between brackets the month Śrāvaṇa (July/August) is mentioned. It follows that the manuscript was copied in the second half of the month July of the year 1929 A.D.

According to the colophon the manuscript was copied from another manuscript which was written in old *devākṣaras* (sc. in *nāgarī*-script). More important, perhaps, is the remark that the manuscript contained 399 folia, which agrees with the number of folia of our manuscript B. It is very likely indeed, that MS C was copied from MS B. From the Variant Readings it becomes clear that both manuscripts correspond to each other to a very high degree. The copyist of MS C indicates with horizontal lines those words in his manuscript, which were apparently illegible or lacking in MS B. Checking these instances confirms the assumption that MS C was copied from MS B. The reason for copying MS B was not because it was in a very bad state of conservation, but to commemorate the birth of a girl of great beauty, for which Kubjikā is acknowledged. It appears then that in the beginning of this century the goddess Kubjikā was still held in esteem by some people in Nepal. It is difficult to explain otherwise why a text dedicated to Kubjikā was selected to commemorate the birth of a girl.

As was already mentioned in Note 10, there is a possibility that among the manuscripts called Śrīkubjikāmata Tantra or Kulālikāmnāya in the National

Archives some of them might contain an incomplete version of the Ṣaṭsāhasra Saṃhitā. One such instance is the present manuscript which contains the next of the 10th chapter. Only the text of the 10th chapter is also found in MS Nr. 2-219/1565 of the National Archives.

Ṭ Nr. 5-4775/209 in the National Archives (Kathmandu); complete; Folia, 102; paper; illustrated; appearance: recent.

For our translation of the first five chapters of the ṢaṭSS extensive use has been made of the *ṭippanī* or commentary on the text. Of this Ṭ there are at least six manuscripts available, of which two are written on palm-leaf (cf. Notes 12 & 13). I have used MS Nr. 5-4775/209 because it reads very well, and appears to be the only manuscript of the Ṭ which is complete. The two palm-leaf manuscripts (cf. Note 13) are incomplete, and rather difficult to read. As far as I can judge, however, they correspond almost exactly with the text of our manuscript. The MSS 5-4776/210 and 1-30/300 are both incomplete, and the order of leaves of the latter is very seriously disturbed. MS 2-219/1565 only contains the commentary on the chapters 1, 2, 9/10. As becomes apparent from the translation and the Notes to the translation, one can hardly do without the Ṭ for a good understanding of the contents of the text, At least one can find in it a confirmation of a proposed translation or interpretation. Apart from a few instances it appears that the explanations as found in the Ṭ are very much to the point. Moreover, the Ṭ contains many drawings and diagrams of the more intricate *maṇḍalas*. The figures of the Mālinī, Yoni and Vajra Gahvara (cf. Appendix I) are found in the Ṭ, but the *akṣaras* which are to be filled in into the figures are never entirely correct.

The Text of Ṣaṭsāhasra Saṃhitā 1-5

The text of the first five chapters is based on three manuscripts which differ considerably in age (A 12th century; B 16th century (?); C 20th century). Thus, generally speaking, between each of the three manuscripts lies a period of approximately four hundred years. Besides this, the relationship between the manuscripts B and C is so close (see above), that one can hardly speak of two different manuscripts. This actually leaves us with the text of two manuscripts (A & BC) on which the critical edition of the first five chapters is based. This number is, of course, very meagre. It is therefore doubtful to what extent the appellation 'critical' for our edition is justified.

It stands to reason that the text of MS A is to be preferred to the text of MS B, because it is of a considerably older age. On the whole this principle has been followed as much as possible. There are, however, some instances where the reading of the MSS BC has been followed, mainly because the reading of A seemed incomprehensible or wrong (cf. 3,8cd). In comparison with the MSS BC MS A is far less accurate with regard to the spelling of words and the congruity between the different components of a grammatical unity. This is, however, no reason to prefer the MSS BC to MS A.

The first concern for the writer of a Tantric text regards the subject-matter which he entrusts to writing to the best of his capacities. One should therefore make a distinction between the meaning or interpretation of a line and the way in which it is actually put in writing. This implies that the words which are used are of primary importance, and that case-endings, congruity between words etc. are of secondary importance. Especially in the case of MS A one finds many inconsistencies with regard to the gender and the number of words. These inconsistencies do not alter the contents of a line, however. In other words in many instances one is able to grasp the meaning of a line, but one is at a loss as to how the grammatical structure of the line is or ought to be. Thus, for instance, the meaning of *ato yan na paro bhūtvā rakṣā kāryā vidhānataḥ* (3,13cd) is perfectly clear ('Henceforth, one should guard according to the rules that which is to be kept secret'), but the grammatical structure of *pāda* 13c is rather puzzling. One should, therefore, be very careful in correcting a line, and restrict emendations to an absolute minimum. There are, however, a few instances in the text, where an emendation seemed unavoidable. In the first chapter the reading of the manuscripts for *śloka* 31b is definitely wrong (A *dvādaśāntān tadantagaḥ*; BC *dvādaśāntaṃ tadaṅgatam*), but from the context its intended meaning is clear; therefore an emendation of the text is acceptable here (*dvādaśāntaṃ tadantagam*).

For the transcription of the Devanāgarī-alphabet I have used the system which is generally accepted and used. The preference as shown in the manuscripts for the use of the *anusvāra* I have not followed. Thus although the manuscripts usually write *paṃca*, for instance, for the text the spelling *pañca* is chosen. Likewise I write *ūrdhva*, *tattva* etc., although in the manuscripts they are almost invariably spelled *ūrddha* and *tatva* [16].

The translation of the text is sufficiently clear in itself, and needs only a few remarks of a more general nature. In rendering the Skt text into English I have tried to follow the original as closely as possible. In some instances this may perhaps have resulted in a rather awkward style, but in this respect the translation shows no great difference with the text itself which does not aim at any literary appraisal either. Some of the more technical terms are not translated, but are explained in the Notes to the translation. The epithets of Devī with the exception of *priyā* are left untranslated, because they do not serve any particular purpose and are of small interest. Moreover, it would create a wrong impression in the reader's mind, when the epithet *varārohā* (lit:

---

[16] In manuscript C we find in a very few instances a correct spelling of such words as *tattva*, for instance.

'the woman with the beautiful buttocks') is translated each time. Only in one passage an epithet of Devī serves a purpose within the context (cf. 3,59b Notes).

Metrics and Grammar

The text of the complete Ṣaṭsāhasra Saṃhitā is composed in the *śloka*-metre with only a few exceptions. As usual the introductory lines are composed in a more elaborate metre, e.g. the *sragdharā*-metre (1,1-5). In chapter 4/5 we find one line in the *triṣṭubh*-metre (4/5,163 = KmT 3,71), which consists of a combination of an *upendravajrā* and an *indravajrā* (= *upajāti*). In the same chapter a line in prose is found (4/5,150).

It appears that the *śloka* is a very important implement for the prospective writer of a Tantra. It serves as the skeleton on which the text is hung. For this reason the writer takes every pain to produce regular octo-syllabic *pādas*, the fundamental characteristic of a *śloka*. Within a *pāda* the writer has every possible freedom with regard to the length of the syllables as long as the fifth and the sixth syllables are short and long, respectively. To achieve this latter condition, a short fifth and a long sixth syllable, even grammar is made submissive to metrics, as we will see below.

The outward appearance of the *ślokas* is very regular throughout the text of the first five chapters. There are only two instances found, where the division between two *pādas* is ignored. In both cases it concerns an enumeration (3,46ab & 93ab). The rule that the *pāda* of a *śloka* should count eight syllables is scrupulously followed with only a few exceptions. When the *pāda* of a *śloka* constitutes an irregularity with regard to its number of syllables, it may contain either too few or too many syllables. in most of the instances the irregularity concerns the difference of one syllable only. Thus an irregular *pāda* may contain either seven or nine syllables. One should make a distinction between these two irregularities, however.

In the case of a *pāda* with only seven or even less syllables, it is very likely that the copy of the text itself is corrupt, and that the original author should not be blamed for this defect of the text. It requires only little knowledge of the Sanskrit language to add a mono-syllabic word with little meaning (e.g. *ca*, *hi*, *tu* etc.) to the text in order to obtain a regular octo-syllabic *pāda*. In case a *pāda* lacks two or more syllables, the chances are very great that in the process of copying a word has been dropped which was originally included in the text. In the first five chapters of the ṢaṭSS there is only one *pāda* which contains less than eight syllables. It concerns 3,73d which has seven syllables only. It is certain, however, that the *pāda* is corrupt. The reading of MS A has the required eight syllables, but unfortunately the first word of the *pāda* is hardly legible. For that reason the reading of MSS BC has been followed, although the result is a *pāda* of seven syllables only.

There occur eight instances of *pādas* with nine syllables (1,41a; 2,7c; 3,23d; 51a; 69c; 105a; 4/5,139c; 145d). Out of these eight instances six might be regarded as examples of the incapability of the author to construct a regular octo-syllabic *pāda*, or it is perhaps better to say that in these six instances the author had no alternative at his disposal to write an octo-syllabic *pāda* with the same contents. This becomes evident from the fact that two of them consist of a single compound (3,23d *sauvarṇatāṃbūlapūritaṃ* (orig. *svarṇa-*?); 4/5,139c *caturbhujādigaṇeśāntaḥ*[17]), while the other four allow no room for another composition (1,41a *daradaṇḍī paścime bhāge*; 2,7c *caturviṃśaṣoḍaśair bhedair*[17]; 3,51a *ucchālanadhūnanaiḥ kaṃpaiḥ*; 3,69c *na jātyākṛtidhanādharaiḥ*). With regard to the two remaining instances of nine-syllabic *pādas* the author could have written an octo-syllabic *pāda* with still the same meaning. In 3,105a the text reads *prathamāhne vācayitvā tu*. In order to obtain an octo-syllabic *pāda* the author might have dropped *tu*, or read *vācitvā* (cf. 3,9c) instead of *vācayitvā*. In both cases the *pāda* becomes octo-syllabic. Yet the author has not done so for good reason, as it appears. The two octo-syllabic *pādas* suffer from the same defect: the fifth syllable is not short with a long sixth syllable. It appears then that a nine-syllabic *pāda* with a short sixth and a long seventh syllable is preferred to an octo-syllabic *pāda* with an ametrical fifth and sixth syllable. In the six other nine-syllabic *pādas* the sixth and seventh syllables are also short and long, respectively. In the last nine-syllabic *pāda* the sixth and seventh syllables are again short and long, respectively (4/5,145d *pīṭhaikaike kathayāmy aham*). Even when *aham* is dropped, there is no way in obtaining a regular octo-syllabic *pāda* with a short fifth and a long sixth syllable.

Within a *pāda* we find several features which enable the writer to construct a regular octo-syllabic quarter with a short fifth and a long sixth syllable. A common characteristic in many Tantric texts is the frequent occurrence of hiatus within a *pāda* (2,5b *-randhrasya ūrdhvagam*) or between two *pādas* (1,35ab ...*tu, etat*...). There are a few irregularities with regard to the Saṇdhi-rules. Thus, for instance, the final consonant of a word is sometimes dropped and the word is connected by Sandhi with the following word (3,10b *śrīmatam idaṃ* > *śrīmata idaṃ* > *śrīmatedaṃ*; 3,36a *samastedaṃ*; cf. 3,41a Notes). In two instances we find an irregularity with regard to the Sandhi-rules in order to 'save' a syllable (4/5,110a *antako aṃbikā* instead of *antako 'ṃbikā*; 4/5,128a *vīro avyakta-* for *vīro 'vyakta-*). The same irregularity is found in 1,53c (*cañcalo āṇavānando*), although no syllable is lost in a correct reading (*cañcala āṇavānado*). For metrical reasons a vowel may be shortened at the joint of a compound (3,45a *rudrair mālinitattvaiś ca* for *rudrair mālinītattvaiś*

[17] Especially in *pādas* beginning with *catur-* hypermeter appears to be an accepted feature in Tantric texts.

ca; 3,101b *vīrayoginimānataḥ* instead of *vīrayoginīmānataḥ*). Likewise at the joint of a compound a vowel may be lengthened for metrical reasons (4/5,27d *asthijāpure* for *asthijapure*; 4/5,28b; 104d; 121b; 121d). A rather curious method for obtaining a short fifth syllable in a *pāda* is the dropping of the nominative case-ending. It is found for all three genders (1,21c *kapāṭās traya vātādyā* for *kapāṭās trayo vātādyā* (cf. 1,21c Notes); 1,36ab *himavān meru candrādi gandhamādana śrīgiriḥ* for *himavān meruś candrādi gandhamādanaḥ śrīgiriḥ*; 2,27a *gandhaṃ ca rasa rūpaṃ ca* for *gandhaṃ ca raso rūpaṃ ca*; 3,70b *sacarācara māyayā* for *sacarācaraṃ māyayā*; 3,82d *na sā prakṛti mānavī* for *na sā prakṛtir mānavī*; 4/5,56a *kālakūṭākhya nāma ca* for *kālakūṭākhyo nāma ca*). Although it appears that the writer had at his disposal several means to help him in constructing a regular *pāda*, this does not mean that he has succeeded in doing so in every instance. Throughout the text there are some fourteen examples where we do not find a short fifth syllable together with a long sixth syllable. Most of these instances are treated in the Notes to the translation.

All the mentioned 'irregularities' serve a useful function in the composition of a correct *pāda*. Besides these there are some other features in the text, which should be mentioned. Thematization of a consonant-stem is found in a few instances (1,14a *himavanta*; 1,28a & 2,17b *śira*; 3,15d *satyavādina* (see Notes); 4/5,51b *jyoti* (*metri causa*!)). The use of *r* as a Sandhi-consonant (4/5,122d *viṣṇu-r-antagā*). There are a few irregular verb-forms (3,9c *vācitvā*; 4/5,4c *-ṣṭhayed*; 4/5,22c *aspṛśyaṃ*). An irregular feminine derivation is found in 1,60c (*svāmī* instead of *svāminī*). As in most Tantric texts there is confusion between the gender of words (cf. 1,14c *kūṭāni* and 1,17c *kūṭās*; 1,36d *sthānam* (neuter) and 1,37d *sthānās*), and no congruity between related words (1,2c *siddhās trīṇy avatāraṃ*; 1,14c *trīṇi kūṭāni ye*; 1,17c *trīṇi kūṭāś*). These irregularities mainly concern male and neuter words. With regard to words of the feminine gender the following should be remarked. There are a few instances where a feminine word ending in *-ī* has become *-yā*. Thus in 3,43a the form *devyā*[*ḥ*] is best understood as the nom. pl. of *devyā*. In *śloka* 4/5,4d there is no doubt that *putryāś* is the nom. pl. of *putryā*. The form *yoginyaś* in *pāda* 3,93d should evidently be understood as an acc. pl. Most likely, the reading *yoginyaś* should be corrected to *yoginyāś*, the acc. pl. of *yoginyā*. There is, however, the possibility that the word *yoginī* is declined according to the mono-syllabic feminine stems in *-ī*, which show an acc. pl. on *-iyas*. With regard to the personal names of some female deities there is sometimes the choice between an instr. sg. and a nom. sg. In 4/5,102d there is no doubt that the form *bhānumatyā* should be regarded as a nom. sg. besides *bhānumatī*, but in 4/5,32a (*nādinyā*), 4/5,81a (*kapālinyā*) and 4/5,106c (*pāvanyā*) it is not clear whether a nom. sg. or an instr. sg. is meant. Most probably, however, these forms are to be regarded as a nom. sg. because in all parallel instances the names of the goddesses occur in the nominative case. When the writer wants to express the idea that a son of Devī is *together* with his consort, he seems to use a compound (cf. 4/5,108a *chagalīsaṃsthito*). Especially in the case of compounds of which the second member has an *a*- or *ā*- as initial vowel, there is no way in deciding whether the first member of the compound contains a female personal name in -*i*/-*ī* or in -*yā* (cf. 4/5,31d *mālinyādikramaiḥ*: *mālinī-ādikramaiḥ* or *mālinyā-ādikramaiḥ*; 4/5,33a *nivṛttyākhyā*: *nivṛtti-ākhyā* or *nivṛttyā-ākhyā*). In my opinion one should acknowledge the fact that especially with regard to female personal names or designations the final -*i*/-*ī* may change into -*yā*. In much the same way a female personal name in -*ā* may change into -*ī* as, for instance, is found in an Indonesian stone-inscription where the name of the goddess Cāmuṇḍā has become Cāmuṇḍī (cf. Damais 1962: 407 ff.)[18]. In theory one can expect the following pattern: -*ā* > -*ī* > -*yā* and -*ī* > -*yā*.

In conclusion attention should be paid to a particular use of the optative mood. In a few instances it appears that the optative mood is used to indicate a subordinate clause without a conjunction: 1,47cd *kāmarūpāṇi paśyeta kāmarūpaṃ tu tat smṛtam*, 'Because She can see [there every] form at will, that [place] is known as Kāmarūpa'; 3,102cd *yācayed bhāvitātmānaḥ ācāryaḥ pratipādayet*, 'When [the pupil] sincerely requests [instruction], then the teacher should teach him'. In one instance the optative mood seems to have replaced the Present Indicative (1,56ad *yas tv aṭec caiva trailokye ... cañcalānanda ucyate*, 'The one who roams about in the Three Worlds ... that one is called Cañcalānanda').

[18] According to Damais (*op. cit.*, p. 413) the forms Cāmuṇḍā and Cāmuṇḍī have geographical implications: "*Cāmuṇḍā* est donc du Nord et *Cāmuṇḍī* du Sud". I do not think that such a rather fundamental statement is corroborated by the facts which we have at our disposal at the time.

PART TWO

ṢAṬSĀHASRA SAṂHITĀ

Critical Text, Translation and Notes

PAṬALA 1

PAṬALA 1

1 [1]saṃvartāmaṇḍalānte[2] kramapadanihitānandaśaktiḥ[3] subhīmā
sṛṣṭinyāye[4] catuṣkaṃ[4] akulakulagataṃ[4] pañcakaṃ cānyaṣaṭkam |
catvāraḥ pañcako 'nyaḥ[5] punar api caturaḥ ṣoḍaśājñābhiṣekaṃ
devyāṣṭau[6] mūrtimadhye ha[7] sa[7] kha pha ra kalā bindupuṣpaṃ[8] kha-mudrā[9] ||
2 bālaṃ[10] kaumāravṛddhaṃ[10] paramaśivakalā cakradevī[11] kramāṇāṃ
śrīnāthaṃ candrapuryāṃ navanavakalitaṃ[12] yugmabhedais[13] tu sāram |
siddhās[14] trīṇy[14] avatāraṃ[14] prathamakaliyuge koṅkaṇe cādhikāraṃ
teṣāṃ vai putraśiṣyā navapuruṣakramās[15] teṣu madhye[16] dvirāṣṭau[17] ||
3 santānaṃ gotrapiṇḍaṃ kramapadasakalaṃ[18] ṣoḍaśāntaṃ[19] kramāntaṃ
śeṣā vai maṇḍalānāṃ[20] paribhramavimalaṃ pūjyasadbhāvavṛndam[21] |
ādāv aṣṭādaśāntaṃ kulakramasakalaṃ maṇḍalotthānapūrvaṃ
saṃskāraṃ triḥkramotthaṃ[22] paśumalakṣayakṛt[23] piṇḍaśuddhiḥ śivāgnau ||
4 madhye viśrāmabhūmau[24] prasaram[25] anubhavaṃ pratyayaṃ svādhikāraṃ
saṃsṛṣṭaṃ yena tasmai namatha[26] guruvaraṃ bhairavaṃ śrīkujeśam ||
5 vṛttyādhyuṣṭakramārthaṃ[27] racitam anubhavaṃ khañjinīmūrtipūrvaṃ
divyaughaṃ devasaṃjñaṃ[28] punar api[29] aparaṃ mānavaṃ triḥkramaugham |
bhedānekair vibhinnaṃ sakalapadakramamaṃ maṇḍalaṃ ṣaṭprakāraṃ
saṅketaṃ[30] kādipūrvaṃ sakalaguṇayutaṃ maṇḍalaṃ bhairavaṃ[31] tam[31] ||

1. A opens with oṃ svasti oṃ (hūṃ) śrīśivāya śrīdevyai gurubhyaḥ śrīkramagaṇapataye namaḥ; B with huṃ śivāya śrīkulagaṇādhipataye namaḥ; C reads oṃ namaḥ śivāya śrīkulagaṇādhipataye namaḥ 2. A śrīsaṃvartāmaṇḍalānte 3. B. kramapatha-; SaṃP -sahitānanda- 4. outside the microfilm of B; C catuṣkam akula-; SaṃP catuṣkaṃ tv akula- 5. AB 'nyaṃ 6. SaṃP divyā- 7. A sa ha; C illegible 8. SaṃP -puṣpā 9. C sva-; BC -mudrāḥ 10. A vṛddhaṃ kaumārabālaṃ 11. SaṃP vaktradevīṃ 12. B -kalitā 13. B yugmā-; BC -bhedas 14. SaṃP trīṇi siddhāvatāraṃ 15. A -kramaṃ; SaṃP -krame 16. BC madhyād 17. SaṃP dviraṣṭau 18. SaṃP padakramasakalaṃ 19. BC ṣoḍaśāraiḥ; SaṃP ṣoḍaśārcaṃ 20. SaṃP maṇḍalāni 21. B -sadbhava- 22. SaṃP tri-; A SaṃP -krameṇa 23. A -malahariṇīṃ 24. BC -bhūmiṃ; SaṃP -bhūmir 25. BC prasavam 26. SaṃP namata 27. A vṛtyādyu-; BC -ṣṭaṃ kra-; SaṃP vṛttādhyuṣṭam anārthaṃ 28. A -jñā 29. SaṃP api hy 30. ABC saṃketa- 31. A bhairavāntam.

1 In the centre of the Saṃvartāmaṇḍala [arises] Ānandaśakti, embedded in [all] the stages of the Tradition, terrifying; in the pattern of creation there are the Four relating to both *akula* and *kula*, the Five, next the Six, [again] Four, another Five, and again Four; there is the consecration according to the sixteenfold instruction; there are the eight goddesses embodied in Her form; there are [the consonants] HA, SA, KHA, PHA, and RA; the *kalā*, and the '*bindu*-flower'; there is the KHA-*mudrā*;

2 there is [the subdivision in] *bāla*, *kaumāra*, and *vṛddha*; She is Cakradevī, the limited energy of Parama Śiva, for [all] traditions.

Śrīnātha was in Candrapurī, provided with the eighteen [Nāthas]; because they were distinguished in couples, there was firmness;
three Siddhas were his incarnations; thus [he made] the Rule in [the country of] Koṅkaṇa at the beginning of the Kali Yuga.
These [three] had nine *putraśiṣyas*; from among these [originated] the sixteen [disciples],
3 then the continuous succession [of teachers], the lineage and families together constituting all the stages of the Tradition, the human body, the completion of the Tradition. There are other groups [bringing about] the purification of the erroneous, and a host of those whose nature is worthy of worship.
In the beginning there was the inclusive group of the eighteen [Nāthas], the whole of the Kula-tradition, preceded by the rise of the [Saṃvartā-]maṇḍala; there was the hallowing sprung from the three ways, destroying the defilement of the uninitiated, the purification of the body in the fire of Śiva;
4 in the centre, in the 'Place of Repose', there is progress, understanding, confidence, and [finally] self-authority — you honour Him Who has emanated [all this], the most eminent among the gurus, Bhairava, Śrīkujeśa!
5 For the sake of the series of three and a half *vṛtti*(?) there is made understanding preceded by [meditation on] the form of Khañjinī; the Divyaugha is called after the gods, another one [is called] Mānava — thus is the threefold way. Distinguished by various parts, [but] for the Tradition complete in [all] its stages, is the sixfold *maṇḍala*; as an agreement it is called Kādipūrva. Thus is the *maṇḍala* of Bhairava, provided with all the qualities.

As introduction the KmT and the ṢaṭSS both open with a *maṅgala*, the so-called Saṃvartāmaṇḍalasūtra. The version of this *sūtra* as found in the ṢaṭSS is considerably longer than in the KmT. The SaṃP which explains the longer version of the *sūtra* (see below), mentions this difference explicitly. After its explanation of the words *api caturaḥ* (1c) it states: *anyatra tadanantaraṃ tattvato maṇḍaleneti coktam; saṃsṛṣṭam ityādibhiḥ pūritam; idaṃ laghusaṃvartārthaḥ; ayaṃ tu bṛhatsaṃvartākatvād adhikataram uktam*, 'elsewhere, immediately after that (*sc. api caturaḥ*), *tattvato maṇḍalena* is said; it is completed with the words *saṃsṛṣṭam* etc.; that is the scope of the shorter Saṃvartāmaṇḍalasūtra; here, however, something additional is said because it concerns the longer Saṃvartāmaṇḍalasūtra'. Thus the shorter Saṃvartāmaṇḍalasūtra reads in its third *pāda* '... *api caturas tattvato maṇḍalena*', and its fourth *pāda* is identical with *pāda* 4b of the ṢaṭSS (*saṃsṛṣṭaṃ yena tasmai* ...). The statement of the SaṃP is correct with regard to the Saṃvartāmaṇḍalasūtra of the KmT, which consists of only one verse corresponding to the lines 1abc and 4b of the ṢaṭSS. Instead of *maṇḍalena* at the end of the third *pāda* which the SaṃP reads, the KmT has *maṇḍaledaṃ* (v.l. *maṇḍaleśaṃ*).

The Saṃvartāmaṇḍalasūtra, in both its versions, is composed in the *sragdharā*-metre (– – – | – ◡ – | – ◡ ◡ | ◡ ◡ ◡ | ◡ – – | ◡ – – | ◡ – –), which is applied correctly in the major part of the text. There are only a few transgressions against the metre. These will be dealt with when discussing each of the *pādas* separately.

The Saṃvartāmaṇḍalasūtra appears to present in a very concise way the line along which from the very beginning the teachings of the Kula-tradition have come down to us. The proposed translation of the Bṛhatsaṃvartāmaṇḍalasūtra should be considered an attempt. Only when the complete ṢaṭSS and its secondary texts have been edited and translated, it might prove possible to understand the *sūtra* to its full extent. As far as I know, the longer version of the Saṃvartāmaṇḍalasūtra is commented upon in only one text, the Saṃvartārthaprakāśa (SaṃP), of which only one MS is available. Among many other topics relating both to the contents of the KmT and the ṢaṭSS, from Folia 4B onwards the Bṛhatsaṃvartāmaṇḍalasūtra is explained. The text quotes every word from the *sūtra*, and explains it. These *pratīkas* have been included in the critical apparatus. The fifth stanza of the *sūtra* is given in full, but not explained.

1a: The *sūtra* derives its name obviously from its opening words (*saṃvartāmaṇḍa-lānte*). In the SaṃP the Saṃvartāmaṇḍala is described: *atasīpuṣpasaṃkāśam akhaṇḍi-tanityoditaṃ sarvagaṃ śāntam*, 'it has the outward appearance of the flower of the hemp, it arises constantly and completely, it is omnipresent and tranquil'. The description is not of much help. Significant is perhaps the reference to the flower of the hemp (*atasīpuṣpa*), which is of a blue colour. The colour blue has some importance in relation with the goddess Kubjikā (cf. Schoterman 1977:937), as well as with Devī in general. Moreover, hemp is sometimes used as a narcotic in Tantric rituals. The SaṃP explains the name Saṃvartāmaṇḍala as the *maṇḍala* of the [goddess] Saṃvartā: 'when Śakti is together with Śiva destroying the worlds (*saṃvartana*), She is called Saṃvartā'. Obviously, the author of the SaṃP mistook the final *-ā* of *saṃvartā* for a feminine ending, while it is clearly the lengthening of a vowel at the joint of a compound (*saṃvarta-maṇḍala*). Apparently the term Saṃvartāmaṇḍala refers to the periodical destruction of the world, and the beginning of a new one (cf. 2,14 Notes). For this reason the Saṃvartāmaṇḍala is called in the SaṃP the 'egg' (*aṇḍa* = *brahmāṇḍa*, 'the mundane egg'). According to the SaṃP Bhairava and His *śakti* Bhairavī or Ānandaśakti reside in the centre of the *maṇḍala* (*tadante tanmadhye*; for *-ante*, 'in the centre', see Gonda 1938: 457 ff.). This Ānandaśakti features in all the stages (*pāda*) of the tradition (*krama*), viz. the tradition according to the Kula-system (SaṃP: *kramaḥ kulakramaḥ*). She appears at the beginning of a new Yuga, in the centre of the Saṃvartāmaṇḍala which marks the period of dissolution between the successive Yugas. When Śiva and His *śakti* are united, creation starts and the Kula-doctrine is proclaimed.

1bc: In the pattern of creation (*sṛṣṭinyāya*) the first phase in the propagation of the Kula-doctrine is symbolized by the series of Four, Five, Six, Four, Five, and Four. This series which amounts to twenty-eight in total, is appropriately called the Aṣṭāviṃśatikrama, 'the Series of the Twenty-eight'. This Aṣṭāviṃśatikrama features in several instances in the ṢaṭSS (cf. 2,21b ff.). The order of the units (4-5-6-4-5-4) is fixed in the texts, but their 'contents' may vary. Thus the SaṃP explains the six units here as follows: 1) Icchā, Jñānī, Kriyā, Buddhi, 2) earth (*pṛthivī*), water (*āpas*), fire (*tejas*), wind (*vāyu*), sky (*ākāśa*), 3) the six *āmnāyas*, the six deities Ḍākinī up to Hākinī, or the six *vijñānārthas* (*tvac*, *cakṣus*, *ghrāṇa*, *jihvā*, *śravaṇa*, *manas*), 4) the four Mahāpīṭhas (Oḍiyāna, Jālandhara, Pūrṇagiri, Kāmarūpa), 5) the five *tanmātras* (*gandha*, *rasa*, *rūpa*, *sparśa*, *śabda*), 6) *sattva*, *rajas*, *tamas*, *guṇātīta*. This explanation of the SaṃP does not correspond with any similar enumeration in the ṢaṭSS or cognate texts, although some of the units are common (cf. Schoterman 1980:344). The enumeration of the SaṃP contains several units well-known from other Tantric texts and Sāṃkhyaphilosophy. In some instances the usual number is increased in order to reach the number required for the Aṣṭāviṃśatikrama. Thus in the first unit which should consist of four parts, the fixed triad Icchā, Jñānī, and Kriyā (KRP F.15A: *śaktitraya*) is completed with Buddhi. The second unit consists of the well-known five *mahābhūtas*. The third unit offers a choice out of three possibilities according to the SaṃP. It consists either of the six *āmnāyas* (cf. Gupta a.o. 1979:41), the goddesses Ḍākinī, Rākinī, Lākinī, Kākinī, Sākinī, and Hākinī, or the six *vijñānārthas* as they are called in the SaṃP, which are the five *jñānendriyas* of the ŚT (1,34) completed with *manas*. In the SvT (10,1094) these five are called the *buddhīndriyas* (cf. ṢaṭSS 21,67 where *tvac*, *cakṣus*, *jihvā*, and *ghrāṇa* are called the *buddhīndriyacatuṣka*). The fourth unit consists of the four Mahāpīṭhas, which are well-known in Tantric texts. In the ṢaṭSS a fifth Mahāpīṭha, the Mātaṅgapīṭha, is sometimes added to these four. The fifth unit consists of the five *tanmātras*. The sixth unit comprises the three *guṇas* completed with a fourth which is 'beyond the *guṇas*' (*guṇātīta*). The SaṃP explains *akulakulagata* (1b) with *akulaṃ laukikaṃ kulaṃ tāntrikam*, '*akula* is everyday life, *kula* is Tantrism'. More likely it refers to Śiva (*akula*) and Śakti (*kula*), the participants in creation when united (*kulākula*; cf. 1,21). The expression *akulakulagata* should be connected with each of the six units of the Aṣṭāviṃśatikrama.

In the second line of the first verse we come across the first metrical irregularity. The reading *catuṣkam akulakulagataṃ* would result in a short seventh syllable (*-ṣkam*) of the line instead of the required long syllable. MS A 'solves' this problem by reading *catuṣkaṃ | akulakulagataṃ*. Only the SaṃP reads *catuṣkaṃ tv akulakulagataṃ*, which is metrically correct. From the eighteen MSS of the KmT at our disposal, sixteen read *catuṣkaṃ akula-* here; only two MSS read *catuṣkam akula-*. The reading of the SaṃP seems to be a correction not attested in any other manuscript. Obviously the ending in an *anusvāra* in *catuṣkaṃ* despite the following vowel of *akula-* functions here as a means of lengthening the syllable *-ṣka* as required by the metre. For this reason I have accepted in the text the reading *catuṣkaṃ akula-*, rather than inserting *tv* as the SaṃP does. To what the 'consecration according to the sixteenfold instruction' (1c: *ṣoḍaśājñābhiṣeka*) exactly refers, is not clear to me. The SaṃP explains it as consisting of the Six Paths (*ṣaḍadhvan*), the nine conditions of existence (*navagati*), and the *cit kalā*. The Six Paths (*bhūta*, *bhāva*, *śākta*, *māntra/āṇava*, *raudra*, *śāṃbhava*; or: *bhuvana*, *pada*, *varṇa*, *dvādaśa* (= *mantra*), *kalā*, *tattva* (cf. ŚT 5,78; Padoux 1975: 261 ff.)) are discussed in the 17th chapter of the ṢaṭSS (= KmT 10). The nine conditions of existence (*navagati*) do not feature anywhere in the ṢaṭSS, as far as I know — the Buddhists reckon six *gatis* usually. The *cit kalā* is the 17th *kalā* of which there are usually sixteen (cf. Padoux 1975: 80). In the ṢaṭSS this 17th *kalā* is also called *mahādīptā* (chapters 15; 17) or *nityā* (chapter 42). Although the enumeration of the SaṃP indeed amounts to sixteen (6+9+1), the explanation is not very convincing. The SaṃP offers another explanation for the number sixteen: sixteen places (*sthāna*) of which the first is called the *bhargasthāna* (*bhargasthānādayaś caiva ṣoḍaśa*). Bharga is a name of Rudra, but what is meant with the *bhargasthāna* I do not know; perhaps it refers to a particular letter of the Skt alphabet (see notes on 1d).

1d: The eight goddesses (*devyāṣṭau*) are the Aṣṭamātṛkā, viz. Brahmāṇī, Māheśvarī, Kaumārī, Vaiṣṇavī, Vārāhī, Aindrāṇī, Cāmuṇḍā, and Mahālakṣmī. The expression *ha sa kha pha ra kalā bindupuṣpaṃ* forms a *bīja* according to the SaṃP: HSKHPHREṂ. The word *kalā* represents the vowel *e*. The '*bindu*-flower' (*bindupuṣpa*) is the *anusvāra* which adorns the *bīja* on its top like a flower (SaṃP: *puṣpavac chirobhūṣaṇam*). The *bīja* HSKHPHREṂ is the so-called *kulakūṭa*, the most prominent sacred syllable of the Kula-tradition (*paṭala* 34). The *bīja* HSKHPHREṂ belongs to Śiva, while the form of the same *bīja* as SHKHPHREṂ (= MS A) belongs to Śakti. A *bīja* beginning with an *h* belongs to Śiva; with an *s* for its first letter it belongs to Śakti (cf. Schoterman 1980: 345 note 7; Appendix II; *paṭala* 34). The explanation of the SaṃP seems correct, but another possibility should also be considered. It is possible to regard *kalā* in the text as a plural instead of a singular. In this way *kalāḥ* refers to the sixteen vowels of the Skt alphabet. Consequently, one should then count sixteen *bījas*: HSKHPHRAṂ, HSKHPHRĀṂ ... up to HSKHPHRAḤṂ. These sixteen *bījas* might then be related to the concept of the 'consecration according to the sixteenfold instruction' in the previous line. We have suggested above (1c) that the *bhargasthāna* of the SaṃP might refer to a particular letter of the Skt alphabet. If this suggestion is correct, the *bhargasthāna* should represent the vowel *a*. As is shown in Appendix II the fifty letters of the Skt alphabet can be represented by a manifestation of Devī (Mālinī) or Śiva (Śabdarāśi). In the list of the fifty manifestations of Śiva the vowel *a* is represented by Śrīkaṇṭha. It is not unlikely, though, that other lists exists featuring other manifestations of Śiva as representatives of one of the fifty letters. In one of such lists Bharga might represent the vowel *a*. The number sixteen seems to be significant. Perhaps it refers to the sixteen disciples (2d): each of them could have possessed his own personal *bīja*, all being variants of the *kulakūṭa*.

The KHA-*mudrā* refers to the Khecarī-*mudrā*, which is dealt with in *paṭala* 10 of the ṢaṭSS (cf. Brunner 1974: 144; Briggs 1973: *s.v.*).

2a: The first *pāda* of the second verse provides a second problem connected with the metre. Obviously, one has to read *bālakaumāravṛddhaṃ*, which produces, however, a short second syllable, whereas the metre requires a long second syllable. As we have seen above (1b), the *anusvāra* is used here again to regulate the metre (*bālaṃ kaumāravṛddhaṃ*). The SaṃP explains this triad with *avasthātrayaṃ*; *bālakrama-kaumārakramavṛddhakramam iti kramatrayam*, which is hardly of any help. Probably it refers to the nine Siddhas (Gagana etc.; see below). These nine are 'classified' according to this threefold division: Gagana, Padma, and Deva are called *bālanāthas*; Kumuda, Kamala, and Rāma are *kaumāranāthas*; Bhairava, Śiva, and Kṛṣṇa are *vṛddhanāthas* (cf. *paṭala* 43). The KnT, moreover, assigns authority (*adhikāra*) to the three groups in the three Lokas: *bhūr*, *pātāla*, and *gagana* (KnT F.18A). The distinction of a unit in three gradations, as we see here (*bāla*, 'child-like'; *kaumāra*, 'juvenile'; *vṛddha*, 'old') represents the same threefold division which is found, for instance, with regard to the *nyāsa* of Mālinī. Here the three stages are called *bhavā*, *sthairyā*, and *saṃhārī* respectively, together forming the threefold cycle of excistence (cf. Appendix II). Another appellation for the three stages is *bāla*, *madhyama*, and *jyeṣṭha* (see below 2b). With the name Cakradevī Devī might be meant in Her aspect as Ānandaśakti (1a) appearing in the centre of the Saṃvartāmaṇḍala. In this way *cakra* refers to the Saṃvartāmaṇḍala. She is called the 'limited energy' (*kalā*; cf. Padoux 1975: 193) of Parama Śiva. As Ānandaśakti She appears for all the traditions (*kramānāṃ*). The SaṃP reads instead of Cakradevī the form Vaktradevī, which is obviously corrupt. Yet the author of the SaṃP troubles himself to explain this evident mistake: *vaktrākhyā yā devī śivavanitā śakravākyapatipālikānām*, 'the beloved wife of Śiva is called Vaktrā for those women who protect the words of Śakra (h.l. = Śiva?)'.

2b: The city of Candrapurī occupies an important place in our text as a centre from which the teachings of Kulālikāmnāya were propagated (cf. Schoterman 1977: 934). The expression *navanavakalita*, 'provided with the eighteen [Nāthas]', is uncertain. On the authority of the SaṃP I have understood *nava* as meaning 'nine', and not 'new'. The SaṃP explains these twice nine as the eighteen-fold line of Nāthas, ending with Śrīnātha, the *divyāmnāyānukrama*. Although the major part of the SaṃP is written in prose, the enumeration of the eighteen Nāthas is composed in the *śloka*-metre. Usually only quotations from other—metrical—texts constitute the metrical parts of the SaṃP. Probably this is also the case here, as we find the same list of eighteen Nāthas in the KnT, in the chapter of the text which is called Ādyolitraya (KnT FF.16A ff.). It is told in the KnT that there was only one Guru in the city Candrapura who belonged to the Western Tradition (*paścima krama*), as opposed to the Siddhānta which has five Gurus; the Vāmadakṣiṇatantras which count four Gurus, or the Bhairavatantras which have three Gurus. Next the KnT provides an enumeration of the eighteen Nāthas ending with Śrīnātha. The list of the KnT runs as follows (the names of the eighteen as found in the SaṃP are put between brackets): 1) Unmanīśāna (Unmanāmnāya), 2) Manonmana (Manonmaya), 3) Samanākhya (Samanā), 4) Vyāpinyākhya (Vyāpinyā), 5) Avyakta (id.), 6) Nandīśa (Nandinyā), 7) Manthāna (id.), 8) Bhairava (Pheruka), 9) Samyākhya (Samayākṣī), 10) Śrījṛmbhākhya (Jaṃbhalā), 11) Kālasaṃkarṣa (Kālasaṃkārṣṇa), 12) Caṇḍasaṃjñaka (Caṇḍanirṇaya), 13) Aghoreśa (id.), 14) Lokākhya (Trailokya), 15) Vimala (Vinaya), 16) Kamala (id.), 17) Carcikākhya (Carcikā), 18) Śrīnātha.

Each of the eighteen Nāthas is accompanied by a *śakti*, the names of which are not mentioned in either of the two texts. Yet it seems that the list of the SaṃP sometimes enumerates the name of the *śakti* instead of the Nātha (cf. Samanā, Vyāpinyā, Nandinyā, Samayākṣī, Jaṃbhalā, and Carcikā). As is usual in similar lists, the names of the accompanying *śakti* are often merely feminine forms of the names of their male consorts. The KnT further states, that Kubjikā or Kālī manifests Herself in three forms (*jyeṣṭha*, *madhyama*, *bāla*) among these *śaktis*:
1) *jyeṣṭhāvali*: Vyāpinī.
25 *madhyamāvali*: Samanā, in the shape (*mūrti*) of Tripurā.
3) *bālāvali*: Manonmanā, in the shape (*mūrti*) of Mālinī.
Obviously, the three manifestations of Kubjikā or Kālī are related to the 2nd, 3rd, and 4th Nātha. In these three manifestations Kubjikā / Kālī descends from the highest heaven (*satyaloka*) for the benefit of mankind (*anugrahārthaṃ lokānām avatīrṇā parā kalā | olikramavibhāgena āgatā satyalokataḥ*). Furthermore, the KnT connects these three stages with three of the Mahāpīṭhas and their Lords. Thus:
1) Oḍiyāna: Oḍḍīśanātha = Nandīśvara.
2) Pūrṇagiri: Śrīṣaṣṭhanātha = Kārttikeya.
3) Kāmarūpa: Śrīcaryānandanātha = Gaṇeśvara.
The KnT is rather cryptic with regard to the name of Kubjikā or Kālī in connection with the first Nātha, Unmanīśāna. She is described with the epithet 'common to all' (*sarvasādhāraṇā*); no distinction is made in that particular stage (*na bhedas tāsu vidyate*); She is *para-rūpeṇa*, hence called *parā kalā*.

The remaining part of line 2b (*yugmabhedais tu sāram*) seems to stand on its own, as the use of *tu* might indicate. Its interpretation is doubtful, but it may indicate that because the eighteen Nāthas were accompanied by their *śaktis* (*yugmabheda*), the line proved to be firm (*sāra*).

2c: The beginning of this *pāda* is metrically incorrect: *siddhās trīṇy avatāraṃ* has a short fourth syllable (*-ṇy a-*) instead of the required long syllable. The reading of the SaṃP has indeed a long fourth syllable, but now the second syllable is short instead of long (SaṃP *trīṇi siddhāvatāraṃ*). It appears virtually impossible to construct a metrically correct line with these three words at its beginning. Apart from the fact that the beginning of this *pāda* is metrically incorrect, the Skt used is at the least peculiar (*trīṇi* instead of *trayas*). The three Siddhas are according to the SaṃP: Candra, Sūrya, and Agni, the well-known triad of Moon, Sun, and Fire. More probably, it refers to three of the four so-called *gurucatuṣka*, 'the four Gurus'. These four (Mitranātha, Oḍḍīśanātha, Ṣaṣṭhanātha, and Caryanātha) feature in the last unit of the Aṣṭāviṃśatikrama (see above; Schoterman 1980: 344). We have seen in the commentary on *pāda* 2b that three of these four were connected with three of the four Mahāpīṭhas, and with three manifestations of Kubjikā or Kālī. Perhaps the 'missing' Siddha, Mitranātha, is related with Kubjikā / Kālī in Her connection with the first Nātha, Unmanīśāna, of which no specific form of the Goddess was mentioned (see above), but which should be Unmanī in comparison with the others (Manonmana & Manonmanā; Samana & Samanā; Vyāpini & Vyāpinī). With the help of these three Siddhas Śrīnātha established the authority (*adhikāra*) of the Kula-tradition at the beginning of our era, the Kali Yuga (*prathamakaliyuge*) from the city of Candrapurī (2b), which was located in the region of Koṅkaṇa — a region of special interest for the Kula-tradition (cf. Schoterman 1977: 934). The SaṃP situates Koṅkaṇa somewhere in the Himālayas (SaṃP *koṅkaṇa iti himālayādideśaviśeṣaḥ*), but this does not seem very likely. Probably Koṅkaṇa denotes the whole strip of land between the Western Ghats and the Arabian Sea (Dey 1971: *s.v.*).

2d: These, viz. the three Siddhas, had nine disciples called *putraśiṣyas* (see below). The nine are Gagana, Kumuda, etc. (see above). The expression *navapuruṣakrama* is difficult to understand. Obviously the first part of the compound (*nava-* = 'nine') refers to the actual number of the *putraśiṣyas*, but *-puruṣa-* is puzzling, unless we understand it literally: 'a male; a human being'. In this way the nine *putraśiṣyas* differ from the three Siddhas, the latter being solely legendary. This assumption may be inferred from the KnT. The eighteen beginning with Unmanīśa up to Śrīnātha are mentioned in the KnT without being provided with any details. The same proves true for the four Gurus (Mitranātha etc.). Only when these nine are enumerated, the KnT becomes very detailed: of each of the nine the place of origin, the *jāti*, the name, *caryānāma*, *pūjānāma*, *guptanāma*, *kīrtināma*, two other names, and the name of the *śakti* is given. From this enumeration it appears that the names Gagana, Kumuda, Padma, Deva, Bhairava, Kamala, Śiva, Rāma, and Kṛṣṇa are the *pūjā*-names of these nine, each ending in *-ānandanātha*. Thus: Gagana is actually called Gaganāndanātha; Kumuda should be Kumudānandanātha, and so on. The SaṃP seems to refer to this nomenclature by explaining *navapuruṣakrama* with *navātmānandā(=a?)nāthādipuruṣāṇāṃ kramam*. In the following list the 'real' names of the nine are given, their place of origin, and caste, as found in the KnT (FF.18B ff.; cf. also Kaulajñānanirṇaya, pp. 68 ff.):

Place of origin (*janmadeśa*)	Caste (*jāti*)	Name (*nāma*)
1) Pauṇḍravardhana in Oḍiyāna	Brahmin	Trivikrama (*sāmavedin*)
2) Koṅkaṇa	Brahmin	Dāmodara (*ṛgvedin*)
3) Auhaladeśa in Pūrṇagiri	Kṣatriya	Udayarāja
4) Mathurā	Brahmin	Govinda
5) Vārāṇāsī	Brahmin	Viṣṇuśarman
6) Kābhauradeśa in Kāmarūpa	Śūdra	Bāhila
7) Śrīśaila	Vaiśya	Dehila
8) Kāśmīra	Śūdra	Sehila
9) Kundāpura in Oḍiyāna	Kalyapāla (liquor-seller)	Māhila

According to the KnT these nine disciples were former Buddhist monks converted by Unmanīśanātha or Tūṣṇīśanātha to the Kulāmnāya as it seems, although the text is here rather difficult to understand (cf. Schoterman 1977: 934). Their sudden conversion to the Kula-doctrine was due to a miraculous deed performed by Śrīnātha. The story runs briefly as follows: 'On the instigation of Śrīśaṃbhunātha (= Śiva) Śrīnātha went to the Gandharvaloka. There the Buddhists (*saugata*) asked him who he might be, and what the object of his coming was. When Śrīnātha told them that he was a Siddha who had obtained the supreme, divine instruction (*divyājñāvaralabdhaka*), the Buddhist monks (*vandaka*) laughed at him, and invited him to prove this statement. Thereupon Śrīnātha pronounced the sacred syllable HŪṂ, and all the lofty *vihāras* of the monks collapsed. The monks acknowledged the authority of Śrīnātha, and were subsequently converted by him' (KnT FF.17B ff.). Another version of the origin of the nine disciples is related in the 43rd chapter of the ṢaṭSS. It simply tells that that the nine were 'created' for the benefit of mankind on the Candragiri.

The first of the nine, Trivikrama, seems to be the most important of the group, as several stories are told about him in the texts. Thus in the same 43rd chapter of the ṢaṭSS it is told that Trivikrama was born in Pauṇḍravardhana where he studied the three Vedas. Afterwards he went to Śrī Laṅkā (*siṃhaladvīpa*), where he became a king and embraced the Buddhist faith. He persecuted the twice-born fiercely. On one occasion he came upon an ascetic practising austerities on a cemetery. The king could not draw his attention, as the ascetic was deeply absorbed in meditation. Finally the ascetic 'wakes up', and converts King Trivikrama to the Kula-doctrine. Apparently the story is concerned with the same Trivikrama as the one whom the KnT mentions, since both were born in Pauṇḍravardhana, and were students of the Vedas. There is yet another story with regard to Trivikrama in the KnT. Discussing the *kīrti*-name of Trivikrama, the KnT says that he was called Śrīvyomānanda, because he forced the sun to shine for twelve successive days above the city of Karṇakubja (KnT F.19B). It is only with regard to Trivikrama, the first of the nine, that several stories are found in the texts. Of the other eight no particulars are mentioned, as far as I know, apart from their different names, place of birth, caste, and *śakti*.

We have seen that these nine were designated as *putraśiṣyas*, 'having their sons for their disciples'. According to the KnT the nine had sixteen disciples: the *vṛddhanāthas* (Bhairava, Śiva, Kṛṣṇa) had eight disciples, the *kaumāranathas* (Kumuda, Kamala, Rāma) only one, and the *bālanāthas* (Gagana, Padma, Deva) seven (cf. 2a; KnT F.18A). These sixteen disciples are enumerated in the KnT (FF.20B ff.), starting with Madhusūdana etc. Again the place of birth, the caste, the 'real' name, the *caryānāma* etc. are given. Among the sixteen there are eight Brahmins, four Kṣatriyas, two Vaiśyas, and two Śūdras. Noteworthy is the fact, that there is one female disciple, a woman of the *śūdra*-caste. A slightly different list is found in the 44th Ch. of the ṢaṭSS, where the first one is called Piṅgeśa or Candrābja.

3a: The term *piṇḍa*, 'family', stands here for *sapiṇḍa* (lit. 'having the same *piṇḍa* or offering to the ancestors'). It includes the members of a family through six generations in an ascending and descending line (cf. Manu 5,60). The expression *ṣoḍaśānta* (BC *ṣoḍaśāra*; SaṃP *ṣoḍaśārca*) refers to the human body compared with a wheel (*cakra*) with sixteen 'ends' (*anta*) or spokes (*ara*). The 'ends' are those parts of the rim of a wheel, which lie between the ends of the sixteen spokes or actually constitute the ends of these spokes. They are held together by the *nemi* (felly). Thus a wheel of sixteen 'ends' also has sixteen spokes. The comparison of the human body with a wheel, in particular with a wheel of sixteen spokes, is frequently found in the Upaniṣads (cf. Śvetāśvatara Up. 1,4; Praśna Up. 6,6). The explanation of these sixteen parts is not always the same, but the number sixteen appears to be fundamental (cf. Johnston 1930: 864 ff.; Buddhacarita 12,18-19). The SaṃP explains the expression with *unmanādiṣoḍaśayogabhāvana*, which refers perhaps to the first eight Nāthas with their female consorts (cf. p. 36). With *pāda* 3a the exposition of the various stages of creation according to the Kula-doctrine ends: from the rise of Ānandaśakti in the centre of the Saṃvartāmaṇḍala up to the human body.

3b: The author of the Saṃvartāmaṇḍalasūtra appears to acknowledge the fact that there exist other *maṇḍalas* besides the one that propagates the pure Kula-doctrine, which may prove beneficial for the people. The word *maṇḍala* denotes here groups of teachers, different from those of the Kulālikāmnāya (SaṃP *maṇḍalānīti jaganmaṇḍalāni gurumaṇḍalāni vā*). Next to these 'organized' groups there are many individuals worthy to be held in esteem (*pūjyasadbhāvavṛndam*).

In this *pāda* of the third verse we find another metrical irregularity: the 9th syllable (sc. *-ri-* in *paribhrama-*) is long by position instead of short as is required by the metre. Usually a short syllable remains short only before a following *-kra*, *-pra*, *-bra* or *-hra* on account of the occurrence of the *r* in the ligatures. Probably we have to accept here aan extension of that rule in order to obtain a short 9th syllable.

3c: Although in the course of time several differences of opinion developed with regard to the contents of the Kula-doctrine proper, as was acknowledged in the previous line, in the beginning (*ādau*) up to the eighteen Nāthas (cf. 2b) no different views existed: during the period which lasted from the beginning of creation up to the eighteen Nāthas, there was only the one Kula-tradition (*kulakramasakalaṃ*). Although the KnT is not very clear on this point, it seems that after the eighteenth Nātha, Śrīnātha (cf. p. 36), there were three others of which the first was called Śāṃbhava (KnT F.16B *śrīnātho 'ṣṭādaśaḥ smṛtaḥ | śāṃbhavāditrayopetaṃ ...*). Another possible reference to this Śāṃbhava and his two companions is found on the same page of the KnT: *śrīnāthādisvagurvantaṃ pūjayed gurumaṇḍalam | śāṃbhavādikrameṇaiva yāvac chrīnātha ciñcinī*, 'one should honour the Gurumaṇḍala from Śrīnātha up to one's own Guru; in proper order from Śāṃbhava up to Śrīnātha and (?) Ciñcinī (KnT F.16B). It is possible to understand *ciñcinī* as the name of one of the three, viz. Ciñcinin, but more likely it is the name of the female consort of this Śrīnātha. In the Ciñcinīmata (cf. Goudriaan & Gupta 1981: 57) the goddess Ciñcinī seems to be identical with Kubjikā.

Summarizing the above, it seems that at the end of the eighteen Nāthas three other Nāthas appeared, of which the second is not mentioned anywhere; the first was Śāṃbhava, the third Śrīnātha. Although the text is not very clear again, these three seem to be identified with the three *avatāras* mentioned in verse 2c (KnT F.17AB). Beginning with these three, anyway, different views arise within the Kula-tradition with regard to the teachings, as it seems.

3d: In this *pāda* the viewpoint mentioned above seems to be confirmed by mentioning a *saṃskāra* 'sprung from three ways' (*triḥkramottha*), which might point to the three Nāthas after Śrīnātha. Although three different opinions arose with regard to the Kula-doctrine, all three obviously stayed within the limits of the Kula-doctrine, since they 'destroy the defilement of the uninitiated' (*paśumalakṣayakṛt*).

As to the expression *piṇḍaśuddhiḥ śivāgnau*, '[there was] the purification of the body in the fire of Śiva', the explanation of the SaṃP is acceptable: 'by means of Mālinī,

Śabdarāśi etc. one is capable to purify one's own body' (*mālinīśabdarāśyādibhiḥ piṇḍaṃ deham ātmānaṃ śodhayati*). Leaving, with the last of the eighteen Nāthas, the mythic part of the Kula-tradition, purification of the body in order to become a member of the Kula-order can only be achieved by 'earthly' means, e.g. by means of ritual. For this there is the sixfold *nyāsa*, consisting of the *nyāsa* of Mālinī, Śabdarāśi, Trividyā, Aghorikāṣṭaka, Dvādaśāṅga, and Ṣaḍanga (cf. Appendix II). The compound *śivāgnau* refers to the sacrificial fire as a manifestation of Śiva on earth, according to the SaṃP (*śivāgnāv iti loke kujāgni*[*r*] *yajñārthaḥ*; cf. Bodewitz 1973: 316 n. 18).

4a: The expression 'Place of Repose' (*viśrāmabhūmi*) is not clear to me, nor in the middle (*madhye*) of what it is thought to be located. According to the SaṃP the *viśrāmabhūmi* is in the centre of the Cakras, through which the central *nāḍī*, the Suṣumṇā, runs (*madhye iti antaścakrāṇāṃ madhye; viśrāmabhūmir iti iḍāpiṅgalayor madhye vakṣye viśrāmabhūmikā ity ukteḥ*). Perhaps *viśrāmabhūmi* refers to the Santānabhuvana or Saṃvartāmaṇḍala (1,29), which is called the 'most excellent refuge' (1,33c: *āśrama parama*), having the Suṣumṇā for its base (1,31a: *suṣumṇādhārabhūta*). In the second chapter of the ṢaṭSS four different locations of this Santānabhuvana are mentioned: 1) above the Brahmarandhra, 2) in the Anāhata Cakra, in the centre of the Mātṛcakra, 3) below the navel, 4) in the Ādhāra Cakra (2,4-15). Possibly the SaṃP has these four places in mind. Otherwise with *antaścakrāṇāṃ* all of the six Cakras might be meant. However, until other passages dealing with the *viśrāmabhūmi* are found, the exact meaning of the term remains doubtful.

4b: With *pāda* 4b the shorter version of the Saṃvartāmaṇḍalasūtra as it is found in the KmT, is taken up. Since all the three MSS of the ṢaṭSS read *namatha*, I have accepted this reading for the ṢaṭSS. In the KmT (1,1d) the reading *namata* has been preferred, although three out of the six palm-leaf MSS also read *namatha*. The SaṃP which reads *namata* mentions the variant reading *namatha* explicitly in its commentary (*namata iti namaskaromi; namatheti ca pāṭhaḥ*).

The epithet *guruvara* ('the most eminent among the Gurus') of Bhairava is explained in the SaṃP in connection with the three groups of teachers (cf. 5b *triḥkramaugha*). Thus the three groups (*divyaugha*, *siddhaugha*, *mānavaugha*) are related respectively to the three *guṇas* (*sattva*, *tamas*, *rajas*); the three Lokas (*svarga*, *pātāla*, *martya*); with the *devas*, the *dānavas*, and the *manuṣyas*; the sun, the darkness (*andhakāra*), and the moon; with fire, ether, and water. Among those three groups of Gurus, the most excellent Guru is the one without any *guṇa*, sc. Bhairava (*gurūṇāṃ tryaughasvarūpāṇāṃ madhye varaṃ śreṣṭhaṃ nirguṇasvarūpam*). Although Bhairava is one, He appears in a manifold form (*sa eka evānaketvaṃ pratibhāti*).

For *śrīkujeśa* the SaṃP gives the variant reading [*śrī*]*kulīśa* (*śrīkujeśam iti kulīśaṃ iti pāṭhaḥ*).

5: The Saṃvartāmaṇḍalasūtra ends in fact with the fourth—half—Sragdharā verse, although a fifth verse in the Sragdharā-metre is added in all the three MSS of the ṢaṭSS. In the KmT there are two MSS which also add an additional verse, which is composed however, in a different metre (*śārdūlavikrīḍitā*). After its comment on the fourth *sragdharā*-verse the SaṃP states: 'In the same Manthāna [the following verse] is said' (*tatraiva manthāne coktam*). Manthāna refers here to the ṢaṭSS, and not to the Manthānabhairava Tantra in which these lines are not found at all. Hereafter, the

SaṃP quotes the fifth verse in full (contrary to the other four verses!), but does not provide any comment on it.

The beginning of the fifth verse is problematic, and I do not know to what it refers. The deity Khañjinī (lit. 'The Limping One'), is an aspect of Devī, just as Kubjikā is (cf. Schoterman 1980: 346). In the second line the Triḥkramaugha is mentioned, which is explained in the commentary on verse 4b (see above). Note that only two groups are mentioned here: the *siddhaugha* is wanting. the sixfold *maṇḍala* is used in the Aṣṭāviṃśatikramapūjā (KnT F.50B ff.). In this *maṇḍala* one should worship the Aṣṭāviṃśatikrama (KnT F.49B: *śrīkramamaṇḍalaṣaṭkoṇe aṣṭāviṃśatikramam arcayet*). In line 5d I have chosen for the reading of the SaṃP (*saṃketaṃ*), since it is metrically correct. The expression *kādipūrva* refers to a particular designation of the texts belonging to this tradition (cf. Śāstri 1905: LXXVIII).

6 śrīmaddhimavataḥ pṛṣṭhe trikūṭaśikharāntagam |
santānapuramadhyastham anekākārarūpiṇam ||
7 tryaśraṃ ca triprakāraṃ ca triśaktiguṇam ujjvalam |
candrasūryakṛtālokaṃ vahnidedīpyavarcasam ||
8 trisandhyāveṣṭitaṃ divyaṃ prākāratripathānvitam |
dvārapālatrayopetaṃ trikapāṭārgalānvitam ||
9 anekaratnasaṃdīptam udyānavanamaṇḍitam |
vasantaguṇasampannaṃ satatānandapūritam[1] ||
10 santānabhuvanaṃ divyaṃ divyādivyair niṣevitam |
tatrasthaṃ[2] bhuvaneśānaṃ vyaktāvyaktaṃ sanātanam ||
11 kāryakāraṇabhāvena kiñcit kālam upekṣayā[3] |
tiṣṭhate bhairavīśānaḥ[4] sa caiko jagataḥ prabhuḥ ||

1. ABC satātānanda- 2. BC tatra taṃ 3. BC apekṣayā 4. A -śānaṃ; C bhairave-; outside the microfilm of B.

6 On top of the Himavat, on the summit of the Trikūṭa, in the centre of the Santānapura, having a manifold appearance,
7 triangular, with three aspects, three Śaktis and three qualities, splendid, supplied with the light of Sun and Moon, with the brilliant lustre of Vahni,
8 invested by the three Sandhyās, heavenly, provided with three walls and three paths, furnished with three door-keepers, three door-panels and three bolts,
9 bright by various jewels, adorned with gardens and groves, endowed with the features of Spring, filled with constant Bliss,
10 —[thus one should visualize] the heavenly Santānabhuvana, frequented by gods and mortals.
[One should imagine] the Lord of the world abiding there, both revealed and unrevealed, eternal.
11 Encompassing cause and effect the Lord of Bhairavī stands [there] for some time, inactive, the sole Master of the world.

The *ślokas* 6-11c are identical with the introductory verses of the KmT (1,2-7c), except for some minor differences which we have accepted, since the three MSS of the ṢaṭSS and the Ṭ are unanimous.

The lines 6-8 are explained in the ṢaṭSS itself (1,12-26), as does the Ṭ which, however, also comments on ṢaṭSS 1,16cd. The *ślokas* 9-11 are not discussed, neither in the ṢaṭSS itself nor in the Ṭ. This is probably due to the fact that these lines do not provide any 'vital' information regarding the Santānabhuvana, but merely add some non-committal epithets (9; 10ab). The importance of the *ślokas* 6-8 may also be deduced from the fact that the introductory *ślokas* of the Śrīmatasāra (F.1B), a text belonging to the same school, display the same epithets applied, however, to Bhairava Himself:

1 *trikūṭaśikhare ramye bhairavaṃ kulanāyakam* |
santānapuramadhyastham anekākārarūpiṇam ||
2 *triguṇātmakasaṃbandhaṃ triprakāraṃ trirakṣaram* |
candrasūryāgnimadhyasthaṃ trisandhyātripathānvitam ||
3 *dvārapālatrayopetaṃ trikapāṭārgalānvitam* |
trailokasya tu kartāraṃ triśaktyā śaktiveṣṭitam ||

The translation and interpretation of śloka 11 are not certain. Probably it refers to Lord Bhairava before creation begins, when He encompasses both cause and effect (11a *kāryakāraṇabhāvena*). In pāda 11b the reading of MS A has been followed (*upekṣayā*) instead of the reading *apekṣayā* (MSS BC). In the KmT *upekṣayā* is found in two of the six palm-leaf manuscripts. the translation 'inactive' for the form *upekṣayā* is based upon the meaning 'to wait; to disregard' of the verb *upekṣ-*, and refers to the state of inactivity of Bhairava before creation.

śrībhairavy[1] uvāca ||
12 devadeva mahādeva uktaṃ ślokārthanirṇayam |
bāhyārthaṃ[2] na śrutaṃ nātha[3] anekopāyabhedataḥ ||
13 adhyātmaṃ[4] na yathā vedmi kulācārārthataḥ prabho |
kathayasva prasādena yena bhrāntir vinaśyati ||

1. BC śrīdevy 2. A -rthe 3. A nātha hy 4. BC -tme.

Śrībhairavī said:

12 O God among gods, O Great God, You have enunciated the plain meaning of the [above] *ślokas*. Their macrocosmic meaning which is differentiated in various ways, I have not heard, O Lord,

13 nor do I know their microcosmic meaning according to the Kula-precepts, O Master. Pray, tell this in Your graciousness in order that [any] misunderstanding vanishes.

In *pāda* 13a the order of the words is unusual: one should expect *adhyātmaṃ yathā na vedmi*. The regular order was changed *metri causa*. The author of the ṢaṭSS keeps strictly to the rule that the fifth syllable of a *śloka* should be short and the sixth long. The reading *adhyātmaṃ yathā na vedmi* would result in a long fifth syllable and a short sixth, however. *Yathā* should be followed by a corresponding *tathā* before *kathayasva* (13c), which is omitted, however. The initial position of *kathayasva* in *pāda* 13c indicates its close relationship with the previous line despite the lack of a corresponding *tathā*. For the expression *anekopāyabhedataḥ* see 3,48 Notes.

śrībhairava[1] uvāca ||
14 himavantaṃ mano[2] yac[3] ca virāmaṃ dvādaśāntagam[4] |
trīṇi kūṭāni ye tatra kathayāmy aparādikāt[5] ||

1. A śrībhairav 2. A illegible 3. A yaś 4. BC -ntakam 5. BC -kam.

Śrībhairava said:
14 The Himavat is the mind, the apex [of the triangle] of the Dvādaśānta. The three peaks which are there, I shall tell [You] beginning with the one in the West.

Mt. Himavat is identified with the mind (*manas*) as in *śloka* 39a. It is the *virāma* of the Dvādaśānta. With *virāma* ('termination; end') the apex of the pyramid on the Brahmarandhra is meant (Ṭ *ūrdhvaparyanta*; cf. 1,29ab), which is situated twelve *aṅgulas* above the Brahmarandhra. The three peaks, or corners of the pyramid are explained in the next *śloka*. The ṢaṭSS starts from the West (*aparādika*), the Ṭ from the N.E. (*īśādi agrakoṇaṃ yāvat*).

15 īraham īlakaṃ caiva īraśaṃ[1] ca varānane |
pūjyās te ca trikoṇānte devīdevau ca madhyataḥ ||

1. B īraṣaṃ; C īra(gh)aṃ; A ī(. .)ṃ.

15 Īraha, Īlaka and Īraśa [are the three peaks], O Varānanā. One should worship these at the end of the triangle. from its centre [arise]Deva and Devī.

The names of the three peaks seem to be artificial, or at least made for the occasion. They are, in fact, no real names but disguised *bījas*. The letters of each name form a *bīja*, in reversed order. Thus: Īraha = HRĪṂ; Īlaka = KLĪṂ; Īraśa = ŚRĪṂ. One should keep in mind that besides 'peak', the word *kūṭa* may also denote a *bīja*. The three *bījas* represent three manifestations of Devī: HRĪṂ = Māyā (MbhT 6,60); KLĪṂ = Kālī (MNT 7,33cd); ŚRĪṂ = Mahālakṣmī (MbhT 7,6 *viṣṇuśaktibīja*). In the MNT Kālikā is called the 'Destructress of the fear of Death' by these three *bījas* (MNT 7,32ab *krīṃ hrīṃ śrīṃ mantravarṇena kālakaṇṭakaghātinī*). The three *bījas* are to be placed at the three corners of the base of the pyramid. The top of the pyramid is identified with Mt. Himavat or the mind. From the centre of the pyramid Deva and Devī appear in the form of one *bīja* which is given in the next *śloka*.

The picture of the Himavat and the Ṭrikūṭa above the Brahmarandhra is that of a pyramid. The distance between the top of the pyramid and its base is twelve *aṅgulas*. The question is, where the top of the pyramid is situated: in the centre of the

Brahmarandhra, or twelve *aṅgulas* above it. Most probably we have to imagine a pyramid turned upside down, with its top on the Brahmarandhra. The Trikūṭa is situated twelve *aṅgulas* above it, formed by the base of the pyramid. The Santānabhuvana is situated then on this base of the pyramid, which is marked out at the three corners by the three *kūṭas*. The Santānabhuvana which is of triangular shape (7a), is bordered by the three peaks of the Trikūṭa. In other words, the Santānabhuvana is located between the three peaks. Perhaps *pāda* 6b should be translated with 'situated between the [three] peaks of the Trikūṭa', as if the text reads *trikūṭaśikharāntargam.*

Although it is not mentioned here, the Santānabhuvana is most likely identical with the Sahasrāra Cakra which is situated above the Brahmarandhra. The three peaks of the Trikūṭa are actually depicted within this Sahasrāra Cakra (Khanna 1979: plate 69 (a detail of Mookerjee & Khanna 1977: plate XIII); Rawson 1973: plate 59). Clearly visible in these drawings is a dot or *bindu*, which symbolizes the oneness of Śiva and Śakti, or Deva and Devī as they are called in the text (15d) (cf. Rawson 1973: frontispiece).

16 bhṛgulākulayogaṃ vai arghinā[1] krūradīpitam |
sānto 'haṃ[2] mālikādyena bhuvanaṃ[3] śivaśaktigam ||

1. A argheśā 2. A saṅmohaṃ 3. BC bhuvanaṃ taṃ.

16 The union of Bhṛgu and Lākula, together with Arghin and illuminated by Krūra—I am [the letter] after the *sa*, with Mālikā at the beginning—[constitutes] the world of Śiva and Śakti.

As is often the case in the ṢaṭSS, *mantras*, *bījas* etc. are presented in a concealed way. Here the syllables of the *bīja* in which Śiva and Śakti are united, are replaced by the names of the fifty Bhairavas or Rudras, each representing one of the fifty letters of the Skt alphabet (see Appendix II). Bhṛgu represents the *sa*, Lākula the *ha*, Arghin the vowel *ū*, and Krūra is the *anusvāra* (*aṃ*). The result of this is the *bīja* SHŪṂ, in which Śiva is represented by the letter H (*sānto 'haṃ*) and Śakti (= Mālikā) by the S (cf. Notes on *śloka* 1d). According to the Ṭ the *bīja* is HSAUṂ, which is not correct: the order of Bhṛgu and Lākula is changed, and Arghin (Ṭ Arghīśa) does not represent the vowel *au* which is alloted to Anugrahīśa. The world mentioned in *pāda* 16d (*bhuvana*) is the Santānabhuvana. The *bīja* of Śiva and Śakti should begin with the letter S (16c *mālikādyena*), and is therefore of the nature of Śakti.

17 mudrā caiva trikūṭaṃ ca trikapāṭārgalais tribhiḥ |
kathitās trīṇi kūṭāś ca dvārapālatrayaṃ[1] śṛṇu ||

1. A -pālā trayaṃ.

17 Both the *mudrā* and the Trikūṭa have three door-panels and three bolts. [Thus] are explained the three peaks. Hear now the three door-keepers.

With *mudrā* which is not found in the lines 6-8, probably the Triśikhāmudrā is meant. Together with the Yonimudrā and the Padmamudrā it is held in high esteem by the

Kulācāryas (ṢaṭSS 10; KRP F,15B *mudrātraya*). The mention of the Triśikhāmudrā here in relation with the Trikūṭa is obvious. The three door-panels and the three bolts are explained in the *ślokas* 21cd-23.

18 tamo'riś caiva dakṣastho vāme caiva niśāṭanaḥ[1] |
kālānalas[2] tadagre tu dvārapālās tv ime matāḥ ||

1. A -nam 2. A -laṃ.

18 Tamo'ri is in the South; in the North is Niśāṭana; at the top of it is Kālānala — these are known as the [three] door-keepers.

The three door-keepers represent three aspects of light. Thus Tamo'ri (lit. 'the enemy of darkness') is the sun; Niśāṭana (lit. 'the night-rover') is the moon; Kālānala or Kālāgni is a form of Agni, the conflagration at the end of time. The three door-keepers are located at the three corners of the triangular Santānabhuvana.

19 lākulabhṛgusaṃvartā[1] vahnigaukārabindugāḥ[2] |
kūṭabhūtās tu kartavyā dvārapālās tathārcane ||

1. B lakula-; A lākulaṃ bhṛgusaṃvarta 2. A -gokāra-.

19 Lākula, Bhṛgu and Saṃvarta, together with Vahni, the letter AU and the *bindu* — thus one should form the door-keepers as *kūṭas* during worship.

Again the *kūṭas* or *bījas* are presented by means of the names of the fifty Bhairavas: Lākula = HA; Bhṛgu = SA; Saṃvarta = KṢA. The letter of Vahni or Agni is the *repha* (RA), and the *bindu* represents the *anusvāra*. In *pāda* 19b I have accepted a case of double Sandhi: *vahnigāḥ aukāra- > vahnigā aukāra- > vahnigaukāra-*. This results in the following three *bījas* for the door-keepers: HRAUṂ, SRAUṂ and KṢRAUṂ. As we have seen in the previous *śloka*, the three door-keepers are actually the sun, the moon and an aspect of Agni. This fits with the syllables allotted to them. The sun and the moon are represented by the HA and the SA respectively. The third door-keeper, Kālānala, is not Agni himself, but an aspect of Agni. Therefore, Kālānala is not assigned the letter RA which belongs to Agni. The Ṭ does assign the letter RA to Kālānala: *dvārapālatrayopetam (= 8c) | dvārapālatrayaṃ kālānalaṃ RA* ... Commenting on *śloka* 7cd the Ṭ explains: *etad dhāmatrayaṃ yathā | kālānalaḥ agniḥ RA* ... There is no doubt, however, that Kālānala should be connected with the letter KṢA. In the KnT (F.49A) the *bījas* of the three door-keepers are also given; here Kālānala is also connected with the KṢA (*hānta*). Kālānala represents Agni at the end of a world-period, when the worlds are destroyed by fire. In this way the identification of Kālānala with the Bhairava called Saṃvarta (= KṢA) becomes probable. We have seen that Saṃvarta points to the periodical destruction of the worlds, as does Kālānala. Moreover, the letter KṢA comes at the end of the alphabet, in which way it is comparable with the fire at the end of a world-period. Besides Kālānala, the sun and the moon are also connected with the concept of Fire or Light. Therefore the *bījas* of all three of them have one basic syllable in common, the RA (19b *vahniga*), the *akṣara* of Agni. The vowel in all three *bījas* is the AU. According to the Ṭ on *śloka* 16d *bhuvana* (= Santānabhuvana) is characterized by the AU. As the three door-keepers belong to this Santānabhuvana, it is only natural that they also should be characterized by the AU. The KnT also has the vowel *au* in the three *bījas*. Following the reading of MS A for *pāda* 19b (*vahnigokārā*) the three *bījas* should be HRŪṂ, SRŪṂ and KṢRŪṂ. In this way the vowel in the three *bījas* is the same as the vowel in the *bīja* of Śiva and Śakti when residing in this Santānabhuvana (*śloka* 16). As MS A often reads *o* instead of *au*, one cannot be sure whether the reading is correct or not here. For this reason the reading of the MSS BC has been followed, although the reading of MS A is not without sense.

In the section of the KnT (MS 5-8541/101 FF.71A ff.) on the three door-keepers, the Dvārapālārcana, we find the *dhyānaślokas* of the three. All three have four hands, in which they hold the same attributes: in their left hands a trident (*śūla*) and a skull-cup (*kapāla*), in their right hands a sword (*khaḍga*; MS 1-239/201[k]: a club (*khaṭvāṅga*)), and a lotus (*padma*). Niśāṭana is of a white colour (*sita*); Tamo'ri is red (*rakta*); Kālānala has a massive form (*sthūla*). The mounts of the three door-keepers point to their relationship with the sun, the moon and Agni: Tamo'ri is seated on a horse (*vājin*); Niśāṭana rides a hare (*śaśa*); Kālānala is mounted on a ram (*meṣa*).

20 dakṣakoṇe tu lakulī vāme vai[1] bhṛgudevatā |
ante saṃvartanāthas[2] tu ante[3] cāgram[4] udāhṛtam /

1. BC ca 2. C saṃvartā- 3. A anta 4. A cogram.

20 In the Southern corner is Lakulin; in the North is the deity Bhṛgu; at the end is Saṃvartanātha — with 'end' the top is meant.

In *pāda* 20a we find one of the few instances where the sixth syllable of a *pāda* is short instead of long. Lakulin is obviously the same Bhairava as Lākula (16a; 19a (MS B Lakula)). The name of this 49th Bhairava is subject to a variety of readings: Lakulīśa (Appendix II), Lakuli (ŚT 2,35a), Lakulānanda (ṢaṭSS 17,154c), Lagūlīśa (Tantrasārasaṃgraha 1,57c). The initial *l* of the name becomes sometimes *n* (ŚT[a] *ibid.*). To obtain a correct metre one should read *lākulo* here, as the form Lākulin of the name is not attested.

Śloka 20 provides the locations of the three door-keepers in the Santānabhuvana, but instead of using their proper names (Tamo'ri etc.) the names of the Bhairavas representing their characteristic syllables are mentioned. Thus Lakulin/Tamo'ri is in the South, Bhṛgu/Niśāṭana is in the North, and Saṃvarta/Kālānala is at the end. The locations of the three door-keepers are, of course, related to the three corners of the triangular Santānabhuvana. The end or the top of this triangle is situated in the West (cf. 1,14d). The Ṭ in its commentary on *śloka* 7cd situates Tamo'ri at the top (*agrakoṇe*), Niśāṭana in the North, and Kālānala in the South. The KnT follows the ṢaṭSS.

21 akulaṃ ca kulaṃ caiva tathā caiva kulākulam |
kapāṭās[1] traya[2] vātādyā durbhedyāḥ sudṛḍhāḥ priye ||

1. A kapāṭas 2. BC tatra.

21 (The three door-keepers are) Akula, Kula and Kulākula. There are [three] door-panels, Vāta etc., difficult to break through, very solid, O Lovely One.

Finally, the three door-keepers are put on the same line as Akula, Kula and Kulākula. Akula stands for Bhairava, the transcendental energy, Who is to be united with His Śakti in order to activate His energy. Kula, 'l'énergie originelle de la manifestation' (Padoux 1975: 196), represents Śakti. Kulākula, hence, is the union of Kula and Akula or Śiva and Śakti, from which the visible creation originates (cf. Padoux 1975: 195 ff.).

After discussing the three door-keepers the doors itself are dealt with in the next lines. In *pāda* 21c the reading of MS A has been followed despite the fact that the form *traya* is grammatically incorrect. It should be *trayo*. The singular *kapāṭas* might be considered to be a 'slip of the pen', but the form *traya* serves a specific purpose, namely to obtain a short fifth syllable in the *pāda*. The grammatically correct form *trayo* results in a long fifth syllable, which should be avoided. The reading of BC (*tatra*) is evidently a non-committal *lectio facilior* in order to obtain a regular metre and a grammatically correct *pāda*. There are a few other instances in the text, where no case-ending is added for metrical reasons (cf. 1, 36a; 36b 2,27a) One wonders, why the author of MS A did not write simply *kapāṭās trīṇi* here, which is metrically correct, while the form *trīṇi* (neuter) with a masculine nom. pl. (*kapāṭās*) is not unusual in our text (cf. 1,2c *siddhās trīṇy*; 1,22c *argalās trīṇi*).

In our translation of the text the word *kapāṭa* has been translated with 'door-panel', which it usually means. Here, however, the word *kapāṭa* clearly denotes the complete door consisting of two leaves. The three doors are identified with Vāta etc. (*vātādyā*), which are explained in the next *śloka*.

22 svarūpaṃ te[1] tu vakṣyāmi vātapittaśaleṣmikāḥ |
argalās trīṇi tatraiva vyāpinī samanonmanā ||
23 rodhasaṃjñā imā trīṇi raudrarūpā mahābalāḥ |
tais tu saṃrakṣitaṃ[2] yac[2] ca na jānante[3] vimohitāḥ ||

1. BC tais 2. A taṃ rakṣitaṃ yaś 3. BC -nti.

22 I will tell You [their] true nature: they are Vāta, Pitta and Śaleṣmika. There are also three bolts: Vyāpinī, Samanā and Unmanā.

23 These three are called 'obstruction'. They are of a fierce nature, and are very strong. What is shielded by these, the foolish-minded do not know.

As already hinted at in the previous *śloka* (21c) the three doors are identified with the three humours of the human body: wind (*vāta*), bile (*pitta*), and phlegm (*śaleṣmika*). The latter is usually called *śleṣman* or *śleṣmaka*, but the form *śaleṣmika* can be understood as a case of an epenthetic *a* (cf. Edgerton 1972: I,29).

The three bolts of the doors are the goddesses Vyāpinī, Samanā and Unmanā. This triad is well-known (cf. Padoux 1975: 83-85; 346), and represents the three highest, and most subtle phases in the process of emanation of sound (Padoux 1975: 83).

Because these three are very difficult to pass for the Sādhaka in his endeavour to reach the complete oneness of Śiva and Śakti which lies beyond these three, they are designated as 'bolts' and 'obstruction'. The Ṭ identifies the three bolts with desire (*kāmā*), wrath (*krodha*), and greed (*lobha*), which are the first three of the Six Enemies (*ṣaḍ ari*; the other three being *māna*, *mada* and *mātsārya* (KA 1,6,1 ff.). The Sādhaka should avoid these three (cf. MNT 8,65cd).

24 icchā jñānī kriyā teṣāṃ guṇās tatra tridevatāḥ |
sṛṣṭipālanasaṃhāre brahmaviṣṇumaheśvarāḥ[1] ||
25 prākārās trīṇi tatraiva sattvaṃ rajas tamas tathā |
pathās[2] trīṇi samuddiṣṭā iḍā piṅgā tu madhyamā ||

1. C brahmā- 2. BC panthās.

24 Icchā, Jñānī and Kriyā [are the Śaktis] of these. There are [three] qualities with three deities: Brahma, Viṣṇu and Maheśvara, related to emanation, maintenance and absorption [respectively].
25 There are also three walls: Sattva, Rajas and Tamas. Three paths are mentioned: Iḍā, Piṅgā and Madhyamā.

The *ślokas* 24 and 25 are the explanation of the *pādas* 7b and 8b. Thus the three Śaktis (7b) are Icchā, Jñānī and Kriyā. The three qualities (7b *guṇa*) are emanation, maintenance and absorption. The three qualities are connected with Brahma, Viṣṇu and Maheśvara (= Śiva), who are not referred to in the *śloka* 6-8. The three walls (8b) are identified with Sattva, Rajas and Tamas, which are known as the Three Guṇas. The three paths (8b) are the three main *nāḍīs* in the human body: Iḍā, Piṅgā or Piṅgalā, and the central *nāḍī* Madhyamā (lit: the Central One), or Suṣumṇā. The name Piṅgā instead of the more usual Piṅgalā is probably *metri causa*, as Piṅgalā would result in a long fifth syllable (*iḍā piṅgalā madhyamā*). The Ṭ explains the epithets of the *pādas* 7b and 8b in a slightly different way. The three Śaktis are the same (Icchā etc.). The three qualities are Sattva, Rajas and Tamas. The three walls are Brahma, Viṣṇu and Maheśvara. The three paths are identical (Iḍā etc.).

26 yogināṃ ca trisandhyā[1] yam[1] āviṣṭaḥ[2] tiṣṭhate prabhuḥ |
santānaṃ paścimāmnāyam etac candragṛhaṃ[3] smṛtam ||

1. BC -sandheyam 2. ABC -ṣṭaṃ 3. A -guhaṃ.

26 What is the Trisandhyā for the Yogins, [with that] invested is the Lord. This is the Santāna(-bhuvana), the Paścimāmnāya, known as Candragṛha.

In *pāda* 26b the reading of the three MSS (*āviṣṭaṃ*) has been emended to the more correct *āviṣṭaḥ*. The reading of *pāda* 26a, for which MS A has been followed, is not correct Skt; the MSS BC intend to read here perhaps *yogināṃ ca trisandhyêyam*. The Trisandhyā is the threefold division of the day (morning, noon and evening), on which the daily worship is performed. According to the Ṭ these three are identical with the three kinds of breathing exercised in Yoga: exhalation (*recaka*), inhalation (*pūraka*), and stopping of the breath (*kuṃbhaka*). Perhaps the mention of *yogināṃ* in the text (26a) points to the explanation of the Ṭ. In the translation of *pāda* 26b we have regarded *āviṣṭaḥ* as directly related to the previous *pāda*. In this way it is the same as *āveṣṭitaṃ* in *trisandhyāveṣṭitaṃ* (8a). It is also possible, however, that *āviṣṭaḥ* refers to the contents of the previous *ślokas*, from *śloka* 14 onwards. In this way all the epithets do not belong to the Santānabhuvana, as is the case in the *ślokas* 6 ff., but to Bhairava (cf. p. 42). The words *tiṣṭhate prabhuḥ* (26b) refer then to *śloka* 11c (*tiṣṭhate bhairavīśānaḥ*).

With *śloka* 26ab the explanation of the introductory verses is completed. It is apparent, however, that the ṢaṭSS does not explain every epithet in these *ślokas*. Moreover, the order of its explanations does not follow the order of the epithets in the text too closely. The Ṭ, on the contrary, explains every epithet in its order of occurrence in the *ślokas* 6-8. The Ṭ then is not an explanation of ṢaṭSS 14-26, but of ṢaṭSS 6-8. The epithets not explained in the ṢaṭSS itself, are explained as follows in the Ṭ: *anekākārarūpiṇam* (6d) = *nānāvarṇadharam*, 'having different colours'; *tryaśraṃ* (7a) = *trīṇi koṇāni*, 'three corners'; *triprakāraṃ* (7a) = emanation (*sṛṣṭi*), maintenance (*pālana*), and absorption (*saṃhāra*) (cf. 1,24c); *ujjvalam* (7b) = *antarbhāsitam*, 'radiant from within'; *śloka* 7cd (instead of *-varcasam* the Ṭ reads *-tejasam*) is explained with *etad dhāmatrayaṃ yathā | kālānalaḥ agniḥ ra dakṣe niśāṭanaḥ | candraḥ sa vāme tamo'riḥ | sūryaḥ ha agrakoṇe | etad dhāmatrayam*. The only word in the *ślokas* 6-8 the Ṭ does not explain is *divyaṃ* (8a).

The Santānabhuvana is called Paścimāmnāya (26c), the Western Tradition, in the ṢaṭSS, whereas the Ṭ refers to it as *paścimagṛha*. Since the Santānabhuvana has the shape of a triangle (7a), the Ṭ identiefies it with the *yoni*, and subsequently with the letter *e*, the *yonibīja*, probably on account of its form resembling a triangle. The reading *candragṛha* (26d) of the MSS BC is also found in the Ṭ here (for the reading of MS A, *candraguha*, cf. *śloka* 30). The Ṭ ends its explanation with the statement, that the Santānabhuvana is also called Saṃvarta.

27 merupaścimadigbhāge[1] pṛthivyāṃ[2] paścime dale |
gandhamādanapūrveṇa vijñeyaṃ tadvidair[3] naraiḥ ||

1. B merau pa-; C meroḥ pa-, 2. A -vyā, 3. A -vidhair.

27 [The Santānabhuvana is located] on the Western side of Mt. Meru, in the Western region of the earth, East of Mt. Gandhamādana — thus the adepts should know.

The location of the Santānabhuvana corresponds with that of the Candraparvata in the KmT (1,56d ff.), and the Candravīpa in the 47th chapter of the ṢaṭSS: *meru(*KmT: *meroḥ)paścimadigbhāge gandhamālyasamīpataḥ* (KmT 1,59cd = ṢaṭSS 47,106ab). The Candraparvata or Candradvīpa, however, is completely round (KmT 1,60b = ṢaSS 47,106d: *samantāt parimaṇḍalam*), whereas the Santānabhuvana is of a triangular form (1,7a). Although the Gandhamālya is not known to me as the name of a mountain, it is most likely identical with the Gandhamādana in *śloka* 27c.

The Ṭ does not comment on the *ślokas* 27-35, nor are they quoted in full.

28 śiraṃ[1] meruḥ[2] samuddiṣṭaṃ[3] śarīraṃ pṛthivī smṛtā |
cūlikādhas trikūṭaṃ tu[4] vijñeyaṃ gandhamādanam ||

1. C′ śiro, 22. A meru, 3. C′ -ṣṭaḥ, 4. BC ca.

28 The Meru is known as the head; the earth is the body; beneath the crown of the head, with three peaks — thus one should imagine the Gandhamādana.

In *śloka* 28 the three localities which were mentioned in the previous *śloka*, are identified with three parts of the human body. The identification of the Meru with the head is also found in *śloka* 39b of this chapter, as well as in the KRP (F.39B: *śiraś ca merunāmānam*). Since the Meru (= the head) rests on the earth, the identification of the latter with the body (*śarīra*) becomes plausible. The second part of this *śloka* proves to be enigmatic at first sight. It is very tempting to regard *trikūṭaṃ* (28c) as the name of a mountain, which it actually is in *śloka* 36c and 40c. Mt. Trikūṭa, however, is not located beneath the *cūlika* (cf. 40cd), whereas the Gandhamādana is (39cd). Moreover, in the previous *śloka* there is no mention of the Mt. Trikūṭa. For these reasons I have regarded *trikūṭaṃ* as an epithet of the Gandhamādana. In the passage of the ṢaṭSS dealing with the Candradvīpa (see above) there are mentioned three peaks (*trīṇi kūṭāni*), but it does not become clear whether they belong to the Gandhamālya or not because the text is difficult to understand and seems to be rather corrupt. The names of the three peaks are here: Trikūṭa (*sic*), Kiṣkindhaka, and Candradvīpa.

29 brahmarandhrasya[1] santānaṃ[2] bhāvagamyaṃ trikoṇagam |
saṃvartāmaṇḍataś[3] cakra[ṃ][3] tatra candraśilā sthitā ||

1. BC brahmā-, 2. BC saṃsthānaṃ, 3. C -maṇḍalāt tac ca; B -maṇḍala tac ca.

29 The Santāna(-bhuvana) of the Brahmarandhra should be regarded as a triangle. From the Saṃvartāmaṇḍala [originates] a circle; there is the Candraśilā located.

The Santānabhuvana or Saṃvartāmaṇḍala when located on the Brahmarandhra, has the shape of a triangle (for other localities of the Saṃvartāmaṇḍala in connection with the body, see 2,4-15). The expression *bhāvagamya* occurs rather frequently in the ṢaṭSS (cf. 2,8b). Its original meaning might be 'to be conceived by the mind (only)' (M.-W.: *s.v.*) which is found in the Meghadūta (*uttaramegha* 25; Mallinātha: *saṃbhāvanayotprekṣyam*), but in the ṢaṭSS its meaning seems to have become less specific. Therefore, *bhāvagamya* has been translated with 'to be regarded; to be imagined', although the idea that the process is chiefly mental, should be kept in mind. In *pāda* 29c the reading of A has been followed, although the form *saṃvartā-maṇḍa*[*la*]*taś* is irregular. The use of *-maṇḍalataś* would, of course, result in a *pāda* of nine syllables. MS C also expresses the idea of an ablative here, while MS B appears to read a nominative (*-maṇḍala*[*ṃ*]).

The image is that of the triangular Santānabhuvana or Saṃvartāmaṇḍala from which a circle originates (29c *cakra*). This circle is probably the Candraparvata of the

KmT, or rather the Candradvīpa of the ṢaṭSS, which is completely round (cf. notes on *śloka* 27). In this circle the Candraśilā is located (KmT 1,61c *tatra madhye śilā ramyā*).

30 sā ca candraguhā proktā visargasthānam āśritā |
yogapīṭhaṃ ca vijñeyaṃ kathitaṃ mayā sphuṭam ||

30 This is called the Candraguhā, associated with the *visargasthāna*. It should be known as the Yogapīṭha — thus I have told clearly.

From the text it appears that the Candraśilā (lit: Moon-rock) is also called Candraguhā (lit: Moon-cave). More likely, though, the Candraguhā is a particular cave on this Candraśilā. In the KmT the Candraparvata where the Candraśilā is located, is described as 'having many caves' (KmT 1,57d *gahvarānekasaṃkula*). The followers of the Kulācāra hold three caves in high esteem: the Candrākhyā, the Yakṣiṇī and the Śaṅkhinī (KRP F.15B). The Candraguhā is most likely identical with the Candrākhyā of the KRP. In *pāda* 30b the Candraguhā is connected with the *visargasthāna*, the place from which creation starts.

Yogapīṭha in *pāda* 30c refers to the circle which originated from the triangular Santānabhuvana on the Brahmarandhra (29c). Yogapīṭha appears to be another name of the Saṃvartāmaṇḍala, when it is located on the Brahmarandhra: it is at the end of the Dvādaśānta, and constitutes the base for the Suṣumṇā (cf. ṢaṭSS 28,15cd; 16ab *visargaṃ ca suṣumnāyā ādhāraṃ dvādaśāntagam* | *kvacic ca yogapīṭhaṃ tu kvacit saṃvartāmaṇḍalam*). In the Catuṣpīṭha Tantra, a Sahajayāna text, Yogapīṭha is included in a list of four Pīṭhas, all of them being philosophical concepts instead of actual localities (Sircar 1973: 11).

31 suṣumṇādhārabhūtaṃ[1] tu dvādaśāntaṃ[2] tadantagam[2] |
etat tu[3] maṇḍalaṃ divyaṃ pūjyaṃ[4] dhyeyaṃ tu[5] sannaraiḥ ||

1. A -bhūtas 2. A -ntān tadantagaḥ; BC -ntaṃ tadaṅgatam 3. BC tan 4. A pūjya 5. BC ca.

31 It has the Suṣumṇā as its base, and comes at the end of the Dvādaśānta. Thus then is the divine circle, which the right people should worship and meditate upon.

In *śloka* 31 the Yogapīṭha is explained in further detail. *Pāda* 31b is rather curious with regard to the formation of the words. Evidently the *pādas* 31ab correspond with ṢaṭSS 28,15cd (*visargaṃ ca suṣumnāyā ādhāraṃ dvādaśāntagam*; see above), of which *visargaṃ* has been allotted to the Candraguhā (30ab). Since the expression *suṣumnāyā ādhāraṃ* ('the base of the Suṣumnā') corresponds to *suṣumṇādhārabhūtaṃ* (31a), *dvādaśāntagam* should correspond to *pāda* 31b. The Yogapīṭha of the Brahmarandhra is found at the end of the Dvādaśānta, *viz.* at the end of the inverted pyramid (see *śloka* 15 Notes). A compound expressing this idea would be *dvādaśāntāntagam*, which looks rather confusing. Perhaps for this reason the author has avoided it, and has split the compound into two parts with a connecting *tad* inserted in between. Thus *pāda* 31b means literally 'going to the end of that, namely the Dvādaśānta', Separation of the parts of a compound does occur (cf. Hazra 1963: 123), sometimes with insertion of an indeclinable word (Hazra 1963: 124), but *tad* is not indeclinable. Another solution for this *pāda* might be the reading of A (*dvādaśāntānta-d-antaga*), in which the consonant *d* functions as an intervening hiatus-bridger (cf. Hazra 1963: 104; Edgerton 1972: I,37). The result, however, is a very confusing compound with one *anta* too much.

32 etac cakravaraṃ divyaṃ[1] yatra viśvaṃ pratiṣṭhitam |
asya madhyād dviraṣṭāntam[2] anekākārabheditam[3] ||
33 viniṣkrāntaṃ varārohe na vijānanti mūḍhadhīḥ[4] |[5]
āśramaṃ paramaṃ divyaṃ divyādivyair niṣevitam[6] ||
34 guruhīnā na paśyanti kalpakoṭiśatair api |
atrasthaṃ tu catuṣkādyaṃ punar yānti[7] hy anekadhā ||

1. BC devi 2. BC viniṣkrāntam 3. BC -bhedataḥ 4. A -dhī 5. *pādas* 33ab omitted in BC 6. A -tāḥ 7. BC yāti.

32 This is the divine, most excellent of [all] circles, on which everything is based. From its centre the Dviraṣṭānta, in a pluriform way,
33 appears, O Varārohā. This the foolish-minded do not recognize. It is the most excellent, divine refuge, frequented by gods and mortals.
34 People without a Guru do not perceive it, not even in a thousand millions of Kalpas! Being there the Four etc. go again in various ways.

The expression Dviraṣṭānta, or Ṣoḍaśānta is a designation of the human body (cf. *śloka* 3a Notes), which is connected with the number sixteen in the next *śloka*. In *pāda* 34cd the Aṣṭāviṃśatikrama is referred to (*catuṣkādya*; cf. *śloka* 1bc), symbolizing the creation. *Punar yānti* (pl!) expresses the idea that after a period of absorption, the visible world appears again from the Yogapīṭha (cf. 47,113cd; 114ab *tatra sthāne layaṃ kṛtvā līlayā parameśvarī | avyaktaliṅgarūpā sā sṛṣṭiṃ saṃhṛtya śāṃbhavī*).

35 samantād dvyaṣṭakād[1] yas[1] tu etat kulakalevaram |
visṛṣṭam ādināthena yogivṛndaniketanam[2] ||

1. BC vyuṣṭakoṭis 2. BC yoga-.

35 That which [originates] from the complete sixteen, is the body according to the Kula-tradition. It is emanated by Ādinātha; it is the abode for innumerable Yogins.

The reading of *pāda* 35a is uncertain. The ligature *-ddvya-* in MS A is scarcely legible. The MSS BC seem to read *-dvyu-*, or perhaps *-ddhyu-*. I have opted for the reading of MS A because of its connection with the body: *dvyaṣṭaka* ('sixteen') corresponds with *dviraṣṭa* in the expression Dviraṣṭānta, which denotes the human body (32c). In the 28th chapter of the ṢaṭSS it is stated that Kubjikā surrounded by sixteen *śaktis* resides together with Bhairava in the Yogapīṭha, which is described as a lotus; from here She 'throws' (*kṣipate*) the sixteen *śaktis* in the human body (ṢaṭSS 28,16cd-17cd *tatpadmakarṇikāmadhye kujeśo bhairavaḥ svayam | kubjikā ca sthitā tatra śaktibhiḥ ṣoḍaśair vṛtā | sā śaktīḥ (MS śakti) kṣipate dehe kramārthe ca krame 'dhvani*). Probably the sixteen *śaktis* are located in the sixteen petals of the lotus, in the pericarp (*karṇikā*) of which Kubjikā and Kujeśa Bhairava reside. The sixteen *śaktis* are most likely the sixteen vowels (cf. 2,17 ff.)

36 himavān meru candrādi[1] gandhamādana[2] śrīgiriḥ |
trikūṭaṃ daradaṇḍī ca sthānam olaṃbasaṃjñakam[3] ||
37 karālaṃbaṃ[4] sasahyākhyam ucchuṣmavanasaṃjñakam |
hradaṃ nīlahradaṃ caiva iti[5] sthānās trayodaśa[6] ||

1. B candrādyā 2. C′ -naḥ 3. A olaṃbha- 4. BC karālāsyaṃ 5. BC ete 6. A -śaḥ.

36 The Himavat, Meru, Candrādi, Gandhamādana, Śrīgiri, Trikūṭa, Daradaṇḍī, the place called Olaṃba,
37 Karālaṃba together with Sahyākhya, [the place] called Ucchuṣmavana, Hrada and Nīlahrada — thus are the thirteen localities.

In the *pādas* 36ab there are two irregularities which are probably due to the rule, that the fifth syllable of a *pāda* should be short and the sixth long. Thus none of three MSS adds a nominative ending to *meru* (36a), which would result in a long fifth syllable in this *pāda* (*meruś*). One might argue that the word *meru* is considered here as a neuter, but this seems highly improbably as the gander of *meru* is always masculine in the text (cf. 1,28a; 39b). In *pāda* 36b all three MSS omit the nominative ending of *gandhamādana*; MS C shows a correction (C′ *gandhamādanaḥ*), which does not seem to be correct as the name *gandhamādana* appears to be of the neuter gender (cf. 1,28d; 39d). Again, the nominative ending seems to be dropped in order to acquire a short fifth syllable in the *pāda* (N.B. due to the *r* in the following *śrī* this combination of two consonants does not necessarily lengthen the preceding syllable; cf. Notes on *paribhrama* (1,3b)).

The Himavat and the Meru are, of course, two well-known mountains. The Candrādi or Candrākhya (1,39c) is most likely identical with the Candraparvata (cf. Notes on *śloka* 1,27). The Gandhamādana has been discussed in *śloka* 28. The Śrīgiri or Śrīparvata, and the Trikūṭa are also familiar mountains. Daradaṇḍī appears to be the name of a cave rather than that of a mountain (ṢaṭSS 47,122 *gartā yā ca kṛkāṭikā daradaṇḍī samākhyātā*; cf. *śloka* 41ab). This assumption is corroborated by the fact that the first part of the name (*dara*) actually means 'cleft' or 'cave'. The next locality, a place called Olaṃba, is not known to me from other sources. The name appears in the MSS as Ulaṃbha/Olaṃbha (MS A), and Ulaṃba/Olaṃba (MSS BC); the Ṭ reads Olaṃba. Since the place is identified with the Mahāpīṭha Oḍiyāna (cf. 1,42), I have opted for an initial *o*-. The preference for Olaṃba instead of Olaṃbha is mainly based on KmT 2,34-40: when Devī goes around in Bhārata Varṣa, She visits, among other places (cf. p. 149), Daradaṇḍī (KmT 2,34); next She goes to the Western Himagahvara (KmT 2,36), where Laṃbikā resides (*yatra tu laṃbikā nāma tiṣṭhate vanapālikā*). It is noteworthy that of the eighteen MSS of the KmT at my disposal nine seem to point to a name U/Ol(l)aṃbikā (among these nine MSS are three palm-leaf MSS: AJ *yatra ulaṃbikā nāma*; H *yatra olaṃbikā nāma*). Moreover, also in the KmT the visit of Devī to this deity is brought in relation with the Mahāpīṭha Oḍiyāna (KmT 2,40cd = ṢaṭSS 4/5,16cd). Accepting a relation between Laṃbikā, the protectress of the forest (*vanapālikā*), in the KmT and a locality called Olaṃba in the ṢaṭSS, one might consider Olaṃba to be a small village in the forest (*vanapallikā*). The name Olaṃba is perhaps derived from Skt *avalaṃba* (cf. Edgerton 1972: II, *s.v.*). The next locality, Karālaṃba, likewise provides a puzzle, since no locality of this name is mentioned elsewhere. The reading Karālāsya (MSS BC) seems to be a *lectio facilior*; the Ṭ reads Karālaṃbha. We have chosen for the reading Karālaṃba for not quite substantional reasons: perhaps the name is related to Kalaṃbakubja (Sircar 1973: 114), or with Kalaṃbāipāda (KJñN 8,18). The KmT (2,50b) mentions as the next place after the residence of Laṃbikā, a locality called Karāla, which is obviously the same as Karālaṃba. To make any sense of the name, one should perhaps expect Karālāṃbā(-sthāna). Sahyākhya, the next locality, probably refers to the Sahya mountain-range, or to a particular forest in this region (cf. 4/5,62b). In the KmT (2,63d) Devī visits after Karāla a forest (*sahyaṃ mahāvanam* = ṢaṭSS 4/5,62b). Ucchuṣmavana, the forest of Ucchuṣma, is most likely a sacred grove dedicated to Ucchuṣma, a manifestation of Śiva. This form of Śiva is mentioned in late Vedic literature (AV-pariśiṣṭa, 36 *ucchuṣmakalpa*). There seems to exist an Ucchuṣmabhairava or Ucchuṣmaśāstra, a text referred to in the Śivasūtravimarśiṇī of Kṣemarāja, in the Tantrasāra and Parātriṃśikāvyākhyā by Abhinavagupta, and in the Svacchandatantra (Kavirāj 1972: 68-69). In the 43rd chapter of the ṢaṭSS we read *piśācocchuṣmacaryā*. In Hindu Tantrism Ucchuṣma seems to be a form of Śiva/Bhairava, as we learn from the TĀ (28,390-391 *deva eva gurutvena tiṣṭhāsur daśadhā bhavet | ucchuṣmaśabaracaṇḍagumataṅgaghorāntakograhalahalakāḥ | krodhī huluhulur ete daśa guravaḥ śivamayāḥ pūrve*). In the KmT as the next stop after Sahya Mahāvana the river Ucchuṣmā is mentioned (KmT 2,82d), which is located in Mahocchuṣmavana (KmT 2,83a; cf. 103b). In the Mālinīstava (KmT 2, *daṇḍaka*) Mālinī is called *mahocchuṣmayāgapriyā*. Also in Buddhist sources Ucchuṣma is the name of a deity (Edgerton 1972: II, *s.v.*; SaṃT 8,38), a fierce variety of Jambhala (Kramrisch 1964: 157), considered to be an emanation from Akṣobhya (Bhattacharya 1968: 239). In the Sādhanamāla we find four *sādhanas* of Ucchuṣma Jambhala (Nos. 291-294). The two ponds, Hrada and Nīlahrada, are most probably located in the vicinity of Ucchuṣmavana, but are not identified with any known locality. The KmT (2,83cd) refers to the two ponds as Mahocchuṣmahrada and Nīla Mahāhrada. Since Ucchuṣmavana is identified with Kāmarūpa (KmT 2,89-90; ṢaṭSS 1,44), the two ponds might be located in the same area. Significant perhaps in this context is the name Nīlahrada: the dark-blue colour (*nīla*) is strongly associated with Devī as Kāmākhyā, living on the Nīla Mahāgiri (KP 72,35) or the Nīlakūṭa (KP 62,1), a mountain located in the region of Kāmarūpa.

38 bāhyārthaṃ[1] kathitaṃ devi sthānāś caiva trayodaśa[2] /
dehasthān[3] saṃpravakṣyāmi yogināṃ kulayoginām ||
39 himavān tu[4] mano[4] yaś[4] ca meruś caiva śiraḥ smṛtaḥ /
candrākhyaṃ[5] cūlikāsthānaṃ tasyādho gandhamādanam[6] ||

1. BC bāhye me 2. A -daśaḥ 3. AB -sthā 4. BC mano virāmaś 5. A -khyāṃ 6. A -naḥ.

38 I have told [You] the macrocosmic significance, O Devī; [these are] the thirteen localities. Now I shall tell [You] how they are located in the body of the Yogins, [especially] of the Kulayogins.

39 The Himavat is the mind; the Meru is known as the head; the Candrākhya is the crest, beneath which the Gandhamādana is located.

In *śloka* 38 it is said that the macrocosmic meaning (*bāhyārthaṃ*) of the thirteen localities has been told (*sc.* the enumeration in the two previous *ślokas*), and that subsequently their location in the body (*dehasthān*) shall be explained. With *dehastha* the microcosmic meaning is meant, of course (cf. *śloka* 12c; 13a *bāhyārthaṃ* and *adhyātmaṃ*). The identification of these thirteen localities with thirteen parts of the human body is valid for Yogins in general, but is of special importance for those Yogins who follow the Kula-doctrine (*kulayogin*).

In *pāda* 39a the reading of MS A has been followed, as the reading of BC has nine syllables in this *pāda*. The Ṭ (*himavān mano virāmam*) points to the reading of BC. The reading of MS A corresponds with *śloka* 14a, while the reading of the MSS BC supported by the Ṭ or perhaps based on the Ṭ, seems to be an attempt to compress the contents of two *pādas* (14ab) into only one *pāda*. An attempt which is not too successful, as the result is a *pāda* of nine syllables.

The Meru is identified with the head (*śiras*)—an identification which follows *pāda* 28a. The Candrākhya (A Candrākhyā; cf. Candrāyā of MS B in *śloka* 36a) or Candrādi (36a) is identified with the top of the head (*cūlikā*). As we have seen before (28c), the Gandhamādana is located beneath the *cūlikā*. No mention is made here of its having three peaks (28c *trikūṭa*). According to the Ṭ Mt. Gandhamādana represents the joint of the neck (*kṛkāṭikā*), which is located in the middle of the crest (*gandhamādanaṃ kṛkāṭikā cūlikāyā madhye*).

40 śrīparvataṃ hutāśas[1] tu dhūmravartis[2] tu mastake |
trikūṭaṃ candrapuryākhyaṃ bāhye yac[3] ca trikoṇakam[4] ||

1. A -śaṃ 2. BC dhūma- 3. A yaś 4. A -kaḥ.

40 The Śrīparvata is the Eater of Oblations, the column of smoke on the head. The Trikūṭa is [the place] called Candrapurī, which has the outward appearance of a triangle.

The Śrīparvata or Śrīgiri (36b) is identified with the 'Eater of Oblations' (40a *hutāśa*), another name for Agni, who appears as a column of smoke (40b *dhūmravarti*) on the top of the head. As the Ṭ explains here, the Śrīparvata is the Brahmarandhra or the abode of Dhūmāgni (Ṭ *śrīparvataṃ brahmarandhraṃ dhūmāgnisthānam*). This Dhūmāgni, 'Smoky Agni' has the shape of a column of smoke with a length of twelve *aṅgulas*. It leads upwards from the Brahmarandhra to the base of the inverted pyramid, on which the Santānabhuvana is located (cf. *śloka* 15 Notes). The twelve *aṅgulas* are identified with the series of A, U, MA, Bindu, Ardhacandra, Nirodhikā, Nāda, Nādānta, Śakti, Vyāpinī, Samanā, and Unmanā, which constitute the Dvādaśānta (ṢaṭSS 28,2-3; cf. Padoux 1975: table opposite p. 346). At the end of this column of smoke, e.g. above Unmanā, resides Parā Śakti consisting of pure througth (*cidrūpā*).

The Trikūṭa is a triangle called Candrapurī (cf. 1,2b). According to the Ṭ it is situated outside the crest (Ṭ *trikūṭaṃ bāhyacūlikā trikoṇasthānam*). Probably the triangular Santānabhuvana or Saṃvartāmaṇḍala when located on the Brahmarandhra, is meant (cf. *śloka* 29ab).

41 daradaṇḍī paścime bhāge yā[1] ca proktā kṛkāṭikā |
meroḥ[2] savyāpasavyena olambaṃ[3] saṃvyavasthitam ||

1. A yaś 2. A meru 3. BC ulaṃbaṃ; A ulaṃbhaṃ.

41 The Daradaṇḍī is on the Western side, and is what is called the joint of the neck. At the left and right side of the Meru Olaṃba is located.

The location of the Daradaṇḍī in the ṢaṭSS provides an example of the way in which the author of the ṢaṭSS incorporated the data of the KmT in his text. In the KmT Devī visits Daradaṇḍī (KmT 2,34d), and goes next to the Paścima Himagahvara (KmT 2,36d) where a forest-deity called Laṃbikā (KmT 2,37ab) or U/Olaṃbikā according to some MSS (cf. *śloka* 36d Notes) resides. From the context it becomes evident, that this locality is identical with the Mahāpīṭha Oḍiyāna (KmT 2,40 ff.). In the ṢaṭSS we find that immediately after the Daradaṇḍī the place called Olaṃba is mentioned (36cd; 41a-d), which is also identified with the Mahāpīṭha Oḍiyāna (*śloka* 42ab). In the fourth/fifth chapter of the ṢaṭSS, which deals with the five Mahāpīṭhas, the first Mahāpīṭha is also referred to as U/Olaṃbikā (cf. p. 149). Obviously the locality called Paścima Himagahvara of the KmT has been omitted in the ṢaṭSS. Instead of this Paścima Himagahvara the author of the ṢaṭSS has included a place called Olaṃba which is identical with Oḍiyāna, just as the Paścima Himagahvara of the KmT is. He may have done this in order to elucidate this passage in the KmT, of which the exact reading is not certain: besides the fact that the name of the deity dwelling in the Paścima Himagahvara is not certain (see above), there is some doubt whether actually a forest-goddess (*vanapālikā*) is meant or perhaps a hamlet in the forest (*vanapallikā*; cf. 4/5,12ab Notes). Although the author of the ṢaṭSS has omitted here the Paścima Himagahvara of the KmT and has replaced it with the locality called Olaṃba, it seems that in the *pādas* 41ab a weak reminiscense to the original Paścima Himagahvara might be found. It is stated in *śloka* 41ab that the Daradaṇḍī is at the Western side, and that it is identical with the joint of the neck (*kṛkāṭikā*). With 'at the Western side' the back of the head, the Meru (cf. 39b), is obviously meant, where the joint of the neck is indeed located. Due to the use of the word *paścime*, however, *pāda* 41a has the irregular number of nine syllables. The author might have used *apare* instead of *paścime* in the same meaning, which would have resulted in a regular *pāda*, however (*daradaṇḍy apare bhāge*). Moreover, the Gandhamādana was already identified with the *kṛkāṭikā* (*śloka* 39d Notes). Yet the identification of the Daradaṇḍī with the *kṛkāṭikā* is also found in ṢaṭSS 47, 122 (*gartā yā ca kṛkāṭikā daradaṇḍī samākhyātā*), which might, however, been based on the present *pāda*. The identification of the Daradaṇḍī with the *kṛkāṭikā* can be made plausible on grounds of popular etymology contrary to the identification of the other localities mentioned in *ślokas* 36-37 with a particular spot on the head. As has been observed earlier (p. 53) the

Daradaṇḍī is most probably a cave — an assumption corroborated by the fact that *dara* denotes a cave, and that the Daradaṇḍī is called a *gartā* in ṢaṭSS 47,122 (see above), which also denotes a cave. Moreover, the *kṛkāṭikā* is indeed a shallow spot at the back of the head, which might easily be called a cave or a hollow. Next to this it is not far-fetched for Indian etymology to discern in the word *kṛkāṭikā* (from: *kṛkāṭa*) a component *kāṭa*, which denotes a hollow also, and is cognate with *garta* and *karta*. The identification of the Daradaṇḍī with the *kṛkāṭikā* becomes thus rather plausible. Returning to the starting point of our exposition it appears that *pāda* 41a has an irregular number of syllables due to the use of the word *paścime*, and that the identification of the Daradaṇḍī with the *kṛkāṭikā*, with which another locality was identified earlier, is based on the word 'cave'. Consequently, it does not appear to be too improbable, that we find in the *pādas* 41ab a reference to the Paścima Himagahvara of the KmT, as *gahvara* also means cave.

The next locality, Olaṃba, is situated North and South of the Meru which represents the head (39b). Olaṃba obviously stands for the two ears at either side of the head. Olaṃba is identical with the Mahāpīṭha Oḍiyāna, which represents the faculty of hearing (1,48c = 4/5,20a). The identification of Olaṃba with the two ears is almost inevitable. The Ṭ is very explicit in its commentary on the *pādas* 41cd: *olaṃbau* (!) *karṇau oḍiyānapīṭham*.

42 pīṭham o-kārasaṃjñaṃ[1] tu madhyabhāge[2] tad ucyate |
karālaṃbaṃ ...... jñeyaḥ .... ||[3]
43 kālānalaṃ (caiva toyaṃ) tatra jālandharaṃ smṛtam |[3]
.... ||[3]

1 AC oṃ-kāra- 2. BC madhye bhāge 3. only in A′, but virtually illegible.

42 [Olaṃba] is the Pīṭha designated by the letter O; it is said to be in the centre.
Karālaṃba should be known as .....
43 Kālānala (is the water); there [the Pīṭha] Jālandhara is known.
....

Olaṃba is identified here with the Pīṭha which is called after the letter O. This is, of course, the Mahāpīṭha Oḍiyāna. The mentioning of its being in the centre (42b) most probably refers to the Mālinī Gahvara (Appendix I), which is of vital importance in our text. In the centre of the Mālinī Gahvara is the letter HA (see fig. 3), which is identical with the Mahāpīṭha Oḍiyāna according to the Ṭ on ṢaṭSS 34,2: *hākāraṃ tad o sthānīyam o-śabdena oḍiyānapīṭham* (cf. p. 185). Lines 42cd-44ab are omitted in all MSS, but are added in the margin of MS A, written in a different hand. Unfortunately, the lines are virtually illegible. They can, however, not be missed, since they explain the next two localities of the enumeration in *ślokas* 36-37: Karālaṃba and Sahya. In the lines 42cd; 43ab the place Karālaṃba is discussed, and is identified with the Mahāpīṭha Jālandhara (43b). According to the Ṭ Karālaṃba is identical with the mouth (*vaktra*), which seems correct as Jālandhara is connected with the faculty of speaking (cf. 1,48d = 4/5,20b). In the *pādas* 43ab the name Jālandhara seems to be explained by relating it to Kālānala, the submarine fire at the end of time, and with water (*toya* = *jala* for *jāla* in Jālan-dhara). Note that the suggested reading *caiva toyaṃ* in *pāda* 43a results in a long fifth and a short sixth syllable, which is not correct. In the *pādas* 43cd the place called Sahya should be explained (see Notes on *śloka* 44ab).

44 .... pūrṇapīṭhaṃ tad ucyate |[1]
ucchuṣmaṃ madhyarandhre tu vāme nīlahradaṃ bhavet ||
45 hradaṃ ca dakṣiṇe śṛṅge olaṃbau[2] dvyaṣṭam[3] aṅgulau |
etad randhradvayaṃ devi trikūṭaśikharaṃ smṛtam ||
46 tṛtīyaṃ brahmarandhraṃ[4] tu ucchuṣmavanasaṃjñakam |
ucchuṣmāc ca samāyātaṃ[5] pravāhaṃ vāmadakṣiṇam ||
47 saṃkrāntaṃ[6] tu varārohe tatrasthā parameśvarī |
kāmarūpāṇi paśyeta kāmarūpaṃ tu tat[7] smṛtam ||

1. only in A′, but virtually illegible 2. BC ulaṃbau; A ulaṃbhau 3. A dvyuṣṭam; BC dviraṣṭam 4. BC -randhre 5. A -tām. 6. BC saṃjātau 7. ABC taṃ.

44 ....; that is called the Pūrṇapīṭha. Ucchuṣma is in the central aperture. At the left [peak] the Nīlahrada should be,
45 and the Hrada at the right peak. The two Olaṃbas are twice eight *aṅgulas*. This pair of apertures, O Devī, is known as the peak of the Trikūṭa.
46 The third one is the Brahmarandhra, which is called the Forest of Ucchuṣma. From [this] Ucchuṣma a [twofold] stream comes forth, left and right.
47 Where [this twofold stream] comes together, O Varārohā, there abides Parameśvarī. Because She can see [there every] form at will, that [place] is known as Kāmarūpa.

Together with *śloka* 43cd which is illegible, *śloka* 44ab deals with the tenth locality called Sahya (37a). From the legible text (*pāda* 44b) we are informed that Sahya is identical with the Pūrṇapīṭha, which is the third Mahāpīṭha Pūrṇagiri. According to the Ṭ Sahya is identical with the 'abode of Laṃbikā' (*laṃbikāsthāna*), which is the uvula (cf. KRP F.39B *ghaṇṭikā laṃbikā jñeyā*). The third Mahāpīṭha Pūrṇagiri represents the faculty of *puṣṭi* (1,49a = 4/5,20c), which should here be understood as 'nourishing; eating' because of the identification of Sahya/Pūrṇagiri with the uvula. In 4/5,21c, however, the opposite of *puṣṭi* is called *klība*, 'impotence'. Obviously *puṣṭi* means 'thriving' in general, either by means of eating or procreation. Contrary to the two preceding Mahāpīṭhas where the location on the head seemed to determine the particular faculty (ears = hearing; mouth = speaking), here the name of the Mahāpīṭha itself appears to be decisive, as the relation between Pūrṇagiri and *puṣṭi* is clearly based on the similarity of their initial syllable (*pū-* & *pu-*). Moreover, the uvula can as easily be related to the faculty of eating as the mouth (*vaktra*) of the previous locality (Karālaṃba = Jālandhara). Instead of the name Sahya the Ṭ uses the name Sasahya for this tenth locality, which is probably caused by a misunderstanding of *śloka* 37a: *karālaṃbaṃ sa-sahyākhyam*.

The eleventh locality Ucchuṣma (44c; Ṭ Ucchuṣmavana, cf. 1,37b; 46b) is located in the central aperture (44c *madhyarandhre*), or is identical with this central aperture according to the Ṭ (*ucchuṣmavanaṃ madhyarandhram*). From *pādas* 46ab it appears that this central aperture is another name for the Brahmarandhra, which is not mentioned in the Ṭ. According to the Ṭ Ucchuṣmavana originates from the centre of the triangular Trikūṭa, and lies between the two eyes, Hrada and Nīlahrada (Ṭ *sa ca kasmād āyātaṃ trikūṭāt trikoṇamadhyād āyātaṃ tatra ucchuṣmavanaṃ madhyarandhram*). The Trikūṭa referred to in the Ṭ is probably the Trikūṭa mentioned in *śloka* 40cd, and in *śloka* 45d, of which Ucchuṣmavana constitutes the third peak (46ab). The other two peaks of the Trikūṭa are in the North Nīlahrada (44d), and in the South Hrada (45a), both of which are called 'apertures' (45c *randhra-dvaya*). From the Ṭ it becomes clear, that Nīlahrada and Hrada are the left and the right eye, respectively. This agrees with the fact, that Ucchuṣma together with Nīlahrada and Hrada is identified with the fourth Mahāpīṭha Kāmarūpa, which represents the faculty of seeing (1,49b = 4/5,20d). The Ṭ relates only Nīlahrada and Hrada to Kāmarūpa: *etayoḥ (sc. Nīlahrada and Hrada) kāmākhyāvidhānam*. The description of the text makes us visualize a triangle, the apex of which is Ucchuṣma, while its base is formed by Nīlahrada and Hrada, the two eyes. From the apex of the triangle a twofold stream comes forth, which debouches into the two pools which Nīlaharda and Hrada actually are (*hrada* = pool): *pravāhaṃ vāmadakṣiṇam* (46d). Of the description of Ucchuṣma, Nīlahrada and Hrada *pāda* 45b with its reference to the two Olaṃbas is rather puzzling. The two Olaṃbas (cf. Ṭ on *śloka* 41cd) are probably the two ears (*śloka* 41cd Notes). The ears are said to be of 'twice eight *aṅgulas*' (*dvyaṣṭam aṅgulau*). It is not clear to what this refers, but perhaps the distance between the eyes and the ears is meant. The Ṭ does not explain this *pāda*. In *pāda* 45b the reading of BC (*dviraṣṭam*) results in a *pāda* of nine syllables. The reading of A (*dvyuṣṭam*) does not make sense, and has been emended to *dvyaṣṭam*, 'twice eight'. The final *-m* of *dvyaṣṭam* serves here as a connecting consonant between two parts of a compound (cf. Hazra 1963: 124; Edgerton 1972: I, 4.60): *dvyaṣṭa-m-aṅgulau*. The insertion of this *-m-* is probably due to a preference for a short fifth and a long sixth syllable in a *pāda*. A regular compound according to MS A would require an additional monosyllabic word in the *pāda* (*ca*, *tu* etc.), but the metrical structure would not be correct (*olaṃbau tu dvyaṣṭāṅgulau; olaṃbau dvyaṣṭāṅgulau tu*). A regular compound according to Mss BC would neither result in a metrically correct *pāda* (*olaṃbau dviraṣṭāṅgulau*).

The place where the twofold stream comes together is Ucchuṣmavana, and is identified with Kāmarūpa. Probably not only Ucchuṣma, but also both eyes constitute this fourth Mahāpīṭha, as we have suggested earlier. The identification of these three places which have the shape of a triangle, with Kāmarūpa is rather obvious due to the fact that a triangle represents the *yoni*, in which form Devī is actually worshipped in Kāmarūpa, modern Gauhati in Assam. The *pādas* 47cd explain the name Kāmarūpa in connection with the faculty of seeing which this Mahāpīṭha represents (cf. 1,49b).

48 pratiṣṭhitaṃ tadā devi devyādhiṣṭhānatāṃ[1] gatam[2] |
śrotukāmā tadoḍrākhyaṃ[3] vaktukāmā tu jālakam[4] ||
49 puṣṭyarthe caiva pūrṇākhye kāmākhyam īkṣaṇecchayā |

1. A vidyā- 2. A gataḥ 3. BC tadoḍḍā- 4. A jālakaḥ; BC jālake.

48 [A place is considered] then to be an acknowledged resort [of the Goddess], O Devī, when Devī has taken up Her abode there.
[Thus when] She wishes to hear, then it is [the place] called Uḍra; [when] She wishes to speak, it is Jālaka;
49 for the sake of thriving She abides in [the place] called Pūrṇa; it is Kāmākhya, when She desires to see.

In this one and a half *śloka* the four Mahāpīṭhas Oḍiyāna, Jālandhara, Pūrṇagiri, and Kāmarūpa are connected with the six last localities of the enumeration in the *ślokas* 36-37: Olaṃba, Karālaṃba, Sahya, Ucchuṣmavana & Hrada &Nīlahrada. For particulars with regard to these identifications I refer to the Notes of the relevant *ślokas* (41cd-47cd).

The *pādas* 48ab serve the purpose of making a distinction between the first seven localities of the enumeration and the six last ones which represent the four Mahāpīṭhas. These six are called a resort or basis (48a *pratiṣṭhita*) of Devī, because She abides (48b *adhiṣṭhānatā*) there for a particular purpose, namely 'hearing', 'speaking', 'thriving', and 'seeing'. In *pāda* 48b the expression *devyādhiṣṭhānatā* can be read in several ways. According to the rules of Classical Sanskrit Grammar one should read *devyā* + *adhiṣṭhānatāṃ*, in which *devyā* is a correct instr. sg. of *devī*. On the other hand it is permissible to regard the expression *devyādhiṣṭhānatā* as a compound of which the first member is *devyā* which stands for *devī* (nom. sg.). As a third possibility the occurrence of double Sandhi might be taken into account (*devyā* for *devyāḥ*), in which *devyā* is the gen sg. of *devī*. The first possibility (*devyā* = instr. sg. of *devī*) is not very probable, as the factual subject of *gatam* (48b) is [*sthānaṃ*] *pratiṣṭhitaṃ* (48a), and not Devī which an instr. sg. for *devyā* would indicate. The second and third possibility (*devyā* = *devī*; *devyā* = gen. sg. of *devī*) do not vary in meaning with regard to the *pāda* 48b. The only difference between these two is the fact, that in the first instance the expression *devyādhiṣṭhānatā* has to be understood as a compound, while in the latter double Sandhi has to be accepted here. Either way, the meaning of the expression *devyādhiṣṭhānatā* remains the same. It is difficult to decide, how to understand *devyā* here. Perhaps one should regard the word *devyā* here as a gen. sg. of *devī* (accepting double Sandhi), because we find in 2,40d an almost identical *pāda* opening with a gen. sg. (masc.). *tasyādhiṣṭhānatāṃ gataḥ*.

In *pāda* 48c there is another instance of which it is difficult to decide what the correct reading is. It is possible to read *tadā* + *uḍrākhyaṃ*, or *tad oḍrākhyaṃ*. In the corresponding *pāda* of the 4th/5th chapter (20a) MS A reads *tu oḍyākhye*, while MSS BC read *tad oḍḍākhye*, in which the same problem features (*tad oḍḍākhye* or *tadā* + *uḍḍākhye*). The only instance where there is no doubt, is the reading of MS A for 4/5,20a, although here hiatus within the *pāda* occurs. Taking into account the reading of MS A for 4/5,20a, perhaps the reading *tad oḍrākhyaṃ* in *pāda* 48c is preferable.

The second Mahāpīṭha Jālandhara is referred to as Jālaka in *pāda* 48d. For the text the reading of MS A (*jālakaḥ*) has been followed on the understanding that the masculine gender has been changed into the neuter (*jālakam*), which agrees better with the neuter gender of the other Mahāpīṭhas mentioned here. Moreover, MS A shows a tendency to write a *visarga* (*-ḥ*) at the end of a line as an indication that the end of a line has been reached (cf. p. 16). The locative of BC (*jālake*), which is also found in 4/5,20b (MS A *jālakaḥ*), is grammatically correct and makes good sense. Apart from the third Mahāpīṭha which shows a locative (49a *pūrṇākhye*), the names of the other two Mahāpīṭhas are definitely neuter nominatives. For this reason the reading *jālakam* seems to be preferable to *jālake*. Perhaps the locative in *-e* of *pūrṇākhye* is influenced by the ending in *-e* of *puṣṭyarthe* (49a). In the 4th/5th chapter (*śloka* 20) the division between locative and nominative is quite different (see 4/5,20 Notes).

kaumāraparvataṃ yac[1] ca anākhyaṃ ṣoḍaśāntakam[2] ||
50 tad vai yad randhragaṃ mārgaṃ tac ca kaumāraparvatam |

1. A yaś 2. BC -ntikam.

The Kaumāraparvata, that is Anākhya, the Ṣoḍaśāntaka.
50 This then is the path, which leads to the [Brahma-]randhra; this is the Kaumāraparvata.

So far, we have seen a series of thirteen localities all situated on, or connected with the head. The Kaumāraparvata appears to be an additional 14th locality (Ṭ *anya[ṃ] caturdaśasthānaṃ kaumāraparvatam anākhyaṃ ṣoḍaśāntam*). The Kaumāraparvata which seems very important since it leads to the Brahmarandhra (50a), is called *anākhya* (lit: 'unmentionable') and *ṣoḍaśāntaka* which refers to the human body as consisting of sixteen parts (cf. 1,3a Notes). In order to account for the Kaumāraparvata being called Ṣoḍaśāntaka here, the Ṭ adds to the thirteen localities again the earth and the head (Ṭ *pṛthivī śiro meruḥ* ||*15*||), which were already mentioned in *śloka* 28ab. In this way the Kaumāraparvata comes at the 16th place. The Kaumāraparvata symbolizes then the totality of the human body.

We have seen, that from the locality called Olaṃba onwards all the remaining localities were identified with one of the four Mahāpīṭhas. The fifth Mahāpīṭha, Mātaṅga, is not mentioned in the enumeration because it is transcendental, and consequently cannot be identified with a particular spot on the human body (cf. 4/5,22ab). The Ṭ, however, seems to lay a connection of the Kaumāraparvata with this fifth Mahāpīṭha, although it does not say so explicitly. After explaining that creation originates from the Saṃvartāmaṇḍala it mentions as a first outcome of creation the four Mahāpīṭhas (in short form), but immediately afterwards the number five is mentioned in relation with the Kaumāraparvata (Ṭ *atrādau vinirgataṃ; catuṣkam o-jā-pū-kā* |*4*| *pañcakādi kaumāraparvataṃ ṣoḍaśāntam*). It does not seem too far-fetched to regard the Kaumāraparvata here as identical with the fifth Mahāpīṭha, although no direct evidence is to be found in the text itself. Its appellation *anākhya*, though, could be understood on the same line as *aspṛśya*, *adraṣṭavya*, and *agamya* (4/5,22c; 23a), with which the Mātaṅga Mahāpīṭha is described.

In the enumeration of the KmT the Kaumāraparvata occupies a rather prominent position compared with the other localities mentioned. It is called Śrīparvata Kumārākhya (2,23c), Kulaparvata (2,22d), and Śrīmatkaumāraparvata (2,24b). A forest full of *liṅgas* (2,25d *liṅgapūrṇaṃ mahāvanam*) is situated there, and because the benignant eye of Devī fell upon this place, it is also called Śrīśaila (2,28). Moreover, when Devī drew with Her toe a line in the sands, a divine river originated (2,29). Abiding on the Kaumāraparvata Davī is described as *avyaktā vyaktarūpiṇī* (2,24d), which agrees with a possible identification of the Kaumāraparvata with the fifth transcendental Mahāpīṭha (see above).

We have assumed that the Kaumāraparvata of the KmT is identical with the Śrīgiri of the enumeration in the ṢaṭSS (p. 149), which is not implausible. Probably because of its prominent position in the KmT the author of the ṢaṭSS has repeated the Kaumāraparvata after the enumeration of the thirteen localities in which it was already included as the Śrīgiri, and stressed its importance by referring to it as the path leading to the Brahmarandhra.

One point of minor importance should be mentioned in connection with the Kaumāraparvata. When Devī is on the Kaumāraparvata She is described as *chāyātmikā* (KmT 2,24c), 'of a shadowy nature'(?). When She abides in Daradaṇḍī, Devī is called *chāyādharī* (KmT 2,35a), which means roughly the same. The meaning of both epithets is rather enigmatic at first sight, but most probably *chāyā*, 'reflection', refers to the old subdivision of Tantras according to the *srotas*-system (cf. 3,35 Notes). It is peculiar, however, that it are just these two localities, the Kaumāraparvata and Daradaṇḍī, which both have caused some difficulty for the author of the ṢaṭSS.

prāṇādyādhāraṇī[1] yā ca adhobhāge kule viduḥ ||
51 pañcagatā ca sā devī tattvākārā śarīragā |
vistareṇa mayā sā tu pūrvagranthe udāhṛtā ||
52 ātmā manaś ca mantraś ca śivaḥ śaktiḥ tathaiva ca |
pāramparyeṇa te jñeyā vṛddhaiś caiva na paṇḍitaiḥ ||

1. BC -dhāriṇī.

The support of the *prāṇa* etc. one knows to be in the lower part of the body.
51 Here Devī is situated in the five, having the shape of the Tattvas, residing in the body. In extenso She has been explained by Me in an earlier work.
52 The Self, the Mind, Mantra, Śiva and Śakti — [only] by tradition these can be learned, not from old and wise teachers.

In the *pādas* 50cd the Mūlādhāra Cakra is described as the 'support' (*ādhāraṇī*) of the *prāṇa* etc. As usual it is located in the lower part of the body (50d). The Ṭ describes this 'support' of the vital airs with the epithets *nālatantukapāṭarūpā tantuprākārā*, 'its door-panels have the shape of hollow threads, its walls are threads'. As the Ṭ confirms, we find a reference here to the ten vital airs in the human body, namely *prāṇa*, *apāna*, *samanā*, *udāna*, *vyāna*, *nāga*, *kūrma*, *kṛkara*, *devadatta* and *dhanañjaya*. Here (50d), as elsewhere, the word *kula* denotes the body (Ṭ *kule śarīre*).

When Devī resides in the Mūlādhāra Cakra She is called *pañcagatā* (51a), 'situated in the five'. It is not clear, what precisely is meant with these 'five'. The ṢaṭSS probably to the series of five in *śloka* 52ab. Since the number five occurs frequently in our text and elsewhere (five Mahāpīṭhas, five Mahābhūtas, five Tattvas etc.), it is uncertain to what *pañcagatā* exactly refers. In the KRP (F.3B) it is explicitly stated that Devī or rather Śakti appears in a fivefold form in the body: *icchā jñānī kriyānandā pañcamī kuṇḍalī matā | tad etad vividhākhyātaṃ śaktiḥ pañcavidhā kule.*

The epithet *tattvākāra* (51b) refers most likely to the five Tattvas, and possibly at the same time to the five Mahāpīṭhas (cf. 4/5,24 Notes). The statement of Bhairava, that He has explained all this in an earlier work (51d *pūrvagranthe*) might refer to the spurious *ślokas* 77 and 78 of the first chapter of the KmT. Here, however, with Tattva the fifty letters of the Sanskrit alphabet are meant, which constitute the human body. Probably, however, the reference to an earlier work should be understood here as a device for avoiding further explanation.

53 tasmin dehe mayā[1] sṛṣṭaṃ siddhānāṃ ca catuṣṭayam |
cañcalo[2] āṇavānando vyāpārīśas tṛtīyakaḥ ||
54 śivānandaś caturthas tu pañcamī tu kulāṃbikā ||

1. A mahā- 2. C′ cañcala.

53 In this body a number of four Siddhas has been emanated by Me: Cañcala, Āṇavānanda, Vyāparīśa as the third,
54 Śivānanda as the fourth, and Kulāṃbikā is the fifth.

In the Ṭ the four Siddhas and Kulāṃbikā (Ṭ Kujāṃbikā) are related with the series of five in *śloka* 52ab, e.g. Cañcala = *manas*; Āṇavānanda = *mantra*; Vyāpārīśa = *ātman*; Śivānanda = Śiva; Kulāṃbikā = Śakti. The names of the four Siddhas do not feature anywhere else in the ṢaṭSS, which is rather striking: one should expect the first four Siddhas emanated by Bhairava, to occupy an important place in the text. In this respect one should notice that two of the four Siddhas have a name ending in *-ānanda* (sc: Āṇavānanda and Śivānanda). In the Ṭ the names of all the four Siddhas end in *-ānanda* (Cañcalānanda, Vyāpārīśānanda)..The reason why in the *ślokas* 53 & 54 only two of the Siddhas have a name ending ending in *-ānanda*, is *metri causa*. In its commentary on the 17th chapter of the ṢaṭSS the Ṭ gives the rules of 'name-giving' for a pupil (*śiṣya*) after his initiation. Among the various names he is given (cf. p. 37), the pupil receives a secret name (*guptanāma*), which should end in *-ānanda*. Most likely the same rule is appropriate here. The names of the four Siddhas mentioned here are probably the 'secret names' of the four Siddhas or Gurus, who feature in the Aṣṭāviṃśatikramapūjā: Mitranātha, Oḍḍanātha, Ṣaṣṭhanātha and Caryanātha. In the Aṣṭāviṃśatikramapūjā these four are connected with the four Mahāpīṭhas — a fact which is nicely linked up with the last six localities of the series of thirteen (see above). The four Siddhas are supplied with a fifth, Kulāṃbikā, who is obviously female and no Siddha. In the *mantras* of the four Siddhas used during the ritual of the Aṣṭāviṃśatikramapūjā (KnT F.54A 'Gurucatuṣka'), the four Siddhas are all connected with an aspect of Devī (Kubjikā, Kuleśvarī etc.). It seems acceptable therefore, that Kulāṃbikā should not be regarded here as the fifth in a series of five, but rather as the female consort of the four Siddhas. This assumption is confirmed in *śloka* 61a of this first chapter, where Devī is clearly connected with Mitranātha or Mitreśāna (see also the Notes on *śloka* 61).

śrīdevy uvāca //
55 ye siddhā deva catvāraḥ pañcamī tu kulāṃbikā |
kathitāḥ ke ca te svāmin kathayasva prasādataḥ ||
śrībhairava[1] uvāca ||
56 yas tv aṭec caiva trailokye cintādhāro[2] mahāprabhuḥ |
kāmarūpāṃśadhārī[3] ca cañcalānanda[4] ucyate ||
57 aṇurūpe[5] sthito yasmāt paryaṭet[6] sarvajantuṣu |
jālapīṭhe svābhāvas tu āṇavānanda[7] ucyate ||
58 samasteṣu ca bhūteṣu vyāpāraṃ kurute tu yaḥ |
pūrṇapīṭhāṃśabhāvaiś ca vyāpārīśaḥ sa ucyate ||
59 ājñāśabdārthaśāstrāṇi yatsakāśāt[8] pravartate |
oḍḍapīṭhāṃśabhāvaiś[9] ca śivānandaḥ sa ucyate ||
60 śaktisāmārthyato[10] buddhir ājñā yasya akhaṇḍitā |
tvaṃ ca vai kubjike svāmi catuṣpīṭhādhikāriṇī ||
61 mitreśānasamāyuktā bhāvitāsi kalevare[11] ||

iti ṣaṭsāhasre[12] śrīmate prathamaḥ paṭalaḥ ||

1. A śrībhairav 2. B antādhāro 3. B -rūpā(..)dhārī 4. BC′ cañcalānandaḥ sa; C dhālānandah sa 5. C -rūpa 6. B paryaṭe 7. ABC āṇavānandaḥ sa 8. B ya(..)kā-māt 9. C aḍḍa- 10. B śaktisāsāmā- 11. B -varo 12. B saṭsasre; C -sāhasra.

Śrīdevī said:
55 Those four Siddhas with Kulāṃbikā as the fifth, about whom You have told, who are they, O Master? Please tell it to Me!
Śrībhairava said:
56 The one who roams about in the Three Worlds, bearing the mind, the Great Lord, that one is called Cañcalānanda, integrally connected with Kāmarūpa.
57 Because he goes around in the form of an atom in all living beings, he is called Āṇavānanda, integrally connected with Jālandhara.
58 The one who concerns himself with all living beings, that one is called Vyāpārīśa, integrally connected with the Pūrṇapīṭha.
59 From whom instruction, the meaning of words and the Śāstras come forth, he is called Śivānanda, integrally connected with the Oḍḍapṭha.
60 Whose mind and authority are unimpaired on account of Śakti, that is You, O Kubjikā, O Mistress, wielding authority in the four Pīṭhas.
61 Together with Mitreśāna You are imagined in the body.

Thus in the Ṣaṭsāhasra, in the Śrīmata the first chapter.

56: In *śloka* 56 and following the names of the four Siddhas are explained, and connected with one of the four Mahāpīṭhas (cf. *ślokas* 53; 54 Notes). Cañcala or more correctly Cañcalānanda 'roams about' in the Three Worlds. The use of the verb *aṭ-* here is caused by the meaning of *cañcala*, 'moving to and fro'. He bears the mind (56b), which refers to *manas* in *śloka* 52a. The expression *-aṃśadhārin* (lit: 'bearing a share of') seems to be synonymous with *-aṃśabhāva* (58c; 59c) and *svābhāva* (57c), all three of them being used in the same context. For this reason we have translated them in the same manner 'integrally connected with'.

57: The name of the second Siddha, Āṇava, is clearly derived from the word *aṇu*, which denotes an 'atom'. For this reason he is described as *aṇurūpe sthito* (57a). According to the Ṭ this Āṇavānanda is connected with *mantra* in *śloka* 52a (see *śloka* 52 Notes), but at first sight no such connection is laid in *śloka* 57, in contradistinction with the previous Siddha Cañcalānanda, who was clearly connected with *manas* of *śloka* 52a by means of the epithet *cintādhāra* (56b). A possible connection with *mantra*, though, might be found in the word *aṇu*. It appears that *mantra* and *aṇu* are interchangeable, or at least their derivatives *māntra* and *āṇava*, in the enumeration of the Six Paths (*ṣaḍadhvan*): the fourth Path is called either *māntra* or *āṇava* (cf. p. 34). Therefore the expression *aṇurūpe sthito* in *pāda* 57a might refer to *mantra* in *śloka* 52a. The use of *aṇu* for *mantra* is perhaps based on the same concept by which the word *bīja* may denote a mystical letter or syllable of a *mantra*. Both *aṇu* and *bīja* express something very minute. Āṇavānda is related to the Mahāpīṭha Jālandhara, which is called here simply Jāla (cf. 48d: Jālaka).

58: The third Siddha, Vyāpārīśa, should be connected with the Self (52: *ātman*). In the *pādas* 58ab his name is explained with the expression *vyāpāraṃ kṛ-*, 'to concern oneself with'. The Ṭ explains *vyāpāra* simply with *karman*, 'action'. The Siddha Vyāpārīśa is connected with the Mahāpīṭha Pūrṇagiri.

59: Śivānanda, the fourth Siddha, is identified with Śiva of *śloka* 52b. Although Śiva is not mentioned by name, the contents of the *pādas* 59ab certainly pertain to Śiva. Because the majority of Tantric texts have the form of a dialogue between Śiva and Devī, in which Śiva answers the questions of Devī, the reference to instruction (*ājñā*), the meaning of words (*śabdārtha*) and the Śāstras becomes understandable. Śivānanda is connected with the Mahāpīṭha Oḍiyāna, which is here simply called Oḍḍa. Noteworthy is the fact that all three MSS have the same reading of the name for this Mahāpīṭha (the reading *aḍḍa* of MS C is obviously a scribal error). Elsewhere MS A reads in most instances Oḍra, while the MSS BC have the form Oḍḍa.

With the fourth Siddha the explanation of the first four Siddhas or Gurus ends. The order of the Mahāpīṭhas with which they are connected, is contrary to their usual order: Oḍiyāna, Jālandhara, Pūrṇagiri, and Kāmarūpa. The Mahāpīṭha Oḍiyāna seems to be the most important one here. We have already remarked that it is situated in the centre of the Mālinī Gahvara (*śloka* 42 Notes). Here in Oḍiyāna resides Śivānanda who is identified with Śiva Himself, and who is united there with His Śakti (61ab).

60: In *śloka* 60 the Śakti of *śloka* 52b is identified with Kulāṃbikā (54b), or as She is called here Kubjikā (60c). From the epithet *catuṣpīṭhādhikāriṇī*, 'wielding authority in the four Pīṭhas', it becomes clear that Kubjikā is the female consort of each of the four Siddhas (cf. *śloka* 54b Notes). The form *svāmi* (60c) which is a vocative fem. sg., supposes a nominative sg. *svāmī* instead of the regular form *svāminī*.

61: Mitreśāna should be the same as Śivānanda or Śiva. United with him Kubjikā resides in the body. This is confirmed in the Ṭ (*sā ca mitreśādisaṃyuktā vartate*). For the 'real' names of the other three Siddhas see the Notes on *śloka* 53; 54.

PAṬALA 2

PAṬALA 2

śrīdevy uvāca ||

1 saṃvartāmaṇḍalaṃ deva kathaṃ tena prabho kṛtam[1] |
śaktibhiḥ purato[2] deva kathayasva prasādataḥ ||

2 anyagranthāvatāre tu bhrāntir adyāpi me prabho[3] |
śrīmatīyaṃ yena nāmabhedeṅa lakṣyate[4] ||

3 kathayasva prasādena sthānaṃ mānaṃ yathākramam ||[5]

śrībhairava[6] uvāca ||

4 saṃvartāmaṇḍalaṃ devi[7] kathayāmy anupūrvaśaḥ[8] |
yogināṃ saṃsadākālaṃ yatra sthāne pravartate ||

1. A kṛtaḥ 2. BC pārato; *pādas* 1cd virtually illegible in A 3. A prabhuh.; *pāda* 2a illegible in A 4. B lakṣyata 5. *pāda* 3b illegible in A 6. A śrībhairav 7. *pāda* 4a illegible in A; perhaps A reads *yaś ca* instead of *devi* 8. A -pūrvakaḥ.

Śrīdevī said:

1 How, O Deva, is the Saṃvartāmaṇḍala made [by You] in that manner, O Lord, in former times together with the *śaktis*? Please tell [that] in Your graciousness, O Deva!

Still I am confused with regard to Your appearances in other texts,
2/3 O Lord. Please tell [me] in Your graciousness the different names by which the tradition of the Śrīmata is characterized, the place and the ideas, [all] in due order.

Śrībhairava said:

4 I will explain [to You], O Devī, the Saṃvartāmaṇḍala in regular order, the [right] time for the Yogins to assemble, [and] the place where it takes place.

In these introductory *ślokas* Devī asks Bhairava how he 'made' (1b *kṛta*) the Saṃvartāmaṇḍala in former times together with the *śaktis*. As it appears from the answer of Bhairava, there are four different Saṃvartāmaṇḍalas to be distinguished (5-14ab). The Ṭ agrees with this number, and mentions the following four Saṃvartāmaṇḍalas: 1) in the Brahmarandhra, 2) in the heart, 3) in the Ādhāra Cakra, 4) in the Tradition (Ṭ *saṃvartāmaṇḍalavyāvarṇanam | brahmarandhrasthaṃ hṛdistham ādhārastham | tathā kramagataṃ ca*). In *pāda* 3b it is uncertain to what *sthānaṃ* and *mānaṃ* exactly refer. *Sthāna* might refer to the place for the Yogins to assemble (4ab) in order to perform the rite of the Saṃvartāmaṇḍala, but no explanation is given by Bhairava with regard to this in the present chapter. Perhaps it anticipates the exposition of the innitiation of a pupil as given in the third chapter of our text (3,18 ff.). With *māna* the doctrine itself of the Kulālikāmnāya could be meant, in which way *māna* is almost synonymous with the more usual *mata*, or it might perhaps be understood as 'honour'. In the latter case *māna* also refers to the third chapter of the ṢaṭSS.

In *pāda* 4c it is difficult to decide whether to read *saṃsadā kālaṃ* or *saṃsadākālaṃ*. In the first case there is an irregular use of the instr. (from *saṃsad*); in the latter one has to accept a nominative fem. *saṃsadā* instead of the masc. *saṃsada*. Most likely *-ā* is added to the consonant stem *saṃsad* (fem.), by which the feminine gender of the word is retained (cf. Edgerton 1972: I,15.9). The *ā* in *saṃsadā-* is necessary for metrical reasons (a long sixth syllable).

5 saṃvartāmaṇḍalaṃ tac ca brahmarandhrasya ūrdhvagam |[1]
khecarīcakramadhyasthaṃ mātaṅgapadamadhyagam ||[1]
6 śrīśailavanamadhyasthaṃ catuḥpīṭhordhvasaṃsthitam[2] |
tatrasthaṃ maṇḍalaṃ divyaṃ divyādivyair niṣevitam ||[3]
7 catuṣkādyaṃ tu yatrasthaṃ kujeśena tu nirmitam |[4]
caturviṃśaṣoḍaśair bhedair aṣṭābhiś ca vyavasthitam ||[5]
8 saṃvartāmaṇḍalaṃ tac[6] ca bhāvagamyaṃ ca yoginām |

1. *śloka* 5 illegible in A 2. BC candrapīṭho-; A -sthitaḥ 3. *pāda* 6d illegible in A 4. *pādas* 7ab virtually illegible in A; perhaps A reads *kubjiśena* instead of *kujeśena* 5. *pāda* 7c illegible in A 6. taś.

5 The [first] Saṃvartāmaṇḍala then is located above the Brahmarandhra, in the middle of the Khecarīcakra, in the centre of the abode of Mātaṅga;
6 it is in the centre of the Śrīśailavana, above the four Pīṭhas. There is the divine Maṇḍala, frequented by gods and others.
7 [It is the place] where the Four etc. are, created by Kujeśa. It is arranged according to the distinction between 24, 16 and 8.
8 Thus the [first] Saṃvartāmaṇḍala should be regarded by the Yogins.

The first Saṃvartāmaṇḍala is located above the Brahmarandhra (5b), whereas the Ṭ situates it in or on the Brahmarandhra (Ṭ *brahmarandhrastha*), a location which agrees with ṢaṭSS 1,29. Furthermore this first Saṃvartāmaṇḍala is situated in the middle of the Khecarīcakra (5c). This refers to the Five Cakras, a very important concept to the tradition of the Śrīmata: *śrīmataṃ tu varārohe ebhiś cakrais tu mudritam* (ṢaṭSS 20,4ab). The Five Cakras are the Devī-, Dūtī-, Mātṛ-, Yoginī- and Khecarī-cakra. The 'highest' Cakra of these Five is the Khecarīcakra. The Five Cakras are dealt with in great detail in the chapters 21 to 25 of our text (cf. KmT Ch. 14-16). These five chapters of the ṢaṭSS are preceded by a chapter entitled Kulābhiṣeka, in which the initiation of the pupil is discussed and the qualities of the Guru. The importance of the concept of the five Cakras for the Śrīmata may be derived from the fact, that they are dealt with immediately after the exposition of the initiation of the pupil into the Kula-doctrine. In *pāda* 5d the first Saṃvartāmaṇḍala is said to be in the centre of the abode of Mātaṅga (*mātaṇgapāda*). this refers to the fifth Mahāpīṭha, which is called Mātaṅga. Like the first Saṃvartāmaṇḍala it is situated above the Brahmarandhra, and in the centre of the Khecarīcakra (4/5,119ab). While the first Saṃvartāmaṇḍala is located in the Forest of the Śrīśaila (6a *śrīśailavanamadhyasthaṃ*), the Śrīśaila itself is stated to be in the Mātaṅga Mahāpīṭha (4/5,119c), and above the Brahmarandhra (19,63cd *brahmarandhrasya ūrdhve tu śrīśailaṃ yatra parvatam*). Consequently an identification between the first Saṃvartāmaṇḍala and the fifth Mahāpīṭha Mātaṅga appears to be evident, while the relation between these two and the Khecarīcakra too seems to be very close. In *pāda* 6b the reading of A has been preferred: *catuḥpīṭhordhva-* (cf. 1,60d *catuṣpīṭhā-*). We have seen in the first chapter that the first four Mahāpīṭhas were identified with a particular part of the head (ears, mouth, uvula, eyes). The fifth Mahāpīṭha and the first Saṃvartamaṇḍala are situated above the Brahmarandhra, in other words above the head with which the other four Mahāpīṭhas were related. The reading of the MSS BC, 'above the Candrapīṭha' (*candrapīṭhordhva-*), also makes good sense (cf. 1,26 ff.).

In *pāda* 7a the expression *catuṣkādyaṃ* refers to the Aṣṭāviṃśatikrama (cf. 2,21 ff.). According to the *pādas* 7ab the first Saṃvartāmaṇḍala is 'arranged' (*vyavasthita*) following a division of 24, 16, and 8. The Ṭ provides most probably the correct interpretation of this line. It connects the numbers with the *akṣaras* of the Skt alphabet, and at the same time with the well-known triad Sūrya, Soma, Agni (= Sun, Moon, Fire). The number 24 are the syllables *ka* to *bha*, the Sūryacakra; the number 16 represents the vowels (*a-aḥ*), the Somacakra; the number 8 stands for the syllables *ma* to *sa*, the Vahnimaṇḍala. Not included in this enumeration are the *ha* and the *kṣa*; according to the Ṭ these two should be 'in the centre' (Ṭ *madhye ha kṣa*). Most likely we have to think of a lotus with respectively 24, 16 and 8 petals; in the pericarp (*karṇikā*) the *ha* and *kṣa* are placed (cf. 2,40b). In the 25th chapter of the ṢaṭSS which deals with the Khecarīcakra, we find the same arrangement of the 48 *akṣaras*, also connected with the triad Sūrya, Soma and Agni. Here the *ha* and *kṣa* are not mentioned either. It seems that only the Ṭ on *śloka* 7ab is aware of the fact that the enumeration does not include the last two syllables of the alphabet, or at least the Ṭ does mention it while the ṢaṭSS remains silent on this point. It should be noted, that *pāda* 7c counts nine syllables instead of the regular eight. It appears that the author of the ṢaṭSS had little chance to produce a regular *pāda* of eight syllables using the words he used, while an alternative with the same meaning seems difficult to find. For the meaning of *bhāvagamya* I refer to the Notes on 1,29b with emphasis on the fact that the process is chiefly mental.

dvitīyaṃ hṛdgate padme draṣṭavyaṃ bhāvarūpiṇam ||[1]
9 yogārthe[2] vartate yasmāt saṃvartāmaṇḍalaṃ tu tat[3] |
mātṛcakrasya madhyasthaṃ navapadmasamanvitam ||
10 śāstrārthasya pravaktāraṃ yogārthaṃ pratipādakam |[4]
dravyādiguṇasaṃyuktaṃ vijñānānandasaṃkulam ||
11 saṃvartāmaṇḍalaṃ tac[5] ca anāhatapade sthitam[6] |

1. *pādas* 8cd illegible in A 2. A grāhyārthe (?) 3. BC tam 4. *pādas* 10ab illegible in A 5. A taś 6. A sthitaḥ.

The second [Saṃvartāmaṇḍala] should be seen in a mental manifestation in the heart-lotus.

9 Because it serves the cause of Yoga, it [is called] Saṃvartāmaṇḍala. It is situated in the centre of the Mātṛcakra, and furnished with nine lotuses.

10 It expounds the contents of the Śāstras; it teaches the essentials of Yoga. It is

endowed with the qualities of the substances etc.; it is full of these bliss of [true] understanding.

11 Thus then is the [second] Saṃvartāmaṇḍala located in the Anāhata-*pada*.

The second Saṃvartāmaṇḍala is situated in the heart (8c), which coincides with the Anāhata Cakra (11b). The expression *draṣṭavyaṃ bhāvarūpiṇam* (8d) appears to have the same meaning as *bhāvagamya* (1,29b; 2,8b), although perhaps more emphasis is laid here upon the fact that it concerns here a mental or meditative manifestation. The meaning of the *pādas* 9ab is not clear to me. At first sight it appears to be an etymological explanation of the name Saṃvartāmaṇḍala, or at least of its first member *saṃvartā-* (9a *vartate*). As the first Saṃvartāmaṇḍala was related with the Khecarīcakra (2,5c), so is the second situated in the centre of the Mātṛcakra (9c). This Mātṛcakra (ṢaṭSS Ch. 23) consists of a central lotus around which are placed eight other lotuses dedicated to the eight Mothers (Brahmāṇī etc.), thus amounting to nine lotuses in total (cf. 9d *navapadmasamanvita*). In the central lotus Piṅgeśa or Piṅganātha together with Guhyakubjikā resides. To what *pāda* 10c refers is not clear. *Dravya*, 'substance', might refer to the materials used during the *pūjā*. On the occasion of the initiation of the pupil, he should learn the true nature of the five or nine *dravyas* (Ch. 17). Since the second Saṃvartāmaṇḍala is connected with the Mātṛcakra of nine lotuses, one is inclined to link the reference to the *dravyas* with these nine *dravyas* mentioned in *paṭala* 17. These nine *dravyas* are: 1) *gandha*, 2) *puṣpa* (Ṭ menstrual blood), 3) *aṃbu* (Ṭ urine), 4) *siddhārtha* (Ṭ saliva), 5) *muditā* (Ṭ a ram's heart), 6) *harṣaṇā* (Ṭ liquor), 7) *āmiṣa* (Ṭ flesh), 8) *candra* (Ṭ semen), 9) *candana* (Ṭ marrow).

tṛtīyaṃ nābhyadhastāt tu saṃvartā vahnir ucyate ||[1]
12 pacate[2] dehināṃ bhakṣyaṃ saṃvartāmaṇḍalaṃ tu tam |[3]

1. *pāda* 11d illegible in A 2. C patate 3. *pādas* 12ab illegible in A.

The third [Saṃvartāmaṇḍala] is located beneath the navel. Saṃvartṛ is called Vahni [here].

12 He consumes the food of men. Thus is the [third] Saṃvartāmaṇḍala.

The third Saṃvartāmaṇḍala is located beneath the navel (11c), or as the Ṭ states 'in the cavity of the navel' (*nābhikandaramadhye*). As far as I know, in *pāda* 11d the only reference is found to a deity called Saṃvartṛ (cf. the goddess Saṃvartā, p. 33; 2,34a) as an explanation of the first member of the compound Saṃvartā-maṇḍala. Perhaps *saṃvartā* is a short form here for *saṃvartāmaṇḍalaṃ*. Either way, the third Saṃvartāmaṇḍala is connected with Vahni or Agni, especially that aspect of Agni which consumes the food in the stomach (Jāṭhara Agni). According to the Ṭ this third Saṃvartāmaṇḍala has the form of Agni (Ṭ *vahnirūpa*), which is a triangle according to the Ṭ on the 16th chapter of the ṢaṭSS: *āgneyamaṇḍalaṃ trikoṇaṃ yathā*

ādhāracakramadhyasthaṃ janmamaṇḍalamadhyagam[1] ||
13 trikoṇaṃ[2] ca catuṣkoṇaṃ ṣaṭkoṇaṃ[3] caiva bāhyataḥ[4] |

tatrotpannaṃ jagat sarvaṃ tatra līnaṃ carācaram ||[5]
14 vaḍavānalamadhyasthaṃ saṃvartāmaṇḍalaṃ tu tam |[6]

1. A -gaḥ 2. B trikoṭyaṃ 3. omitted in BC 4. A bāhyatā 5. *pādas* 13cd illegible in A 6. *pādas* 14ab illegible in A.

[The fourth Saṃvartāmaṇḍala] is in the centre of the Ādhāra Cakra, in the middle of the Janmamaṇḍala.
13 There is a triangle, a square, and a hexagon at the outer side. There the complete world originates; in here the animate and inanimate world is retracted.
14 It is in the centre of Vaḍavānala. Thus is the [fourth] Saṃvartāmaṇḍala.

The fourth Saṃvartāmaṇḍala is situated in the lowest of the Six Cakras, the Ādhāra or Mūlādhāra Cakra (12c). this place is identified with the Janmamaṇḍala, 'The Circle of Births' (12d: Ṭ *ādhāraṃ janmasthānam*), which is most probably the *yoni* (see below). The place is described as having the form of a triangle, a square and a hexagon, respectively, e.g.  . *Śloka* 13cd refers to the periodical emanation and reabsorption of the world. Next the fourth Saṃvartāmaṇḍala is located in the centre of the Vaḍavānala, the submarine fire or the fire in the lower regions (14a), which agrees with the fact that the fourth Saṃvartāmaṇḍala is located in the lowest of the Six Cakras. Moreover, Vaḍavānala and Saṃvartaka are both a designation for the Fire of Dissolution, which destroys the world at the period of universal destruction (Dowson 1968: s.v. *aurva*; MBh 6,8,26; BhP 4,30,45). The close relationship between Vaḍavānala and Saṃvartaka is very clearly illustrated in a passage from the Gorakṣa Saṃhitā (p. 6), where Saṃvartaka is called Saṃvartānala (*saṃvartānalamadhyasthaḥ saṃvartānalasaṃsthitaḥ | saṃvartāsṛṣṭirūpastho bhairavas tena cocyate*). The Ṭ locates the Vaḍavānala in the upper part of the *yoni* (*yonyagratala*), and identifies it with the Saṃvartāmaṇḍala. The first two Saṃvartāmaṇḍalas were identified with the Khecarīcakra and the Mātṛcakra, respectively (see above). The Ṭ identifies this fourth Saṃvartāmaṇḍala with the Devīcakra (Ṭ *tathaiva devīcakram iti vyākhyāyate*). This agrees with the description of the Devīcakra as we find it in the 21st chapter of the ṢaṭSS, where the triangle, the square and the hexagon are mentioned in connection with this Devīcakra. The third Saṃvartāmaṇḍala is not related with any of the five *cakras*, at least no mention is made of it. Possibly one might connect it with the Dūtīcakra, which is considered to be the stomach (*udara*; *paṭala* 22).

The description of the four Saṃvartāmaṇḍalas ends with *pāda* 14cd. We have seen that the Ṭ agrees with the ṢaṭSS with regard to the number of Saṃvartāmaṇḍalas (cf. p. 69), but the location of the third and fourth Saṃvartāmaṇḍala is not the same in the ṢaṭSS and its commentary:

ṢaṭSS:	Ṭ:
1) Brahmarandhra,	Brahmarandhra,
2) heart,	heart,
3) below the navel,	Ādhāra Cakra,
4) Ādhāra Cakra.	Krama.

The texts do not offer an explanation for this obvious inconsistency, but perhaps the Ṭ related the description of the four Saṃvartāmaṇḍalas with *śloka* 16 where the *kramāvatāra* (16a) is mentioned in connection with the Saṃvartāmaṇḍala.

yasmin śāstre ca yat proktaṃ guruṇā pratipāditam[1] ||
15 tasmin tac ca pramāṇaṃ syād yad yathā vedanā bhavet |[2]
athātaḥ kathayiṣyāmi guhyād guhyatara[ṃ] param ||[2]

1. A -pāditaḥ 2. *pādas* 15bcd illegible in A.

What is stated in a Śāstra, or explained (orally) by a Guru,
15 that has authority in that particular text, valid for every way of thinking.
Next I will tell [You] something else, which is even more secret than secret!

In the *pādas* 14cd; 15ab the reader of the ṢaṭSS is urged to accept the sole authority of the ṢaṭSS with regard to the concept of the four Saṃvartāmaṇḍalas, as it is explained in the previous lines. No matter what other texts may say about the subject (14c), or what is transmitted orally by a Guru (14d), the student should follow the exposition of the ṢaṭSS which is true for all other doctrines (15ab). The meaning of *vedanā* (15b) is uncertain here. Obviously it belongs to the root *vid-*, 'to know', and is used instead of the more usual *vedana* (neuter). The preference for the feminine *vedanā* which does occur rarely, might be due to metrical reasons (a long sixth syllable).

In *pāda* 15d the MSS BC read both *guhyatara* (A illegible), which is wrong on both grammatical and metrical grounds.

16 ādau kramāvatāraṃ tu akathyam[1] itare jane |
paratattvāt kujeśena śaktiś cānandasaṃjñikā[2] ||
17 saṃvartāmaṇḍale kṣiptā[3] ṣoḍaśāre śiropari |[4]
karṇikāyāṃ sthitā jñānī[5] a-kārādyā[6] kriyā dale ||
18 tāś ca ṣoḍaśabhedena śaktayaḥ parikīrtitāḥ |
preraṇāc chrīkujeśasya tais tu ṣoḍaśabhiḥ[7] kṛtam[7] ||[8]
19 krodhīśādibhṛgvantaṃ[9] ca[9] rudrāṇāṃ ca dvikaṃ dvikam |
dvikaṃ saptadaśaṃ yac[10] ca tasyādyaṃ sahajākṣaram ||
20 krodhaśvetodbhavaṃ varṇaṃ tena tan na kalātmakam |[11]

1. A a[ka]thyam 2. A cāna(..) 3. B kṣiptvā 4. *pādas* 17ab illegible in A 5. B jñāti 6. BC -dyāḥ 7. B ṣoḍaśa niṣkṛtam 8. *pāda* 18c illegible in A 9. A -bhṛgvāntaṃ [ca] 10. A yaś 11. *pādas* 20ab illegible in A.

16 In the beginning there is the uninterrupted line of descent. One should not tell this to other people. From the Paratattva Kujeśa sent His Śakti called Ānandā
17 in the Saṃvartāmaṇḍala, [specifically] in the sixteen-petalled [lotus] above the

head. As Jñānī She abides in its pericarp; as Kriyā She represents the [sixteen vowels] beginning with the *a* in the petals.

18 These [vowels] are called *śaktis*, of which there are sixteen different ones. By the instigation of Śrīkujeśa then these sixteen have linked themselves,

19 two by two, with the Rudras from Krodhīśa up to Bhṛgu. With regard to the seventeenth pair: the first is a natural syllable;

20 the [other] syllable originates from Krodha and Śveta. Therefore this seventeenth pair] has not the nature of the *kalās*.

From the Paratattva, 'The Ultimate Tattva', Śrīkujeśa sends His Śakti Ānandā (cf. 1,1a) down in the Saṃvartāmaṇḍala, which is located above the head (17a *śiropari*). According to the fourfold division of the Saṃvartāmaṇḍala (see above), it follows that Ānanda Śakti descends into the first Saṃvartāmaṇḍala, which is situated above the Brahmarandhra (2,5b). This Saṃvartāmaṇḍala has the form of a lotus with respectively sixteen and thirty-two petals (see below). In the pericarp (*karṇikā*) of the lotus Ānandā Śakti manifests Herself as Jñānī or Jñānaśakti (17c). Jñānī belongs to the well-known triad of Icchā, Jñānaśakti, and Kriyā. The second one is almost always called Jñānaśakti, and but rarely Jñānī. For this reason perhaps the Ṭ considers *jñānī* to be the nominative sg. masc. of *jñānin* (Ṭ *tasya (sc. padmasya) ṣodaśārasya karṇikāyāṃ sthito jñānī; jñānaśaktir yasya vidyate 'sau jñānī; sa ca kailīśaḥ (wr.f. kaulīśaḥ?)*). Needless to say that the Ṭ is clearly wrong here. Thus we find Jñānī in the pericarp of the lotus. As Kriyā She manifests Herself in the sixteen petals of the lotus, which represent the sixteen vowels of the alphabet, e.g. *a* to *aḥ*. These sixteen vowels are called *śaktis* (18ab). Outside the row of sixteen petals there is a series of thirty-two petals (cf. 38ab), in which thirty-two Rudras or Bhairavas are situated. As we have seen before (1,16 Notes), the Rudras or Bhairavas stand for the fifty *akṣaras* of the alphabet, in their male form obviously. By the instigation of Śrīkujeśa (18c) the sixteen vowels or *śaktis* unite themselves in pairs with the Rudras (18c; 19ab). Since the sixteen *śaktis* link themselves in pairs (19b *dvikaṃ dvikam*) with the Rudras, thirty-two Rudras are required. These are the Rudras from Krodhīśa up to Bhṛgu (19a), i.e. from *ka* up to *sa* (cf. Appendix II). The *śaktis* link themselves with the Rudras in the following way: *a* + *ka* & *kha* = *ka*, *kha*; *ā* + *ga* & *gha* = *gā*, *ghā*; ..... *aḥ* + *ṣa* & *sa* = *ṣaḥ*, *saḥ*. According to the Ṭ this union of one *śakti* with two Rudras represents Ānandā Śakti as Icchā.

In *pāda* 19c a seventeenth pair is mentioned, which can only consist of the two remaining syllables of the alphabet: *ha* and *kṣa*. The first of this seventeenth pair is called a 'natural' syllable (19d *sahajākṣara*), the *ha*. The second one is a combination of the Rudras Krodha (*ka*) and Śveta (*ṣa*): *krodhaśvetodbhava* (20a). This combination forms the syllable *kṣa*. As is explained in the 7th chapter of the ṢaṭSS the *kṣa* is regarded to be an 'artificial' syllable in contradistinction to the other 49 letters of the Skt alphabet. The Mālinī Gahvara consists of the 49 letters (*a-ha*) only; the *kṣa* being formed by combining *ka* with *ṣa*. The sixteen vowels are connected with the thirty-two Rudras. Consequently, there are no vowels left to be connected with this seventeenth pair *ha* and *kṣa*. Therefore, the text states that this pair is *na kalātmakaṃ* (20b), in which *kalā* (a 16th part) refers to the sixteen vowels. Thus the seventeenth pair is not to be connected with any of the sixteen vowels, which were already used up with the preceding sixteen pairs (*ka* up to *sa*). This leaves us with the question where this seventeenth pair is located in the lotus. The only place left for the *ha* and the *kṣa* is in the pericarp of the lotus, a fact which is confirmed in *śloka* 40b. Although the *ha* and the *kṣa* cannot be connected with any of the sixteen vowels or *śaktis*, they do have a *śakti* of their own. Except the *ha* and *kṣa* also Jñānī abides in the pericarp, as we have already seen (17c). Probably Jñānī functions as the *śakti* for this last pair. It should be mentioned that the syllable *ha* represents Bhairava (1,16c *sānto 'ham*), while the Rudra or Bhairava representing the *kṣa* is called Saṃvartaka (cf. Appendix II). Thus Bhairava (*ha*) and Saṃvartaka (*kṣa*) reside in the pericarp of the lotus together with their *śakti* Jñānī. Despite the fact that no vowels are left for these two, it seems possible to connect the *ha* and the *kṣa* with a particular vowel. In the Mālinī Gahvara Jñānaśakti stands for the vowel *e* (cf. Appendix II), which has the shape of a *yoni* (cf. 1,26 Notes) — a shape which is rather appropriate here, as from the pericarp of the lotus the other 48 letters of the alphabet are 'born'. Although the text nor the Ṭ suggest it, it does not seem too far-fetched to assume that both the *ha* and the *kṣa* should be connected with the vowel *e* in the pericarp of the lotus.

Summarizing the above, we are informed that Śrīkujeśa sends His Śakti Ānandā down from the Paratattva to the first Saṃvartāmaṇḍala, which is located above the Brahmarandhra. It has the form of a lotus with sixteen and thirty-two petals. As Jñānaśakti She abides in the pericarp of the lotus together with Bhairava and Saṃvartaka. In the row of sixteen petals the sixteen vowels are located, and Śakti manifests Herself here as Kriyā. In the row of thirty-two petals the consonants *ka* up to *sa* are situated. The vowels and the consonants unite themselves by the instigation of Śrīkujeśa. The result of this union between vowels (*śaktis*) and consonants (Rudras) is, of course, creation. In the following lines of this chapter the beginning of creation is described, namely the Aṣṭāviṃśatikrama

śrīkaṇṭhinyāditaḥ[1] kṛtvā tripādinyāvasānakam[2] ||
21 catuṣkādyaṃ kṛtaṃ tais tu aṣṭāviṃśapadakramam |
mārgaṃ ca saṃpravakṣyāmi[3] yenāyātaṃ[4] krameṇa tu ||

1) B -ādinaḥ 2) A -sānagaḥ 3. A saṃ[pra]vakṣyāmi 4) A yenāyāta (?).

Beginning with Śrīkaṇṭhinī one ends with Tripādinī:
21 by these the Aṣṭāviṃśapadakrama, the Four etc., is brought about. I shall tell [You] the way and the order in which it is attained.

Starting with *śloka* 20cd the fifty letters of the Skt alphabet are brought in connection with the Aṣṭāviṃśatikrama, which marks the beginning of creation according to the Kulālikāmnāya. Again, we find the combination of the vowels or *śaktis* with the consonants or Rudras. As the name Aṣṭāviṃśatikrama already indicates, in the first place it concerns only twenty-eight of the thirty-four consonants. The remaining six consonants are related to the Aṣṭāviṃśatikrama in a special way (cf. 29cd ff.). In the *pādas* 20cd the vowels are mentioned, which are to be connected with the twenty-eight consonants. They are the vowels from Śrīkaṇṭhinī up to Tripādinī. The *śakti* Śrīkaṇṭhinī stands for the first vowel, the *a*. Although in 7,18cd (see Appendix II) Vāgeśvarī is mentioned as this particular *śakti*, the name Śrīkaṇṭhinī is readily understood. It is related to Śrīkaṇṭha, the Rudra or Bhairava who represents the vowel *a* (7,46cd). Thus the *śakti* Śrīkaṇṭhinī indicates the vowel *a*. The śakti Tripādinī is more enigmatic: no *śakti* by this name is found in the enumeration of the 7th *paṭala*, neither has a Rudra been found by the name Tripāda. In *śloka* 30a the 17th pair (*ha* & *kṣa*) is mentioned. This indicates that we have to arrange the consonants in pairs, as was already pointed out in the *ślokas* 16-20ab. Consequently, the twenty-eight consonants (see above) are connected with the vowels in pairs. Of the sixteen vowels only fourteen are required for the group of twenty-eight Rudras divided in pairs. Since in *śloka* 30c the *aṃ* and the *aḥ* are connected with the remaining six consonants, it follows that the fourteen vowels to be connected with the twenty-eight consonants are the *a* up to the *au*. In this way the *śakti* Tripādinī should represent the fourteenth vowel, the *au*. It is perhaps possible to account for the fact, that the vowel *au* is represented by a *śakti* called Tripādinī. The name Tripādinī might refer to the Gāyatrī-metre, which consists of three *pādas*. In 7,36ab (see Appendix II) the *śakti* Gāyatrī represents the thirteenth vowel, the *o*; the *au* being represented by the *śakti* Sāvitrī. If we accept a possible relation of the name Tripādinī with the Gāyatrī-metre, the fourteenth *śakti* Sāvitrī can also be understood in this context: Sāvitrī is a particular form of the Gāyatrī-metre. Moreover, the most famous Gāyatrī-verse (ṚgV 3,62,10) is dedicated to the god Savitṛ. In this way the connection between the *śakti* called Tripādinī and the vowel *au* becomes plausible. Apart from the above one should keep in mind that the vowels *o* and *au* are easily confounded in manuscripts. Especially the *au* is quite often written as *o*. In the same way the names of the accompanying *śaktis* might have been confused so that perhaps the *śakti* Gāyatrī could represent the vowel *au*.

22 prathamam unmanāyātaṃ[1] catuṣkaṃ niṣkalaṃ ca yat |
bhāvayec cittamadhye[2] tu samanāyās[3] tu pañcakam[4] ||
23 vyāpinyā[5] tu[5] bhavet ṣaṭkaṃ śaktigocare |
nādānte[6] pañcakaṃ proktaṃ catuṣkaṃ nādagaṃ tataḥ ||
24 niṣkalā bhāvagamyās[7] te śūnyarūpā[8] vicintayet |
unmanādau tu sthānāni aṅgulānāṃ[9] dvikaṃ dvikam[10] ||

1. A -yātāṃ 2. B cinta- 3. A samanā yas 4. A -kaḥ 5. A vyāpinyādyā [tu] 6. A nādyāye 7. A [bhā]va- 8. B -rūpādi; C rūpaṃ; 9. A aṅgulaṃ tu 10. A -kaḥ.

22 The first, the Four, comes forth without a vowel from Unmanā; one should visualize it [thus] in the mind. The Five belong to Samanā.
23 The Six exist by means of Vyāpinī. The Four relate to Śakti. The Five are said to be in the Nādānta. The Four, finally, are in the Nāda.
24 They should be considered without vowels. One should regard them as 'empty'. The [six] places from Unmanā onwards are each of two *aṅgulas*.

The Aṣṭāviṃśatikrama in its fixed subdivision (4-5-6-4-5-4) is connected with Unmanā (22a), Samanā (22d), Vyāpinī (23a), Śakti (23b), Nādānta (23c) and Nāda (23d), respectively. These six are known from a series of twelve in total, explaining the origin of the *bīja* OṂ. In the ṢaṭSS this list of twelve is discussed in the 28th chapter (cf. Padoux 1975: table after p. 346). The twenty-eight consonants are 'without a vowel' (*niṣkala*) and 'empty' (*śūnyarūpa*), which has the same connotation. It means that they originate as *k*, *kh*, etc. (*anacka*) and not as *ka*, *kha*, etc. Only in a second phase are the 'empty' consonants provided with a vowel (*śloka* 25ab). The first component of the Aṣṭāviṃśatikrama, the Four, should be visualized in the mind (22c *citta*), which agrees with the list of Padoux (see above). Each of the six places is said to measure two *aṅgulas* (24cd). The total of *aṅgulas thus amounts to twelve (6 × 2 = 12)*. The complete series of twelve 'ends' at a distance of twelve *aṅgulas* above the Brahmarandhra, the so-called Dvādaśānta (cf. 1,15 Notes). Since only six out of the twelve are mentioned in this passage, the author has assigned two *aṅgulas* to each of the six in order to reach the number twelve.

25 śrīkaṇṭhinyā anantinyā krodhaś[1]caṇḍāntagaiḥ[2] śivaiḥ |
catuṣkādyaṃ kṛtaṃ tais tu o-jā-pū-ka[3] tu bhālake[4] ||

1. B krodho 2. A caṇḍā(..)ai 3. BC -kan 4. A bhācake.

25 By Śrīkaṇṭhinī and Anantinī together with Krodha, Caṇḍa, Antaga and Śiva — by these are brought about the first Four on the forehead: O, JĀ, PŪ and KĀ.

The first component of the Aṣṭāviṃśatikrama is the series of Four. It consists of the four Mahāpīṭhas Oḍiyāna, Jālandhara, Pūrṇagiri and Kāmarūpa. Their names are given in the text by means of their initial syllables (25d *o*, *jā*, *pū*, *ka*). This practice is also observed in the case of the other components of the Aṣṭāviṃśatikrama in the following *ślokas*. The vowels or *śaktis*, Śrīkaṇṭhinī and Anantinī, stand for the *a* and *ā*, respectively (cf. Appendix II). It is peculiar, however, that in both instances the feminine form of the name of the particular Rudra (Śrīkaṇṭha & Ananta) has been used, and not the name of the *śakti* in the corresponding Mālinī-system, namely Vāgeśvarī and Amoṭī (cf. Appendix II). Another problem with regard to the names of the two *śaktis* is their actual name. In the translation of *pāda* 25a *śrīkaṇṭhinyā* and *anantinyā* have been regarded as the instr. sg. fem. of a nom. sg. of an *ī*-stem. It is possible, however, to regard both words in the text as a nom. sg. fem. on *-yā* derived from an original *ī*-stem (cf. Hazra 1963: 97). This problem is found very frequently in our text (see also 2,20c; 23a) especially with regard to the names of female deities, and it is often impossible to decide whether an instr. sg. fem. is meant by the author or a nom. sg. fem. *Pāda* 25b contains the names of the four Rudras or Bhairavas with which the two *śaktis* are to be united: Krodha, Caṇḍa, Antaga and Śiva. These four represent the *ka*, *kha*, *ga*, and *gha*, respectively (cf. Appendix II). In the list of Rudras as given in Appendix II, the Rudra for the syllable *ga* is called Pracaṇḍa (MS A), whereas the MSS BC give Pañcārtha as the name for this particular Rudra, a name which seems to point to Pañcāntaka, the Rudra for the syllable *ga* in the ŚT (2,29 ff.). In the 13th chapter of the ṢaṭSS we find the Rudra Pañcānana for the *ga*. The name Antaga, as we find it here, resembles most Pañcāntaka of the ŚT. The grammatical structure of *pāda* 25b is, at least, to be called striking. We observe successively a nom. sg., a Dvandva-compound in the pl., and an instr. pl. which should obviously be sg. in the present enumeration. As all the MSS agree on the instr. pl. of *śivaiḥ*, one should expect a reading *krodhacaṇḍāntagaśivaiḥ*, which is grammatically correct, but offends against the metre: a short sixth syllable instead of a long one. Thus the instr. pl. of *caṇḍāntagaiḥ* might be due to metrical reasons. Why all three MSS are so persistent in writing the nom. case for Krodha, remains puzzling, as there is no metrical need for it. Perhaps the final *-ś* of *krodhaś* should be explained by the fact that a superfluous *ś* is often written before an initial *c-* in the manuscripts, just as before an initial *t-* an additional *s* is written.

In *pāda* 25c (= 21a) we have translated *catuṣkādyaṃ* with the 'first Four', which is not correct actually, as it means literally 'beginning with the Four'. One might assume an inverted compound here (*catuṣkādya* for *ādyacatuṣka*) because of the octosyllabic nature of the *pāda*. Rather one should supply a not mentioned *aṣṭāviṃśapadakramam*, as is the case in 21b. For the sake of clarity, however, the present translation has been chosen. The location of the first Four is on the forehead (25d; Ṭ *lalāṭe*). Thus the first component of the Aṣṭāviṃśatikrama consists of the following syllables and Mahāpīṭhas:

1) ka = Oḍiyāna,
2) kha = Jālandhara,
3) gā = Pūrṇagīri,
4) ghā = Kāmarūpa.

26 anenaiva kramenānyā mā-pu-śa-caṃ-ku-saṃjñakam[1] |
mahantāryāṃ[2] yathā sthāne tathā ca kathayāmi te ||
27 gandhaṃ ca rasa rūpaṃ ca sparśaṃ[3] śabdaṃ ca pañcamam |
kulākulapravāhe tu kathitaṃ jñānapañcakam[4] ||

1. A -kaḥ 2. A mahāntāryāṃ 3. A sparśa 4. A -kaḥ.

26 In the same sequence there are others: [the Five] called MĀ, PU, ŚA, CAṂ and KU. I will tell You how they are situated in the place of Mahantārī.
27 Smell, taste, form, touch and sound as the fifth; these are called the five Jñānas, [and are located] in the continuous stream of Kula and Akula.

The second component of the Aṣṭāviṃśatikrama is the Five, which is represented by a series of five goddesses; hence the fem. pl. *anyā(ḥ)* in *pāda* 26a. The five goddesses are referred to with the first syllables of the names in *pāda* 26b. According to the Ṭ they are called in full Mātaṅgī, Pulindī, Śabarī, Campakā and Kubjikā. The five names correspond with those given in the 47th chapter of the ṢaṭSS, in which the Aṣṭāviṃśatikrama is also explained. In the 47th chapter, however, these five are called the Vimalapañcaka. In the *mantras* of this second component of the Aṣṭāviṃśatikrama the five goddesses are connected with five Nāthas: Anādivimalanātha, Sarvajñavimalanātha, Yogavimalanātha, Siddhavimalanātha and Samayavimalanātha (cf. KnT F.53B). In the T. the five goddesses are called the Mahantārikāpañcaka, 'The Five of the [goddess] Mahantārikā'. In the ṢaṭSS this goddess Mahantārikā or Mahantārī (26c) is only mentioned in this particular context, and as one of the six Dūtīs (ṢaṭSS 47; cf. Schoterman 1977: 936). It is probably the same deity which features in the Sādhanamālā (No. 90) as Mahattārī, an aspect of the Green Tārā (De Mallmann 1975: 10; 369).

The five goddesses are in the 'place of Mahantārī' (26c). It is not clear whether this refers to an exact locality on the human body, or that it is only a figure of speech to express the idea that the Five belong to Mahantārikā as in Mahantārikāpañcaka. I have at least not been able to find a particular place on the body which is related to Mahantārī. The Five are connected with *gandha* etc. (27ab), which are the well-known Tanmātras. Note that in *pāda* 27a *metri causa* (a short fifth syllable) the word *rasa* has no nominative case-ending (*raso*) in all the three manuscripts. The same phenomenon was also noticed in 1,21c; 36a; 36b. *Pāda* 27c is not clear to me: the Five are in the *kulākulapravāha*, 'the continuous stream of Kula and Akula'. We have seen in 1,21 that Kula and Akula may stand for Śakti and Bhairava, respectively. The combination of the two as expressed by Kulākula, may denote the process of visible creation (cf. 1,21 Notes). Although the Five definitely form part of the creation, it is doubtful whether this is meant here. Compared with the other descriptions of the components of the Aṣṭāviṃśatikrama we lack an exact location of these Five on the human body. The Ṭ situates the Five in the *prāṇapatha*, 'the path of the breath', which it explains with the expression *nāsāpravāha*, 'the stream (of breath) from the nose'. Obviously the Ṭ locates the Five in the two nostrils. Basing our assumption on the use of *pravāha* in the text and in the Ṭ, one could assume that *kula* and *akula* stand here for the two nostrils, (Iḍā & Piṅgalā), or perhaps *prāṇa* (exhalation) and *apāna* (inhalation). I have, however, not been able to find any textual evidence for this usage of *kula* and *akula*, although such an identification does not seem implausible at first sight. In *pāda* 27d the Five are called 'The five Jñānas' (*jñānapañcaka*). There are two possibilities to account for this designation. In view of the fact that the next component of the Aṣṭāviṃśatikrama is connected with Kriyā (28a), one is tempted to connect this second component with Jñānī or Jñānaśakti. The second possibility seems to be more acceptable, however. Another designation for the series of *gandha* etc. besides Tanmātra, is Jñānendriyārtha (ŚT 1,34a; see also the commentary by Rāghavabhaṭṭa). In this way the first member of the compound *jñāna-pañcaka* might refer to the five Jñānendriyārthas or Tanmātras. Closely related to the five Jñānendriyārthas are, of course, the five Jñānendriyas (ŚT 1,34ab; see also 1,1cd Notes): the ears (*śrotra*), the skin (*tvac*), the eye (*dṛś*). the tongue (*jihvā*), and the nose (*nāsikā*). Perhaps the location of the Five in the nose, as suggested in the Ṭ, is somehow related to first mentioned Tanmātra or Jñānendriyārtha *gandha* (27a), which corresponds with the Jñānendriya *nāsikā*.

The following vowels and consonants belong to the Five: *i, ī, u*; *ṅ, c, ch, j, jh*. Thus the second component of the Aṣṭāviṃśatikrama is as follows:

1) ṅi = Mātaṅgī,
2) ci = Pulindī,
3) chī = Śabarī,
4) jī = Campakā,
5) jhu = Kubjikā.

28 ghaṭasthāne[1] kriyāṣaṭkaṃ ku-khiṃ-ṣa[2]-ma-su-ras tathā |
mi-u-ṣa[3]-ca[4] hṛdisthā tu ā-svā[5]-ma-a-vi[6] nābhigam[7] ||

1. BC ṣaṭ sthāneṣu 2. A śa 3. A śa; BC a 4. A ma 5. A thā 6. A dhi 7. A -gaḥ.

28 In the Ghaṭasthāna there are the Six of Kriyā: KU, KHIṂ, ṢA, MA, SU, and RA. In the heart are MI, U, ṢA, and CA. In the navel are Ā, SVĀ, MA, A, and VI.

Pāda 28ab deals with the third component of the Aṣṭāviṃśatikrama, namely the Six, which are here called the 'Six of Kriyā'. They are located in the 'Place of the Jar' (*ghaṭasthāna*), which is according to the Ṭ the throat (*kaṇṭha*) or the uvula (*kaṇṭhakūpa*). The names of the Six are according to the Ṭ: Jakārā, Khiṅkinī, Ṣaṣṭhī, Maṇi, Sundarī, and Ratnasundarī. Obviously the first goddess, Jakārā, does not correspond with the shortened form of the name *ku* (28b). In the 47th chapter of the

ṢaṭSS the following names are listed: Kukārā, Khiṅkinī, Ṣaṣṭhāṃbā, Maṇi, Suśirāṃbā, and Ratnasundarī. These names agree with the shortened forms in *pāda* 28b (cf. also AgniP 143,11). These Six are called Nugrahaṣaṭka (*nugraha* = *anugraha*), 'The Beneficent Six', in the 47th chapter of the ṢaṭSS. Their opposites are called Ugraṣaṭka, 'The Wrathful Six', and include the well-known series of the goddesses Ḍākinī, etc. (cf. *śloka* 30). In the enumerations of the components of the Aṣṭāviṃśatikrama usually the Ugraṣaṭka is mentioned as the third component (ṢaṭSS 47; AgniP 143 (cf. Schoterman 1980: 344); 1,1b Notes). It appears, that when performing the Aṣṭāviṃśatikramapūjā one has the option between the Nugrahaṣaṭka or the Ugraṣaṭka in the ritual. Perhaps the choice depends on the purpose for which the *pūjā* is performed: beneficial or malevolent. The texts remain silent on this point, however. The third component of the Aṣṭāviṃśatikrama in its Nugrahaṣaṭka-form is the following:

1) ñu = Kukārā,	4) ḍṛ = Maṇi,
2) ṭū = Khiṅkinī,	5) ḍhṛ = Suśirāṃbā,
3) ṭhū = Ṣaṣṭhāṃbā,	6) ṇṝ = Ratnasundarī.

The next component, the Four, is located in the heart (28c). Their full names are Mitranātha, Oḍḍanātha, Ṣaṣṭhanātha, and Caryanātha (ṢaṭSS 47; KnT F.54A; 1,53; 54ab Notes). For the second one the Ṭ has the abbreviation *jā*, and records the full name as Jyotīśa. The Four are referred to as the Siddhacatuṣka. The following vowels and consonants belong to this group:

1) tṝ = Mitranātha,	3) dḷ = Ṣaṣṭhanātha,
2) thḷ = Oḍḍanātha,	4) dhḹ = Caryanātha.

The fifth component, the Five, is situated in the navel (28d). The five full names are Ādhāra, Svādhiṣṭhāna, Maṇipura, Anāhata, and Viśuddhi (Ṭ; ṢaṭSS). Obviously the Five represent five out of the Six Cakras. In the Ṭ the Five are called 'The Five Jewels' (Ratnapañcaka). The accompanying vowels and consonants are the following:

1) nḹ = Ādhāra,	4) bai = Anāhata,
2) pe = Svādhiṣṭhāna,	5) bhai = Viśuddhi.
3) phe = Maṇipura,	

29 vā-jye[1]-rau-aṃbikā[2] nāma maṇḍalaṃ[3] tritaye sthitam[4] |

1. A je 2. BC aṃbidhā 3. BC maṇḍala 4. A -taḥ.

29 VĀ, JYE, RAU, and Aṃbikā — the group of this name is situated in the triangle.

The last component of the Aṣṭāviṃśatikrama, the Four, is located in the *tritaya* (29b). Both the MSS BC and the Ṭ read *maṇḍalatritaye* in *pāda* 29b. The Ṭ explains it with *trikoṇāsthāne ante* and with *nābhyadhaṃ kandasthāne*, 'at the end of the triangle', and 'below the navel, in the place of the bulb (*kanda*)'. Especially the designation *kandasthāna* seems to point to the Mūlādhāra Cakra as the location of this last component (cf. Gupta a.o. 1979: 173), although probably more specifically the *yoni* is meant here, which has a triangular shape. The names of the Four are Vāmā, Jyeṣṭhā,

Raudrī, and Aṃbikā: the Devīcatuṣka (T). The following vowels and consonants are allotted to this final component of the Aṣṭāviṃśatikrama:

1) mo = Vāmā, 3) rau = Raudrī,
2) yo = Jyeṣṭhā, 4) lau = Aṃbikā.

With the explanation of the Devīcatuṣka the exposition of the Aṣṭāviṃśatikrama is completed. As we have remarked earlier (p. 33), the order of the components of the Aṣṭāviṃśatikrama appears to be fixed (4-5-6-4-5-4 = 28), but their 'contents' may vary. Thus instead of the Nugrahaṣaṭka as the third component, one may also include the Ugraṣaṭka (see above). In the description of the Aṣṭāviṃśatikrama as found in the 47th chapter of the ṢaṭSS, it is not the Devīcatuṣka which features as the sixth component, but a series of four goddesses called the Vṛddhacatuṣka or Aṃbācatuṣka (Kuṇḍalyāṃbā, Vṛddhāṃbā, Bhīmāṃbā, Laṃbāṃbā). Moreover, in the actual ritual of the Aṣṭāviṃśatikrama (KnT FF.50B ff.) the combinations of vowels and consonants as seen in the previous lines, are not found. In the Aṣṭāviṃśatikramapūjā each of the members of the six components have their own *mantra* with a particular *bīja*, which has nothing to do with the above mentioned vowel/consonant combinations. The *mantras*, for instance, of the first component (Pīṭhacatuṣka) run as follows:
LMYRŪṂ Śrī Oḍiyānapīṭha Śrī Oḍeśvaranātha Śrī Oḍāvvā Pā Pū ||1||
VMYRŪṂ [*Śrī*] *Jālandharapīṭha Śrī Jāleśvaranātha Śrī Jālāvvā Pā Pū* ||2||
RMYRŪṂ Śrī Pūrṇagiripīṭha Śrī Pūrṇeśvaranātha Śrī Pūrṇāvvā Pā Pū ||3||
YMYRŪṂ Śrī Kāmarū[*pa*]*pīṭha Śrī Kāmeśvaranātha Śrī Kāmāvvā Pā Pū* ||4||
(= KnT F.50B; Oḍāvvā, etc. = Oḍāṃbā; Pā Pū is short for *pādukāṃ pūjayāmi* (cf. AgniP 144,3)).

Although the present stage of research does not permit a description of the Aṣṭāviṃśatikrama and its *pūjā* in full detail, some particulars should be mentioned here. As the Aṣṭāviṃśatikrama consists of six components, it is almost inevitable that the diagram used for the *pūjā* has the form of a hexagon (KnT F.49B *śrīkramamaṇḍala*[*ṃ*] *ṣaṭkoṇe aṣṭāviṃśatikramam arcayet*). Starting from its western corner the six components are worshipped in its corners, ending with the last Four in the south-western corner. Another feature pertaining to the Aṣṭāviṃśatikrama is the fact that the actual number of twenty-eight may be enlarged to thirty-one. To the first component, the four Mahāpīṭhas, a fifth (Candrapīṭha; cf. 1,27; 29 Notes; 2,6b Notes) and a sixth (Mātaṅgapīṭha) can be added; to the third component—when the Ugraṣaṭka is used—a seventh goddess called Yākinī can be added, thus bringing the total number of members of the *krama* up to thirty-one (KnT F.50A *candrapīṭhamātaṅgapīṭhayoginībhir ekatriṃśatikramaḥ*).

The description of the Aṣṭāviṃśatikrama from *śloka* 20cd onwards serves a purely philosophic or speculative purpose. As it is one of the basic principles of the Kulālikāmnāya, the Aṣṭāviṃśatikrama is here connected with creation in general, and with the origin of the alphabet in particular. The practical application (*pūjā*) of the Aṣṭāviṃśatikrama is not discussed in this chapter, but in the 47th. It is apparent that the Aṣṭāviṃśatikrama cannot 'cover' all of the fifty letters of the alphabet; it is only connected with the vowels *a* up to *au*, and the consonants from *ka* up to *la*. Consequently two vowels (*aṃ* & *aḥ*) and six consonants (*va-kṣa*) are left outside the Aṣṭāviṃśatikrama proper, although they certainly belong to the alphabet. As this second chapter of the ṢaṭSS is primarily concerned with the origin of the alphabet consisting of fifty letters, it appears that the relation of the Aṣṭāviṃśatikrama with this process might be due to its important place in the ritual of the Kulālikāmnāya School. It seems probable therefore, that because of its prominent place in ritual, the

Aṣṭāviṃśatikrama is raised here to a more philosophical level, namely the creation of the alphabet. This development may be a later aspect of the Aṣṭāviṃśatikrama, its original significance lying in the sphere of ritual. Anyway, although the description of the Aṣṭāviṃśatikrama (20cd-29ab) in connection with the origin of the alphabet ends here, there remain eight letters of the alphabet not mentioned yet. In the following lines (29cd ff.) these eight are discussed.

aṣṭāviṃśordhvagair varṇaiś catuḥkhaḍgabhṛgu'ntagaiḥ[1] ||
30 dvikaṃ saptadaśaṃ[2] śeṣam ekaikāya[3] trikaṃ trikam[4] |
krūrasenābhidhair[5] divyair[6] ḍādihāntābhidhānakam[7] ||

1. BC -bhṛgontagaiḥ 2. A saptā- 3. A ekaikāyas; BC ekāikāyās 4 -kaḥ 5. A -bhiddhair 6. A deśar 7. A -dhānakaiḥ.

With the letters after the twenty-eight, i.e. the four from Khaḍga to Bhṛgu —
30 there is the final seventeenth pair. For each of them there is a trio by [the addition of] the divine [vowels] called Krūra and Sena. This is called [the group] from ḌA to HA.

In *pāda* 29d the reading of MS A has been accepted. Apparently the initial vowel of *anta* is lost. Loss of an initial vowel occurs, especially after a word ending in an *anusvāra* (*-ṃ*), but in most cases it is restricted to such small particles as *api*, *iti*, etc. (cf. Edgerton 1972: I, p. 32). In Archipelago Sanskrit the loss of an initial vowel is much more common due to metrical reasons (Schoterman 1979: 326 ff.). It has already been noted that in the appellation Nugrahaṣaṭka *nugraha* stands for *anugraha* (cf. 2,28 Notes), but this was not for metrical reasons (see below). In *pāda* 29d, however, the initial vowel of *anta* is dropped for metrical reasons. A correct compound would result in a long fifth syllable (*-bhṛgvantagaiḥ*). The reading of BC is either *-bhṛgontaga* or *-bhṛgo'ntaga*, as the *avagraha* (') is not written, which is quite normal. The name of this 48th Rudra can be Bhṛgas or Bhṛga, at least according to BC. The Rudra representing the 48th letter of the alphabet, however, is always called Bhṛgu (cf. Appendix II), or has a name based on it (Bhṛgvīśa, etc.). In view of the fact that the name of the 48th Rudra is always an *u*-stem masc., the reading of MS A appears to be correct. Consequently, besides *anta* the form *nta* has to be accepted, but only as a Sandhi variant of the former. The reading of the MSS BC is most likely due to the frequent change of *u* to *o* and *o* to *u*, as is amply attested in manuscripts.

As we have mentioned at the end of the Notes on *śloka* 29ab, the present lines deal with the two remaining vowels (*aṃ* & *aḥ*) and the six remaining consonants (*va*, *śa*, *ṣa*, *ha*, *kṣa*). The four consonants after (lit: 'above'; *ūrdhva*) the twenty-eight run from Khaḍga (= *va*) up to Bhṛgu (= *sa*). Apparently they are the 15th and 16th pair of consonants, whereas the *ha* and the *kṣa* are the 17th, and last pair (30a). Similar to the enumeration in *śloka* 19 ff the *ha* and the *kṣa* are mentioned somewhat separately (cf. 2,7cd Notes). These six consonants are subdivided into two series of three consonants each (*va*, *śa*, *ṣa* & *sa*, *ha*, *kṣa*) for obvious reasons: there are only two vowels 'left' for six consonants. For each of the two vowels there is one series of three consonants (30b). Instead of the gen. sg. fem. *ekaikāyās* (BC) in *pāda* 30b, the reading of A has been emended. Since *ekaika* obviously refers to the two vowels the male gender seems more appropriate here, because they are represented here by two Rudras

(30c). The dat. sg. masc. *ekaikāya* is also quoted in the Ṭ, where it is explained with a gen. sg. masc., however (Ṭ *ekaikāya trikaṃ trikam; ekaikasya ca kārasya* ...). The reading of BC is most likely based upon a misinterpretation of the *s* between *ekaikāya* and *trikaṃ*, which belongs rather to *trikaṃ* than to *ekaikāya*. An additional initial *s*- before a word beginning with a *t* is sometimes found (thus: *ekaikāya s-trikaṃ*). The reading of BC seems therefore a hypercorrection which is quite understandable: the vertical stroke to denote an *ā* in Devanāgarī-script might easily be forgotten by a copyist, and a fem. gender of the word corresponds nicely with the fact that the sixteen vowels are regarded as females, especially as *śaktis* (cf. 2,18ab). The two vowels then to be connected with the six consonants are represented by the Rudras Krūra and Sena, who stand for the *aṃ* and the *aḥ*, respectively (30c). The latter is usually called Mahāsena, though (cf. Appendix II). The use of Sena instead of Mahāsena here has led the author of the Ṭ astray. He quotes *pāda* 30a wrongly (*krūrasenādibhir divyair*), and 'explains' next that Krūrasena represents the *aṃ* and that with *ādi* the *aḥ* is meant. As a matter of fact the name Krūrasena does occur in the ṢaṭSS for the Rudra representing the *anusvāra*. In this way the author of the Ṭ was in the first place misguided by the wrong quotation from the text itself (*-ādibhir* instead of *-ābhidhair*), although he should have realized that instead of the plural the dual would have been more appropriate. Anyhow, the Ṭ reaches the correct result: the six consonants are to be connected with the 15th and 16th vowel. The names of the six goddesses belonging to the six vowel/consonant combinations are Ḍākinī, Rākiṇī, Lākinī, Kākinī, Śākinī, and Hākinī (30d). To these six a seventh may be added called Yākinī (wrongly spelled Yakṣiṇī) or Vajrayākinī (KnT F.52B). The group of six goddesses is called the Ugraṣaṭka, 'The Wrathful Six', the Mahāṣaṭka, 'The Magnificent Six', or the Nigrahaṣaṭka, 'The Punishing Six'. It is perhaps this last designation which caused their opposite group to be called the Nugrahaṣaṭka (2,28b Notes) instead of the more correct Anugrahaṣaṭka. The main occupation of the Ugraṣaṭka seems to lie in devouring those people who do not know the contents of the Kulālikāmnāya-texts or follow other doctrines (ṢaṭSS 47). The vowels and consonants belonging to the Ugraṣaṭka are the following:

1) vaṃ = Ḍākinī,
2) śaṃ = Rākiṇī,
3) ṣaṃ = Lākinī,
4) saḥ = Kākinī,
5) haḥ = Śākinī,
6) kṣaḥ = Hākinī.

31 sṛjitam[1] ugraṣaṭkaṃ tu ka-nā[2]-dṛ-madhyasaṃsthitam |
bhāle[3] prāṇapathe[4] kaṇṭhe[5] hṛnnābhau nābhyadhaḥ[6] priye ||
32 tṛtīyam ugraṣaṭkaṃ tu ka-nā-dṛ-madhyasaṃsthitam[7] |
etat kramāvatāraṃ tu śrīmatīyaṃ[8] prameyagam ||
33 saṃvartāmaṇḍalāntasthaṃ kujeśena tu nirmitam |
athānyaṃ saṃpravakṣyāmi saṃvartāmaṇḍalaṃ tu yat[8] ||

1. A sṛjetam 2. A -rā- 3. A bāla 4. A prānta- 5. B kaṇṭha 6. A -ādhaḥ
7. A ka-ṇā-dṛg-; BC dṛ-nā-ka-madhyagam sthitaṃ 8. A -maṭeyaṃ 9. B yam.

31 [By these] is emanated the [first] Ugraṣaṭka in the KA, NĀ, and DṚ. [The second Ugraṣaṭka] is on the forehead, in the path of the breath, on the throat, in the heart, in the navel, and below the navel, O Lovely One.

32 The third Ugraṣaṭka is located in the KA, NĀ, and DṚ. Thus the line of descent according to the Śrīmata [becomes] accessible as an object of knowledge.

33 It is brought about by Kujeśa in the centre of the Saṃvartāmaṇḍala. Next I shall tell [You] another [concept of] the Saṃvartāmaṇḍala.

With *śloka* 30 the speculation on the origin of the fifty letters of the Skt alphabet ends. The Ugraṣaṭka which represents the last group of vowels and consonants of the alphabet, is discussed in the following lines (31-32ab) in greater detail. It appears to have a triple location with regard to the human body. The first Ugraṣaṭka is located in three places which are indicated by their first syllable (31b). The subdivision of the Ugraṣaṭka is again in pairs (*vaṃ* & *śaṃ*; *ṣaṃ* &*sah*; *haḥ* & *kṣaḥ*; or: Ḍākinī & Rākiṇī; Lākinī & Kākinī; Śākinī & Hākinī). The first pair is located in both ears (*ka* for *karṇa*), the second in the two nostrils (*nā* for *nāsāpuṭā*), and the third pair is situated in the two eyes (*dṛ* for *dṛṣṭi*). The locations of the second Ugraṣaṭka (31cd) correspond exactly with those of the six components of the Aṣṭāviṃśatikrama (25 ff.). The locations of the third Ugraṣaṭka appear to be identical with those of the first Ugraṣaṭka. The reading of the MSS BC shows a reverse order of the locations (eyes, nostrils, ears), but both the Ṭ and MS A have the same order as in *pāda* 31b. The Ṭ, however, has a slightly different reading: instead of *ka-* it reads *śro-*, in which *śro* stands for *śrotrau* which also denotes the two ears. The reason why the first and the third Ugraṣaṭka are located in exactly the same places is puzzling. Perhaps this was also the opinion of the copyists of the MSS BC, who therefore changed the position of the third Ugraṣaṭka in order to distinguish it more clearly from the first Ugraṣaṭka.

After this short digression on the Ugraṣaṭka Bhairava continues with another exposition of the fifty letters of the alphabet, especially in relation with the first Saṃvartāmaṇḍala. We do not find much new information in the following lines, however. The main purpose of these lines seems to lie in establishing a connection of the *mantras* and the letters of the alphabet — a connection which is quite obvious. Towards the end the sole authority of the Śrīmata against other Schools is emphasized, and the important position of the Guru in transmitting the teachings of the Śrīmata.

34 saṃvartas[1] tu[1] kṣa-kāraḥ[2] syād varṇānte saṃvyavasthitaḥ[3] |
maṇḍalaṃ tasya tad rūpam[4] ādikṣāntakrameṇa[5] tu ||

1.BC saṃvartasya 2. ABC -kāra 3. A -tā 4. BC proktam 5. A adi-; ABC -kṣāntā-.

34 Saṃvarta then is the letter KṢA, located at the end of the [other] letters. This is the form of his *maṇḍala*, from A to KṢA.

Saṃvarta is the name of the Rudra or Bhairava representing the consonant *kṣa* (Appendix II), the last letter of the Skt alphabet which begins with the vowel *a* (34d). Thus in this *śloka* the fifty letters of the alphabet are called the *maṇḍala* of Saṃvarta. Most likely the *śloka* is the explanation of the name Saṃvartāmaṇḍala (cf. p. 33; 2,11d).

35 a-kārādi smṛtā varṇāḥ pañcāśat[1] kathitā mayā |
yasya[2] madhyād varārohe kramaṃ divyaṃ[3] vinirgatam[4] ||
36 catuṣkaṃ pañcakaṃ ṣaṭkaṃ[5] catuṣkaṃ pañcakaṃ catuḥ |
padabhedaiḥ[6] samutpannam asya[7] madhyād varānane ||
37 mantragrāmam aśeṣaṃ tu mantrarūpaṃ tu taṃ smṛtam[8] |
āgamāḥ[9] saptavaktrānte[10] teṣāṃ[11] tu jananī parā ||

1. A tpañcāśat 2. BC asyā 3. A divya 4. A -taḥ; BC vinirmitam 5. A ṣaṭka 6. A -bhedai 7. BC asyā 8. A smṛtaḥ 9. A āgamā 10. A -vaktraurthā(?) 11. A teṣā.

35 The fifty letters beginning with the A have been told by Me. From amidst this [group of fifty], O Varārohā, the divine line originates:
36 the Four, Five, Six, Four, Five, and Four. From among this comes forth in different stages, O Varānanā,
37 the complete body of *mantras*. [Therefore the *maṇḍala*] is designated as 'having the form of *mantras*'. [Next] the Āgamas [originate from it] at the end of the Seven Mouths. For them the Supreme [Śakti] is the mother.

The Saṃvartāmaṇḍala consists, as we have seen in the previous *śloka*, of the fifty letters of the alphabet. From these fifty originates the 'divine line' (35d *kramaṃ divyaṃ*), which refers unmistakably to the Aṣṭāviṃśatikrama (36ab). Since the Saṃvartāmaṇḍala encompasses all the fifty letters, it follows that all the *mantras* are based on it or originate from it (36cd; 37a). Therefore the Saṃvartāmaṇḍala is called 'having the form of [all] *mantras*' (37b). The *mantras* originate from it in different stages (36c *padabhedaiḥ*). This probably refers to the fact that the first *mantra* to arise is OṂ after which all the other *mantras* come into existence. After the *mantras* the Āgamas come forth (37c). With the term Āgama probably the Tantras are meant here, as there is often hardly any distinction between the two (cf. Goudriaan & Gupta 1981: 7). The Āgamas originate or come forth from the Seven Mouths (of Śiva). This refers to the classificatory system of the Tantras, the Āmnāyas. Usually there are five mouths, but the number six and seven is also found (cf. Gupta a.o. 1979: 41 ff.; Goudriaan & Gupta 1981: 17). Here there are seven mouths (37c), which according to the Ṭ are the following: above (*ūrdhva*), on the head (*mūrdhni*). East, South, North, West, and the mouth called Picuyoni. The explanation of the Seven Mouths in the Ṭ seems somewhat artificial at first sight, as there appears to be little difference between the first and the second mouth. In the 47th chapter of the ṢaṭSS the Mouths are discussed briefly. In the first instance five mouths are enumerated: *ūrdhva*, *pūrva*, *vāma*, *dakṣiṇa*, and *paścima*. These five are connected with five vital airs (*prāṇa*, *apāna*, *samāna*, *udāna*, *vyāna*), and with the *nāḍīs*. After these five a sixth mouth is mentioned, which is not manifest (*avyakta*). Although the text is not very clear, it seems that also a seventh mouth is mentioned: it is called Pātāla, and is situated 'below'; it serves the purpose of emanation (*pātālākhyam adhovaktraṃ sṛṣṭārthaṃ saṃprakīrtitam*). It is not clear, however, whether this refers to the sixth mouth or to a seventh mouth. In the ṢaṭSS these six mouths are connected with the concept of Ṣaḍadhvan (cf. p. 34). The Ṭ on this passage in the 47th chapter admits of no doubt as to the number of mouths. It enumerates the five mouths with all particulars (*prāṇas* & *nāḍīs*), and states next that there are a sixth and seventh mouth: *ṣaṣṭhaṃ vyomakavaktram; saptamam adhovaktraṃ sṛṣṭivaktraṃ picuvaktram*. Thus the sixth mouth is called Vyomaka ('sky'; cf. *avyakta* of the ṢaṭSS), and the seventh mouth which is 'below', is called Picuvaktra which corresponds with Picuyoni of the Ṭ on the present *pāda* (37c). From the description of the mouths as found in the 47th chapter of the ṢaṭSS it appears that the first five mouths are the most important, as they are connected with the *prāṇas* and the *nāḍīs*. The name of the seventh mouth (Picuyoni or Picuvaktra) refers most probably to a text called Picumata (cf. Goudriaan & Gupta 1981: 41; 42n.). The Seven Mouths are also discussed in the 42th chapter of the ṢaṭSS, but in a more speculative way. Although the text is sometimes rather confusing, one may draw up the following table:

	Vaktra	Śakti	Devī	Cakra	(location)	Adhvan	Aṣṭāviṃśatikrama
1	Aja	Icchā	Vyāpikā		Dvādaśānta		Four
2	Īśāna	Jñānī	Hākinī	Ājñā	*ūrdhva*	Tattva	Five
3	Tatpuruṣa	Kriyā	Śākinī	Viśuddha	East	Kala	Six
4	Aghora	Raudrī	Kākinī	Anāhata	South	Varṇa	Four
5	Vāma	Vāmā	Lākinī	Maṇipura	North	Mantra	Five
6	Sadyo	Jveṣthā	Rakiṇī	Svādhiṣṭhāna	West	Pada	Four
7	Pātāla	Ambikā	Ḍākinī	Ādhāra	*adhas*	Bhuvana	

In the first mouth resides Śiva as the Ādideva together with His Ādiśakti. He is described as 'The endless One' (*anantākhya*), 'Having the nature of Ether' (*vyomarūpa*), etc. In the seventh mouth resides Devī as Guhyaśakti. Here the worlds originate, as the place is called *jagadyoni*, 'matrix of the world'. In the Ṭ on this passage this seventh mouth is again called Picuvaktra. Besides the term mouth (*vaktra*) we find in this 42th chapter also the appellation *srotas* ('Current'), which points to the oldest subdivision of the Tantras (cf. Goudriaan & Gupta 1981: 16): *evaṃ śaktir adhovaktre ūrdhvasrote śivaṃ viduḥ*. It appears that among the Seven Mouths one has to distinguish an upper and a lower mouth with in between an intermediate group of five mouths. The union of Śiva (upper mouth) and Śakti (lower mouth) is, of course, the ultimate goal.

Pāda 37d refers to Parā Śakti as the Mother *par excellence*, especially with regard to the letters of the alphabet and the sacred texts. Probably there is a connection here with Mālinī who is called the 'Mother of all Beings' (KmT 2,2a *jananī sarvabhūtānāṃ*), and after the explanation of the Mālinī-system the 'Supreme Matrix' (ṢaṭSS 7,39c = KmT 4,107c *parā yoniḥ*) of the *mantras*, and the 'Mother of the Rudras and Yoginīs' (ṢaṭSS 7,41ab = KmT 4,109ab *rudrāṇāṃ yoginīnāṃ ca sā mātā tu nigadyate*), in which the Rudras and Yoginīs stand for the consonants and vowels, respectively.

38 ṣoḍaśāraṃ mahāpadmaṃ dvātriṃśaṃ caiva bāhyataḥ |
svaraṣoḍaśarūpeṇa śaktayas tāḥ prakīrtitāḥ ||
39 pīṭhākṣarās tu te bhadre ṣoḍaśāre prakalpitāḥ[1] |
siddhā dvātriṃśa[2] ye proktā dvīpās[3] te tu[4] varānane ||
40 dvātriṃśāre niyoktavyā ha-kṣau[5] karṇikayā[6] nyaset[7] |
ha-kāraḥ prāṇabhūtas tu tasyādhiṣṭhānatāṃ gataḥ[8] ||
41 varṇāntas tu kṣa-kāras tu saṃvartaś[9] caiva ucyate[10] |
a-kārādi-kṣa-kārāntaṃ saṃvartāmaṇḍalaṃ tu tat[11] ||

1. A -kalitā 2. A tu triṃśa 3. BC dīpās; A bījās 4. BC ca 5. A -kṣā 6. A karṇika 7. A vinyaset 8. A gatā 9. A saṃvartāś 10. BC cocyate 11. BC tam.

38 There is a lotus with sixteen petals, and beyond these are thirty-two petals. In the shape of the sixteen vowels these are called *śaktis*.

39 These [so-called] *pīṭhākṣaras* are arranged in the sixteen petals [of the lotus], O Bhadrā. The thirty-two Siddhas, O Varānanā, are called *dvīpas*.

40 They are to be placed in the thirty-two petals [of the lotus] In the pericarp [of the lotus] one should put the HA and the KṢA. The letter HA has become the base of that [lotus] as the breath.

41 The letter KṢA comes at the end of the [other] letters, and is called Saṃvarta. The Saṃvartāmaṇḍala then runs from the A to the KṢA.

The *ślokas* 38-41 are merely a further explanation of the *ślokas* 17-20ab. The fifty letters are arranged in a lotus with two rows of petals: sixteen and thirty-two. In the centre of the lotus, the pericarp, the HA and the KṢA are placed; in the row of sixteen petals the sixteen vowels are put, and in the outer-row of thirty-two petals the thirty-two consonants from *ka* to *sa* are located.

As we have seen before, the sixteen vowels are called *śaktis* (cf. 2,18b). A new feature is their designation *pīṭhākṣaras* (39a). Likewise, the thirty-two consonants or Siddhas are called *dvīpas*, or in full *dvīpākṣaras*. The readings of BC (*dīpās*), and A (*bījās*) are incorrect. This division of the fifty letters of the alphabet in *pīṭhas and dvīpas* is clearly stated in the 15th chapter of the ṢaṭSS: *uddhāraṃ tu dvibhir bhedaiḥ pīṭhadvīpākṣaraiḥ priye | pīṭhāḥ ṣoḍaśabhedena dvīpās triṃśaṃ caturyutāḥ* (cf. KnT F.80A *svarāḥ ṣoḍaśa pīṭhākhye dvīpākhye vyañjanāni ca*). From *pādas* 39cd it does not follow that the *ha* and the *kṣa* are also considered to be *dvīpākṣaras*, as their number is explicitly stated to be thirty-two (39c), e.g. from *ka* to *sa*. From the lines of the 15th chapter and of the KnT as quoted above, it appears that the *ha* and the *kṣa* are also *dvīpākṣaras*. The Ṭ confirms this in its commentary. It follows the reading of MS A (*bīja* instead of *dvīpa*): *bījarūpāḥ ha-kṣau karṇikasthitau*.

In *pāda* 40b the reading of the MSS BC has been followed, because it is metrically correct and understandable. The form *karṇikayā* is the instr. sg. of *karṇikā* according to the rules of correct grammar. One should, however, expect a loc. sg. here (*karṇikāyāṃ*), which is metrically incorrect (long fifth syllable). The use of the instr. instead of the loc. is attested (cf. Hazra 1963: 115). Another possibility is the assumption that the form *karṇikayā* is a loc. sg. actually (cf. Edgerton 1972: I,9.46). The reading of MS A (*karṇika vinyaset*) is metrically correct, but is difficult to explain from a grammatical point of view. The word *karṇikā* is always of the fem. gender. For metrical reasons it occurs that sometimes an *ā*-stem has a nom. sg. ending in *-a* (cf. Edgerton 1972: I,9.8), but a nom. sg. is out of place here. Another possibility to explain the reading of MS A is to assume a masc. *karṇika* besides the fem. *karṇikā*, to which the Ṭ seems to point (*ha-kṣau karṇikasthitau*). In that case the word is not inflected for metrical reasons: the loc. sg. *karṇike* would result in a long fifth syllable. We have seen this phenomenon before (1,21c; 36a; 36b; 2,27a), but in those cases it concerned the nom. sg., whereas here we have a loc. sg. Although the last possibility should not be ruled out beforehand, for the moment the reading of BC seems to be the most probable version of the text.

The letter *ha* is put on a par with the breath (40c). The fifty letters of the alphabet are not only connected with a particular Rudra/Bhairava or manifestation of Mālinī, but are also related to a part of the human body. The letter *ha* is related to the breath (cf. Appendix II). The letter *kṣa* comes at the end of the alphabet (41a), and is represented by the Rudra called Saṃvarta (41b; cf. 34a), from whom the Saṃvartāmaṇḍala derives its name, as is suggested in the *pādas* 41cd (cf. 2,34 Notes).

42 mantragrāmam aśeṣaṃ tu tatrotpannaṃ tu sarvadā[1] |
etat kramāvatāraṃ tu śrīmatīyaṃ[2] prameyagam ||
43 akathyaṃ bhinnajātīnāṃ bhaktihīne śaṭhe[3] priye |
anyagranthasahasrais[4] tu lakṣakoṭiśatair api ||
44 yat phalam arcite[5] granthe śruteś[6] caiva tu yat phalam |
śrīmatasya varārohe[7] ślokaikenāpi[8] tat phalam ||
45 yena jñātaṃ gurusthānaṃ[9] vartanaṃ dṛśyate sphuṭam |
tasyākhyeyam idaṃ jñānam anyathā mama drohakṛt ||

iti śrīkulālikāmnāye divyaughasadbhāve[10] śrīkubjikāmate ṣaṭsāhasre saṃhitāyāṃ śrīśrīmate dvitīyaḥ paṭalaḥ ||[11]

1. A -dhā 2. A -teyaṃ 3. C saṭhe 4. B -gra[n]tha- 5. A -taṃ 6. A -taṃ 7. B ca varārohe 8. A ślokekaināpi 9. BC guroḥ sthānaṃ 10. A divyogha- 11. BC end with only *iti dvitīyaḥ paṭalaḥ*.

42 The complete body of *mantras* arises from here, at all times. Thus one should consider the line of descent of the Śrīmata.
43 It should not be told to people belonging to other groups, nor to someone devoid of *bhakti*, nor to a pretender, O Lovely One.
The fruit which is acquired from other texts, how numerous they may be,
44 [in short] what fruit is acquired in [whatever] text held in steem, or from oral tradition, that [same] fruit is acquired by merely one single *śloka* of the Śrīmata, O Varārohā!
45 To him who acknowledges the position of the Guru and perceives clearly the process, to him this knowledge may be communicated — in every other way an offence is committed to Me!

Thus in Śrīkulālikāmnāya, in the Divyaughasadbhāva, in the Śrīkubjikāmata, in the Ṣaṭsāhasra Saṃhitā, in the Śrīśrīmata the second chapter.

After the statement that from this Saṃvartāmaṇḍala which encompasses all the fifty letters of the alphabet, all the *mantras* originate (42ab; cf. 37ab), and that in this way the Śrīmata is transmitted (42ab; = 32cd), the usual warnings are given to prevent that the information falls into the wrong hands. Thus one should not instruct a follower of (*sc*. opposite) groups (43a), nor one who is bereft of sincere devotion towards his Guru (43b *bhaktihīna*), nor a cheat (43b *śaṭha*). In the *pādas* 43cd the numbers *sahasra* (1000), *lakṣa* (100.000), *koṭi* (ten millions), and *śata* (100) are rendered in the translation by the expression 'how numerous they may be', as these high numbers symbolize only the futility of studying whatever other text where only one line of the Śrīmata would serve the purpose.

In *pāda* 44a the word *arcita* (held in esteem) is used in all the three MSS. One gets the impression, however, that perhaps a contamination with *arjita* ('acquired') might be supposed. For this reason both meanings are found in the translation. With 'process' (45b *vartana*) the order in which the creation is explained to the pupil by his Guru, is probably meant. The pupil should gain an insight into the successive phases of creation, as they are expounded in the first two chapters of the ṢaṭSS.

PAṬALA 3

PAṬALA 3

śrīdevy uvāca ||
1 śrīmate[1] tu mahājñānaṃ sūcitaṃ tu mahāprabho[2] |
kathayasva vidhānaṃ tu vyākhyākāle tu[3] lekhayet[3] ||
2 śrīmataṃ tu sureśāna yādṛśaṃ[4] saṃprakāśyate[4] |
yādṛśena vidhānena tat sarvaṃ ca vadet[5] prabho ||
śrībhairava[6] uvāca ||
3 vyākhyālekhanakāle[7] ca śrīmataṭasya kulānvaye |
vidhihīnasya[8] vighnāni yāni te kathayāmy aham ||
4 vyādhayaś ca prakupyanti rājānaḥ svajane[9] api |
svagṛhe kalaho[10] nityaṃ jāyate saha mānuṣaiḥ ||
5 gotrāṇāṃ[11] caiva udvegaṃ kalahaṃ ca parasparam[12] |
mahāhāni[13] viyogaṃ ca suhṛdbhir saha jāyate ||
6 kapotaś ca[14] gṛhe nityaṃ kākādyāś ca viśanti ca |
pariśocaṃ[15] tu[15] śvānābhyā[m][15] akāle maraṇāni ca ||
7 gaganaṃ garjate caiva garbhapātaḥ prajāyate |
ulkāpāto diśāṃ[16] dāgho[17] gṛhe dāhaś[18] ca jāyate ||
8 rātrau svapnāti raudrāṇi paśyate satataṃ priye |
caṇḍavegaprakopena[19] vātā[20] vānti[20] subhīṣaṇāḥ ||
9 prapaśyanti[21] gṛhasthāne vyālāś[22] caiva phaṇotkaṭāḥ[22] |
vācitvā nāradādyas tu tasya vighnā[23] bhavanti[23] ca ||
10 rakṣanti siddhayoginyāḥ[24] śrīmatedaṃ mahākulam |
vidhvaṃsakānāṃ[25] deveśi śivaravaḥ prajāyate ||
11 piṅgalānāṃ[26] gṛhe śabdaṃ nityaṃ kupyanti[27] pārvati |
adṛṣṭamudgarāghāto[28] vidhihīne ca jāyate ||
12 evamādīni vighnāni jāyante[29] vidhivarjite |
ācāryasyāpi[30] śiṣyasya[30] samayaghne viśeṣataḥ ||
13 tadarthas tu vidhiḥ[31] kāryo[31] vyākhyākāle ca lekhane |
ato yan na paro bhūtvā rakṣā kāryā vidhānataḥ[32] ||
14 vyākhyālekhanakāle ca cuṃbake na prakāśayet[33] |
aśuddhasyāpi kṣudrasya tārkikasya[34] śaṭhasya ca ||

1. BC -taṃ 2. A -prabhu 3. BC ca lekhane 4. BC yādṛśānāṃ pra- 5. BC vada 6. A -bhairav 7. A vyākhya- 8. BC -hīnaś ca 9. BC -janāny 10. A kalahe; BC kalajño 11. C gotriṇāṃ; B gotṛṇāṃ 12. B -paro; C -parau 13. B mahā-[hā]ni; C sumahāhāni 14. BC sva- 15. BC pariveśo candrasūryābhyām 16. A diśā 17. A dāghau; B dāghā 18. A dāhaṃ 19. A -prakāśena 20. A rātrāv ante 21. BC prapaśyati 22. BC vyālāṃś ... balotkaṭān 23. A vighnāṃ bhaveti 24. BC -yoginyaḥ 25. BC -kāni 26. BC piṅgalāś ca 27. BC kurvanti 28. A -ghātā 29. A jāyate 30. A ācāryasya viśeṣesya 31. A vidhiṃ kāryaṃ 32. BC vidhānavit 33. A prakāśitaḥ 34. A tarkikasya

Śrīdevī spoke:

1 The great knowledge of the Śrīmata has been revealed [by You], O Great Lord. Please relate [next] the precepts how it should be caused to be written down at the occasion of its explanation.

2 To what kind of people, O Sureśāna, the Śrīmata is explained and in what way — please tell all that, O Lord!

Śrībhairava spoke:

3 I will tell You the obstacles someone encounters who is bereft of the [right] method when the Śrīmata is explained and written down according to the Kula-tradition.

4 Diseases will rage; kings will become angry even with their own subjects. In one's own household constant quarrels arise among its members.

5 In families there will be commotion and mutual quarrels; between close friends great loss and separation occurs.

6 In one's house pigeons, crows etc. constantly enter; there is the wailing of two dogs, [the portent of] untimely deaths.

7 The sky thunders, miscarriages occur. Meteors fall down, fires arise in the open air and in one's house.

8 At night one sees constantly terrible things in one's dreams, O Lovely One. Raging with turbulent speed winds blow, very fearful!

9 Cobras with immense hoods are seen in the courtyard, making the clouds thunder. Thus are the obstacles for him [who is bereft of the right method].

10 The Siddhas and Yoginīs guard this Śrīmata, the great Kula [-tradition]. For those who obstruct [the Śrīmata], there is the howling of jackals, O Deveśī.

11 In one's house the angry screeching of ichneumons is constantly heard, O Pārvatī. The one bereft of the right method receives blows from invisible hammers.

12 These and other obstacles occur for the one bereft of the right method, for the teacher and his pupil alike, in particular for one who violates the Samaya.

13 Therefore one should adhere to the right procedure when explaining and writing down [the Śrīmata]. Henceforth, one should guard according to the rules that which is to be secret.

14 On the occasion of explaining and writing down [the Śrīmata] one should not reveal it to a rogue, nor to an impure one, a vile person, a sceptic, nor to a deceiver.

15 codya saṃcālakasyaiva śāstram etan[35] na sūcayet |
subhaktasya suśāntasya dhārmike[36] satyavādine ||
16 gurudevāgnibhakte ca kathanīyaṃ na durjane |
padārthasyākṣarārthasya[37] carcācarcaṃ[38] na kārayet ||
17 atra bhrāntigataṃ[39] jñānaṃ tatrānyaṃ[40] pariprcchayet |
ācāryo budhyamāno[41] 'pi sacchiṣye[42] pratipādayet ||
18 tithiṃ pūrṇāṃ samāsādya riktā sā[43] sūryayo[r][43] bhavet |
aṣṭamyāṃ ca caturdaśyāṃ duṣṭarikṣavivarjite[44] ||
19 susame mandire ramye puṣpaprakaraśobhite |
sudhūpadhūpite sthāne kuṅkumāgurucandane[45] ||
20 kṛtvā maṇḍalakaṃ tatra caturaśraṃ samantataḥ |
svastikair lāñchitaṃ[46] kṛtvā koṇe dīyā[t][47] tu dīpakān[48] ||
21 ghṛtaprabuddhā[49] dīpās[50] tu śālipiṣṭamayạ̄ḥ[51] śubhāḥ[52] |
svastikopari saṃsthāpya[53] kalaśaṃ tu suśobhanam ||
22 ratnasauvarṇapuṣpaṃ tu paripūrya[54] samantataḥ |
cūtapallavaśobhāḍhyaṃ sitasūtreṇa veṣṭitam ||
23 ācchādya vastrayugmena tatpṛṣṭhe sthāpya pustakam |
pūrṇapātraṃ tadagreṇa sauvarṇatāṃbūlapūritam[55] ||
24 ity evaṃ kulakuṃbhaṃ ca natvā caiva punaḥ punaḥ |
āmantrayet kumāryāṣṭau[56] catasro[57] vā varānane ||
25 yogeśvaryā[58] ca[58] yoginyaḥ pūjayet kuladīkṣitāḥ |
suvastrair kusumair dhūpair aliphalgusamanvitaiḥ ||
26 bhakṣair[59] nānāvidhair devi pūjāṃ kṛtvā yathāvidhi[60] |
tadante prārthayec[61] cājñāṃ kulajānāṃ kulāgate ||
27 śiṣye[62] vyākhyā mayā kāryā avighnena prasidhyatu |
labdhānujñas[63] tu vīrendraḥ[64] pūjayec ca kulakramam ||
28 saṃpūjya pustakaṃ tatra vidhinā ca varānane |
dehasthā devatās tatra pūjayed bhaktito guruḥ ||
29 ācāryaṃ pūjayec chiṣyo gobhūhemāṃbarādibhiḥ |
tato maṅgalanirghoṣaiḥ pustakaṃ vācayet tataḥ ||
30 ādivṛttau[65] ca yat proktam[66] aṣṭāviṃśapadakramam |[67]
avatāraṃ[68] kramād[68] yātaṃ[68] kriyāśaktyāditaḥ[69] kramāt ||[70]

---

35. C dan 36. BC tyāgine 37. A paratrasyā-; C parārdhasyā 38. BC -carcir 39. A bhrāntiṃ gataṃ 40. A tatrānyā 41. A budho mānau 42. A taccheṣaṃ 43. BC sūryeṇa yā 44. A duṣṭā-; C -ṛkṣa- 45. BC -gurucarcite 46. BC lāñchanaṃ 47. BC deyās 48. B dīpakāḥ; C dīpikāḥ 49. A -prabodhā 50. A dīpāṃs 51. A -mayāṃ 52. A śubhā 53. B [saṃ]sthāpya 54. BC -pūrṇaṃ 55. BC suvarṇa- 56. C -aṣṭau 57. A catvāro 58. BC yogeśvarāya 59. BC bhakṣyair 60. A -vidhim; C -vidhiḥ 61. A prāṣaye 62. A śiṣyaṃ 63. A -jñās 64. BC yogīndraḥ 65. BC -vṛtte 66. BC coktam 67. pāda 30b omitted in BC; C acknowledges this deficit by eight horizontal strokes 68. BC avatārakramāyātaṃ 69. C kuryā-; B kuyaśi[ ]āditaḥ 70. pādas 30cd put between square brackets in C

15 Even when urged by one's closest friend, one should not reveal to him this Śāstra. To someone with sincere devotion, or with complete peace of mind, to someone who follows the Dharma, to someone who [always] speaks the truth,
16 to someone with devotion to his guru, the Gods and Agni — [to these people the Śrīmata] may be told, not to wicked people. One should not discuss the meaning of [separate] words nor syllables:
17 in that case knowledge leads to fallacy. If this happens, he should direct him to another [teacher]. A teacher, even an alert one, should care to teach [only] a sincere pupil.
18 On the *tithi* [called] Pūrṇā — there should be neither sun nor moon — or on the eighth or fourteenth day of the month free from inauspicious constellations,
19 on a smooth, enjoyable spot bright by scattered flowers; on a place heavily scented with incense, [provided] with saffron, aloe and sandal;
20 there he should make a *maṇḍala* in the form of a regular square. He should mark it with svastikas, and at [each] corner he should put a lamp.
21 The lamps should burn on ghee and rice-flour, and be bright. On the [central] svastika he should place a beautiful jar,
22 filled to the brim with gems, gold and flowers. It is brightly decorated with mango-twigs; around it a white thread is knotted.
23 He covers [the jar] with a pair of garments, and places the book on top of it. In front of the jar is the Pūrṇapātra filled with gold and betel.
24 Thus [are the preparations]. Having paid homage to the Kula-jar, again and again, he should invite eight or four virgins, O Varānanā,
25/26 and honour these women consecrated in the Kula[-tradition] with the thought: "The Yoginīs are on the same line with Yogeśvarī". With beautiful garments, blossoms, incense and with all kinds of nourishment including liquor and meat, he should honour them properly. Next he should ask the permission of the Kulajās with regard to the one who has entered the Kula[-tradition] with the words:
27 "I intend to explain [the Śrīmata] to [this] pupil. Let it succeed without hindrances". Having obtained [their] consent, the Vīrendra should worship the Kulakrama.
28 Having honoured the book there according to the rules, O Varānanā, next the guru should honour with devotion the deities of the body.
29 The pupil should then honour his teacher with [a gift of] cows, land, gold, garments etc. Next he should read out loud the book with a pleasant voice.
30/31 When the teacher tells the Aṣṭāviṃśapadakrama which is told in the initial gloss, the descent coming from the tradition starting with the Kriyā Śakti onwards, and the sixteen Śaktis — when he thus recounts the Aṣṭāviṃśa-

31 śaktiṣoḍaśakaṃ tatra[71] aṣṭāviṃśapadakramam |[72]
kathayed yas tu ācāryaḥ sa gurur nābhiṣecakaḥ ||
32 śrīmate pañca cakrāṇi ṣaṭkūṭaṃ tripurārṇave |
puruṣaṃ haṃsabhede tu yo vetty evaṃ gurus tu saḥ ||
33 anyagranthasya lakṣeṇa śrutenaiva tu yat phalam |
śrīmatasya tu deveśi pañcaślokena[73] tat phalam ||
34 prameyam anyagranthasya yo vetti surasundari |
kramaṃ[74] tu kaulikaṃ sarvaṃ buddhyāsau hy avicārataḥ ||
35 kvacic ca dakṣiṇacchāyā[75] kvacit siddhāntikā[76] smṛtā |
saṃsphuṭā[77] ca kulacchāyā devyādau cakrapañcake ||
36 samastedaṃ sphuṭaṃ devi mayā te pratipāditam |
matprasādena cakre 'smin budhyate cakrapañcakam ||
37 te narā matsamā jñeyāḥ siddhās te[78] 'tra mahītale[79] ||
śrīdevy uvāca ||
38 deva loke tvayākhyātaṃ[80] kubjikākhyaṃ mahāmatam |
kulamārgaprapannānāṃ[81] mukhyabhūtaṃ kulāgamam ||
39 anulomavilomena samastavyastayogataḥ |
agrārthaṃ pṛṣṭhataḥ khyātaṃ pṛṣṭhārtham[82] agraṃ[82] bodhitam[83] ||
40 yāgasya mukhyatā nāsti niḥsaṃdigdhakarī[84] parā |
caturviṃśasahasrasya[85] tasyaivārdhasya[86] cārdhataḥ ||
41 tanmadhyād dhyuṣṭasaṃkhyaṃ[87] tu sahasraṃ yad udīritam |
tatsāraṃ[88] vada[89] deveśa[90] kulamārge ca saṃsphuṭam[91] ||
42 niḥsaṃdigdhakaraṃ cādya[92] pāraṃparyakramāgatam[93] |
saṃvartāmaṇḍalaṃ yac[94] ca aṣṭāviṃśapadāṅkitam[95] ||[96]
43 kathaṃ[97] pīṭhādhipā devyā[ḥ][98] śarīre saṃvyavasthitāḥ |
yadartham api cāmnāye yan na pṛṣṭo 'si bhairava ||
44 adhyātmanā pravāhena tat sarvaṃ kathayasva me |
kenopāyena grantho 'yaṃ labhyate[99] saṃsphuṭaṃ[100] vada[101] ||
śrībhairava[102] uvāca ||
45 rudrair mālinitattvaiś[103] ca bhāṣāvakrakramotkramaiḥ[104] |
anyatantrāvatāraiś[105] ca padaiḥ siṃhāvalokanaiḥ ||

71. BC tantraṃ 72. pāda 31a put between square brackets in C 73. BC -ślokais tu 74. BC kramas 75. A dakṣiṇach[ ] 76. A siddhāntakī; C siddhāntikī 77. BC sasphuṭā 78. C ta- 79. A mahātale 80. B -khyāte 81. B -pannaṃ 82. A pṛṣṭhārtham agra; BC antaḥpṛṣṭhena 83. C bhāvitam; B bhavitam 84. A ni[ḥ]- 85. C caturviṃśat- 86. BC -ārthasya 87. C -saṃkhye. 88. A -sāra; C -saṃsāraṃ; B -sāsāraṃ 89. A deva-; C ca 90. A deveśi 91. BC sasphuṭam 92. BC vākyaṃ 93. A -gataḥ 94. A yaś 95. A -taḥ 96. pādas 42cd omitted in BC 97. A kāma- 98. BC devyaḥ 99. A labheta 100. A tat saṃsphuṭaṃ; BC sasphuṭaṃ 101. C padam; omitted in A, but added in the same hand under the line 102. A -bhairav 103. A mā(lini)- 104. BC bhāṣācakra- 105. A -tārāś

padakrama on that occasion, then he is a [true] guru, and not one who inaugurates by mere sprinkling.

32 The one who knows that the Five Cakras [are taught] in the Śrīmata, the sixfold Kūṭa in the Tripurārṇava, and the Puruṣa in the Haṃsabheda, that one is a [true] guru.

33 The result gained by hearing 100.000 [verses] of another collection, the [same] result is gained by [hearing only] five *ślokas* of the Śrīmata, O Deveśī.

34 The one who knows the complete bulk of another collection, O Surasundarī, believes himself [to know also] the complete Kula-tradition out of lack of discrimination.

35 Sometimes it is called the 'Southern Reflection', sometimes 'Siddhāntika'. In truth, though, it is the 'Kula Reflection' with regard to the Five Cakras beginning with the Devī Cakra.

36 All this I have explained to You clearly, O Devī. Due to My graciousness the Five Cakras are understood among [the members of] this circle:

37 these people are to be regarded equal to Me; they are the Siddhas here on earth.

Śrīdevī spoke:

38 O Deva, You have told the Great Teachings of Kubjikā on earth, the sacred lore of the Kula[-tradition] which is the most important for those who have embraced the Kula Path.

39 Whether told in correct or in reversed order, whether as a whole or fragmentarily, whether from the beginning to the end or from end to the beginning, it is [always] understood.

40 The pre-eminence [of the Kula-tradition] is not second to sacrifice: it [represents] real supremacy and causes certainty.
From the half of the half of the 24.000 —

41 from that is enunciated the 3500. O Deveśa, tell its quintessence clearly with regard to the Kula Path,

42 i.e. at first the Saṃvartāmaṇḍala which leaves no room to ambiguous thought, which is established in the uninterrupted tradition, and which is characterized by the twenty-eight steps.

43 How are the Lords of the Pīṭhas distributed over the body of Devī? Whatever topic with regard to the Tradition You are not [specifically] asked about [by Me], O Bhairava,

44 please tell all that to Me of Your own accord. [Furthermore,] tell Me clearly by what means this collection [of texts] is obtained.

Śrībhairava spoke:

45 By means of the Rudras, the essence of Mālinī, by means of ambiguous or inverted order of speech, by means of the occurrences of manifestations of Me in other Tantras, by the 'Lion's Look',

46 punaruktaiś[106] ca māṇḍūkaplutyarthaiḥ[107] pīṭhagranthanaiḥ[108] |
catuṣkādyabjavajraiś[109] ca[110] mātṛkādyakṣarārcanaiḥ ||
43 vāḍavānalasaṃbhūtaiḥ kubjigotraiś caturvidhaiḥ |
etaiḥ[111] ṣoḍaśabhedais tu bhāva[ṃ] bhinnaṃ tu bhāmini[112] ||
48 sabāhyābhyantare jñeyaṃ sa vettā[113] kubjikāmate |
durlabhaṃ pṛcchitaṃ bhadre kalau prāpte kulacyutāḥ[114] ||
49 adhyuṣṭakoṭayas[115] teṣāṃ yāsyanti narakārṇave |
yena mūrkho[116] 'pi gatvā tu guruvṛddhasya cāgrataḥ ||
50 abhiṣicyānyathātmānaṃ[117] kariṣyanti[118] bṛhattvatā[m] |
abhiṣekena dīkṣāyāṃ puṣpāñjalighaṭena ca ||
51 ucchālanadhūnanaiḥ[119] kaṃpaiḥ patanair bāhyapratyayaiḥ[120] |
etanmātreṇa saṃtuṣṭā bṛhattvena tu darpitāḥ ||
52 kiṃ tu tena na[121] jyeṣṭhatvaṃ[122] śṛṇu tvaṃ[123] bhavate yathā |
anuṣṭhātari jyeṣṭhatvaṃ guṇajñe[124] ca[124] kriyākule[125] ||
53 jñānajñeyavidhānajño[126] na jyeṣṭho nābhiṣiñcitaḥ[127] |
atha mūrkho 'pi yasyāsti kṣudhānidrājarājayaḥ ||
54 sa jyeṣṭhaḥ kim anarthais tu[128] anuṣṭhānāgamair[129] guṇaiḥ |
jyeṣṭhajyeṣṭhataro[130] meghaḥ[130] sarveṣām uparisthitaḥ[131] ||
55 sṛṣṭipālanasaṃhāre[132] hānādānaṃ[133] ca nirmitam[134] |
yadi jyeṣṭhābhiṣekena[135] jāyate ca bṛhattvatā ||
56 tadā meghābhiṣekena[136] sarvasyāpi bṛhattvatā |
saṃbhāṣyāsanagauṇye[137] ca ājñā tasyāpi bhūtale ||
57 kurvanti guṇajyeṣṭhasya dīkṣājyeṣṭhasya tan na hi |
dīkṣājyeṣṭhair[138] guṇajyeṣṭhāḥ pūjyā vandyāḥ sadā mate[139] ||
58 kalisthā[140] ke[140] ca bhāṣāṇi mudrābandhaiś[141] ca[141] chomakaiḥ[141] |

---

106. BC -uktaś 107. A māṇḍūkaṃ plutyarthaiḥ 108. BC -granthakaiḥ 109. BC catuṣkānya-; A -vajrāś 110. BC tu 111. A etat 112. BC bhāvini 113. A sacetā 114. BC kalicyutāḥ 115. A adyuṣṭa- 116. B mūrkhyo 117. A abhiṣecyā- 118. BC kathiṣyanti 119. A ucālana- 120. C -pratyatyayaiḥ 121. A hi 122. A jyeṣṭhāṃ tu 123. BC -ṣva 124. A -jña ya 125. A -kulaḥ 126. C -vijñāna-; B -vitāna- 127. BC -ṣiñcite 128. omitted in BC 129. BC cānu- 130. BC -tarā meghāḥ 131. BC -tāḥ 132. C -hārau 133. BC -dāne 134. A -taḥ; BC vinirmale 135. A jyeṣṭho 'bhi- 136. A megho 'bhi- 137. A -bhāṣyamaṇagauryāś 138. A -jyeṣṭhā 139. A (suti) 140. BC kale sthāne 141. A -bandanac chramakaiḥ

46 by means of repetitions, by means of the 'Frog-leap', by means of combining the Pīṭhas, by means of the 'Lotus-vajras' beginning with the Four, by means of honouring the syllables, the Mātṛkās etc.,

47 and by means of the fourfold lineage of Kubjī, sprung from Vaḍavānala. By these sixteen different ways, O Bhāminī, is reality differentiated.

48 [The teachings of Kubjikā] ought to be known both with regard to their macro- and microcosmic meaning; then one [is regarded to be] an expert in the teachings of Kubjikā.

It is a difficult [question] You have asked Me, O Bhadrā. When the Kali Yuga has come, there will be people who have fallen from the Kula-tradition.

49/50 From among these three and a half crore will enter the Hellish Sea. Because of this it will happen that people, even if they are fools, having gone before an experienced teacher and having been sprinkled, will falsely make themselves authorities [solely] on the ground of the sprinkling at the occasion of the initiation, and the flowers, *añjalis* and [ritual] pitchers.

51 By jerking upwards, shaking, trembling and flying through the air — which are all only outward proofs [of the initiation] — merely by these they are satisfied, and made arrogant by their state of authorities.

52 By that, however, [genuine] superiority is not defined. Hear Thou in what way there is superiority for someone who performs religious actions, but who knows also its virtues, and is [at the same time] devoted to the practical side of it.

53 The one who only knows the procedure which has to be known for [acquiring the true] knowledge, that one is not superior, nor is the one who is initiated only by sprinkling. [If such should be the case,] then one might even be a fool who has mastered hunger, sleep and old age.

54 If such a one is a superior, what is the use then of the knowledge behind religious practice and virtues, which are then rendered superfluous? A cloud is more superior than superior: it is above everything.

55 In emanation, maintenance and absorption alike, taking and leaving is produced [on either side].

When by means of sprinkling by a superior authority is produced,

56 then there is authority for everyone because of the sprinkling by clouds! Should one have merely spoken [with someone] about the meritoriousness of the *āsanas*, it would then follow that one gains [from that conversation] authoritative insight [with regard to the subject] on earth!

57 One obeys the one whose superiority is based on virtues, and certainly not the one whose superiority is based on his initiation. By those who borrow their superiority from the initiation as such, the ones who borrow their superiority from virtues should always be worshipped and honoured — [thus it is said] in the texts.

58 In the Kali Yuga there are all kind of languages together with the forming of

saṅketair nāgamoktāś[142] ca kiṃ tu varṇavivakṣayā ||
59 triyugoktakramo hy eṣa kalau prāpte[143] krameśvari |
bhaviṣyanti narā mūḍhā dīkṣāmātreṇa garvitāḥ[144] ||
60 darpitānāṃ ca gopyaivaṃ[145] na kathyaṃ[146] ca guṇākṣaram |
darpair[147] vyākulitās teṣu[148] nirguṇās te śaṭhāḥ sadā ||
61 kiṃcid[149] yauvanagarveṇa lakṣmīgarveṇa kiṃcana[150] |
kiṃcid[151] vidyābalenāpi anuṣṭhānena darpitāḥ ||
62 etat sarvaṃ vinaśyeta santānaṃ na vinaśyati |
hemāyaskārakāṇḍārāś[152] carmaraṅgopajīvinaḥ ||
63 ācāryatve[153] bhaviṣyanti mūḍhā mūḍhābhiṣecitāḥ[154] |
ajñātvāgamasadbhāvaṃ[155] mithyājñāvākyabhāṣakāḥ ||
64 dīkṣāṃ[156] sarve[156] prakurvanti[156] pāpiṣṭhāḥ samayacyutāḥ |
tīvrājñā[157] na[157] ca teṣāṃ vai asadvākyapralāpakāḥ ||
65 yācayitvā tv aṭitvā tu poṣayanti kuṭumbakam[158] |
katham ājñā bhavet teṣāṃ yādṛśī bhavate śṛṇu ||
66 cintitārtho[159] bhavet tasya[160] ruṣṭena[161] patate paśuḥ |
tuṣṭena[162] bhavate rājyaṃ dehaṃ rugvyādhivarjitam ||
67 vartamānaṃ bhaviṣyaṃ ca kathed yaḥ[163] suvicārakah.[163] |
āgamārthaiḥ[164] śrutair dīkṣā[165] atha jñānāvalokanaiḥ ||
68 anarthaṃ te dvibhis tyaktvā mūrkhā[166] mithyāvabhāṣakāḥ[167] |
tena devi mayā hy etac chrīmataṃ tu[168] samuddhṛtam[168] ||
69 īdṛglokā bhaviṣyanti caturthe tu kalau yuge |[169]
na jātyākṛtidhanādhāraiḥ[170] saṃjñāyuktair[171] mahārgalaiḥ ||
70 etair mudritaṃ etad dhi[172] sacarācara[173] māyayā[174] |[175]
na gurur nāgamas teṣāṃ na[176] saṃskārāḥ[177] śivātmakāḥ ||
71 kalau yugasya doṣās te jāyante adhamā[178] narāḥ |
anyad manasi cānyac[179] ca karmaṇānyad[180] vyavasthitam[181] ||
72 lokānāṃ duṣṭacintānāṃ[182] tena vyastasamastakam[183] |
śrīmataṃ kathitaṃ kaule yāgaṃ[184] guptataraṃ[184] mahat ||

---

142. BC āgamoktaiś 143. A prāptiṃ 144. A -taḥ 145. BC gopyevaṃ 146. BC kathec 147. BC darpa- 148. BC te tu 149. BC kecid 150. A kiṃcina; BC kecana 151. A kiṃ sad; BC kecid 152. A hemāyaskara-; C hemāyaḥkāra- 153. A ācāryo na 154. A muḍhe 'bhi-; B -ṣecināḥ 155. BC ājñā- 156. A dīkṣā sarvāni kurvanti 157. A tīvrajñānaṃ 158. A kaṭumbakam; C kuṭaṃbakam (C′ kuṭumbakam) 159. A -rtha- 160. BC yasya 161. B tuṣṭena 162. BC saṃtuṣṭe 163. BC so jñādhārakaḥ 164. A -rtha 165. BC dīkṣām 166. A mūrkho 167. B mith[y]ā-; A śiṣyā bhaviṣyati 168. C tantra mudritam; B tantram uditam 169. after pāda 96b BC insert pāda 70c 170. C jātyāṃ kṛtidhanadaraiḥ; A -[dhā]nādāraiḥ; B -dhanadhāraiḥ 171. A saṃyuktaiś ca 172. BC viśvaṃ 173. A sācārācara; BC carācaraṃ 174. BC māyayā samyak 175. between pādas 70bc BC insert *āryā* 176. A ni 177. A saṃskāra 178. BC cādhamā 179. A cānyaś 180. A karma cānyad 181. A -tā 182. BC -cetānāṃ 183. A -kaḥ 184. A yāga guptatarā

mudrās and secret signs, which are not in accordance with the sacred texts; not to say anything about the [true] meaning of the letters.

59 The tradition as told in the three [previous] Yugas has become thus in the Kali Yuga, O Krameśvarī. There will be stupid men behaving haughtily only because they have received the inauguration.

60 The true value of the syllables should be shielded from these haughty men, and not be told to them. Among them are those confused by their [own] haughtiness: they lack theoretical background and are always deceitful.

61 Sometimes they are blinded by the arrogance of their youth, sometimes by pride of their wealth, sometimes also by pride of their magic powers or by their ritualistic performances.

62 All this is likely to disappear, [but] the continuity [of the Kula-tradition] does not vanish.

Goldsmiths, blacksmiths, Kāṇḍāras, people who earn their livelihood with skins or on the stage,

63 will act as teachers. They are fools initiated by fools. Being ignorant of the essence of the sacred texts, they proclaim words of false authority.

64 All perform the inauguration, these most wicked people unfaithful to the Samaya. They do not possess sharp authority, those twaddlers of untrue words.

65 By begging and wandering about they [only] thrive their own household. How can there be [real] authority for them? Listen what kind of so-called authority this is.

66 The aim on which he has concentrated his thought, is realized for him. When he is angry, cattle dies; when he is pleased, the kingdom prospers and his body is free from pain and diseases.

67 Anyone who tells the present and the future, [is regarded] a trustworthy guide. There is initiation [based] on the contents of sacred texts which are [only] heard, and by glances full of wisdom;

68 Laying aside twice [true insight] as something superfluous, they are fools speaking false words.

Therefore, O Devī, I have revealed this Śrīmata.

/70 Such people will there be in the fourth [Yuga], the Kali Yuga. The whole world is no [longer] defined by strong bolts based upon birth, appearance and wealth, and provided with mutual understanding, [but] by illusion. For these people there is no [true] guru nor sacred text, nor do they possess *saṃskāras* according to the Śaiva tradition.

/72 In the Kali Yuga such are the defilements, and such despicable people there are. These foul-minded people have one thing in mind, another thing they actually do, yet to another thing they are inclined. Therefore I have told the Śrīmata according to the Kula-tradition, both fractionally and as a whole. It is a great ritual, very well guarded.

73 kiṃ tu bauddhāś[185] ca[186] bodhyena[186] manyante cānyaśāsane[187] |
dayāṃ[188] mithyā vadiṣyanti arhantāś[189] ca nirdayāḥ[189] ||
74 bhaviṣyanti kalau viprā abrahmā[190] brahmavādinaḥ |
sāṅkhyayogaṃ vadiṣyanti yogavarjitacetasāḥ[191] ||
75 mīmāṃsābhāṣyayogena garvayiṣyanti[192] cādhamāḥ |
kāpālikāḥ[193] kālavaktrāḥ[194] praveśyanty[195] anyaśāsane ||
76 bhairavīye svamārgeṇa lajjayiṣyanti mānavāḥ |
granthasthāyina[196] yogīndrāḥ kariṣyanti akṛtyatām ||
77 śūdrāṇāṃ dvijā[197] bhaktinā[197] āvariṣyanti[198] mohitāḥ |
digaṃbarāś ca śaivākhye[199] śaivā viprajane jaḍāḥ[200] ||
78 vānaprasthā gṛhasthānaṃ[201] gamiṣyanti ca dāsatām |
brāhmaṇānāṃ magānāṃ ca samatvaṃ[202] jāyate kalau ||
79 māṭhāpatye[203] sthitā ye tu bhaviṣyanti[204] ca[204] darpitāḥ |
kṣatriyā āhave bhagnāḥ kariṣyanti prabhutvatām[205] ||
80 brāhmaṇāś ca kariṣyanti rasavedāgnivikrayam |
mātā pitā[206] ca putrā ye na namiṣyanti[207] cādhamāḥ ||
81 kulācāryā[208] bhaviṣyanti pitṛdevāgninindakāḥ |
cuṃbakena tu bhāvena paṭhitvāgamasaṅgraham ||
82 na guruṃ pūjayiṣyanti pratyakṣaṃ śāstradaṃ śivam[209] |
śāstradas tu śivaḥ sākṣān na sā[210] prakṛti mānavī ||
83 pūjitāpūjitaṃ[211] sarvaṃ na jñāsyante[212] narādhamāḥ |
bhasmair jaṭais tu saṃtuṣṭāḥ kecin nagnatvadarpitāḥ[213] ||
84 kecin mudrākapālais tu kecid daṇḍatridaṇḍakaiḥ |
daṃbhakauṭilyapāṣaṇḍair[214] anyonyaṃ bhāṣayanti ca ||
85 gurudravyaṃ[215] gamiṣyanti devadravye[216] tu[216] cāpare[216] |
itthaṃ[217] nirarthakā lokā bhaviṣyanti kalau yuge ||
86 tena devi mayā hy etac[218] chrīmataṃ[219] mudritaṃ kalau |
avyaktaliṅgino hy atra bhaviṣyanti jaḍāḥ[220] priye ||
87 vyaktaliṅgī ca nirlajjo[221] viplaviṣyati[222] śāsanam[223] |
tathā te[224] kathayiṣyāmi kathanīyaṃ ca yādṛśe ||
88 brāhmaṇe vā[225] narendre vā vicchūdre vātha cāntyaje |
kriyāyukte adarpiṣṭhe kathanīyaṃ na durjane ||

---

185. A bodhaś 186. BC subodhena 187. BC nāśamanāsanam 188. A dayā 189. A āruru( )ś ca nindayaḥ 190. A abrahmo 191. BC yogavartitacetasaḥ 192. A varjayiṣyanti 193. A kapālokā 194. A -vaktrāś ca 195. A praviśyanti 196. BC -sthā ye na 197. BC ca dvijā bhaktim 198. A r-āvariṣyanti; C ācariṣyanti 199. A -khyo 200 A jatāḥ 201. BC -sthānāṃ 202. BC saṃbandham 203. A māṭhāpitṛ- 204. BC te bhaviṣyanti 205. BC prabhoḥ kriyām 206. BC pitāś 207. A namaṣyanti 208. A -cārya 209. A śikaḥ 210. A sa 211. A pūjitapūjitaṃ; BC pūjite pūjitaṃ 212. BC jñāsyanti 213. BC -darśitāḥ 214. A -pāśāṇḍā; C -pākhaṇḍair 215. A -dravya 216. BC -dravyam upācaret 217. BC ete 218. A eta[c]; BC etaṃ 219. BC śrīkramaṃ 220. A mahā- 221. A nilajā 222. A viplavanti stu 223. A śāsanaḥ 224. C ne; C′ na 225. A ca

73 Nevertheless, the Buddhists, in all their wisdom, set their mind on another doctrine, and Jains without compassion will speak falsely of compassion.
74 In the Kali Yuga there will be *vipras* who are not Brahmins, but who speak about the Brahman. People whose mind is bereft of yoga, will speak of the Sāṅkhya Yoga.
75 Despicable people will boast by means of the Mīmāṃsābhāṣya. Kāpālikas and Kālavaktras will be forced to another doctrine.
76 People will be caused to be ashamed on account of their own 'path' which is dedicated to Bhairava. Prominent Yogins, steadfast in their scriptures, will perform things not to be done.
77 Twice-born will approach Śūdras with devotion in their blindness. Digambaras will be regarded as Śaivas; Śaivas will act as *vipras* in their stupidity.
78 Vānaprasthas will return to their homes, and become slaves. In the Kali Yuga Brahmins and Magas will be put on the same line.
79 Those who are in charge of the monasteries, will become arrogant. The Kṣatriyas, though broken in battle, will act as if they are [still] powerful.
80 Brahmins will sell philtres, the Vedas and Agni. Children will not honour their parents, those base creatures.
81 Teachers of the Kula-tradition will become those who scorn the Pitaras, the Gods and Agni. Having recited the sacred texts with a roguish inclination,
82 [pupils] will not pay homage to their guru, [although] he is the personification of Śiva giving the Śāstras. Indeed, [the guru] is the personification of Śiva in his capacity of giving the Śāstras (sc. to the pupil); he is not of human origin then.
83 Everything is a matter of honour to whom honour is due — that those low people do not realize. [Some] are completely satisfied with ashes and matted locks, others are blinded by nakedness,
84 others are blinded by *mudrās* and skulls, some by staffs or triple staffs. They will accuse each other of hypocrisy, dishonesty and heresy.
85 Some will put their hands upon the possessions of the guru, others upon the possessions of the gods. Such then will be the worthless people in the Kali Yuga.
86 Therefore, O Devī, is the Śrīmata impressed by Me on the Kali Yuga. People whose distinguishing mark is invisible will be stupid in this Yuga, O Lovely
87 The one who stands for his characteristic [will appear] shameless, and the doctrine will be ruined. Thus I will tell You to what kind of people [the Śrīmata] may be told.
88 To a Brahmin, to a Kṣatriya, or to a Vaiśya, a Śūdra, or Antyaja [the Śrīmata] may be told [as far as] they are dedicated to religious practice, and completely free from infatuation; not to wicked people.

89 yasya jñātaṃ[226] gurusthānaṃ[227] vartanaṃ dṛśyate sphuṭam[228] |
tasyākhyeyam idaṃ[229] ratnaṃ[229] yadi bhaktiḥ suniścalā ||
90 kathanīyaṃ kulācārye krīḍājñe samayānvite |
siddhanātha[ḥ] sthito yasmin kāle[230] ca[231] tasya[231] preraṇāt[231] ||
91 tasmin kāle kathed etad yogasārasamuccayam[232] |
śubhe vāre śubhe rikṣe[233] śubhakāle[234] śubhālaye ||
92 śubhe dine[235] ca rātrau ca śubhadravyasamanvite |
puṣpadhūpānvite divye aliphalgvanvite[236] priye[237] ||
93 candanāgurukarpūrasugandhāmodamodite[238] |
tatas tv āmantrayet tatra yoginyaś[239] ca kumārikāḥ ||
94 samayīsādhakāḥ putrā[240] ācāryā ye kulānvaye |
bṛhatsthānagatā[241] ye ca mātaṅgā[242] yadi vā[243] dvijāḥ[244] ||
95 namasyed bhāvayuktena nātra doṣo vidhīyate ||
śrīdevy uvāca ||
96 etad deva virodhaṃ[245] tu mātaṅgasya dvijasya tu |
jyeṣṭhakanyasakatvaṃ ca nirguṇasya guṇasya ca ||
śrībhairava[246] uvāca ||
97 etad[247] devi bhaṇiṣyāmi[248] bhāvādvaitaṃ sadā kuru |
kriyādvaitaṃ na kartavyam ekānte vātha[249] vandayet ||
98 kramaṃ[250] pūjya[250] tataḥ paścāt pustakaṃ ca samarcayet[251] |
ācāryaḥ[252] pūjayet paścād yoginīś ca kumārikāḥ ||
99 mālāṃ pradāpayet paścād maṇḍalasthāpanaṃ[253] kuru |
dakṣiṇāṃ dīyate[254] tatra gohiraṇyaṃ ca vāsaṃ[255] ca[255] ||
100 asaṃpattau phalaṃ puṣpaṃ tāṃbūlādyaṃ[256] pradāpayet |
namaskṛtvā ca taṃ cakraṃ pātrāṇy utkṣipya satkaraiḥ[257] ||
101 dīpakān[258] bodhayet paścād vīrayoginimānataḥ |
nānāpānavarair[259] divyair yāvad ānandatāṃ[260] vrajet ||
102 ājñāṃ[261] yācya gṛhītvā[262] tu pustakaṃ grāhayet tataḥ |
yācayed bhāvitātmānaḥ[263] ācāryaḥ[264] pratipādayet ||
103 paraṃ sūkṣmaṃ tathā sthūlaṃ kramaṃ ca trividhaṃ smṛtam[265] |
dvādaśānte paraṃ proktaṃ sūkṣmaṃ ca brahmarandhragam ||
104 tasyaivādhaḥsthitaṃ[266] sthūlaṃ catuṣkādīni maṇḍale |

226. C jñānaṃ 227. BC guro[ḥ] sthānaṃ 228. A yathā 229. BC prayatnena 230. A kālaṃ 231. BC cittasthapreraṇā 232. A yāga- 233. B rekṣe; C ṛkṣe 234. A śubhava(str)e 235. BC 'hani 236. A -phalgunvite; B -phalgvānvite 237. BC śubhe 238. BC -karpūraiḥ su-; C sugandhāgandhamodite (C′ corrects) 239. BC yoginyau 240. A putra 241. A bṛbhasthāna- 242. BC mātaṅgo 243. A ca 244. BC dvijaḥ 245. BC viruddhaṃ 246. A -bhairav 247. A etaṃ 248. A bha(vi)ṣyāmi 249. A mātha 250. A kramapūjā 251. AB samardhayet 252. A ācārya 253. BC maṇḍalotthāpanaṃ 254. BC dāpayet 255. A vāsa ca; BC vāśanam 256. A tāṃbolādya 257. B sa(jva)raiḥ; A śaṅkārai 258. A dīpakaṃ 259. A nānāpābharaṇair 260. A addhāyan nandatāṃ 261. B ājñaṃ 262. BC gṛhitaṃ 263. B -tmāta 264. A ācārya 265. A smṛtaḥ 266. A tasyaivādha[ḥ]-

89 The one who recognizes the position of the guru, and who clearly perceives the proceedings, to him this gem might be told, at least when his devotion does not waver.
90 It might be told to a teacher of the Kula-doctrine who understands the [meaning of] *krīḍā*, and who sticks to the Samaya. When a Siddhanātha is present, and on his command,
91 then one might tell this compendium of Yoga.
On a propitious day, under an auspicious constellation, at the right time, in an appropriate place,
92 on an auspicious day or night, [in a place] provided with auspicious materials, with flowers and incense, agreeable, with liquor and meat, O Lovely One,
93 which causes intoxication by the strong fragrant odour of sandal, aloe and camphor. Next he should invite there Yoginīs and virgins,
94 Samayins, Sādhakas, Putras and what other teachers there are in the Kula-tradition, Mātaṅgas and twice-born, no matter who, as long as they are authorities.
95 [Those] he should honour sincerely. No transgression is committed by that.
Śrīdevī spoke:
96 Is there no incompatibility between a Mātaṅga and a twice-born, as there is superiority and inferiority between respectively someone with virtues and someone without virtues?
Śrībhairava spoke:
97 This, O Devī, I will explain to You. Never make any distinction between someone's rank, but discern between someone's [ritual] actions. On a lonely spot he should then greet respectfully [the Yoginīs etc.].
98 Having honoured the tradition, next the teacher should venerate the book. Then he should worship the Yoginīs and the virgins:
99 a wreath he should offer [them]. Next [he should order]: "Form a circle!". On that moment a *dakṣiṇā* is presented: cows, gold and garments.
100 In case one cannot afford it, one might give fruit, flowers, betel etc. Having [thus] honoured that circle, and having raised the cups with steadfast hands,
101 he should light the lamps. Next, in honour of the Vīras and Yoginīs, [he should enjoy] all kinds of divine, superb drinks until he reaches a state of bliss.
102 Having asked for consent and [subsequently] having obtained it, he should next make [his pupil] familiar with the book. When [the pupil] sincerely requests [instruction], then the teacher should teach him [beginning with the following words]:
103 "*Para*, *sūkṣma* and *sthūla*: thus the tradition is known in a threefold way. In the Dvādaśānta *para* is proclaimed to be; *sūkṣma* is in the Brahmarandhra;
104 situated below that one is *sthūla*, i.e. the [series of] Four etc. in the *maṇḍala*".

pūrvaṃ tu kathitā pūjā eṣā vai śeṣikā[267] kriyā ||
105 prathamāhne[268] vācayitvā tu saṃvartāmaṇḍalāntagam[269] |
kramasṛṣṭidine[270] tasmiṃ kārayec ca mahotsavam ||
106 cakrakrīḍāṃ samāśṛtya tad[271] dinaṃ kṣapayed[272] budhaḥ |
evaṃ tu prathame divi[273] pratyahaṃ bhaktitaḥ punaḥ ||
107 kurute vidhivat prajño[274] baliṃ rātrau prayatnataḥ |
yāvat samāpyate[275] granthas tāvat kuryād imaṃ[276] vidhim[277] ||
108 anyathā prāpyate 'nartho[278] mahatā[279] yoginīkule |
yathā[280] cittānusāreṇa kartavyaṃ tu dine dine ||
109 ity evaṃ kathitaṃ devi śrīmatīyaṃ mahākulam |
nāpuṇyair[281] labhyate[282] lokair[283] yoginīgarbhavarjitāḥ[284] ||
110 yoginīgarbhasaṃbhūtā aṃbā[285] vai koṅkaṇāṃbikā[286] |
kathyate bhaktiyuktānāṃ saṃsārārṇavabhīruṇā ||
111 ādau madhyāvasāne ca[287] pūjā kāryā yathāvidhi |
dine dine prakartavyā yathā śaktyā prapūjayet[288] ||
112 puruṣaṃ śṛṇūyāt pūrvaṃ pūrvāmnāyī[289] ca yaḥ[290] smṛtaḥ[291] |
tena dṛṣṭena so vetti śarīre devatāṣṭakam[292] ||
113 kalaśasyābhiṣekaṃ ca kārayec[293] ca[293] punaḥ punaḥ |
niḥśaṅkaṃ nirvikalpaṃ ca tena jānanti deśikāḥ[294] ||

iti kulālikāmnāye śrīdevyaughasadbhāve śrīkubjikā[ma]te
ṣaṭsāhasre saṃhitāyāṃ śrīśrīmate tṛtīyaḥ paṭalaḥ ||[295]

267. A śeśakī 268. BC prathame 'hni 269. A -gaḥ; BC -ntikam 270. A kāmasṛṣṭidinais 271. A tu 272. A kṣipayed 273. BC divase 274. BC prājño 275. A samāghate 276. A ayaṃ 277. BC vidhiḥ 278. BC naryo 279. BC mahāntaṃ 280. A athavā 281. A nāpuṇye 282. BC labhate 283. BC loke 284. A -tā 285. A ājñāṃ 286. A -ke 287. BC tu 288. BC -pūjanam 289. B pūrva[ ]; C pūrvā [ ]ye 290. A ya; C yaṃ; B iyaṃ 291. BC smṛtam 292. B devatmastakam 293. BC kārayitvā 294. A deṣikaḥ 295. BC iti śrīmate ṣaṭsāhasre saṃhitāyāṃ tṛtīyaḥ paṭalaḥ

The [accompanying] *pūjā* has been told earlier. Now follows the remaining part of the ritual.

105 Having read aloud [the text] up to the Saṃvartāmaṇḍala on the first day, he then should celebrate a Mahotsava on that day on which the tradition is emanated.

106 The wise should pass [the rest of] the day in practising *cakrakrīḍā*. Thus he does on the first day, and on every following day, with devotion,

107 according to the rules, the intelligent one. At night time he offers a *bali* with care. Until the text is completely gone through, he should follow this rule.

108 Otherwise there occurs a disappointing event amidst the assembly of the Yoginīs by the extensiveness [of the text]. As it is conform to the mind [thus] it should be done day after day.

109 Herewith, O Devī, I have told You the Great Kula-doctrine of the Śrīmata. It is not obtained by impure people: they are bereft of the *yoginīgarbha*,

110 and born from the *yoginīgarbha* is The Mother, Koṅkaṇāṃbikā! It is told to people who possess [genuine] devotion, by [a teacher] who dreads the ocean of the Saṃsāra.

111 At the beginning, in the middle and at the end *pūjā* should be performed according to the rules. Day after day it should be performed. One should worship according to capacity.

112 The one who is known as a Pūrvāmnāyin [teaching]: "The Puruṣa one should hear first", [that one] knows the eight deities of the body due to that opinion of his.

113 The teachers [who ordain]: "Again and again one should perform the inauguration by means of a pitcher"; they know it therefore in an easy way, not bothered by alternatives.

Thus in the Kulālikāmnāya, in the Śrīdevyaughasadbhāva, in the Kubjikāmata, in the Ṣaṭsāhasra Saṃhitā, in the Śrīśrīmata the third chapter.

COMMENTARY

In comparison with the two preceding chapters, the third chapter of the ṢaṭSS is of a more narrative character. It does not deal with the basic concepts regarding the macro- and microcosmic ideas held in esteem by the followers of the Śrīmata. Probably because of this, the Ṭ on this third chapter is merely marginal: it shortly indicates its contents, and concludes with the statement that everything in this chapter is sufficiently clear, and hence no detailed explanation is necessary (*tṛtīyapaṭala āraṃbhaḥ || śrīdevy uvāca | śrīmataṃ tu mahājñānam ityādi tṛtīyapaṭalāvadhir yāvat vyākhyālekhanavidhis tathā guruśiṣyasamayalakṣaṇādikaṃ spaṣṭārtham || iti ṣaṭsāhasre tṛtīyaḥ paṭalaḥ* ||). Because of this more general character of the third chapter we have abstained from the method followed in the first two chapters, namely to add an explanation immediately after the translation of a *śloka*. The contents of the verses in the first two chapters of the ṢaṭSS are frequently of such a highly intricate nature, that a translation of these verses becomes only understandable when immediately followed by extensive notes. The translation of the third chapter as well as the next chapter is suffficiently clear in itself. For this reason we present the translation of the third and fourth/fifth chapter of the ṢaṭSS in a whole, while the Notes are given after the complete translation because they are not of primary importance for understanding the translation.

The central subject of the third chapter of the ṢaṭSS regards the transmission of the text itself by the teacher to his pupil, and the proper ritual connected with this procedure (*ślokas* 18-29; 91-95; 98-108). The calamities one is likely to meet when not strictly following the rules prescribed for the above-mentioned ritual are vividly described as well as the horrors of the Kali Yuga. Besides this we find a vehement fulmination against those teachers who restrict the initiation of a pupil to a mere sprinkling with water. In relation to this, the characteristics of the true teacher and pupil are explained. In this the third chapter of the ṢaṭSS has only a loose relationship with the third chapter of the KmT. In the latter we also find an exposition on the characteristics of the true teacher and his pupil, but the contents of this passage (KmT 3,40-134) have little in common with the similar passage in the ṢaṭSS.

1: The 'great knowledge of the Śrīmata' (1a *śrīmate tu mahājñānaṃ*; note that the *pratīka* of the Ṭ (see above) follows the reading of BC) refers to the contents of the two preceding chapters. Devī inquires after the prescribed rules (*vidhāna*) with regard to the exposition of the text by the teacher to his pupil (*vyākhyā*), the suitable occasion for this (*kāla*), and how the text should be written down by the pupil (cf. 3a *vyākhyālekhanakāle*). As we shall see below, the teacher recites the text while the pupil notes it down at the same time in order to procure a copy of the text for himself.

4: In the *pādas* 4ab we have translated the verb *prakupyanti* (4a) two times. It is also possible to regard the two *pādas* as a unity: 'Like diseases kings rage over their subjects'.

6: Pigeons (Skt: sg.!) and crows are regarded as ominous birds, especially when they perch down on a house or a palace (cf. Kohlbrugge 1938: 123; Negelein 1912: 215 ff.). Mainly because of their resemblance to a jackal dogs are also considered as ominous animals (cf. Negelein 1912: 302 ff.). In *pāda* 6c two dogs are mentioned. This probably refers to the two dogs of Yama, King of Death. Although the wailing of a dog is a bad portent as such, the relation of these two dogs to Yama seems to be the more important here, as it is the cause of untimely deaths (6d). In *pāda* 6c BC have a different reading: 'When there is a halo around the sun or the moon', which is also a bad portent.

7: In *pādas* 7ab (note the alliteration of *gaganaṃ garjate ... garbha-*) the thunder of the sky causes the occurrence of miscarriages or premature births. The falling of meteors (*ulkāpāta*) is frequently mentioned as an omen. The expression *ulkāpāta* does not necessarily refer only to meteors, but may also denote thunder, lightning etc. (cf. Kohlbrugge 1938: 39). It is easily imagined that the falling down of meteors or the striking of lightning may cause houses to be set afire (7d). The explanation of the expression *diśāṃ dāgho* (7c) is uncertain. It may refer here to a natural phenomenon as *ulkāpāta*, or it may be the result of the falling down of meteors. As a natural phenomenon the burning of the sky-regions is a bad portent (cf. Kohlbrugge 1938: 34 ff.), and a Brahmin should not recite the Vedas, for instance, 'while the sky is preternaturally red' (Manu 4,115 *digdāha*, trs. Bühler). It is also possible, however, to regard *diśāṃ dāgho* as the result of the falling down of meteors. In this way it stands on the same line as *gṛhe dāha* (7d), and might refer to a forest-fire as a contrast to the fire in one's house (cf. Negelein 1912: 196 *nagara-grāma-dāhaṃ ca diśāṃ dāhaṃ tathaiva ca*). In our translation we have opted for the second possibility.

8: In *pāda* 8a *svapnāti*, 'he sleeps', is probably wrong for *svapnānte* (cf. Negelein 1912: 282 *yadi paśyati svapnānte ...*), or one might read *svapnāni raudrāṇi*, 'horrible dreams', although in correct Skt *svapna* is usually of the masculine gender.

9: Snakes are regarded as very ominous animals, especially when they are found inside the house (cf. Negelein 1912: 282 ff.). The relation between snakes and rain is amply attested for in India and elsewhere. Note that in *pāda* 9c *vācitvā* is incorrect for *vācayitvā*. Nārada (9c) is the name of a well-known Ṛṣi, but this does not make any sense here. We have translated *nārada* here with 'cloud' on the following grounds. The Ṛṣi Nārada is supposed to be the messenger between the gods and men. In this capacity he travels between heaven and earth, and can therefore easily be identified with a cloud. Moreover, the name Nārada can be explained as 'the Water-giver' (cf. *nīra-da*, 'water-giver; cloud'), and he is described as bearing a water-pot and appears on a cloud (cf. Gonda 1969: 221).

10: In *pāda* 10b the form *śrīmatedaṃ* is wrong for *śrīmatam idaṃ*, which would result in a *pāda* of nine syllables, however. The reading of A in *pāda* 10c (*vidhvaṃsakānāṃ*) is not correct with regard to the metre: the fifth syllable is long instead of short, whereas the reading of BC (*vidhvaṃsakāni*) is metrically correct. The reading of A, however, fits better in the context. The jackal is one of the most inauspicious animals in India because it ostentatiously devours corpses (Negelein 1912: 284). Its howling is also considered a bad omen with disastrous effects (Negelein 1912: 286).

11: The literal translation of *pādas* 11ab runs: 'in one's house the sound of ichneumons [is heard]; they are constantly angry'. The reading of BC seems to be a *lectio facilior*: 'in one's house the ichneumons constantly make noises'. We have translated *piṅgala* with 'ichneumon', but it is also possible that some kind of owl is meant (cf. Negelein 1912: 220).

The receiving of blows by an invisible hammer (11c) is not known to me as a bad portent or as the effect of one. It is, however, inauspicious when one dreams about a hammer (cf. Negelein 1912: 350). In Buddhist literature we find the story of Ambaṭṭha who is threatened by a *yakkha* with a hammer invisible to other people, when he fails to answer a question of the Buddha (Dīghanikāya: Ambaṭṭha Sutta).

12: *Samayaghna*, 'one who violates the Samaya' (12d). In this context *samaya* refers to the eight rules of conduct, which are to be strictly followed. The eight rules are enumerated in the 17th chapter of the ṢaṭSS. The first Samaya prescribes: 'One should always honour the authority of one's guru, the Śāstra, one's personal *mantra* (*iṣṭamantra*), Bhairava, spirituous liquor, Devī, and oneself'. The other seven Samayas run likewise, prescribing what to do and what to leave.

14: With *tārkika* (14d) a sceptic or dialectician is probably meant. The Śrīmata should not be told to such a person, because he might raise a different opinion with regard to some of the topics related to him by his teacher. In this context one should understand *śloka* 16cd, where it is advised not to discuss the meaning of separate words or syllables with the pupil.

15: *Saṃcālaka* (15a) is probably wrong for *saṃcāraka*, 'leader; guide' (the consonants *l* are *r* are easily interchanged). Note that in *pāda* 15c the genitive is used twice (*subhaktasya*, *suśāntasya*) instead of the locative which we find in 15d (*dhārmike*) and 16ab (*-bhakte*, *durjane*). Probably the use of the genitive in *pāda* 15c is brought about by the occurrence of the genitive in *pāda* 15a. In *pāda* 15d the form *satyavādine* is a dative sg. from *satyavādin* according to correct grammar. In view of the fact, however, that in the same *pāda* the more correct locative (*dhārmike*) is found, it becomes plausible that *satyavādine* is to be regarded as a locative sg. from *satyavādina*. In the same way one should regard the form *tyāgine* (BC for *dhārmike*) as a loc. sg. from *tyāgina*, which stands besides the more correct *tyāgin*.

16: In the compound *gurudevāgnibhakta* (16a), 'someone with devotion to his guru, the Gods and Agni', *agni* refers most probably to the sacrificial fires, because the deity Agni is included among the Gods (*deva*). This reference to the sacrificial fires points to the fact that the pupil should fulfil his sacrificial duties properly.

17: From *pāda* 17b it appears that a guru should send his pupil to another teacher, when the pupil wants to discuss or question single words or topics told to him by his guru (cf. 14d; 16cd).

18: Pūrṇā (18a) is the name of an auspicious *tithi*, 'lunar day'. It may denote the 5th, 10th or 15th day of a lunar fortnight, but it is particulary connected with the 15th day of the moon at full moon. The meaning of *pāda* 18b is uncertain. Like Pūrṇā Riktā may also denote a particular *tithi*: the 4th, 9th or 14th day of a lunar fortnight. On the other hand *rikta* may simply mean 'empty'. Taken together with *sūryayor* ('sun & moon', cf. *pitarau* 'father & mother') it may denote a day without sun or moon, perhaps an eclipse of either the sun or the moon, or twilight. In this way the ceremony should be performed on the 5th, the 10th or the 15th day of a lunar fortnight when there is no sun nor moon. The reading of BC (*riktā sūryeṇa yā bhavet*) might indicate that the appropriate time for the ceremony is at night.

In *pāda* 18d the form *-rikṣa-* in the compound is noteworthy. According to the sandhi-rules the complete compound should be *duṣṭarkṣavivarjite*, which would, however, result in a *pāda* of only seven syllables. It is not unusual in the manuscripts of our text, that instead of *ri* simply *ṛ* is written. Thus MS A writes almost invariably *pṛya* instead of *priya*. Here we find the reverse: instead of *ṛkṣa rikṣa* is written. MS C 'solves' the problem by accepting a hiatus within the compound, and writes *duṣṭa*| *ṛkṣa-*.

19: In *śloka* 19 the place is described where the initiation of the pupil should take place. The word *mandira* usually denotes a temple, or at least some kind of building. It is, however, doubtful whether we should translate it in this sense here. Tantric initiations and other rituals generally take place at some lonely spot, where there is no danger of being watched by others. In the 20th chapter of our text another initiation is described, the so-called Kulābhiṣeka, of which the preparations are very much like the present ritual. In the case of the Kulābhiṣeka the place for the ceremony is described as follows: *sugupte nirjane sthāne gandhapuṣpādivāsite* | *tāṃbūlādisamākīrṇe candanāguruvāsite* (MS B), ' on a secluded and lonely place, scented by perfumes and flowers, strewn with betel etc., fragrant by sandal and aloe'. This description of the place harmonizes very well with the present description except for the fact that no *mandira* is mentioned. It is important, that the place is 'secluded' (*sugupta*) and 'not accessible to others; lonely' (*nirjana*). It is possible to translate *mandira* with 'the place where one abides; spot', as we have done in our translation of this *śloka* (*mand-*, 'to stay; to rest'). As in chapter 20, however, the actual place of the ritual is simply called *sthāna*. It is therefore very tempting to see in *mandire* an adjective belonging to *sthāne* in *pāda* 19c. Unfortunately an adjective *mandira* is not attested for. Perhaps *mandire* in the text actually stands for *mandre*, 'pleasant; agreeable', which appears to be an important qualification for the place (cf. *ramye* in the same *pāda*). Moreover, the epithet *susama*, 'smooth; flat', is hardly appropriate for a temple, but does fit for some place in the woods where one finds a clearance with a smooth or flat surface: the surface of the ground has to be flat for the purpose of drawing a *maṇḍala* on it (*śloka* 20), and perhaps for the gathering to sit on. The *pāda* 19d of MS A obviously is not grammatically quite correct, although its meaning is clear. The reading of BC (*kuṅkumāgurucarcite*, 'covered with saffron and aloe') is more correct, but seems to be a *lectio facilior*.

21-23: These three *ślokas* describe the putting down of the so-called Kula-jar (24a *kulakuṃbha*) on the central svastika of the square. The compound in *pāda* 22a seems to be of the same kind as the one in *śloka* 19d. In our translation we have connected it with the following *paripūrya* (22b), however, which is not grammatically quite correct. Perhaps 'being filled to the brim' (*paripūrya*) does not refer to the gems, gold and flowers mentioned in *pāda* 22a. In the case of the similar ceremony of the Kulābhiṣeka (Ch. 20; see above) the *kuṃbha* is described as follows: *ādāya kalaśaṃ divyam akṛṣṇa[ṃ] śubhalakṣaṇam* | *pūrayed alinā vātha vāriṇā vātha suvrate* | *sahiraṇyaṃ prakartavyaṃ vastrayugmaṃ tu veṣṭayet* | *cūtapallavasaṃchannaṃ candanāguruvarcitam* (wr.f. *-carcitam*? cf. BC in 19d), 'having taken a beautiful jar, white, with auspicious marks, he should fill it with liquor or water, O Suvratā; together with gold this should be done; [next] he should wrap two vestments around it; [the jar] is covered with mango-twigs, and smeared with sandal and aloe' (MS B). Again the description fits nicely to the Kula-jar of the present ceremony. Consequently one might argue that *paripūrya* refers to liquor (*ali*) or water (*vāri*), both of which are not mentioned here. Thus one might translate the *pādas* 22ab with '[the jar with] gems, gold and flowers, and having it filled to the brim [with liquor or water]'. In *pāda* 22a *-sauvarṇa-* is the Vṛddhi-form of *suvarṇa* in compounds. The 'book' (23b *pustaka*) most likely refers to a manuscript of the ṢaṭSS, which the teacher is going to recite for his pupil. The Pūrṇapātra (23c), or 'Vessel of Plenty', is a bowl filled with rice or valuable items to be distributed as presents among the leading figures in the ceremony. In our case its contents are likely to be presented to the guru in the first place, and perhaps also to the other participants, viz, the virgins (cf. *śloka* 24).

24: The teacher invites eight (24c) or four (24d) virgins (*kumārī*) to be present at the ceremony. Although with *kumārī* simply a virgin may be meant, in this context there may be something more to it. According to the KRP (F.50B ff.) there are four kind of Yoginīs in the Kula-tradition: *kulajā mantrajāś caiva yogajā[ḥ] sahajās tathā | caturvidhā samākhyātā yoginyaḥ kulaśāsane*. The fourth kind of Yoginī, the Sahajā, is explained in this text with *kumārī sahajā jñeyā* (KRP F.51A), ' the Sahajā Yoginī should be known to be a virgin'. Probably the *kumārīs* of our text refer to this fourth kind of Yoginī. It is not clear why the teacher has the option to invite either eight or four *kumārīs* on the occasion of the ritual. Moreover the sequence is peculiar: first the number eight is mentioned, next the number four. The reverse would be more likely, although the sequence may be due to metrical reasons. The numbers four or eight may refer to the four or eight points of the compass. It is possible that the 'four' in *pāda* 24d do not refer to virgins, but to another group of female participants. Although the text is vague at this point, it seems that the number 'four' here might refer to four Yoginīs, who are actually addressed in *śloka* 25a. Moreover in *pāda* 93cd of the third chapter we read *tatas tv āmantrayet tatra yoginyaś ca kumārikāḥ*, where a distinction is made between Yoginīs and Kumārikās. Although Yoginī is a general name for a female Yogin, here the designation Yoginī may denote one of the four kinds of Yoginīs in particular, the Yogajā (see above; KRP F.51A: *kṣetrapīṭhādisaṃbhūtā yoginyo yogajā matā[ḥ]*).

26: In *pāda* 26d the Kulajās, 'women born in the Kula-tradition', are mentioned. As we have seen above (*śloka* 24 Notes) the Kulajā is also one of the four kinds of Yoginīs. A Kulajā Yoginī is defined in the KRP (F.51B) with *kulāṣṭakaniḥkrāntā*, 'a woman come forth from the Kulāṣṭaka'. The Kulāṣṭaka is explained in this context as the Eight Samayas (KRP F.7B), 'the eight rules of conduct' (cf. *śloka* 12 Notes). Thus it appears that there are three types of Yoginīs present at the ceremony: the Sahajā, the Yogajā and the Kulajā. The Kulajās are mentioned only incidentally: they are not explicitly invited as the Sahajās and Yogajās were (*śloka* 24cd), nor is their number mentioned. Therefore one might assume that the general term Yoginīs in the *ślokas* 25a and 93d of this third chapter actually refers to the Kulajā Yoginīs. In the latter case there are only two types of Yoginīs present, the Sahajā and Kulajā Yoginīs, who are respectively eight and four in number. Especially in instances as these it is a pity that the Ṭ does not consider it necessary to provide any explanation. Obviously for those well-versed with the ritual proceedings of the Kula-tradition there is no problem here, but for the modern reader of these texts questions like these arise quite frequently. In *pāda* 26d the expression *kulāgate* refers to the pupil who is about to be initiated.

27: In *pāda* 27c Vīrendra, 'Chief among the Adepts', refers to the teacher. In Tantric texts *vīra* is a designation of the adepts in Tantric lore such in contrast to the laymen who are called *paśu*, 'cattle'. A Tantric Vīra is the same as a Yogin, as the reading of BC indicates here (*yogīndra* instead of *vīrendra*). The Kulakrama (27d) which is honoured by the teacher refers to the line of teachers who handed down the Kula-doctrine.

28: The 'book' (28a *pustaka*) refers, again (cf. 23b), to a manuscript of the ṢaṭSS, which the teacher had previously placed on top of the Kula-jar (see above). 'The deities of the body' (28c *dehasthā devatās*) probably refers to the fifty goddesses of the Mālinī-system, and the fifty Rudras or Bhairavas of the Śabdarāśi-system. The deities of both systems are connected with a particular part of the human body (cf. Appendix II). The 'honouring of the deities of the body' actually means that the teacher consecrates the body by means of *nyāsa* for the following ritual, the body thus becoming consecrated to Mālinī (= Śakti) and Śabdarāśi (= Śiva). Another group of 'deities of the body' which might be intended are the gods and goddesses of the five Mahāpīṭhas among which we also find the goddesses of the Mālinī-system (cf. Appendix III). These are explained in the next chapter of our text, and are already introduced in the present chapter by a question of Devī (43ab *kathaṃ pīṭhādhipā devyā[ḥ] śarīre saṃvyavasthitāḥ*). With regard to this consecration of the body by means of the 'deities of the body' one may wonder whose body is actually consecrated. It may refer to the body of the teacher himself, but more likely the body of the pupil is meant, which is consecrated by the teacher. In this way a kind of *varṇamayī dīkṣā* (cf. Gupta a.o. 1979: 85) is performed.

29: The subject of *vācayet* (29d) is the teacher.

30-31: The *ślokas* 30; 31ab possibly refer to the introductory stanzas of the ṢaṭSS (1,1-5), which seem to be of primary importance (cf. *śloka* 33). In *pāda* 31d the expression *abhiṣecaka*, 'a sprinkler', refers to the kind of guru who initiates his pupil by a mere sprinkling with water. To this kind of guru and initiation our text is heavily opposed (cf. *ślokas* 50 ff.).

32: The Five Cakras (32a) are explained in the chapters 21-25 of our text with an introductory chapter on the Kulābhiṣeka (Ch. 20). The text states implicitly that the Śrīmata is characterized by these Five Cakras (20,4ab *śrīmataṃ tu varārohe ebhiś cakrais tu mudritam*; cf. *śloka* 2,5 Notes). From *pāda* 32a it follows that the Tripurārṇava (32b) and the Haṃsabheda (32c) are also the names of texts, characterized by the Ṣaṭkūṭa and the Puruṣa respectively (cf. *śloka* 112). Both texts have not been edited so far, and according to Kavirāj (1972: *s.v.*) are only mentioned in other texts: no manuscript of either of the two texts seems to have been found. Consequently, it is not possible to verify the statement of the ṢaṭSS. For the same reason it is not possible to define with any certainty the nature of the Ṣaṭkūṭa and the Puruṣa. Possibly the Ṣaṭkūṭa is a particular *mantra* consisting of six *bījas*, whereas Puruṣa might possibly refer to the well-known Puruṣa-hymn (cf. *śloka* 112 Notes).

33: It is not clear to which five *ślokas* the text refers in *pāda* 33d. It is possible that the five introductory verses (1,1-5) are meant, although actually they are not composed in the *śloka*-metre. Since *śloka* may also denote a verse or stanza in general, the expression *pañcaśloka* can refer to the five ($4^1/_2$ actually) stanzas in the *sragdharā*-metre at the beginning of the first chapter. Another possibility is that the expression refers to the five chapters in which the Five Cakras are explained (see above).

35: From the *pādas* 35ab it appears that the Kula-tradition (35d *kulacchāyā*) is sometimes referred to as the 'Southern Reflection' or as the 'Siddhāntikā [Reflection]'. The mention of Dakṣiṇa and Siddhāntikā indicates that we find here most probably a reference to the old subdivision of Tantras according to the *srotas*-system. According to this classification of Tantras there are three different 'streams' (*srotas*): Dakṣiṇa (South), Vāma (Left) and Siddhānta (Established) or Madhyama (Middling) (cf. Gupta a.o. 1979: 41; Goudriaan & Gupta 1981: 16ff.). According to the text the Kulacchāyā is sometimes called or identified with the Dakṣiṇa and the Siddhānta. This same connection is mentioned in the 13th chapter of the ṢaṭSS, where it is stated that Samayā Kubjikā (cf. Schoterman 1977: 936) is the same in the Vāma and Dakṣiṇa Tantras (MS B F.97B *vāmadakṣiṇatantreṣu sāmānyā samayā parā* (= KmT 7,10cd)). The use of *chāyā* in connection with the *srotas*-system is not known to me from other sources (cf. 1,49cd; 50ab Notes).

36: Note that in *pāda* 36a *samastedaṃ* is wrong for *samastam idaṃ*, which would result in a *pāda* of nine syllables, however (cf. 10b). *Cakra* in *pāda* 36c should be understood as 'circle or group of insiders'.

38: In *pāda* 38a the reading *devaloke* instead of *deva loke* is theoretically possible, but makes no sense in the context. *Kubjikākhyaṃ mahāmatam* (38b) refers, of course, in the first place to the Kubjikāmata Tantra and its contents.

39: The teachings of the Kubjikā School are the ultimate truth. Consequently it makes no difference whether they are told in fragments or as a whole, in correct order or reversed order: they are the only Truth, in what form whatsoever stated.

40-41: In the *pādas* 40ab the author of the ṢaṭSS takes a firm stand against pure ritualism. Possibly Vedic ritualism is meant in particular with its elaborate sacrificial proceedings, which may easily cause doubt or uncertainty. The teachings of the Śrīmata, however, are clear and leave no room for doubt (40b *niḥsaṃdigdhakarī*; cf. 42a). *Parā* (40b) may stand for *paratā*. In the *ślokas* 40cd; 41ab the 'history' of the Kubjikāmata Tantra — already mentioned in 38b — is explained. 'The half of the half of 24.000' means 6.000. From these 6.000 the thousand numbering *dhyuṣṭa* (41a) originates. Since we are dealing with texts the numbers denote the number of verses of a text. Thus there is a text of 24.000 verses, one of 12.000 verses, one of 6.000, and a text with *dhyuṣṭa*-thousand of verses. The *mūla*-text of the Kubjikā School should contain 24.000 verses. This number is indeed mentioned in the colophons of the Manthānabhairava Tantra, but this text should not be regarded as the basic text of the Kubjikā School, which is rather the Kubjikāmata Tantra. A version of 12.000 verses is not known to me. The 6.000 verses undoubtedly refer to the Ṣaṭsāhasra Saṃhitā, which contains indeed approximately 6.000 verses. The number of verses called *dhyuṣṭasaṃkhyaṃ sahasram* should refer to the Kubjikāmata Tantra, which contains approximately 3500 verses (Schoterman 1977: 932). Consequently *dhyuṣṭa* ought to mean 'three and a half'. Unfortunately the word *dhyuṣṭa* is not attested for in any text or dictionary. The only Skt numeral which sounds familiar with *dhyuṣṭa* and also means 'three and a half', is *adhyuṣṭa* which is the Skt counterpart of Prakrit *addhuṭṭha*. Perhaps we have to accept a form *dhyuṣṭa* besides *adhyuṣṭa* (cf. 1,5a; 3,49a), or emend *pāda* 41a to *tanmadhyādhyuṣṭa-*.

Although it is not explicitly stated here, the four versions might be connected with the four Yugas. In the first Yuga the *mūla*-text counted 24.000 verses, a number which gradually decreases in a regular way (24.000-12.000-6.000) until in the fourth Yuga, the present Kali Yuga, there are only 3.500 verses left of the original. Thus in our time we possess the Kubjikāma Tantra of 3.500 verses. This phenomenon of a decreasing original text through the various Yugas is frequently met with in Tantric texts. It is peculiar, however, that the author of the ṢaṭSS places his text chronologically before the KmT, while in reality it comes after the KmT. Although the author of the ṢaṭSS does not mention his text in so many words, his intention seems clear: the identification of the ṢaṭSS with the 6.000 verses is too obvious to be overlooked. Perhaps we have to see in this an attempt to establish the authority of a later text, *in casu* the ṢaṭSS, at the cost of the original text, the KmT.

43: The Lords of the Pīṭhas and their distribution over the body of Devī are explained in the next chapter (cf. *śloka* 28 Notes). The reading of BC, 'the Lords of the Pīṭhas [and] the Devīs', is also possible since in the next chapter both male and female deities are enumerated in connection with the different parts of the human body. The reading of BC could be meant by MS A also, when one does not regard the form *devyāḥ* as the gen. sg. of *devī*, but as the nom. pl. of *devyā*, which is perfectly acceptable. One might even prefer the latter interpretation of the *pādas* 43ab because of the more regular distinction between the two *pādas* at the caesura.

45-47: In these three *ślokas* there are enumerated sixteen different ways in which the teachings of Kubjikā are possibly veiled or handed down in a disguised form. Consequently, by recognizing a particular method used for obscuring the true teachings it becomes possible for the adept to learn the teachings of Kubjikā from texts which appear at first sight to teach something else. The teachings of Kubjikā are the only Truth, in what form soever stated (cf. *śloka* 38). The exact meaning of the sixteen is not always clear. 1) The Rudras refer to the Śabdarāśi-order of the alphabet, i.e. the fifty *akṣaras* from *a* to *kṣa* each identified with a particular Rudra or Bhairava (cf. Appendix II), 2) the 'essence of Mālinī' refers to the Mālinī-order of the alphabet, i.e. the fifty *akṣaras* from *na* to *pha* each identified with a particular manifestation of Mālinī/Devī (cf. Appendix II), 3) & 4) both ambiguous and inverted order of speech may lead to true knowledge, at least when it is recognized as such, 5) although in a veiled form, the teaching of Kubjikā is present in all other Tantras since it is the Ultimate Truth; it is only in the Kubjikāmata Tantra, the Ṣaṭsāhasra Saṃhitā and other texts of the same school, that the teachings of Kubjikā are openly revealed, 6) 'words' (45d *padaiḥ*); in comparison with the others *pada* seems to be somewhat insignificant and vague. For this reason I have connected it with the preceding *anyatantrāvatārais*. By doing so, however, the number sixteen may be obtained by reading in *pāda* 45a 'by means of Mālinī, by means of the Tattvas'. The Tattvas refer then to 'essences' which constitute the human body, 7) The 'Lion's Look' might refer to a particular way of going through a text: proceeding onwards in the teachings but at the same time keeping in mind what has been learned earlier and connecting it with the newly learned things, 8) repetitions, 9) the 'Frog-leap' is a grammatical term meaning 'the skipping of several *sūtras* and supplying from a previous *sūtra*' (the usual name is *maṇḍūkapluti*). Note that the caesura is neglected, a feature not frequently found in our text. One is tempted to assume that the author has deliberately done so, having in mind the literal meaning of the compound ('the frog leaps over [the caesura]'), 10) the 'combining of the Pīṭhas' is puzzling. Perhaps the various texts belonging to the different Pīṭhas are meant. Since the traditional Pīṭhas form a whole as the different parts of Devī's body, the texts belonging to these Pīṭhas might also constitute a unity representing the body of Devī, 11) the 'Lotus-vajras beginning with the Four' refer to the Aṣṭāviṃśatikrama (cf. 1,1); it is not clear, however, why they are referred to as 'lotus-vajras' here, 12) the Mātṛkās are a designation for the sixteen vowels; *ādi* ('etc.') refers to the consonants, 13-16) the 'fourfold lineage of Kubjī' refers perhaps to the sons and daughters of the Goddess in the four Mahāpīṭhas (cf. *paṭala* 4/5).

This effort to account for each of the sixteen ways by which the teachings of Kubjikā could be learned is only an attempt and far from perfect. All three manuscripts agree with each other on the text in essentials. One might assume that the list is traditional within the school, but so far I have not been able to trace a similar enumeration in other texts of the school nor in texts outside it.

48: For *sabāhyābhyantare* see 1,12; 13. Perhaps the expression *anekopāyabhedataḥ* (1,12d) refers to the sixteenfold division of Reality (47d *bhāva*), as we find it in the *ślokas* 45-47ab. In *pāda* 48b the reading of BC (*sa vettā*) has been followed. The reading of A, *sacetā*, is perhaps a shortening of *sacetasā* which would result in a *pāda* of nine syllables, however.

49: It is not clear why only 'three and a half crore' of people (49a) will enter the Hellish Sea in the Kali Yuga. Perhaps there is a relation with the number of *ślokas* of the KmT (see above). The Hellish Sea (49b *narakārṇava*) refers to the Kali Yuga, and the Saṃsāra.

50-57: In these *ślokas* we find a strong opposition against those initiations which are merely ritual performances and have little or no import at all (cf. *śloka* 40a). In the Kali Yuga initiations are still performed, but they have been reduced to an obsequious performing of the prescribed rules. Consequently, even fools can perform an initiation, as long as they know how to perform the ritual. The people of the Kali Yuga, however, still value these 'empty' initiations, because they are completely blinded by the more or less spectacular phenomena which occur at initiations (shaking, flying through the air etc.). These phenomena are regarded as sufficient proof for the validity of an initiation. Although ritual actions (*anuṣṭhāna*) form part of the initiation, one should be well aware of their theoretical implications and values (*guṇa*). It is not sufficient to know only the proper rules for the performance of an initiation (*vidhāna*) in order to acquire real authority (*bṛhattvatā*) or become superior (*jyeṣṭha*). True insight (*jñāna*) is only acquired by profound knowledge of the basic nature of the ritual action. The value of an initiation does not depend on the ritual nor on the person who performs it, but the main reason for its validity lies in the actual contents of the instruction. Therefore teachers who derive their superiority or authority only from their being initiated (*dīkṣājyeṣṭha*) should be inferior to those teachers who derive their authority from true knowledge of the theoretical implications (*guṇajyeṣṭha*).

58: The text of *śloka* 58 seems to be corrupt, but its contents are sufficiently clear. Apparently in the Kali Yuga people speek different languages (58a), which leads to mutual misunderstanding. The idea is perhaps that of a Babel of tongues. In *pāda* 58d *varṇa* means possibly 'syllable' or 'letter'. It refers to the fact that in the Kali Yuga the letters or the texts are not understood in the proper way. With 'letters' possibly *bījas* might be meant.

59: We have seen in *śloka* 48d that in the Kali Yuga people have fallen from the Kula-teachings (*kulacyuta*). The same applies to the tradition (*krama*) itself of the Kula School: people set value on outward things only. In *pāda* 59b Devī has the epithet *krameśvarī*, 'Lady of the Tradition'. In most of the instances the epithets given to Devī do not appear to have any specific function (Bhāminī, Varārohā, Priyā etc.), but here the epithet *krameśvarī* is very functional indeed.

60: The word *guṇa* should be understood here as 'theoretical implication and value' (cf. *ślokas* 50-57 Notes).

61: The *pādas* 61cd refer to the fact that in the Kali Yuga people are blinded by outward phenomena such as flying through the air etc. (cf. *śloka* 51ab). The same applies obviously to the performers of such acts. In our translation the words *vidyābala* and *anuṣṭhāna* have been regarded as two independent nouns. It is also possible to understand the compound *vidyābala* as an adjective to *anuṣṭhāna*: 'they are blinded by their ritualistic performances, the power of which lies in [pure] magic'.

62: Goldsmiths and blacksmiths (cf. Ruben 1939) are looked upon with awe; their forges are situated at the fringe of the village. Kāṇḍāra is the designation for the member of a certain kind of mixed caste. The occupation of its members is not known to me. Possibly they are reed-cutters (cf. *kāṇḍa*, 'reed; cane'). People who earn their livelihood with skins are flayers; those who earn their livelihood on the stage are, of course, actors. Both groups do not rank high in Indian society. The people mentioned in *śloka* 62cd have in common that they all have a rather low social status in society. Goldsmiths and blacksmiths may also have a magical function (cf. the Pasěks in modern Bali).

64: For Samaya see *śloka* 12 Notes.

67: It requires no great wisdom to tell the present, and it is difficult to check any prediction of the future. Yet, teachers who tell these things are regarded as trustworthy guides by the blinded people of the Kali Yuga. The contents of the *pādas* 67cd are uncertain. The meaning is probably that initiation is performed by teachers who know the contents of the sacred texts only from the hearsay of others — they did not really study the contents —, and who look upon their pupils with glances which seem full of wisdom, but which are actually destitute of any real wisdom.

68: I do not understand why true insight is ignored twice (68a *dvibhis*) by the foolish teachers. Perhaps it denotes a strong affirmation.

69-70: The idea which is expressed in the *ślokas* 69cd & 70ab, is that in the Kali Yuga old-established values are lost. Before the Kali Yuga the whole world was neatly defined or arranged by 'bolts' (*argala*) or concepts based on descent (*jāti*), appearance (*ākṛti*), wealth (*dhana*) and mutual understanding (*saṃjñā*). In the present Kali Yuga, however, all this is left, and is everything ruled by illusion (*māyā*). The whole world is turned topsy-turvy (cf. 73 ff.). More or less the same picture is described in the Bhagavadgītā (1,40 ff.). Note that *pāda* 69c has nine syllables.

72: In *pāda* 72b 'fractionally' (*vyasta*) refers to the fact that every other Tantra is believed to contain at least some part of the Kula-doctrine. In the *pādas* 72cd the words *kaule* and *yāgaṃ* are not incorrect, but one wonders why *kaule* instead of *kule* is used and for what reason the Śrīmata is called a 'ritual' (*yāga*). It is very tempting to read instead *kalau yuge*, 'in the Kali Yuga', although one ignores the caesura in that case.

75: The Mīmāṃsābhāsya (75a) is best known as the oldest existing commentary on the Mīmāṃsasūtra, by Śabarasvāmin. Otherwise, one might assume that the expression *mīmāṃsābhāṣya* refers in a more general way to the mode of arguing of the Mīmāṃsakas. It follows, however, that at the time of compilation of the ṢaṭSS the doctrine of the Mimāṃsakas had gained considerable influence — and so much influence that the author of the ṢaṭSS judged it appropriate to warn against it. In other places of the ṢaṭSS the followers of the Mīmāṃsa-doctrine are likewise condemned: in the 17th chapter, for instance, one is earnestly warned to avoid the company of the Mīmāṃsakas (*varjayet ... mīmāṃsakāṃs tathā*). Contrary to the Mīmāṃsakas, the author of the ṢaṭSS seems to be in favour of the Kāpālikas and the Kālavaktras, who 'are forced to embrace another doctrine' (by misguided public opinion?). The Kālavaktras are most probably identical with the Kālamukhas, who in their turn are closely related to the Kāpālikas (cf. Lorenzen 1972: *passim*).

76: In the *pādas* 76ab probably people are meant, who stick to the old texts and doctrines which are no longer understood in the Kali Yuga, and are therefore accused by the ignorant people of performing obsolete and immoral practices. The same may apply to the Yogins who are 'steadfast in their scriptures': because the blind and foolish people of the Kali Yuga do not understand the true doctrines any longer, the Yogins who perform rituals according to these texts are believed to do improper things.

77: The Digambaras ('sky-clothed') most probably refers to one of the two types of Jain ascetics, i.e. to those who go around naked. Because of this nakedness they are easily mistaken for Śaiva ascetics by the blinded people of the Kali Yuga. *Viprajana* (77d) refers to the Brahmins, the upholders of the orthodox religion (cf. *śloka* 74) against the (Tantric) Śaiva ascetics.

78: The third phase in the life of an orthodox Hindu consists of leaving his family and homestead, and taking up the life in the forest (*vānaprastha*; cf. Sprockhoff 1979). In the Kali Yuga the misled *vānaprasthas* return to their families again, where only slavery awaits them (78b). The reason for this slavery is the following: one can only leave one's family and take up a life in the forest, when a son is left behind to take care of the family. When the *vānaprastha* returns to his family, he is likely to become submissive to the son he left earlier in charge of the family.

In *pāda* 78c the term *maga* refers to the Magas or Śākadvīpa-Brahmins, who worshipped the Sun (Gonda 1963: 63; Pandey 1971: *s.v.*).

79: In *pāda* 79a the reading of BC seems to be the most acceptable. The compound *māṭhāpatya* should refer to the position/function of the head of a Maṭh, who is usually called *maṭhādhipati* or *maṭhapati*. The derivation *māṭhāpatya* from *maṭhapati* is perfectly understandable, although not quite correct.

80: The Brahmins of the Kali Yuga are depicted as selling *rasavedāgni* (80b). They obviously sell their knowledge of the Vedas and their sacrificial fires (sc. the performances of oblations by them) for good money. Next to these two, sell they also *rasa*. We have translated *rasa* intentionally with 'philtre', which seems to indicate the state of debauchery the Brahmins have reached in the Kali Yuga better, than the translation 'spirituous liquor' for *rasa*. Moreover, for the Tantrics liqour is not despicable at all. Theoretically one might consider another translation of the compound, in which *rasa* denotes the number six: 'Brahmins selling the six Vedas and Agni'. Five Vedas are accepted, viz. the traditional four Vedas plus the Purāṇas as the fifth Veda. When Brahmins succeed in selling six Vedas in the Kali Yuga, this fact clearly bears testimony of the cunning on the part of the Brahmins and the utmost stupidity of the prospective buyers. Yet, I do not think this latter translation is meant by the author of the ṢaṭSS, especially since compounds as *rasavikraya* and *rasavikrayin* are attested for, in which *rasa* means 'philtre' or 'love-potion'.

The exact grammatical construction of *pādas* 80cd is not clear, although the intended meaning is obvious: in the Kali Yuga children have no respect for their parents. Perhaps one should emend *mātā pitā ca* (80c) to *mātāpitarau* or *mātāpitarā* (archaic dual).

81: In the Kali Yuga the teachers of the Kula-tradition do not worship any longer the Ancestors (*pitṛ*), the Gods (*deva*) and Agni. As in *śloka* 16a (*gurudevāgni-*) *agni* denotes here the sacrificial fires.

83: Ashes and matted locks (83c) are the most striking outward characteristics of ascetics, Sādhus and the like. The 'characteristics', however, can also easily be adopted by imposters. The same applies to nakedness (83d). It is, of course, possible here to see a reference to the Jain Digambaras who were mentioned in *śloka* 77c, but a more general application of the term seems likely, since Śaiva ascetics also used to go around scarcely clothed.

84: It does not take much trouble for an imposter to learn a number of *mudrās* in order to impress his audience, nor would it take great pains for him to walk around with a skull (*kapāla*), in which way he is easily mistaken for a real Kāpālika, for instance. Religious mendicants often possess a single or triple staff (84b).

In *pāda* 84c *daṃbha* ('hypocrisy') and *kauṭilya* ('dishonesty') are abstract nouns, whereas *pāṣaṇḍa* means 'heretical' or 'an heretic'. In view of the first two members of the compound, however, *pāṣaṇḍa* has been translated as an abstract nouns also ('heresy').

85: According to the *pādas* 85ab in the Kali Yuga people rob the gurus and the gods of their possessions. The possessions of the gods (*devadravya*) are probably the temple treasures. Note that the verb *gamiṣyanti* is connected both with an acc. (85a) and with a loc. (85b).

86: In *pāda* 86b the use of *mudritaṃ*, 'marked; impressed', is significant in this context. We saw earlier (69cd; 70ab) that in the Kali Yuga the whole world was no longer defined (*mudrita*) by descent etc.; lawlessness prevailed. In order to restore the situation in which everybody knows his place, the Śrīmata is told by Bhairava (cf. 72c).

87: For *pādas* 87ab see *śloka* 76.

89: For *pādas* 89ab see 2,45ab. In *pāda* 89c *idaṃ ratnaṃ* refers, of course, to the Śrīmata.

90: *Krīḍā* (90b) may refer to the ritual copulation which constitutes a basic part in the ritual (cf. 106a *cakrakrīḍā*), representing the union of Śiva and His Śakti.

Obviously, to people who consider this part of the ritual as mere debauchery or partake in it only for sensual pleasure, the Śrīmata should not be told. For Samaya (90b) see *śloka* 12 Notes. With *siddhanātha* (90c) a true teacher of the Kula-tradition is evidently meant.

91: For *rikṣe* (91c) see *śloka* 18 Notes.

93: In *pāda* 93d the word *yoginyaś* should be an acc. pl. in this context. The acc. pl. of *yoginī* is, however, *yoginīs*, which we find in exactly the same *pāda* of *śloka* 98d. It is not clear why A reads here *yoginyaś*, while it has the correct form in 98d together with BC. The reading of BC for *pāda* 93d (*yoginyau*, 'two Yoginīs') is not very likely. There is no indication at all that only two Yoginīs are present at the ritual. Probably *yoginyaś* is incorrect for *yoginyāś*, the acc. pl. of *yoginyā*. For Yoginī and Kumārikā see *śloka* 24 Notes.

94: Samayins, Sādhakas and Putras are probably three kinds of teachers or adepts, who were initiated by different *dīkṣās*. For Putra see KmT 2, *daṇḍaka*. A Mātaṅga belongs to the lowest level in Indian society, and can be compared with a Caṇḍāla. It is an accepted fact that people of low birth play a significant part in Tantric religion, or at least are entitled to receive instruction in the Tantric teachings (cf. 88b). A Mātaṅga fits nicely in this pattern of course, but in our text he appears to occupy a rather special position. We have already seen (2,5) that the first Saṃvartāmaṇḍala is located in the abode of Mātaṅga (*mātaṅgapadamadhyaga*) above the Brahmarandhra, and that it is equalized with the Khecarī Cakra (cf. 2,5 Notes). Furthermore, besides the four traditional Mahāpīṭhas (Oḍiyāna, Jālandhara, Pūrṇagiri and Kāmarūpa) our text recognizes a fifth Mahāpīṭha, the Mātaṅga Pīṭha, which is incorporated in all the four other Mahāpīṭhas (cf. 4/5,22). The author of the ṢaṭSS has probably deliberately put the Mātaṅga on a par with the Twice-born, i.e. the Brahmins: two classes of people between whom normally quite a difference of position exists. He does so in order to indicate that for him no difference between the very low Mātaṅga and the very high Brahmin really exists. It only matters whether they have authority or not. As if expecting or perhaps even provoking the following question by Devī, He adds that 'no transgression is committed by that' (95b).

96: Devī, of course, takes up the lead offered to Her by Bhairava, and asks Him to account for this seeming contradiction. In *pādas* 96cd *jyeṣtha* and *guṇa* refer to the Brahmin, while *kanyasa* and *nirguṇa* refer to the Mātaṅga. The form *guṇasya* (96d) is noteworthy. One would rather expect *saguṇasya* or *suguṇasya*, which is impossible, however, since it would result in a *pāda* of nine syllables. Thus *guṇa* should be regarded here as an adjective rather than a substantive.

97: In only two *pādas* (97bc) Bhairava solves the dilemma of Devī: one should not judge anyone on his status or rank, but look at his actual doings (sc. in religious practices).

99: The word *maṇḍala* (99b) does not refer to a mystic drawing which was already made in the initial phase of the ritual (cf. 22 ff.), but here has its basic meaning 'circle' (cf. *śloka* 100c where the word *cakra* is used instead). The teacher thus invites the Yoginīs and the Kumārikās to form a circle. Although not explicitly stated here, one might assume that the circle also includes male attendants, an assumption to which *śloka* 101b seems to point.

100: The cups which are raised (100d), probably contain liquor (*ali*), which is available on the ritual ground (cf. 92d).

101: The teacher lights the lamos which were placed on the four corners of the square (cf. 20d ff.).

102: For *pāda* 102a see *śloka* 26cd ff.

103-104: In a very concise way the teacher here explains the three phases of the creation, only mentioning the name of each phase and its location with regard to the human body. Thus *para* ('beyond') is in the Dvādaśānta, or rather at the 'End of the Twelve'; *sūkṣma* ('subtle') is in the Brahmarandhra; *sthūla* ('gross') is situated below the Brahmarandhra, i.e. on the human body. The third phase, *sthūla*, is further defined with *catuṣkādīni maṇḍale* (104b), which refers to the Aṣṭāviṃsatikrama (cf. 1,1 Notes) and to the Saṃvartāmaṇḍala. In the 28th chapter of the ṢaṭSS this threefold division of the creation is explained in greater detail. Moreover, a fourth phase is mentioned, *parāpara*, which, however, has no direct relation with creation as such, and is therefore omitted here. For a concise survey of the four phases of creation as described in the 28th chapter of the ṢaṭSS the following table has been drawn up:

I] parāpara	Parama Śiva	
II] para	Para Śiva & Parā Śakti	
	1) Unmanā	
	2) Samanā	
	3) Vyāpinī	
	4) Śakti	
	5) Nādānta	
III] sūkṣma	6) Nāda	
	7) Nirodhikā	
	8) Ardhacandra	
	9) Bindu	
	10) MA	
	11) U	
	12) A	(cf. Padoux 1975, table after page 346).
IV] sthūla	The fifty letters of the alphabet (*a-kṣa*), and Śiva & Śakti.	

In *pāda* 104c *pūrvaṃ* refers to *śloka* 28 ff.

105: *Vācayitvā* (105a) should be supplied with *pustakam* (cf. 29d). As becomes clear from the following lines, the text is recited by the teacher in parts to the pupil until the complete text is recited and at the same time noted down by the pupil (cf. 107cd). Keeping in mind the actual size of the ṢaṭSS, viz. 6000 *ślokas*, one can easily imagine that it takes several days before the complete text has been recited and noted down. On the first day of recitation the teacher reads the text as far as the Saṃvartāmaṇḍala (105b), by which probably the five introductory verses are meant (1,1-5). In *śloka* 30; 31ab we saw perhaps also a reference to this part of the text to be recited on the first day of the ritual. This first day is referred to by *kramasṛṣṭidine* (105c). It indicates that on this day the *krama* starts — again — because of the recitation of the text, expecially its introductory stanzas.

After the recitation of this first part of the text the teacher should celebrate a *mahotsava*, 'great festival' or 'great rejoycing' (105d). Gonda has made it acceptable that the basic meaning of *utsava* is 'the generating; stimulating; producing' (Gonda 1947: 151), which corresponds nicely to the designation of this first day as *kramasṛṣṭi-dina*, 'the day on which the tradition is emanated'. The character of this *mahotsava* is not explicitly stated here, but it should perhaps be connected with *cakrakrīḍā* in the next *śloka*.

106-108: The term *cakrakrīḍā* (106a) means literaly 'sporting with/of the circle'. With 'circle' the participants of the ritual are meant (cf. 100c; 99b *maṇḍala*), and *krīḍā* was mentioned in *pāda* 99b where it was stated that the Śrīmata may be told to a teacher of the Kula-doctrine (*kulācārya*) who understands the meaning of *krīḍā* (*krīḍājña*). The expression *krīḍā* perhaps denotes 'amorous sport' which precedes the actual ritual copulation. Together with the *bali*-ritual at night (107b) *cakrakrīḍā* constitutes the Mahotsava (105d). Thus the ritual on the first day consists of recitation of the Saṃvartāmaṇḍala (cf. 105 Notes) followed by the celebration of the Mahotsava which includes *cakrakrīḍā* for the rest of the day and the *bali*-ritual at night. This procedure is to be continued day after day (108d) until the complete text of the ṢaṭSS has been recited by the teacher and noted down by the pupil (107cd). It is imperative that this course of action is strictly followed on each day otherwise there may occur a 'disappointing event' (*anartha*) amidst the assembly of the Yoginīs (108ab). This remark probably contains a warning for the participants in the ritual: they should not give themselves over to the celebration of the Mahotsava too enthusiastically, because due to the extensiveness of the text (108b *mahatā*) they are liable to become exhausted during the course of the ritual. In other words: they should not spend their physical powers during the Mahotsava too freely, because at the end they may not be capable to perform the Mahotsava anymore.

109: The meaning of the expression *yoginīgarbha* (109d lit. 'the womb of the Yoginīs') is enigmatic. Possibly it refers to the Yoginīs as 'spiritual mothers', or as representatives of the 'spiritual motherhood of the Kula-doctrine' (cf. 110ab).

110: The 'Mother of Koṅkaṇa' (110b *koṅkaṇāṃbikā*) is born from the *yoginīgarbha* (110a). Why especially Koṅkaṇāṃbikā is mentioned in this context is not clear to me. The region of Koṅkaṇa and its local goddess, however, appear to be important to the doctrine of the Śrīmata (cf. Schoterman 1977: 934). In *pāda* 110d the teacher is defined as one 'who dreads the ocean of the Saṃsāra', i.e. the cycle of re-birth (cf. 49b). In other words: he is anxious to get out of this cycle, and in order to succeed in this he necessarily should be a true teacher of the Kula-doctrine.

111: On every day of the recitation a *pūjā* should be performed three times: at the beginning, in the middle and at the end. Probably the three *pūjās* coincide with the three Sandhyās (dawn, noon, evening).

112: In *śloka* 112 we find a reference to the Pūrvāmnāyin, the follower of the Eastern Tradition. For him the recitation of the Puruṣa appears to be of crucial importance. We have seen in *śloka* 32c that the Puruṣa was the characteristic of a text called Haṃsabheda. It follows then that this Haṃsabheda text was important for the Pūrvāmnāyins. The teachers of the Eastern Tradition are not considered to be inferior to those of the Śrīmata (*śloka* 32d). Possibly the Pūrvāmnāyins follow the same ritual as the teachers of the Kula-doctrine, but precede the ritual by reciting(?) the Puruṣa-hymn (112a *pūrvaṃ*). We have assumed that the Puruṣa of the Haṃsabheda may be identical with the well-known Puruṣa-hymn in the Ṛgveda (10,90). In stanzas 12 and 13 of this Puruṣa-hymn there are eight deities enumerated in relation with a particular part of the human body, but in the next stanza another four are mentioned. In this way the total number of deities in the Puruṣa-hymn becomes twelve, whereas in *pāda* 112d the number eight is given. Assuming that with the Puruṣa of the Haṃsabheda the Vedic Puruṣa-hymn is meant, it would follow that the 14th stanza of the hymn is not included.

133: In the final *śloka* of the third chapter it appears that Bhairava again strongly fulminates against those teachers who initiate only by sprinkling water over the heads of their pupils (cf. 50 ff.).

PAṬALA 4/5

PAṬALA 4/5

śrībhairava[1] uvāca ||
1 pūrvaṃ[2] saṃsūcitaṃ devi pīṭhavyāptiḥ[3] śarīragā |
tāṃ ca te[4] kathayiṣyāmi akathyā[5] bhaktivarjite ||
2 pūrvaṃ[6] devasya devyāś ca saṃvāde ca parasparam |
saṃvāde niścaye jāte saṃbandhe[7] guruśiṣyayoḥ ||
3 tasmin kāle idaṃ vākyam ato[8] vadati[9] niścayam[10] |
gaccha tvaṃ bhārate varṣe adhikārāya sarvataḥ ||
4 pīṭhopapīṭhakṣetreṣu kuru sṛṣṭim[11] anekadhā |
pratiṣṭhayed yadā kāle putrāḥ[12] putryāś[13] ca pālakāḥ ||
5 ekatra militānāṃ ca catustriṃśacchataṃ[14] bhuvi |
etat kṛte tu me tubhyaṃ saṃgamo[15] 'tra[15] bhaviṣyati[15] ||
6 śatakoṭipravistīrṇaṃ[16] yāsyantīdaṃ[17] kulaṃ punaḥ |
gaccha tvaṃ bhārate varṣe kuru sṛṣṭiṃ[18] tvam īdṛśam[18] ||
7 pañca[19] devāś[20] ca pañcaiva yoginyaḥ[21] pīṭhapañcakam |
ekaikasya parīvāraṃ[22] kathayāmi samāsataḥ ||
8 vasvaṣṭavatsarārdhaṃ[23] tu ādipīṭhe parigrahaḥ[24] |
dikkāṣṭhā[25] ṛtavaś[26] caiva dvitīyasyāntagaṃ tv imam ||
9 māsārkās tu rasās[27] tristhe agnīndutridharāḥ[28] svarāḥ |
parivāraś[29] caturthasya grahā nandās tu pañcakam ||
10 pañcamasya idaṃ[30] devi parivāram udīritam[31] |
etāni bhārate varṣe yāvat pīṭhāny[32] asthāpyate[32] ||
11 tāvan na me tvayā sārdhaṃ saṃgamaṃ[33] ca[33] prajāyate |
deśāṃ[34] gatās[34] tu[34] deveśi[34] meror[35] vāmaṃ ca dakṣiṇam ||
12 yatra ulaṃbikā nāma tiṣṭhate vanapallikā[36] |
raktāṃbaradharā devī raktasthā ratilālasā ||
13 tatra sā gahvarāntasthā guhā[37] gahanavāsinī |
yāvat saṃtiṣṭhate kālaṃ tāvad[38] yogimayaṃ[39] khilam ||
14 tais tu saṃtoṣitā devī[40] nayopāyair[41] anekadhā |

---

1. A -bhairav 2. A pūrva 3. A -vyāpti 4. omitted in BC; A ti 5. BC akathyāṃ 6. A pūrva 7. B sabandhe 8. BC devo 9. A vaditi 10. BC niścitam 11. A sṛṣṭir 12. B putrā; C putra; A putrān 13. BC pautrāś 14. A catutriṃśatśataṃ; BC catustriṃśaśataṃ 15. A sa ca gotraga eṣyati; B saṃgamo 'tra bhaviṣyanti 16. A -stīrṇe 17. BC yāsyatedaṃ 18. A sṛṣṭi ... īdṛśaḥ 19. BC evaṃ 20. A vedāś; BC siddhāś 21. A yoginaḥ 22. A parīvarāt 23. A vasvaṣṭaṃ 24. BC -graham 25. C -kāṣṭhāḥ 26. B satavaś; C ( )tavaś; A dhatavaś 27. A rasā 28. A -dharā 29. A -varā 30. BC imaṃ 31. A -taḥ 32. BC pīṭhān na sthāpyate 33. BC saṃgamas tu 34. B devā deśāṃ gatā devi; C devā deśaṃ gatā devi 35. A meru 36. A -palikāṃḥ 37. C guhāṃ 38. A (tāvad) 39. A (yo)gi-; BC -mayā 40. A devi 41: A tayopāyair

Śrībhairava spoke:

1 Formerly, O Devī, I have explained the inherence of the Pīṭhas with the human body. This I will tell You [again, but more in detail]; it should not be told to someone without [true] devotion.

2 Formerly on occasion of a conversation between both Deva and Devī, when the conversation became decisive with regard to the relation between teacher and pupil,

3 on that moment [Deva] emphatically said [to Devī] the following words: "Go to Bhārata Varṣa [to establish] the authority [of the doctrine] everywhere;

4 in Pīṭhas, Upapīṭhas and Kṣetras create offspring in a manifold way. When [Your offspring] is completed, You will have sons, daughters and guardians:

5 of all of them together the number will be 134 on earth. When this is accomplished, there will be an union between You and Me here [again];

6 on their side they will form a community on earth encompassing millions of people. Go to Bhārata Varṣa, and create such an offspring!".

7 There are five Devas and also five Yoginīs, and a number of five Pīṭhas. I will tell You Your retinue in each of them briefly.

8 In the first Pīṭha Your retinue consists of respectively eight, eight and six; respectively ten, ten and six is this complete [retinue] in the second [Pīṭha];

9 respectively twelve, twelve and six in the third [Pīṭha]; thirteen, thirteen and seven respectively is Your retinue in the fourth [Pīṭha]; respectively nine, nine and five

10 is Your retinue in the fifth [Pīṭha], O Devī, mentioned. As long as these Pīṭhas are not established [by You] in Bhārata Varṣa,

11 no union takes place between You and Me. She has gone, O Deveśī, to [different] lands. North and South of the Meru [She went next].

12 Where there is a small village in the forests named Ulaṃbikā, and a goddess dressed in red, standing in [a pool] of blood, delighting in amorous enjoyment,

13 there She took Her abode in a cave, dwelling secretly in the abyss. As long as She stayed there, the whole place was filled with Yogins.

14 The goddess was pleased by these in every aspect, in many ways. Then

tataḥ prasannagaṃbhīram uvācedaṃ kujeśvarī[42] ||
15 anekopāyaracanā vivekaguṇaśālinī |
ramate tatra suśroṇi pañcāśārṇamayā[43] tanuḥ ||
16 sūkṣmādiśabdasaṃghasya[44] uḍḍitā[45] tiṣṭhate sadā |
uḍḍitā[46] yena uḍḍīśe[47] teṇedam uḍḍiyānakam[48] ||
17 śabdasaṃghasya viśrāmaṃ vinā tena śrutir na hi |
bhaviṣyanti purāvasthā|aṣṭau koṭiguṇāśrayāḥ ||
18 āgatya khecarīcakrād ādhārīśaḥ prabhus tava[49] |
aṣṭau te mānasāḥ putrā bhaviṣyanti ca ṣaḍguṇāḥ ||
19 śākinyaṣṭakamātā[50] tvam aṣṭau siṃhāsanādhipāḥ |
tattvādhāragatā[51] śaktiḥ kathitā dehagā śṛṇu ||
20 śrotukāmā tu[52] oḍḍākhye[53] vaktukāmā tu jālake[54] |
puṣṭyārthe[55] caiva pūrṇākhye[56] kāmākhye cekṣaṇecchayā[57] ||
21 ebhiḥ sthānaiḥ sthitā devī pīṭhāṃś[58] ca[59] svaguṇojjvalān |
mūkāndhabadhirāḥ klībāḥ sattvā jāyanti tair vinā ||
22 pañcamaṃ yan mahāpīṭhaṃ pīṭhe pīṭhe vyavasthitam |
aspṛśyaṃ[60] tam adraṣṭavyaṃ[61] mātaṅgavanam āśritam ||
23 agamyaṃ ca gamaṃ[62] nityam abhakṣaṃ[63] bhakṣaṇe[64] ratam[65] |
yena kāryena cāmnāyaṃ śarīre pūjayanti ca ||
24 bhuktimuktipradās teṣām anyaśāstrāntakārakāḥ[66] |
kāṭhinyoṣṇadravaṃ[67] śīghraṃ[68] chidraṃ caiva kalevaram[69] ||
25 teṣāṃ bhāvā ime jñeyā ojāpūkais tu pīṭhajaiḥ[70] |
teṣāṃ sthānāni vakṣyāmi ye yatraiva vyavasthitāḥ ||
26 oḍra[71] ādhāravyāptis[71] tu sthānāni kathayāmy aham |
kṛttisthāneṣu[72] rudrāṇī[72] rudraśākī[73] tu mūrdhaje ||
27 pāṇyaṅghryoś[74] caiva govaktrā sumukhī smaśrunāmake[75] |
vānarī[76] tu dvijāvāse[77] kekarā[78] asthijāpure ||
28 kālarātris tu snāyuni bhaṭṭikā[79] sthairyakāpure |
māndhātā[80] romapīṭhe ca ādhārīśo vyavasthitaḥ ||
29 yas tu ādhārabhūtas tu sthāvare jaṅgame sthitaḥ[81] |
ādhārīśas tu sa[82] prokto[82] na tu kāṣṭhāsmamṛṇmayaḥ ||

---

42. A kuleśvaraḥ 43. B pañcāśa varṇamayā 44. A -saṃgasya 45. BC uḍḍito; A uḍratā 46. A uḍritā 47. A uḍrīśe 48. A uḍriyānakam 49. A tathā 50. BC sākiny-; A śāśinyaṣṭāmātā 51. BC tvaṃ tv ādhāragatā 52. BC tad 53. A oḍyākhye 54. A. jālaka(ḥ) 55. A puṣṭyākhye 56. A -khyaṃ 57. A cakṣa- 58. BC pīṭhāṃ; A pīṭhāś 59. BC sva 60. A apṛśaṃ 61. A adṛṣṭavyaṃ 62. BC gamen 63. BC abhakṣa 64. A bhakṣaṇi 65. A rataḥ 66. A -śāstrānti-; BC anyeṣāṃ bhrāntikārakāḥ 67. A kaṇṭhinyoṣṇadrava 68. A śīghraṃ 69. A -varaḥ 70. BC -jāḥ 71. BC oḍḍiānas tu 72. A hṛdi sthāne tu rudrāṇāṃ 73. A -sākī 74. A -ṅghriś 75. A -nāmike 76. A vāṇarī 77. BC dvyāvāme 78. A kiṅkarā 79. A bahikā 80. A māndāta 81. A sitaḥ 82. A saṃproktaṃ

Kujeśvarī said the following words with a distinct, low voice:

15 "[A Goddess] whose arrangement is in different ways, and who abounds in the qualities of true knowledge abides there, O Suśroṇī. Consisting of the fifty letters is Her body.

16 Constantly She is connected with the totality of speech, i.e. *sūkṣma* etc. Because She is connected [thus] in Uḍḍīśa, therefore this place here [will be known] as Uḍḍiyānaka".

17 It is the repose of the totality of speech: without it there is consequently no hearing. There will be the places of 'towns', the eight recipients of crores of qualities.

18 Coming from the Khecarīcakra, Ādhārīśa will become your lord. You will have eight sons in human shape, endowed with six qualities.

19 You will be the mother of the eight Śākinīs. Eight in number will be the Siṃhāsanādhipas.

You are the base of reality as Śakti; You are told to be in the human body: listen [to that].

20 When You desire to hear, You are in the place called Oḍḍa; when You desire to speak, You are in Jālaka; for thriving You are in the place called Pūrṇa; when You wish to see, You are in Kāmākhya.

21 With these places Devī is connected; [one should consider these] Pīṭhas as splendid by their own qualities. Without these [four Pīṭhas] people are mute, blind, deaf and impotent.

22 The fifth Pīṭha, that one is in each of the other [four] Pīṭhas: it can not be touched, nor seen; it is dependent on the Mātaṅgavana.

23 [Although] inaccessible, one has constantly access to it; [although] it stands for fasting, one enjoys eating there. By what [ever] sacred performance people honour the Āmnāya with regard to the body,

24 [these Pīṭhas] grant them enjoyment and liberation; to [the followers of] other Śāstras they cause destruction.

Firmness, heat, fluidity, motion and aperture — these constitute the human body.

25 The nature of these should be known by means of O JĀ Pū and KA, which originate from the [five] Pīṭhas. I will tell [You] their localities, and which [sons, daughters etc.] are stationed where.

26 Oḍra is inherent to the base; now I will tell [You] the localities [of Oḍra]. In the skin is Rudrāṇī; Rudraśākī is in the hair on the head;

27 Govaktrā is in the hands and feet; Sumukhī is in the [town] called 'beard'; Vānarī is in the place of the teeth; Kekarā is in the town of the bones;

28 Kālarātri is in the sinews, and Bhaṭṭikā is in the town of firmness. As Māndhātṛ Ādhārīśa is situated in the pores of the skin.

29 The one who constitutes a firm base in both the immovable and the moving, that one is called Ādhārīśa: such a one is not made of wood, stone or mud.

30 pañcāśad dhi yutā[83] ye ca sṛṣṭāḥ siṃhāsanādhipāḥ |
tais tu tan mālitaṃ sarvaṃ mālinyā-śaktisaṃyutam[84] ||
31 siṃhaśabdena sthānāni dehānte adhipās tu ye |
siṃhāsanādhipās te tu[85] mālinyādikramaiḥ[86] śritāḥ[86] ||
32 vāmano nāma nādinyā yugmaṃ caiva kamūrdhvajam[87] |
cūlīsiṃhāsanaṃ[88] sṛṣṭaṃ devyā vācakam ūrdhvajam[89] ||
33 harṣaṇaś[90] ca nivṛttyākhyā[91] siṃhavaktra[ḥ] pratiṣṭhikā[92] |
mahābalaś ca vidyākhyā[93] mahākālaś ca śānti ca ||
34 ete[94] bhālordhvagā[95] jñeyāś caturbhir muṇḍamālikā[96] |
ekavaktraś ca grasanī sthitāḥ[97] kāmaṭhamaṇḍale[98] ||
35 cakṣuryugme sthitāś[99] caiva bhairava[ḥ] priyadarśanī |
pracaṇḍo guhyaśaktiś ca nāsāyāṃ ca vyavasthitā[ḥ] ||
36 ādhārīśādhikāraṃ tu etaṃ te kathitaṃ mayā |
nirāśrayā[t] tṛtīyam[100] tu antahīnena maṇḍitam ||
37 antarikṣeṇa śobhāḍhyam ādhārīśārcanākṣaram[101] |
caturbhujo gaṇādhyakṣo[102] gajavaktro mahotkaṭaḥ[103] ||
38 airāvatyo[104] vināyakyaḥ ṣaḍ ete praticārakāḥ |
eteṣāṃ caiva saṃyogaḥ[105] purā prokto[106] 'pi yan mayā ||
39 ādipīṭhaparivāraṃ[107] kathitaṃ tu varānane ||
iti prathamapīṭhāvatāraḥ ||
śrībhairava[108] uvāca ||
40 etad dhy[109] anantare devi[110] karālaṃbaṃ[111] gatā punaḥ |
mahājvālālisaṃdīptaṃ[112] dīptānalasamaprabham ||
41 mahājvālāvalīḍhopaṃ[113]. devyās[114] tejo[114] mahādbhutam |
saumyaṃ cograsya[115] śabdasya tat sthānaṃ paramaṃ smṛtam ||
42 dhṛto[116] yena pratāpo 'syās tenedaṃ jālasaṃjñakaṁ |
māyājālaṃ[117] dhṛtaṃ yena pravaraṃ taṃ ca yoginām[118] ||
43 tena jālandharaṃ[119] nāma māyājālaniyāmakam[120] |
kiñcit kālasya paryāye[121] prabhūtakiraṇojjvalam[122] ||
44 vicitraracanānekā[123] pasyaty[124] agrendrajālakam[124] |
kasyaiṣā racanā divyā pūrvan nāsīd[125] ihādhvare[126] ||
45 mattejasāṃ prabhāvena tuṣṭā[127] na[127] tvaṃ[127] palāyitā[127] |
karālavadane tubhyaṃ māyājālaniyāmike[128] ||

83. B yutya 84. A -tāḥ 85. A stu 86. A -krame(r vṛtāḥ) 87. A -jāḥ 88. A mūla- 89. A -jāḥ 90. A haśaṇaś 91. B -khyau; C -khyo 92. A prati( ) 93. A divyākhyā 94. BC etair 95. A bālo- 96. A muṇḍi- 97. AB sthitā 98. BC kamalamaṇḍale 99. A (sthit)āś; BC sthitā 100. A tṛtīyā 101. BC -ekṣaram; A -kṣarāḥ 102. B gaṇāvyakṣo 103. BC balotkaṭaḥ 104. A erāvatyo 105. A saṃyugāḥ 106. A proktā 107. BC ādipīṭhe parīvāraṃ 108. A -bhairav 109. omitted in BC 110. B devī 111. C karālasvaṃ 112. A maho- 113. A maho- 114. A divyaṃ tejaṃ 115. A cāgrasya 116. B [ ]to; A dhṛta 117. A -jālā 118. A yoġināḥ 119. A jālāndharaṃ 120. A -niyāmakaḥ 121. A paryāyet 122. A -laḥ 123. A vivṛtiracanā- 124. A paryaṇtyā indrajāvat 125. A nāsrad 126. BC ivā- 127. A tuṣṭānāṃ tv apralāpitaḥ 128. C -niyāmake

30 The Siṃhāsanādhipas who are created together with the fifty, by them this whole [body] is garlanded and related to the Śaktis of Mālinī.
31 With the word '*siṃha*' the [various] locations [on the body are meant] the lords who are on the body, these then are the Siṃhāsanādhipas connected with the series of Mālinī etc.
32 The one called Vāmana forms a couple with Nādinī, which originates above Brahma; as the *siṃhāsana* of the crest it has been created above the mouth of Devī.
33 Harṣaṇa and the one called Nivṛtti, Siṃhavaktra and Pratiṣṭhikā, Mahābala and the one called Vidyā, Mahākāla and Śānti:
34 these are to be known above the forehead; by these four is constituted the garland of skulls. Ekavaktra and Grasanī are located on the head.
35 In the pair of eyes are located Bhairava and Priyadarśanī. Pracaṇḍa and Guhyaśakti are established on the nose.
36 Thus I have told You the sphere of influence of Ādhārīśa.
The third [letter] after the [letter] 'without support', adorned with [the letter] 'without end',
37 and brilliantly endowed with [the letter called] 'atmosphere' — that is the syllable for praising Ādhārīśa.
Caturbhuja, Gaṇādhyakṣa, Gajavaktra, Mahotkaṭa,
38 Airāvatya, and Vināyakya: these are the six servants. The relation between them [and their localities?] has previously been told by Me.
39 [Herewith] I have told [You] Your retinue in the first Pīṭha, O Varānanā.
Thus is the manifestation [of Devī] in the first Pīṭha.

Śrībhairava spoke:
40 Immediately hereafter, O Devī, She went on to Karālaṃba: [the place] was set on fire by the streams of mighty flames; it had the radiance of a blazing fire;
41 it appeared as to be touched by mighty flames! The *tejas* of Devī is indeed a great marvel! [Yet] it is [at the same time] cool: it is thought to be the place *par excellence* of the 'fierce word'.
42 Because Her brilliance is endured [there], [the place] is consequently called Jāla. Because the illusion of Māyā is controlled [here], it is [the place] for Yogins pre-eminently,
44 and is therefore called Jālandhara since it restrains the illusion of Māyā. After the expiration of some time [Devī], whose arrangement is in various wonderful ways, saw before Her an Indrajālaka flaming by intense beams. [Devī spoke:] "Who is responsible for this divine fabrication? Formerly it was not on this path.
45 By the might of My *tejas* you are [obviously] silenced; you have not been scared away. [Therefore] for you are [the epithets] 'Big Mouth' and 'Restrainer of Māyā's illusion'".

46 jālandharādhipatye[129] tvaṃ[130] bhaviṣyasy[131] acireṇa[131] tu |
āgatya khecarīcakrāc chrīsiddhakuṇḍalīyakaḥ[132] ||
47 aśeṣārthavido nāma sa[133] te[133] nātho bhaviṣyati |
bhaviṣyanti[134] karālinyo daśaiva duhitā[135] tava ||
48 bhaviṣyanty uttarānandā[136] daśa siṃhāsanādhipāḥ. |
praticārāś ca ṣaḍ bhadre evamādikrameṇa tu ||
49 uṣṇatve saṃsthitā mālā śivā ca dahanātmake[137] |
durgā ca pacanākhye tu pāvanī varṇagocare[138] ||
50 harṣaṇī sarvabhakṣāṅge[139] spṛṣṭāspṛṣṭeṣu[140] carcikā |
suprabhā ca dyutisthāne prabhā ca pratibhāpure ||
51 caṇḍā[141] caiva[141] prabhāvasyā[142] rugminī[143] jyotigahvare[144] |
anyaiś caiva[145] guṇaiḥ[145] samyak[145] kuṇḍalīśo vyavasthitaḥ ||
52 śakuniś[146] caiva cāmuṇḍā locane ca tṛtīyake |
sumato[147] vajriṇī cāsye[148] nando vai kaṅkaṭā tathā ||
53 gopālaḥ kālikā caiva dvibhir dantaiś[149] ca[149] cordhvagaiḥ[149] |
pitāmahaḥ śivā caiva pallavo ghoraghoṣikā ||
54 adhodantadvibhir[150] jñeyā[151] meghanirghoṣa khi[r]varā[152] |
bāhye[153] vinirgatair[153] daṃṣṭraiḥ[153] pañcakaṃ[154] ca[154] dvijā[n]take[155] ||
55 śikhivaktras tathā māyā jihvāsiṃhāsanasthitāḥ[156] |
mahādhvajaś ca vāgeśī vācāyāṃ[157] ca niyojitā[ḥ] ||
56 kālakūṭākhya[158] nāma[158] ca[158] śaktir nārāyaṇī sthitā |
suṣumṇāyāṃ ca vijñeyā niścayena mahātmane ||
57 jālandharādhipatye[159] te[159] kuṇḍalīśaparigrahe |
kuṇḍale[160] caturasre tu tryasre[161] caiva ṣaḍasrake ||
58 kuṇḍe[162] īśāgniyukto[162] yaḥ kuṇḍalīśaḥ sa ucyate |
yasyoddhārita[163] tasyādyaṃ[163] viṣamāṅgena[164] carcitam ||
59 vibhāgabhūṣitaṃ[165] kṛtvā bījaṃ vai kuṇḍalīyakam |
meghavarṇo[166] bṛhatkukṣir ekadaṃṣṭro gaṇeśvaraḥ ||
60 vighnarājo[167] mahānandaḥ[167] ṣaḍ ete putrakās tava[168] |
iti[169] dvitīyapīṭhasya kathito[170] nirṇayo mayā[171] ||
61 vyāptibhūto varārohe tāny[172] eṣāṃ[172] kulayoginām ||

---

129. A jālā- 130. A 'sau 131. A tvad bhaviṣya( )cinā 132. A -kāḥ 133. A so 'pi 134. BC bhaviṣyati 135. B duhitās; C duhitāḥ 136. A -nde 137. A duha- 138. BC vartma-; A -gocarī 139. A -bhakṣāṅgī 140. A sṛṣṭāsṛṣṭeṣu 141. A pracaṇḍa ca 142. C -veśyā; B -veśma 143. BC rukminī 144. BC jyotisaṃkare 145. A caryaguṇe 146. A śaṃkuniś 147. BC sumano 148. A cāsya 149. A pṛṣṭhe hy ada(ṃṣṭra)jau 150. A adhodaṃṣṭra- 151. A jñeyo 152. A kharparā 153. A bāhyavinirgate daṃṣṭrā 154. A pañcavaktra 155. A dvijāntare 156. A -siṃghāsani-; BC -sthitā 157. BC bhāṣāyāṃ 158. A kāla( )khya nāma ca; BC kālakūṭaś ca nāmano 159. A jālāndharāddipatyan te; BC -patye hy ete 160. A kuṇḍalaṃ 161. A (tryasre); BC tryaste 162. B kuṇḍe aiśāgni-; A kuṇḍalīyāgni- 163. A yasya rudhati tasyādya 164. A svaśamāṅgena 165. BC -sūcitaṃ 166. A (me)gha-; BC -varṇā 167. B vighnarā( )ḥ; C vighnarājo [ ]nandaḥ 168. A tathā 169. BC etad 170. A kathita 171. A mahat 172. A ( )ny eṣā

46 Soon you will become the ruler of Jālandhara. Coming from the Khecarī-cakra there will be Śrīsiddhakuṇḍalīyaka,
47 called Aśeṣārthavida: he will be your lord. You will have ten daughters, Karālinīs.
48 There will be ten Siṃhāsanādhipas of supreme bliss, and six servants, O Bhadrā; in this order [I will explain them]:
49 In the heat is Mālā; Śivā is in [the town] characterized by 'burning'; Durgā is in [the town] called 'cooking'; Pāvanī is in realm of colours;
50 Harṣaṇī is in that part [of the body] where everything is consumed; Carcikā is in [the town] which is both touched and not touched; Suprabhā is in the place of splendour; Prabhā is in the town of lustre;
51 Caṇḍā then dwells in brightness; Rugminī is in the cave of light. United with the other qualities stands Kuṇḍalīśa.
52 Śakuni and Cāmuṇḍā are located in the third eye; Sumata and Vajriṇī are in the mouth; Nanda and Kaṅkaṭā,
53 Gopāla and Kālikā are [associated] with the two [rows of] the upper-teeth; Pitāmaha and Śivā, Pallava and Ghoraghoṣikā
54 are to be known by the two [rows of] the lower-teeth; Meghanirghoṣa and Khirvarā are [associated] with the teeth which appear at the front: the five among the [other] teeth;
55 Śikhivaktra and Māyā are located in the *siṃhāsana* of the tongue; Mahādhvaja and Vāgeśī are connected with the voice;
56 the one called Kālakūṭa and his *śakti* Nārāyaṇī are known to be in the Suṣumṇā for sure, O Mahātmanā.
57 These are in the sovereignty of Jālandhara, in the retinue of Kuṇḍalīśa. The one who is in the circle, the square, the triangle and the hexagon, —
58 in the *kuṇḍa* associated with Īśa and Agni, that one is called Kuṇḍalīśa. The first [letter] after the one taken [previously] 'covered' with the [letter called] Viṣamāṅga,
59 and adorned with the [letter called] Vibhāga, that is the *bīja* of Kuṇḍalīśa. Meghavarṇa, Bṛhatkukṣi, Ekadaṃṣṭra, Gaṇeśvara,
60 Vighnarāja, and Mahānanda — these are Your six servants. Thus I have told the arrangement of the second Pīṭha
61 completely revealed, O Varārohā; these things are [only] for the Kula-yogins.

iti dvitīyapīṭhāvatāraḥ[173] ||
śrībhairava[174] uvāca ||
62 evam[175] uktvā maheśāni gatā sahyaṃ[176] mahāvanam |
saṃpūrṇamaṇḍalārcibhiḥ[177] pūrayantī jagattrayam ||
63 jagac charīram ity uktaṃ tālūrdhvasthā[178] tu yā[179] kalā[179] |
rudrādyantajagatsāraṃ[180] jīvitaṃ cāmṛtena tu ||
64 niḥśeṣa[ṃ][181] nikhilaṃ[182] viśvaṃ[182] lokālokāntasaṃsthitam[183] |
yāvat saṃtiṣṭhate tatsthā nayopāyair anekadhā ||
65 kurvantī[184] vividhopāyaiḥ sā kāryaracanā[n] bahūn[185] |
tejobhābhiḥ[186] pradīpyantī[187] caṇḍākṣiṇyāpy[188] atheritā[188] ||
66 tasmin adrau[189] sthitā devī dedīpyārci[r][190] ghanojjvalā[190] |
tat pradeśaṃ sthiraṃ jātam anyad[191] dagdhaṃ carācaram ||
67 āpūritam idaṃ sarvam anekaracanādibhiḥ |
paśyate parvataṃ mātā kalpānte[192] muditekṣaṇā[193] ||
68 tāvac caṇḍākṣiṇī tv agre paśyaty[194] amitatejasā[195] |
divyāmṛtena pūryantīṃ[196] divyaughaguṇaśālinīm[197] ||
69 uvācedaṃ mahādevī sādhu[198] pūrṇamanorathe |
yenedaṃ pūritaṃ sthānaṃ tenedaṃ pūrṇarūpiṇī ||
70 bhaviṣyaty ādhipatyatvaṃ[199] parvato[200] 'yaṃ[201] tapotkaṭaḥ |
viṣuvena tu yogena yenedaṃ saṃskṛtaṃ tvayā ||
71 tena pīṭheśvarī tvaṃ hi bhaviṣyasi yuge yuge |
jīvaskandhāsanaṃ[202] tubhyaṃ dvāparāntādhikāriṇī ||
72 bhaviṣyati[203] bhave[204] siddhaḥ[205] kuraṅgīśaḥ[206] patis tava |
saṃpūrṇamaṇḍalādhāro granthādhāro[207] maheśvaraḥ[208] ||
73 dvādaśaiva bhave[209] tubhyaṃ bhaviṣyanti kumārikāḥ |
tebhyas tv[210] ekaikakoṭis[210] tu ādhipatyādhikārikāḥ ||
74 bhaviṣyanti tathā putrāḥ pratīhārās[211] tadardhataḥ[212] |
adhyātmaṃ[213] saṃpravakṣyāmi yathā[214] devyā puro vṛtāḥ[215] ||
75 haṃsāvalī dravākhye tu sutārā[216] sainyakāśraye[217] |
harṣā[218] śleṣmākhyapīṭhe[219] tu vāṇī aśrunivāsinī ||
76 śubhākṣī[220] bījarā[y]e[221] tu mahānandā tu majjagā |

---

173. B dvitī( )tāraḥ; A -tārā 174. A -bhairav 175. A etan 176. A sahya 177. A -rcībhiḥ 178. A tatrūvasthā 179. C [ ] 180. A rudrādyānta-; BC -sāre 181. A niśeṣa 182. A nikhile viśve 183. A -sthitaḥ; BC -sthitā 184. A -ntīṃ 185. BC bahu 186. A -bhāti 187. A -ntīṃ; C -nti 188. A -kṣinyo paṣe smṛtā 189. A yadrau; illegible in B 190. BC dīpyārciḥ sughanojjvalā 191. A anya 192. A -nta 193. A -kṣaṇāt 194. B paśyanty; A paśyante 195. A 'mita- 196. BC pūrantīṃ 197. A divyogha- 198. BC sā[ ] 199. BC -patye te 200. A paryato 201. B yan; C yat 202. A -skandā- 203. A bhaviṣyanti; BC bhaviṣyasi 204. BC bhavet; A bhava 205. A siddhi 206. A kuruṅgīśaḥ 207. A grantha-; C granthyā; B grānthyā- 208. BC maheśvarāḥ 209. C bhavet; A bhava 210. A te nya kakoṭis 211. A pratīhāra; BC pratīcārās 212. A tad ucyateḥ 213. A -tma; BC -tme 214. C yadā 215. BC vṛtā 216. A sudhārā 217. A sinyakā priye; BC saitya- 218. A harṣa 219. A (kle)ṣmā- 220. A subhakṣi 221. A bhīja-

Thus is the manifestation [of Devī] in the second Pīṭha.

Śrībhairava spoke:
62 After She had spoken thus, O Maheśānī, She went to Sahya, the great forest; [there] She filled the three worlds with the lustre of the Saṃpūrṇamaṇḍala,
63 — 'world' means [in this context] the human body, [or] the *kalā* which is above the palate: it is the quintessence of the 'world' beginning and ending with the Rudras, and subsisting on Amṛta —
64 [filling] completely, entirely and wholly [the three worlds] which encompass both the worlds and beyond.
As long as [Devī] abides there, She accomplishes by means of the various ways of Her wisdom,
65 and by all kind of [other] means the many arrangements of Her task, at the same time setting alight [the three worlds] with the splendour of Her brightness. Then She was addressed by Caṇḍākṣiṇī [with the words]:
66 "On that mountain stands Devī, brilliant in Her lustre, bright as the lightning. This region has become lasting, while the rest of the world was burnt.
67 Filled is this complete [region] by the various kinds of Her arrangements". The Mother with a joyful glance sees the mountain, at the end of the Kalpa.
68 Suddenly [Devī] of infinite splendour, sees before Her Caṇḍākṣiṇī becoming filled with the divine Amṛta, abounding in the qualities of the divine hosts.
69 [To her] Mahādevī said the following: "Very good, O you whose desire is satisfied! Because this place is filled [by you], therefore [you] will possess a complete form here.
70 There will be [for you] sovereignty [over this place]; this mountain will become abounding in *tapas*. Since you have completely formed [this region] in every detail,
71 you will be the mistress of this Pīṭha in every Yuga. The *jīvaskandha* will be your 'seat'; your authority will reach the end of the Dvāpara-yuga.
72 In this existence you will have the Siddha Kuraṅgīśa as husband: this great lord is the support of both the Saṃpūrṇamaṇḍala and the Book.
73 Twelve daughters you will have in this existence: from each of them there will be a crore of [other daughters] who will yield authoritative power.
74 Besides, you will have [twelve] sons, and half that [number of] servants". I will tell [You] how the 'towns' are covered by Devī in a microcosmic way.
75 Haṃsāvalī is in [the town] called 'fluidity'; Sutārā is in the place of *sainyaka*; Harṣā is in the Pīṭha called 'phlegm'; Vāṇī abides in the tears;
76 Śubhākṣī is in the realm of semen; Mahānandā is in the marrow; Sunandā is

sunandā medavāhe[222] ca koṭarākṣī ca raktagā ||
77 viśvākṣī[223] viṣṇuvāhe[224] ca svedavāhe[225] yaśovatī[226] |
viśālākṣī śrutau pīṭhe[227] sundarī cāmṛtānugā[228] ||
78 śeṣair guṇaiḥ kuraṅgīśaḥ[229] saṃsthitaḥ[230] parameśvaraḥ[230] |
vāliś[231] ca[231] mohinī[232] caiva nandaḥ prajñā[233] tathaiva ca ||
79 siṃhāsanādhipās[234] te[234] vai bhūṣaṇau vāmadakṣiṇau[235] |
daśagrīvaḥ[236] sthitaḥ[236] kaṇṭhe tathā ca śikhivāhinī ||
80 hayagrīvaś ca lāmā ca hayaś[237] caiva vināyakī
bāhuyugme sthitā[ś] caiva yojayed varavarṇini ||[238]
81 sugrīvaś[239] ca[239] kapālinyā vāmahaste[240] kapālake |
gopatiḥ pūrṇimā caiva vāmadakṣakaradvaye ||
82 jhaṅkarī bhīṣmakopetā[241] dakṣahastāṅgulīṣu ca |
śikhaṇḍī[242] kurdanī[243] caiva vāmahastāṅgulisthitā[ḥ][244] ||
83 śūladaṇḍe sthitā[ś][245] caiva khaṇḍalo dīpanī tathā |
triśūle ca sthitāv etau jayantī śukra eva ca ||
84 śūlam etad viboddhavyaṃ[246] caṇḍākhyo bhīṣaṇī tathā |
ekaskandhe[247] sthitās[247] te tu jñeyā[ḥ] pūrṇākhyasaṃjñake ||
85 kuraṅgīśaparīvāram[248] etad jñeyaṃ kulāṃbike[249] |
ku-śabdena bhavet[250] pṛthvī[251] raṅgayed yo navāṃbunā[252] ||
86 kuraṅgīśas[253] tu saḥ prokto na[254] raṅgo[254] yas tu kutsitaḥ |
kuṇḍalīśatṛtīyaṃ[255] tu kṛtvārghīśaśirogatam[256] ||
87 svāṅkitaṃ[257] vai[258] kuraṅgīśaṃ[259] mantram etad udāhṛtam[260] |
āmodaś ca pramodaś[261] ca durmukho[262] sumukhas[262] tathā ||
88 vighnakartā ca vighneśaḥ ṣaḍ ete pālakāḥ smṛtāḥ |
tṛtīyasya tu pīṭhasya pūrṇasaṃjñasya[263] pārvati ||
89 kathitaṃ tu parīvāram etad dhi kulayoginām ||
iti[264] tṛtīyapīṭhāvatāraḥ[265] ||
śrībhairava[266] uvāca ||
90 evam[267] uktvā gatā pūrṇaṃ yatrocchuṣmā[268] mahānadī |
mahocchuṣmavanāntasthā divyādivyaughavāhinī ||
91 mahocchuṣmavanaṃ yatra yatra nīlaṃ[269] mahāhradam |

222. A -vāhī 223. A viśvakṣī; C biṃbākṣī 224. B (viṇḍu)-; A -vāhī 225. A -vāhī 226. BC yaśasvinī 227. B pāthe 228. BC amṛtā- 229. A kuruṅgīśaṃ 230. A -sthitaṃ parameśvarī 231. A bhālāṃ ca; B bālīśa 232. C mohanī 233. A prājña 234. A siṃhāsanādhipatyāsthe 235. A mama dakṣiṇau 236. A daśagrī( )ta 237. A jayaś 238. in BC pāda 80cd comes after pāda 82cd 239. A daśagrīva 240. A vā( )ste 241. B bhīṣmakorṇatā 242. BC śikhaṇḍiḥ 243. A dahanī 244. A (-sthitāḥ) 245. BC sthitaś 246. A -vyā 247. A -skande ( )s 248. A kuruṅgeśaparivāraṃ ca-m 249. BC kulānvaye 250. B bhave 251. A pṛṣye 252. A navāṃbhuvā; B navāstunā 253. A kuruṅgiśas 254. A (na) raṅgī 255. A -tṛtīyas 256. A kṛtvādi(kṣī)śirogataḥ 257. A svāṅkita; BC khaṅkitaṃ 258. B khe vai; A kha 259. BC kuraṅgīśa; A kuruṅgīśa 260. A -taḥ 261. A prabodhaś 262. A sumukho durmukhas 263. BC -jñas tu 264. omitted in AB 265. A -pīṭhādikāraḥ 266. A -bhairav 267. BC pañcam 268. A -ṣma 269. A līnaṃ

in the flow of fat; Koṭarākṣī is in the blood;
77 Viśvākṣī is in the flow of Viṣṇu; in the stream of perspiration is Yaśovatī; Viśālākṣī is in the Pīṭha of the two ears; Sundarī is in the Amṛta.
78 Associated with the other qualities stands Kuraṅgīśa, the supreme lord. Vāli and Mohinī, Nanda and Prajñā,
79 they are the Siṃhāsanādhipas of the [ear-]ornaments, both left and right; Daśagrīva and Śikhivāhinī are located on the throat;
80 Hayagrīva and Lāmā, Haya and Vināyakī, stand on the pair of arms — [there] one should fix them, O Varavarṇinī;
81 Sugrīva and Kapālinyā are in the skull in the left hand; Gopati and Pūrṇimā are on the left and right hands;
82 Jhaṅkarī together with Bhīṣmaka is on the fingers of the right hand; Śikhaṇḍin and Kurdanī are situated on the fingers of the left hand;
83 on the shaft of the trident are located Khaṇḍala and Dīpanī; on the trident [itself] stand Jayantī and Śukra —
84 [trident] may also be simply denoted as 'spear' —; the one called Caṇḍa and Bhīṣaṇī are situated on one shoulder. These then one should know in the [Pīṭha] called Pūrṇa.
85 This is to be known as the retinue of Kuraṅgīśa, O Kulāṃbikā. With the word '*ku*' the earth is meant; the one who colours [the earth] with fresh water,
86 that one is called Kuraṅgīśa; a colour which is despicable is not meant. Having made the third [letter] after Kuṇḍalīśa and above Arghīśa,
87 and marked by its self — thus is the *mantra* of Kuraṅgīśa mentioned. Āmoda, Pramoda, Durmukha, Sumukha,
88 Vighnakartṛ, and Vighneśa: they are known as the six guardians. Of the third Pīṭha which is known as Pūrṇa, O Pārvatī,
89 I have told [You Your] retinue — this is [intended] only for the Kula-yogins.

Thus is the manifestation [of Devī] in the third Pīṭha.

Śrībhairava spoke:

90 After She had spoken thus, [Devī] went all the way to Ucchuṣmā, the big river, which is situated in the forest called Mahocchuṣma, and which bears along its stream the host of gods and mortals.
91 In the forest Mahocchuṣma where one finds the [pools] Nīla and Mahāhrada,

tatra sā ramate devī vāmadakṣekṣaṇāntagā[270] ||
92 ubhayos taṭamadhyasthā ramitvā cāṃbikāhvayam[271] |
yāvat paśyati viśvāṅgī tattvāṅgī tāvat paśyati ||
93 kāmabhogakṛtāṭopā vasantaracanojjvalā |
drāvayantī dravantī sā[272] īkṣaṇair bhuvanatrayam[273] ||
94 dṛṣṭvā prahasitā mātā[274] kā tvaṃ kasmād ihāgatā |
tāṃ dṛṣṭvā mohitā mātā jānanty[275] api na jānatī[276] ||
95 viśrāmya ca muhūrtaikaṃ yāvad ālokayet punaḥ |
mahocchuṣmā[277] ihāyatā[278] mamārthe[279] śokavāhinī ||
96 sādhu kāmini sarvatra yat tvayā darśitaṃ mama |
kāmānandaphalā[280] vyāptis tena kāmeśvarī bhava ||
97 kāruṇye kāmarūpaṃ tu mamāgre vividhaṃ kṛtam |
tenedaṃ kāmarūpaṃ tu kāmarūpanirīkṣaṇam ||
98 bhaviṣyati purā[281] kalpe cakrānandaḥ patis tava |
vāyuskandhopaviṣṭo[282] 'sau tadbhedaṃ tu[283] prakāśakaḥ[284] ||
99 aśeṣārthavido[285] nāthaḥ[285] sarvajñaḥ parameśvaraḥ |
kāmuke kāmukaṃ śūnyaṃ kāmadevo[286] bhaviṣyati ||
100 bhaviṣyanti[287] guṇānandās[287] trayodaśaguṇānvitāḥ |
yoginyo[288] yogasampannās[289] tāvaḍ[290] ḍikkarikāḥ[291] śubhāḥ ||
101 putrās trayodaśa hy evaṃ saptaivaṃ[292] prāticārakāḥ[293] |
bhaviṣyanti jagaddīpā[294] jagadānandakārakāḥ[295] ||
102 spandanākhye prabhā[296] devi[296] prasūtiḥ parivartane[297] |
śaṃsā ākuñcanākhye tu bhānumatyā prasāraṇe ||
103 śrībalā vapanagrāme hāriṇī valgane[298] tathā |
hariṇī dhāvane caiva mālinī jṛmbhane tathā[299] ||
104 kandukī[300] hasane caiva muktāvalī[301] tu jalpane |
gautamī ghūrmaṇe[302] caiva kauśikī[303] śoṣaṇāpure ||
105 yā ca śukodarī[304] devī sā naiḥsvanapade[305] sthitā |
śeṣabhāvair mahāsiddha[ḥ] svājñānando[306] vyavasthitaḥ[307] ||
106 vāyuvegā[308] ca bhānuś ca skandhe[309] caiva dvitīyake |
pāvanyānantahetuś[310] ca[310] hṛtpradeśe vyavasthitaḥ ||
107 surājo[311] lambikā[311] śaktir[311] udare[311] saṃvyavasthitaḥ[311] |

270. A -dakṣekṣadhontagā 271. A caṃbikā svayam 272. A sa 273. A -trayaḥ 274. A mātu 275. A (jānas tv) 276. A jānante 277. BC tāvocchuṣma 278. A imā- 279. A mahārthe 280. BC -phala 281. A purā(ṅ) 282. A -skandaupravi( ) 283. BC ca 284. A -kā 285. A -vidu nāthā 286. A kāmavi( )ṃ 287. A bhaviṣyati guṇānandos 288. A yoginyā 289. A -pannā 290. A tāva 291. A dikarikā 292. BC saptaiva 293. BC prati- 294. A jagaddhepā 295. BC -kārikāḥ 296. BC mahādevī 297. AB parivartate 298. A vallane; C valāte 299. BC punaḥ 300. A kaṇḍukī 301. A -valli 302. A jūrmaṇe 303. A kauṣakī 304. AB sū- 305. A ca nesvapade 306. A -nde 307. A -tā 308. A -vegāś 309. A skande 310. A yāvanyā; BC -ntadehe tu 311. A sugajā aṃbhikā prāṇe rocane ṣa vyavasthitaḥ

there Devī rested inbetween the left and the right eye.
92 Abiding amidst the shores of both [pools] Aṃbikā rejoiced, and [made] the proclamation: "As long as Viśvāṅgī sees, that long Tattvāṅgī sees;
93 one has a multitude of *kāma* and *bhoga*, the other is bright by the arrangement of spring; one makes the three worlds 'run' with her glances, [the other] runs to the three worlds with her glances".
94 Having seen [Devī], the mother started laughing [and said]: "Who are you; why have you come hither?". Having seen her, the Mother was stupefied: although She knew, She did not understand.
95 Having paused for a moment, as soon as She looked again [She knew] instantly 'She is Mahocchuṣmā who has come here, for My sake, leading away sorrow'.
96 [Next She spoke:] "Very good, Kāminī, in every aspect, what you have shown to Me: the omnipresence [of you here] which results in the bliss of *kāma*; therefore be Kāmeśvarī!
97 [Because this region] has been made [by you] in your kindness as a manifold form of *kāma* before my eyes, therefore it [shall be known] as Kāmarūpa, [where there is] the observing of the forms of *kāma*.
98 You will shortly have a husband in this kalpa, namely Cakrānanda; he is engaged in the *vāyuskandha*, making clear the distinction of that.
99 Your lord knows everything completely, he is the all-knowing, supreme lord. For the one who wishes he [provides] the [feeling of] wishing; he is the void; Kāmadeva he will become!
100 There will be [thirteen] Yoginīs blissful through their merits, provided with thirteen qualities, in possession of yoga, so much youthful and beautiful.
101 Likewise you will have thirteen sons, and seven servants; they will be the 'lights of the world', bringing about bliss for the people".
102 Prabhā is in [the town] called 'quivering', O Devī; Prasūti is in 'turning around'; Śaṃsā is in [the town] called 'bending'; Bhānumatyā is in 'stretching out';
103 Śrībalā is in the town [called] 'cutting off'; Hāriṇī is in 'jumping'; Hariṇī is in 'running'; Mālinī is in 'yawning';
104 Kandukī is in 'laughing'; Muktāvalī is in 'chattering'; Gautamī is in 'shaking'; Kauśikī is in the town [called] 'panting';
105 the goddess Śukodarī then, she is located in the place of 'sighing'. The Mahāsiddha Svājñānanda is associated with the other constituents.
06 Vāyuvegā and Bhānu are on the other shoulder; Pāvanyā and Anantahetu are situated in the region of the heart;
07 Surāja and his *śakti* Laṃbikā stand in the belly; Saṃhārī and Sundara are in

saṃhārī[312] sundaro nābhyāṃ mahāmātryārjuno[313] viduḥ ||
108 chagalīsaṃsthito[314] dakṣe stane ca parikīrtitāḥ[315] |
bhīmo vai pūtanā devī stane yukte dvitīyake ||
109 droṇakaḥ caiva[316] āmoṭī[317] kṣīre ca parisaṃsthitā[ḥ][318] |
bhasmakaḥ paramātmī ca paramātmagatā viduḥ ||
110 antako aṃbikā prāṇe icchā ketudhvajas tathā |
hastapṛṣṭhe vijānīyās tathā caivaṃ nitaṃbake ||[319]
111 viśālākṣo mahākālī kalyānaḥ[320] kusumāyudhā[320] |
guhyasthāne[321] sthitā[321] caivam[321] anyaṃ[321] caivam[321] ataḥ[321] śṛṇu[321] ||
112 śukrā[322] devī caturvaktraḥ śukre ca parisaṃsthitā |
kāmākhye[323] maṅgalā[324] hy ete yugmāś ca varavarṇini ||
113 śeṣabhāvāś[325] ca ye devi cakrānando vyavasthitaḥ |
madyaiś ca dviprakāraiś[326] ca[327] jñānadravyasamudbhavaiḥ ||
114 cakram ānandayed yas tu cakrānandaḥ sa ucyate |
trisiddhyādyaṃ[328] ca[329] yad bījaṃ sarasvatyā[330] vibhūṣitam[331] ||
115 mahābilagataṃ[332] pūjyaṃ[333] cakrānandaṃ[334] tv anena tu |
laṃpaṭo ghaṇṭakarṇaś ca sthūladanto gajānanaḥ ||
116 bṛhatkukṣiḥ sunandaś ca mahotkaṭas tathāparaḥ |
saptaite kathitā bhadre praticārās[335] tu cānvaye[336] ||
117 etat te kathitaṃ devi kāmākhyasya[337] tu nirṇayam |
caturthasya tu pīṭhasya gopyāt[338] gopyataraṃ param ||
iti caturthapīṭhāvatāraḥ[339] ||
śrībhairava[340] uvāca ||
118 etat proktaṃ tu gātrānte[341] caturthaṃ pīṭhavācakam[342] |
koṣṭhordhva[ṃ][343] cordhvagaṃ dharmi pīṭha[ṃ] mātaṅgasaṃjñakam[344] ||[345]
119 brahmarandhrasya cordhve[346] tu khecarīcakramadhyastham |
śrīśailaṃ cocyate yatra kramaṃ tatra parāparam ||
120 tatra sā tu[347] gatā devī niṣkalābhāvarūpiṇī |
cinmātrā bhāvagamyā sā pīṭhārthaṃ[348] sthāpane sthitā ||
121 hārikā candram ārūḍhā hārī vai īkṣaṇāpure |
gandhārī gandhaviśrāme[349] vīrā ca kamaṭhāpure ||
122 nakhī[350] ca hṛtpradeśe tu jvālinī tu[351] śikhāpure[351] |

---

312. A sandārī 313. A mahāma-; BC mahāmātryajano 314. A chagalīśa sthitā; BC jagalīśaṃ sthitā 315. A -tā 316. A siddha 317. B āmotī 318. A -taḥ 319. pādas 110cd omitted in BC 320 BC nitaṃbe parikīrtitaḥ 321. BC pūṣpāyudhā ca kalyāna guhye caiva vyavasthitaḥ 322. BC śukra 323. B kākāmākhye 324. BC saṃsthitā 325. A śe( )arṇaddhaś 326. BC dviḥ- 327. BC tu 328. B -dyas 329. BC tu 330. B -tyād 331. A -taḥ 332. BC -bilaṃ gataṃ 333. B pūjyeś; B′C pūjyaś 334. B cacakrā- 335. BC pratī- 336. A cāryate 337. BC kāmākṣasya 338. A gopyā 339. BC caturthaḥ pī-; omitted in A. 340. A -bhairav 341. A gotrānte 342. A -kaḥ 343. A koṣṭhārddha 344. A -kaḥ 345. pādas 118cd omitted in BC 346. BC ūrdhve 347. BC nu 348. A -rtha 349. A cogaviśrāme 350. B narkhī; C nar(gh)ī 351. BC śikhināpure

the navel; Arjuna is together with the Mahāmātrī — thus they know;
08 together with Chagalī they are known to be in the right breast; Bhīma and the goddess Pūtanā are associated with the other breast;
09 the Siddha Droṇaka and Āmoṭī are situated in the milk; Bhasmaka and Paramātmī are in the *paramātma* — thus they know;
10 Antaka and Aṃbikā are in the breath; Icchā and Ketudhvaja are to be known on the back of the hands; likewise are on the buttocks
11 Viśālākṣa and Mahākālī; Kalyāna and Kusumāyudhā stand in the secret parts; hear next the other [pair]:
12 the goddess Śukrā and Caturvaktra are in the ovary. These auspicious couples, O Varavarṇinī, are in [the Pīṭha] Kāmākhya.
13 The other constituents which there are, O Devī, [with those] Cakrānanda is associated. The one who with two kind of *madya*, viz. originating from knowledge and from real substance,
14 brings the circle in a state of bliss, that one is called Cakrānanda. The *bīja* which is the first after the three *siddhis*, adorned with Sarasvatī
15 and gone in the *mahābila* — with that [*bīja*] Cakrānanda should be worshipped. Laṃpaṭa, Ghaṇṭakarṇa, Sthūladanta, Gajānana,
16 Bṛhatkukṣi, Sunanda, and Mahotkaṭa as the last one: thus are told the seven servants, O Bhadrā, in the [Kula-]tradition.
17 Thus I have told You, O Devī, the arrangement of Kāmākhya, the fourth Pīṭha; it should be extremely carefully guarded!

Thus is the manifestation [of Devī] in the fourth Pīṭha.

Śrībhairava spoke:
18 Thus is proclaimed the fourth Pīṭha-description with regard to the body. Above the body, being at the top, O Dharmī, is the [fifth] Pīṭha called 'Mātaṅga'.
19 It is above the Brahmarandhra, in the centre of the Khecarīcakra. Where [in this Pīṭha] the Śrīśaila is mentioned, there the Parāpara Krama is.
20 There went Devī then, without 'parts', in a transcendent form: one should envisage Her there as only consisting of mind. She was there for the sake of establishing this [fifth] Pīṭha.
21 Hārikā has ascended the moon; Hārī is in the town of 'seeing'; Gandhārī is in the abode of 'smell'; Vīrā is in the town of the tortoise;
22 Nakhī is in the region of the heart; Jvālinī is in the town of the crest;

sumukhī[352] nābhimadhye tu piṅgalā viṣṇu-r-antagā[353] ||
123 brahmarandhre sukeśī ca śeṣabhāvās[354] tathāntyaje |
śrīphalaṃ[355] caiva tārā[ṃ] ca ūruyugme[356] vilakṣayet ||
124 kaśmalaś[357] ca tathā[358] caṇḍo[358] jñeyau[358] jñānakriyāyutau[358] |
jānvante[359] saṃsthitau[359] hy etau jñātavyau[360] sādhakena tu ||
125 caṇḍālaś caiva sāvitrī gāyatrī ceṭakas[361] tathā |
jaṅghāyāṃ saṃsthitā hy ete yugmarūpe tu[362] dehagāḥ ||
126 mātaṅgo dahanī caiva phetkārī bāhujas[363] tathā |
dakṣapāde tathā vāme yugaṃ yugaṃ vilakṣayet ||
127 eṣā mātaṅgapīṭhasya pañcamasya mayā tava |
vyāptiḥ[364] proktā na cānyeṣām ante kulayoginām[365]
128 vīro[366] avyaktanāma[366] ca mātaṅga[367] antyajās[367] tv ime |
mātā kuṇḍalinī proktā tasyāṅge yā[368] vyavasthitā[368] ||
129 mātaṅgaḥ procyate so 'tra na mātaṅgo yathetaraḥ |
antyam[369] antyaṃ[370] tathāntyaṃ[371] ca koṭibhāgaṃ vicāryate[372] ||
130 antyajaḥ sa tu vijñeyo yathā loke na cetaraḥ |
heraṃbho[373] dhūlisaṃjñaś ca piśācaḥ[374] kubjavāmanaḥ ||
131 pañcaite pālakā[375] bhadre bhaviṣyanti kulādhvare[376] |
pañcamasya tu pīṭhasya vyāptir eṣā[377] udāhṛtā[378] ||
132 snehād bhaktyā[379] ca deveśi kule ca prakaṭīkṛtā ||
iti pañcamapīṭhāvatāraḥ[380] ||
śrībhairava[381] uvāca ||
133 pālakā yatra saṃsthāpyās[382] tatra te kathayāmy aham |
caturbhujo gaṇādhyakṣo gajavaktro balotkaṭaḥ ||
134 airāvatyo[383] vināyakyo meghavarṇas tu saptamaḥ |
bṛhatkukṣyekadaṃṣṭrāś[384] ca gaṇeśo vighnarāṭ tathā ||
135 mahānando mahodaś ca pramodo[385] durmukhas tathā |
sumukho vimukhaś caiva vighnakartā ca laṃpaṭaḥ ||
136 ghaṇṭākarṇaḥ[386] sthūladaṃṣṭro[387] gajānanas tathāparaḥ |
bṛhatkukṣiḥ sunandaś ca mahotkaṭas tathāparaḥ ||
137 heraṃbho[388] cūlisaṃjñaś ca piśācaḥ kubjavāmanaḥ |
ete triṃśad mayā khyātāh. pīṭhapañcakapālakāḥ[389] ||

---

352. BC sumukhā 353. C śiṣnam antagā; B sistam antagā 354. A -bhāvā 355. A -phalaṃś 356. BC kuru- 357. B kasmalaś; A kaśmalaṃś 358. A [tathā] śaṇḍo jñeyau jñā(nanā)kṛyute jā( ) 359. B jātvante sthitau; C jātvanante sthitau; A tatra saṃsthitau 360. BC -vyaḥ; A -vyo 361. A cedakas 362. BC -ṇa 363. A (bahukas) 364. A vyāptaiḥ 365. A -nāḥ 366. illegible in A 367. BC mātaṅgo antyajā 368. A ye vyavasthitāḥ 369. A antye-m 370. BC antya 371. A -ntya(ś) 372. BC vidhīyate 373. C heraṃbo; B hiraṃbo 374. A piśāca 375. A pālaka 376. A kulā( ) 377. BC evam 378. BC udīritā 379. A bhaktyāś 380. BC pañca[ma]- | 381. A -bhairav 382. A -sthāpya 383. A eravatyo 384. illegible in A 385. A pramado 386. B kaṇṭākarṇaḥ; C karṇākarṇaḥ 387. illegible in A 388. BC hiraṇyamukho. After *hiraṇyamukho* B repeats the names from *vimukhaś* (135c) up to *ghaṇṭākarṇaḥ* (136a); C has four horizontal strokes before *cūlisaṃjñaś* (137a) 389. BC pīṭhā pañcakapālakāḥ

Sumukhī is in the centre of the navel; Piṅgalā is in Viṣṇu;
123 in the Brahmarandhra is Sukeśī. The other constituents are connected with Antyaja.
One should imagine Śrīphala and Tārā in the two thighs;
124 Kaśmala and Caṇḍa are to be known connected with Jñāna and Kriyā — they are situated on the knees; thus these two [pairs] are known by the Sādhaka;
125 Caṇḍāla and Sāvitrī, Gāyatrī and Ceṭaka: these are situated on the shanks; thus they are in pairs on the body;
126 Mātaṅga and Dahanī, Phetkārī and Bāhuja: these one should imagine in pairs on [respectively] the right and the left foot.
127 Herewith I have told the inherence of You with the fifth [Pīṭha], the Mātaṅgapīṭha. [This should] not [be told] to other people; [it should only be told] at the end to Kulayogins.
128 Vīra and the one called Avyakta: these are [respectively] Mātaṅga and Antyaja. The Mother is called Kuṇḍalinī, who is contained in the body of him,
129 namely the one who is called Mātaṅga here. There is no one other as Mātaṅga. The one who is examined millions and millions of times,
130 that one is known as Antyaja: like him there is no other in this world. Herambha, the one called Dhūli, Piśāca, Kubja, and Vāmana:
131 these will be the five guardians, O Bhadrā, on the Kula-path. Herewith is explained [Your] inherence with the fifth Pīṭha.
132 Out of love and attachment [to You], O Deveśī, I have made this clear with regard to the Kula[-doctrine].

Thus is the manifestation [of Devī] in the fifth Pīṭha.

Śrībhairava spoke:
133 Where the guardians are to be placed [on the body], that I will tell You. Caturbhuja, Gaṇādhyakṣa, Gajavaktra, Balotkaṭa,
134 Airāvatya, Vināyakya, Meghavarṇa the seventh, Bṛhatkukṣi, Ekadaṃṣṭra, Gaṇeśa, Vighnarāj,
135 Mahānanda, Mahoda, Pramoda, Durmukha, Sumukha, Vimukha, Vighnakartṛ, Lampaṭa,
136 Ghaṇṭākarṇa, Sthūladaṃṣṭra, Gajānana next, Bṛhatkukṣi, Sunanda, Mahotkaṭa next,
137 Herambha, the one called Cūli, Piśāca, Kubja and Vāmana: thus I have named the thirty guardians of the five Pīṭhas.

138 pīṭhatrike triṣaṭkaṃ[390] ca caturthe sapta eva ca |
pañcame pañca vijñeyā dehasthān[391] kathayāmy aham ||
139 dakṣakaniṣṭhikāyāṃ[392] ca yāvad vāmakaniṣṭhikā |
caturbhujādigaṇeśāntāḥ[393] karāṅguliṣu saṃsthitāḥ ||
140 dakṣapādāṅgulīlagnā[394] yāvad vāmapadaṃ gatāḥ |
vighnarājāditaḥ kṛtvā ghaṇṭākarṇāntagā[395] viduḥ ||
141 meṣonmeṣe[396] vyāye āye[397] nirodhe[398] ca vijṛmbhane |
hikkāchikkontake[399] caiva kāse ca daśame sthitāḥ ||
142 sthūladantāditaḥ kṛtvā vāmanāntā[400] vyavasthitāḥ |
yo jānāti prayatnena kulācāryaḥ sa ucyate ||[401].
143 na kevalam ime pīṭhā dehamadhye vyavasthitāḥ |
dinamadhyodayaṃ teṣāṃ ṣaṭ ṣaṭ ca[402] ghaṭikā[ḥ] smṛtāḥ ||
144 udayaṃ pañcapīṭhānāṃ pīṭhaikaike vidur budhāḥ[403] |
māse dināni ṣaṭpañca ca varṣe ca kathayāmy aham ||
145 śatāni trīṇi ṣaṣṭiś[404] ca dināḥ[405] saṃvatsare[405] sthitāḥ |
udayaṃ pañcapīṭhānāṃ pīṭhaikaike kathayāmy aham ||
146 dvāsaptati dināny eva[406] pīṭhe pīṭhe vilakṣayet |
evaṃ vyāptaṃ samastaṃ hi[407] pīṭhānāṃ pañcakena tu ||
147 yathā bāhye[408] tathā dehe jñātavyaṃ tu kulakrame[409] |
pīṭhāṃśakas[410] tu yo[411] yasya nāmamadhye pravartate ||
148 taṃ tathāhaṃ pravakṣyāmi anuṣṭhānātmanāṃ[412] priye |
pañcaiva[413] pīṭhabījāni OṂ-kārādyantā[ś][414] cāntimāḥ[414] ||
149 ādau deyā ime paścād varṇanyāsaṃ tu kārayet ||
150 oḍrapīṭhe[415] A U O[416] GHA ṬA THA PHA RA[417] SA[418] kīrtitāḥ ||
jālapīṭhe Ā Ū AU[419] CA ṬHA DA BA LA HA surapūjite || pūrṇapīṭhe I E
AṂ KHA JA ḌHA NA MA ŚA parikīrtitāḥ || kāmapīṭhe Ī AI AḤ KA CHA
ḌA DHA[420] BHA VA suśobhane[421] || mātaṅgapīṭhe Ṛ Ṝ Ḷ Ḹ GA JHA[422]
TA PA YA ṢA[423] udāhṛtāḥ ||
151 sva-svapīṭhodaye pīṭhān[424] pūjayed yaḥ samāhitaḥ |
likhitvā pustake vātha paṭhate ca dine dine ||
152 vāmadravyābhipūjyaṃ[425] ca kṛtvā yaḥ paṭhate sadā |

---

390. illegible in A 391. A -sthā 392. A dakṣaṃ ka-; BC dakṣe kaniṣṭhikāyāś 393. A caturbhujā( )ṣāntaṃ 394. B dakṣā-; BC -ṅgule lagnā 395. A -karṇīntaghā 396. A -meṣī 397. A āyā 398. A niroddha 399. A -chiko-; BC -chikko[ ]ke 400. A vāmanāntar 401. After śloka 142 BC add: pañcānāṃ caiva pīṭhānāṃ praty ekaike śṛṇuṣva tat (B taḥ) | nāmaśa(bda)navasaṃketā tathā ṣoḍaśabhir yutā || saṃketaiś ca varārohe dhyānamantrādhikaṃ dhiye (C dhipe) | pūrvagranthe mayā coktam (C proktam) atra kiñcid udāhṛtam || 402. A ṣaṭ 403. illegible in A 404. A ṣaṣṭi 405. A di(vāne) vatsare 406. A evaṃ; B aiva 407. A te 408. A bāhya 409. A -kram(aṃ) 410. A pīṭhā( ); B pīṭhā( )akas 411. A (yad) 412. A -nā 413. BC vaktre ca 414. BC Ṛ-kārādyānimāntimaḥ 415. BC oḍḍa- 416. BC U; after this letter both B and C write two horizontal strokes 417. BC LA 418. A SI 419. C Ṛ 420. C DHA VA 421. B subhane; C śobhane 422. C DHĀ 423. A ŚA 424. A pīṭhe 425. A -dravyāni pūjyaṃ

138 In the [first] three Pīṭhas there are thrice six [of them]; in the fourth [Pīṭha] there are seven; in the fifth [Pīṭha] one should discern five. I will tell You how they are located on the body.
139 From the little finger of the right hand to the little finger of the left hand is the series from Caturbhuja up to Gaṇeśa: they are located on the fingers.
140 Attached to the toes of the right foot up to the [toes of the] left foot one should know the series from Vighnarāj up to Ghaṇṭākarṇa.
141 In the shutting of the eyes, in the opening of the eyes, in exhaling, in inhaling, in keeping the breath, in yawning, in hiccups, in sneezing, in belching, and as the tenth in coughing [the others] are located:
142 thus are located [the guardians] from Sthūladanta up to Vāmana. The one who knows this carefully, he is called a kulācārya.
143 These Pīṭhas are not only distributed over the body. The appearance of these [five Pīṭhas] is at noon; the two times six [letters] are known as *ghaṭikās*.
144 The wise know the appearance of the five Pīṭhas for each Pīṭha separately. In [one] month there are thirty days. I will tell You [how many days there are] in [one] year:
145 in [one] year there are 360 days. I will tell You the appearance of the five Pīṭhas for each Pīṭha separately.
146 One should discern in every Pīṭha 72 days. In this way the whole [of the year] is pervaded by the five Pīṭhas.
147 Both outward and on the body [the five Pīṭhas] should be known in the Kula-tradition. Which part of the Pīṭhas occurs in the name of which [Pīṭha],
148 that I will tell You for the benefit of those who are dedicated to religious practices, O Lovely One. The five *bījas* of the Pīṭhas are preceded and followed by the syllable OṂ.
149 These [five *bījas*] are placed first; next one should perform the *varṇanyāsa*.
150 In the Pīṭha Oḍra the A U O GHA ṬA ṬHA PHA RA and SA are mentioned. In the Pīṭha Jāla are the Ā Ū AU CA ṬHA DA BA LA and HA, O Surapūjitā. In the Pīṭha Pūrṇa are mentioned the I E AṂ KHA JA ḌHA NA MA and ŚA. In the Pīṭha Kāma are the Ī AI AḤ KA CHA ḌA DHA BHA and VA, O Suśobhanā. In the Pīṭha Mātaṅga are said the Ṛ Ṝ Ḷ Ḹ GA JHA TA PA YA and ṢA.
151 The one who devoutly honours the [five] Pīṭhas with regard to the appearance [of the letters] for each Pīṭha — namely having written down [the letters] in a book or when one recites them every day,
152 and having honoured the *vāmadravyas*, recites them constantly — for him

na tasya mandire vyādhir na ca mārī pravartate[426] ||
153 nāgnir dahati tadveśma hiṃsyante[427] na ca hiṃsakaiḥ[428] |
śāntir vṛddhir bhaved devi dvipade ca catuṣpade ||
154 ājñā ca[429] visphured[429] divyā[430] trikālaṃ paṭhate tu yaḥ |
deśakṣobhaṃ purakṣobhaṃ strīpumāṃ kṣobhanaṃ bhavet ||
155 vibhūtir[431] vipulā[431] tasya pīṭhānāṃ sevanād[432] bhavet |
rātrau suptasya deveśi jāyate śubhadarśanam ||
156 etat sarvaṃ varārohe labhyate guruvaktrataḥ[433] |
guruvaktraṃ pitā mātā mātāmahapitāmahāḥ ||
157 anye[434] 'pi[434] ye[434] gurusthāne te guruḥ parikīrtitāḥ |
guruvaktraṃ bhaved anyat tac[435] ca[435] śaktimukhaṃ smṛtam ||
158 tadvibodhena[436] sidhyanti sarvakāryāṇi bhūtale |
kulamārgaḥ[437] samartho[437] 'smin vyākhyāto[438] yas tu cānvaye ||
159 sa guruś cānyagurvarthas[439] tatsakāśāt pravartate[440] |
yasyaiva[441] śāṃbhavī[441] dīkṣā sadyaḥpratyayakārikā[442] ||
160 sa gurur nānyavedhaiś[443] ca kuñjakaiḥ śākta-cāṇavaiḥ[444] |
śāstraṃ[445] tasya[445] guroḥ[445] pārśvād viveko[446] devapūjanam[447] ||
161 snānaṃ dhyānaṃ tapo[448] homam avatāraṃ[449] kramasya ca |
mantraṃ[450] mudrā tathā vidyā tatsakāśāt phalapradā[451] ||
162 tasmāt pūjyaḥ sadā so hi ātmanena[452] dhanena ca ||
163 guroḥ[453] samo naiva[454] hi martyaloke tathā viśeṣena hi[455] cāntarikṣe[455] |
yas tārayed duḥkhamahārṇavaughāt kiṃ tasya kartuṃ kṣamate sa śiṣyaḥ ||
164 na mātā na pitā caiva[456] na putro[457] na ca bāndhavaḥ[458] |
upakāraṃ[459] hi kurvanti yādṛśaṃ kurute[460] guruḥ[460] ||
165 yatprasādāt prasidhyanti[461] sarvamantrāś ca bhūtale |
sa guruḥ pūjyate kiṃ na[462] sākṣād devo maheśvaraḥ ||

iti kulālikāmnāye[463] śrīmate ṣaṭsāhasre[464] saṃhitāyāṃ[465]
pañcamaḥ paṭalaḥ ||

---

426. A -ti 427. BC hiṃsanti 428. BC hiṃsakāḥ 429. BC visphurate 430. A devyā 431. A vibhūte vipulāṃ 432. A sevanāṃ 433. A -vaktragaḥ 434. A anyaṃ caiva 435. A taś ca; BC tattva- 436. A tad vibodhyati 437. BC kulaśāstrasya martyo 438. ABC -tā 439. A -guruvaṃ 440. A prava[rta]te 441. BC yasya śāṃbhavīye 442. A -kārakā 443. B nānyabhedaiś 444. A śāktadānnavai 445. A śastrād asya guruḥ 446. BC vivekaṃ 447. A -pūjanaḥ 448. BC japaṃ 449. C avatāra 450. AC mantra 451. A phalaṃ pradā 452. BC ātmanā ca 453. A guru 454. B naita 455. A bhi (yā)ntarikṣe 456. B tv eva 457. BC putrā 458. BC -vāḥ 459. BC upacāraṃ 460. A guru(vesanīn) 461. A -nte 462. illegible in A 463. omitted in BC 464. A -sa- 465. omitted in BC.

there is no disease in his body, nor does death occur [for him].
153 Fire does not burn down his house, nor are [his kinfolk] hurt by wild beasts. There will be peace and prosperity, O Devī, for men and animals.
154 Unlimited, divine power will be his share, when he recites it three times: he will be able to disturb lands and towns, and to excite men and women.
155 There will be an extensive abundance for him as the result of worshipping the [five] Pīṭhas. When he sleeps at night, O Deveśī, auspicious dreams occur for him.
156 All this, O Varārohā, is obtained [by him] on the authority of the Guru. The authority of a Guru [have] the father, the mother, the maternal grandfather, and the paternal grandfather:
157 what other people there may be in the position of a guru, [only] these are called [rightly] 'Guru'. [Yet] the authority of a Guru can be one other thing, e.g. that which is called *śaktimukha*.
158 When one realizes this, then all one's enterprises are successful on earth. The Kula-path is suitable for this [purpose]. The one who is explained in the [Kula-]tradition [as a Guru],
159 he is a [real] Guru and an example for other Gurus. For whom there is the Śāṃbhavī Dīkṣā which effects instant faith, from the presence of such [a Guru],
160 that one is a [real] Guru, and not by means of other *vedhas*, namely the *kuñjakas*, *śākta* and *āṇava*. The Śāstra [one obtains] through this Guru, [as well as] true knowledge, [the proper rules for] worshipping the gods,
161 bathing, meditation, asceticism, oblations, the manifestations of the [Kula-] tradition, *mantras*, *mudrās* and secret knowledge — [obtaining these] from the presence of such [a Guru] it bears fruit!
162 Consequently [such a Guru] should be revered constantly, both by means of spiritual and material means!
163 Among mankind nobody equals the Guru, and certainly not [anyone] in the intermediate space; the pupil then is indulgent to perform the meanest task for him, who will save him from streams of the great ocean of sorrow.
164 Neither the mother, nor the father, nor a son or relative can offer such a help, as the Guru can provide.
165 [The Guru] thanks to whose graciousness all the *mantras* are successful on earth, such a Guru is venerated; why not? He is the personal manifestation on earth of God, of Maheśvara!

Thus in the Kulālikāmnāya, in the Śrīmata, in the Ṣaṭsāhasra Saṃhitā the fifth chapter.

COMMENTARY

Introduction

The first thing to note with regard to the present chapter of the ṢaṭSS is its actual number. In the captions of this chapter we have deliberately left this question open by denoting it as '*paṭala* 4/5'. The chapter preceding the present chapter is unmistakably the third: this number is found in the colophons of all the three MSS, as well as at the beginning (*tṛtīya paṭala ārambhaḥ*) and the end (*iti ṣaṭsāhasre tṛtīyaḥ paṭalaḥ*) of the Ṭ. With regard to the chapter following the present chapter we see the same: both the MSS and the Ṭ agree that it is the sixth *paṭala*. This leaves us with the question which number should be assigned to the present chapter, four or five. Either way, one chapter is missing. The three MSS agree in their respective colophons that the present chapter is the fifth, thus omitting a fourth paṭala. On the other hand the Ṭ, which comments upto line 150 of the text, begins its commentary with *caturtha paṭala ārambhaḥ*, and finishes with *iti ṣaṭsāhasre caturthaḥ paṭalaḥ*. Consequently, according to the Ṭ the present chapter should be the fourth, thus omitting a fifth chapter.

Whereas the three MSS of the ṢaṭSS do not seem to bother about this obvious incongruity in the sequence of their chapters, the Ṭ seems to be aware of it. Thus the author of the Ṭ begins his commentary on the sixth chapter with the words: *tathā pañcame paṭale yāvat pīṭhavyāptiḥ ṣaṣṭhe paṭale yāthā*, indicating that the fifth chapter begins after what is called the *pīṭhavyāpti*, 'the pervasion [of Devī] into the [five] Pīṭhas'. In this way the fifth chapter might begin after *śloka* 132 of the text, which ends the description of the five Pīṭhas. There seems to be a break in the text at this point: the names of all the guardians are repeated and they are connected with different parts of the body or with some physical phenomenon. It is noteworthy in this regard that the strict division of the guardians over the five Pīṭhas as we saw it before, is abandoned. Thus the first five of the six guardians belonging to the first Pīṭha are taken together and identified with the fingers of the right hand; the last of them joins the first four of the second Pīṭha as the five fingers of the left hand etc. Another indication for the assumption that after 132 a new part begins could be found in the fact that line 132 is only a half-*śloka*, which appears often at the end of a section or chapter in a text.

The present chapter of the ṢaṭSS is the first of this text which has a direct relation to the KmT. Its contents are based on the second chapter of the KmT, and quite a few lines are almost literally repeated. As we shall see in the notes, the ṢaṭSS has added much to the text of the KmT. The quintessence of the present chapter in the ṢaṭSS and of the second chapter of the KmT are the same: Devī goes around in Bhārata Varṣa, visiting various places where She obtains daughters, sons and guardians. The number of places visited by Devī on Her tour varies between the two texts, as we shall shortly see.

In the KmT (2,24 ff.) Devī successively visits the Śrīmatkaumāraparvata or Śrīparvata, north of which is situated a great forest full with *liṅgas* (2,25d: *liṅgapūrṇa mahāvana*); the Mt. Trikūṭa; the Daradaṇḍī; the Western Himagahvara; Karāla; the great forest of Sahya; the river Ucchuṣmā; a place not mentioned by name, but described as *mātaṅgakulasaṃbhava* (2,102d) and possibly identified with the river Triśrotrā (2,111b); Devīkoṭa; Aṭṭahāsa; Kollagiri; Ujjenī; Prayāga; Varaṇā (= Vārāṇasī); Viraja; Ekāmraka, and other places (2,116d). The most important of this enumeration are the Western Himagahvara, Karāla, the forest of Sahya, the river Ucchuṣmā, and the locality not mentioned by name: in these five places Devī obtains daughters, sons and guardians, all of whom are mentioned by name. The five places are, of course, identified with the five Mahāpīṭhas (Oḍiyāna, Jālandhara, Pūrṇagiri, Kāmarūpa and Mātaṅga). The present chapter of the ṢaṭSS only mentions these five places at this instance, but in the first chapter of our text the others preceding the Western Himagahvara in the KmT are mentioned in this context. Thus (I-V denote the five Mahāpīṭhas):

	KmT 2,24-116	*ṢaṭSS 1,36-37*	*ṢaṭSS 4/5,26-132*
	—	Himavan	—
	—	Meru	—
	—	Candrādi	—
	—	Gandhamādana	—
	Kaumāraparvata/Śrīparvata	Śrīgiri	—
	Trikūṭa	Trikūṭa	—
	Daradaṇḍī	Daradaṇḍī	—
I	Paścima Himagahvara	Olaṃba	Ulaṃbikā
II	Karāla	Karālaṃba	Karālaṃba
III	Sahya Mahāvana	Sahyākhya	Sahya Mahāvana
IV	Ucchuṣmā Nadī	Ucchuṣma Vana	Ucchuṣmā Mahānadī
	Nīla	Hrada	Nīla
	Mahāhrada	Nīlahrada	Mahāhrada
V			
	Devīkoṭa, etc.	—	—

N.B.: the fifth Pīṭha, Mātaṅga, has no 'real' locality (cf.: ṢaṭSS 4/5,120).

The names of the daughters, sons and guardians obtained by Devī in the five Mahāpīṭhas agree almost completely in both texts. The ṢaṭSS, however, deals more extensively with the subject. All the daughters, sons and guardians are connected with specific parts of the human body, or with a particular physical phenomenon. Moreover, the sons of Devī are provided with a *śakti* of their own. The names of these *śaktis* are the same as the different manifestations of the goddess Mālinī, and their respective location on the human body is the same as in the Mālinī-system as it is explained in the seventh chapter of the ṢaṭSS (Appendix I). The order, however, of the Mālinī-*śaktis* as given in the present chapter differs widely from the order of the Mālinī-system proper (cf. p. 225).

The connection of the daughters etc. of Devī with a particular part of the body or a physical faculty as it is found in the ṢaṭSS, might be due to the fact that the ṢaṭSS appears to put more stress on the practical side of the worship than the KmT (Schoterman 1977: 932): this connecting with the human body could be related with the practise of *nyāsa*.

The appearance of the Mālinī-*śaktis* as consorts of the sons in the ṢaṭSS can be explained from the form of Devī on Her visit to Bhārata Varṣa. As we have pointed out before (Schoterman 1977: 935-937), it appears that the goddess who actually visits the various places is Kubjikā or Mālinī as a manifestation of Devī. This specification of Devī as Kubjikā/Mālinī is only found in the KmT in this phase of the text, as it is missing in the ṢaṭSS. Yet the author of the ṢaṭSS seems to have understood this identification: not only are the fifty Mālinī-*śaktis* inserted in the text as consorts for the sons in each of the five Mahāpīṭhas, but in a row of lines taken directly from the

KmT (ṢaṭSS 4/5,12-19ab) two lines are inserted which are not found in the KmT (4/5,15cd-16ab). Here it is stated beyond doubt that the goddess has a body consisting of the fifty letters of the Skt alphabet (4/5,15d), which refers clearly to Mālinī.

1: It is doubtfull to which occasion *pūrvaṃ* (1a), 'formerly', precisely refers. Most likely the reference is to the first chapter of the text (41cd ff.), where the four Pīṭhas are connected with the ears, the mouth, the uvula, and the 'central aperture' (*madhyarandhra*) respectively. The fifth Pīṭha has no actual geographical location (see Introduction to this chapter). As the connection of the four Pīṭhas with the body in 1,41cd ff. only becomes clear in the Ṭ and not in the text itself, one might perhaps consider *pūrvaṃ* as a reference to 1,48cd; 49ab (= 4/5,20), where this connection with the body is explicitly stated.

2: Again, the *śloka* begins with *pūrvaṃ* (2a) referring to a conversation between Bhairava/Deva and Devī, especially on the topic of the relation between teacher and pupil (2d). This refers to KmT 2,18cd (*tvaṃ gurur mama deveśi ahaṃ te na vicāraṇāt*, 'You be My teacher, O Deveśī, and I will be Yours — no doubt about that!').

3: The term *bhārata varṣa* (3c), 'King Bharata's realm', indicates India, of course.

4: In the present chapter only the five Mahāpīṭhas are discussed, which are visited by Devī on Her tour in India. The other Pīṭhas, Upapīṭhas, Kṣetras and Upakṣetras (4a) are not mentioned by name in the text of this chapter. The mentioning of '*pīṭha*' in this series might, of course, refer to the five Mahāpīṭhas, but no Upapīṭhas, Kṣetras or Upakṣetras are mentioned as being visited by Devī. Probably this mentioning of other places besides the five Mahāpīṭhas refers to KmT 2,115 ff., which mentions several places visited by Devī after Her stay in the fifth Mahāpīṭha: Devīkoṭa, Aṭṭahāsa, etc. (cf. p. 148). In 4c the verb *pratiṣṭhayed* is noteworthy as a denominative from *pratiṣṭha*, 'standing firmly, steadfast'.

5: According to 5ab the daughters, sons and guardians who are obtained by Devī on the occasion of Her visit to the five Mahāpīṭhas, number 134 in total. In reaching this number the female consorts are not included in the enumeration. In *pāda* 5d the reading of the MSS BC is chosen, as it harmonizes with KmT 1,50d.

6: The meaning of *pāda* 6ab is that the daughters and sons of Devī will create their own — numerable — offspring in due course, which will adhere to the Kula-doctrine.

7: Instead of *pañca* (7a) the MSS BC read *evaṃ*, 'thus'. This change between *pañca* and *evaṃ* is explicable, since there is but a small difference between *e* and *pa*, and between *va* and *ca* in writing. Moreover, an *anusvāra* not placed exactly above the *akṣara pa* (A reads *paṃca*) but slightly behind it, may have helped to cause the reading *evaṃ* for *pañca* (*paṃca*). The reading of A (*vedāś*) is a common permutation for *devāś*, which is obviously meant here.

8: In the next lines the number of daughters, sons and guardians in each Mahāpīṭha is given by making use of the numeral value some Skt words have. These symbolic words always start with the units, followed by the tens, the hundreds and the thousands. This method of presenting a number in a 'concealed' way is usually found in metrical texts or inscriptions, where writing the figure in numerals would disturb the metre (cf. Sircar 1965: 228 ff.).

Thus in the compound *vasvaṣṭavatsarārdhaṃ* (8a) the number of daughters, sons and guardians of the first Mahāpīṭha is given: *vasu* means 'eight' (the eight Vasus); *aṣṭa* means, of course, also 'eight'; *vatsarārdha*, 'half of the year', denotes the number 'six' because a year (*vatsara*) has twelve months, and half (*ardha*) of it makes 'six'. In this way there are eight daughters, eight sons and six guardians in the first Mahāpīṭha. As we shall see with regard to the other Mahāpīṭhas, the number of the daughters and the sons is equal in each of the Mahāpīṭhas. Consequently, the question which are mentioned first, the daughters or the sons, has no practical value, since the number is always the same: there are both eight daughters and eight sons in the first Mahāpīṭha. However, one might surmise that with *vasu* the eight daughters are meant, and with *aṣṭa* the eight sons, since when both groups are mentioned by name (26cd ff.), the names of the daughters always precede those of the sons. On the other hand the Ṭ explains each compound by giving the number of daughters and sons of the respective Mahāpīṭhas the other way around. Thus, in case of the first Mahāpīṭha, it states clearly that with *vasu* the sons are meant (*vasuśabdena aṣṭa tasmāt putrā aṣṭau*), and that *aṣṭa* refers to the eight daughters (*aṣṭa duhitāṣṭakam*). For the second Mahāpīṭha the number of the offspring and guardians is found in the *pāda* 8c (*dikkāṣṭhā ṛtavaś*). The reading is based on the Ṭ, since none of the MSS of the text itself furnishes a satisfactory reading. The word *dik* (from *diś*), 'quarter', stands for the ten quarters (East, South, West, North; the four intermediate quarters; zenith and nadir) and denotes the number 'ten'. *Kāṣṭhā* has the same meaning as *diś* in this context, and subsequently also denotes 'ten'. The last word indicates the number of the guardians: *ṛtavaś*, 'the seasons', denotes the number 'six', as there are usually six seasons counted in a year. Unfortunately, this reading is only found in the Ṭ. The reading of BC does not make any sense. MS A reads *dhatavaś*, which might be wrong for *dhātavaś*. The word *dhātu*, however, usually denotes the number 'five', which is impossible, as there are definitely six guardians in the second Mahāpīṭha (cf. 4/5,59cd; 60ab).

9: In *pāda 9a māsa*, 'month', means of course 'twelve'. *Arka*, 'sun', also denotes the number 'twelve'. *Rasa*, 'flavour', means six, as there are believed to be six basic kinds of *rasa* (*madhura*, *āmla* etc.).

The way in which the number of the daughters and sons of the fourth Mahāpīṭha is presented is peculiar, and differs from what we have seen with regard to the first three Mahāpīṭhas. The number of daughters and sons is 'hidden' in the compound *agnīndutridharāḥ* (9d): *agni*, 'fire', denotes the number 'three' (there are three sacrificial fires: Gārhapatya, Āhavanīya and Dakṣiṇa); *indu*, 'moon', means 'one'; *tri* is, of course, 'three'; *dharā*, 'earth', means again 'one'. Thus the compound should be read as '3-1-3-1'. As both the daughters and the sons are mentioned with this compound, it follows we should divide it into 3-1 & 3-1. In the notes to *śloka* 8 we have already remarked that these symbolic words always start with the units, followed by the tens etc. Thus there are thirteen daughters and the same number of sons, and not thirty-one. Note that as in English and other languages, in Sanskrit the word 'thirteen' is the reverse of the numeral: *trayodaśa & 13*. One might wonder why the author uses this system of expressing the number 'thirteen', while 'twelve' was represented simply by *māsa* or *arka* (see above). The explanation is probably that no symbolic word exists for the number 'thirteen'. The number of guardians is described with *svarāḥ* (9b), which denotes 'seven', as there are seven notes on the musical scale (*niṣāda*, *ṛṣibha*, *gāndhāra*, *ṣaḍja*, *madhyama*, *dhaivata*, *pañcama*). In *pāda* 9d the respective numbers are given as *grahā nandās tu pañcakam*. *Graha*, 'planet', here denotes the number 'nine'; *nanda* refers to the nine Nandas of Pāṭaliputra, and subsequently also means 'nine';

pañcaka is, of course, 'five'. The Ṭ has a different reading of this *pāda: grahā nandārtha pañcame*. Here the number 'five' is represented by *artha*, which can symbolize the number 'five' in its meaning 'object of the senses', of which there are five. *Pañcame*, 'in the fifth', refers then to the fifth Mahāpīṭha. Since the text itself every time mentions the number of the specific Mahāpīṭha (*ādipīṭhe*, *dvitīyasya*, *tristhe*, *caturthasya*), the reading of the Ṭ seems to be preferable to the reading of the three MSS.

10: In *pāda* 10d the reading of BC appears to be a *lectio facilior*, in which the gender of *pīṭha* is changed from neuter to masculine for metrical reasons. The form *a-sthāpyate*, in which the *a-* is an alpha privans, is permissible, although such formations are rather rarely met with.

11: For *pāda* 11c the reading of A has been chosen, although the form *gatās* is not correct since the subject (Devī) is singular. Probably one should read *deśāṃ gatā stu deveśi*, in which the word *tu* is enriched with an initial *s-*. This phenomenon is sometimes found with words beginning with an *t-*. Both A and B read *deśāṃ* (acc. pl.), which refers most likely to those places visited by Devī before She comes to Ulaṃbikā (1,36-37; p. 149). In *pāda* 11c it is said that She goes to a place which lies to the South (*dakṣiṇa*) and North (*vāma*) of Mt. Meru. Obviously this is the location of Ulaṃbikā, a small vilage in the forest (12ab ... *ulaṃbikā* ... *vanapallikā*). Also in 1,41cd the location is situated to the South and North of Mt. Meru. The corresponding place in the KmT is called *paścima himagahvara* (KmT 2,36d).

12: In the village of Ulaṃbikā there is a local goddess, who is only described with the term *devī* (12c). No specific name of this deity is mentioned here. The corresponding passage in the KmT, however, reads *raktā* instead of *devī* (KmT 2,37c) which is probably the name of this local goddess ('The Red One'). This supposition is corroborated by a spurious line in two MSS (A&B) in the 22nd chapter of the KmT, where the local deity Raktā is enumerated as the first of the four deities of the four Mahāpīṭhas (*raktākarālacaṇḍākṣīṃ mahocchuṣmāṃ* ...... *naumi*). That one should regard *raktā* as a personal name becomes also evident from the Ṭ, which reads *olaṃbikā nāma vanapallikāḥ* ... *tatra oḍyāne raktā devī* ... One may wonder why the ṢaṭSS has replaced Raktā of the KmT by the non-committal *devī*, while in the case of the other Mahāpīṭhas the local goddess is explicitly mentioned by name. Perhaps this is due to the fact that the *pāda raktāṃbaradharā devī* was already 'standardized' at the time of composition of the ṢaṭSS. We find, for example, in the Pañcasarasvatīmantra from Bali (Goudriaan & Hooykaas 1971: No. 800) five *ślokas* for five different forms of the goddess Sarasvatī. The difference between these five forms of Sarasvatī lies only in the particular colour she has: the five *ślokas* are completely identical except for five different colours mentioned in each of them: the second Sarasvatī is described as *raktāṃbaradharā devī raktamālyānulepanā* | *raktapuṣpapriyā devī* ... || (cf. also Goudriaan & Hooykaas 1971: Nos. 801-803).

13: It is not clear who is the subject in this *śloka*, but probably it is Devī Herself. A hint to this could be found in the use of the word *gahvara* (13a) which is easily connected with Mālinī, the form in which Devī visits Bhārata Varṣa (see Introduction to this chapter). In *pāda* 13b it is uncertain how to read the *pāda*: *guhāgahana-* or *guhā gahana-*. We have opted for the first possibility and translated *guhā* with 'secretly', which is, however, actually Vedic (*gúhā*). It seems, however, that Raktā is not aware of Devī's presence, and only notices that the place suddenly becomes filled with Yogins

(13d), probably because Devī also practises austerities while abiding in the cave. Taking *pāda* 13b as one compound it means 'dwelling in the abyss of a cavern', which also makes good sense.

14: In *pāda* 14a *devī* refers to the goddess Raktā. Because Devī observes that Raktā is pleased with Her practising yoga, She addresses Herself to her. Devī speaks with a 'distinct (*prasanna*), low (*gaṃbhīra*) voice' (14c). Since we have assumed earlier that Devī is hiding in a deep cave, Her voice will be low and sonorous. She is called here Kujeśvarī, a common name for Devī in the ṢaṭSS and the KmT.

15: *Pāda* 15cd is not found in the KmT at this instance (see: p. 150).

16: *Sūkṣmādi-* in *pāda* 16a refers to the creation in general, and to the phases in which 'speech' (*śabda*) originates in particular, e.g. *sūkṣma* and *sthūla* (cf. 3,103; 104 Notes). The lines 15cd and 16ab are inserted by the author of the ṢaṭSS between lines taken directly from the KmT to stress the importance of Mālinī here as the female representative of the fifty *akṣaras*, which form the basis of creation in Tantric concepts.

The pseudo-etymological explanation of the name Oḍiyāna in 16cd is not clear to me: BC both read *uḍḍito* in *pāda* 16b, while A reads here *uḍratā* which is probably wrong for *uḍritā* (cf. 16c). The meaning of both words is unfortunately uncertain: both readings are obviously past passive participles, but it is puzzling from which verbs they are derived. The form *uḍḍita* is likely to be connected with the verb *ud-ḍī-*, 'to fly upwards', which has, however, *uḍḍīna* for its p.p.p. Besides, the meaning 'flown up' does not seem to make any sense in the context. The form *uḍrita* of MS A is perhaps even more enigmatic, since it cannot be connected with any known Skt verb. We have chosen for the reading *uḍḍitā*, which the KmT reads also in this instance, and translated it with a non-committal 'connected with'.

17: *Pāda* 17ab is not found in the KmT, and seems to anticipate *śloka* 20a, in which the Mahāpīṭha Oḍiyāna is related to the faculty of hearing. As we have seen in 1,42, this Mahāpīṭha represents the two ears at both sides of the head (Mt. Meru). Without it there is deafness (Ṭ *tena pīṭhena vinā badhiratvam*). With the term *purāvasthā* (17c), 'the places of towns', those particular physical places are meant, to which the daughters of Devī are related. Instead of the term *pura*, we find also synonyms such as *gocara*, *sthāna*, *āvāsana*, *gahvara*, *āśraya*, *pīṭha*, *rājya*, *grāma*, *pada*, *viśrāma*, and *pradeśa*. The sons of Devī are not connected with 'towns' etc. but here the term *siṃhāsana* is used (cf. 31).

18: The lord of the goddess Raktā will be Ādhārīśa, who will descend from the Khecarīcakra (cf. 2,5 Notes). In the KmT the name of the future husband is Mitrānanda (KmT 2,47b). From him Raktā will receive eight sons, who are described as *ṣaḍguṇa* (18d), 'endowed with six qualities'. It is doubtful to which this refers: perhaps the six actions of a king in foreign politics are meant (Manu 7,160), but this does not seem very likely. The KmT has the same reading (KmT 2,42b), and the number 'six' is again referred to with regard to the eight sons in KmT 2,48b where the sons are described with *ṣaṭkulādhipatīśvarāḥ*, 'Masters of the group of six commanders (*adhipati*)'. It seems that *guṇa* and *kula* are used here much on the same line, but the meaning of both words differs considerably. It, requires, however, only a small emendation to remove this difference: instead of *ṣaḍguṇāḥ* one should read *ṣaḍ gaṇāḥ* in *pāda* 18d, 'the six groups'. Obviously this refers to the six guardians of the first

Mahāpīṭha, who are not mentioned otherwise in the text, while the sons and daughters are. The guardians in each of the five Mahāpīṭhas are designated by the names *praticāraka* (38b), *putraka* (60b), *pālaka* (88b; 133a), and *praticāra* (116d), but never in the text itself are they called *gaṇas*. The Ṭ, however, uses the designation *gaṇa* in its commentary on 4/5,8a, which deals with the number of daughters, sons and guardians of this first Mahāpīṭha. It seems therefore acceptable to read *ṣaḍ gaṇāḥ* instead of *ṣaḍguṇāḥ* in *pāda* 18d. The translation of *pādas* 18cd should then run as follows: 'You will have eight sons in human shape, and there will be a group of six attendants'. Since, however, all the MSS of both the KmT and the ṢaṭSS unanimously read *ṣaḍguṇāḥ* we have not altered the text.

Note that the sons and (possibly) the guardians are mentioned before the daughters, who are referred to in *pāda* 19a immediately followed by the sons for the second time (19b).

19: Raktā will become the mother of the eight Śākinīs. These are obviously the eight daughters: Rudrāṇī, Rudraśākī etc. (27 ff.). Only in this instance are the daughters of Devī given a name for the group in total besides their personal names. The eight Śakinīs are most likely manifestations of the goddess Śākinī, who belongs to the so-called Ugraṣaṭka, 'The Six Terrible Ones': Ḍākinī, Rākinī, Lākinī, Kākinī, Śākinī, and Hākinī or Yākinī. For the Siṃhāsanādhipas (19b): 31 ff.

From *pāda* 19c up to *pāda* 26d fourteen lines are found in the text, which are not found in the KmT. The reading of BC for *pāda* 19c (*tvaṃ tv ādhāragatā śaktiḥ*) seems to be a *lectio facilior*. What exactly is meant with *tattvādhāragatā* is not clear to me, but a relation to the name of the lord of this Mahāpīṭha, Ādhārīśa, seems probable. Moreover, the first Mahāpīṭha is called *ādhāravyāpti* (26a). (For the meaning of *ādhāra* here, see 24 Notes).

20: = 1,48cd; 49ab.

21: In *pāda* 21c it is explained in what state people would be without the four Mahāpīṭhas (21d *tair vinā*): they would be mute (*mūka*; because Jālandhara = *vaktra*, the mouth), blind (*andha*; because Kāmākhya together with Hrada and Nīlahrada represents the eyes), deaf (*badhira*; Oḍiyāna represents both ears), and impotent (*klība*; Pūrṇagiri stands for *puṣṭi*, 'thriving').

22: The fifth Mahāpīṭha, Mātaṅga, which is treated in the *ślokas* 118-132, has no physical faculty as the other four have, nor any specific geographical location: it is transcendent.

24: In *pāda* 24b the reading of A corresponds with the reading of BC: *anyeṣāṃ bhrāntikārakāḥ*, 'causing confusion among others'. The reading of A might also be translated with 'making the other Śāstras superfluous'. In *pāda* 24cd five constituents of the body are enumerated: firmness (*kāṭhinya*), heat (*uṣṇa*), fluidity (*drava*), motion (*śīghra*), and aperture (*chidra*). These five are connected with the five Mahāpīṭhas, although in the next *śloka* (25b) only four out of the five Mahāpīṭhas are mentioned. In the enumeration of the daugthers in each of the five Mahāpīṭhas one particular daughter is connected with each of this series of five constituents. Oḍiyāna: Bhaṭṭikā (28b *sthairyakā-pura* = *kāṭhinya*); Jālandhara: Mālā (49a *uṣṇatva*); Pūrṇagiri: Haṃsāvalī (75a *dravākhya* [*pura*]); Kāmākhya: Hariṇī (103c *dhāvana* = *śīghra*); Mātaṅga: Sukeśī (123a *brahmarandhra* = *chidra*). Although this series of five constituents as enumerated in the *pādas* 24cd are not known from other texts, as far as I know, the connstituents are most probably identical with the well-known five *tattvas/bhūtas/skandhas*. Thus: *kāṭhinya* = *pṛthivī*; *uṣṇa* = *tejas*; *drava* = *jala*; *śīghra* = *vāyu*; *chidra* = *ākāśa*. It should be remarked, however, that in the series mentioned above of *tattvas tejas* comes before *jala*, while usually the reverse is found. Since the first Mahāpīṭha is connected with 'firmness' (*kāṭhinya*, *sthairyakā*, or *pṛthivī*), the compound *tattvādhāragatā* (19c) might be seen in this context: 'in the *tattva* [called] Ādhāra'. The word *ādhāra* can easily be connected with the concept of 'firmness' (cf. 28b Notes). The inversion of *tattvādhāra-* from *ādhārattva-* is probably *metri causa*.

25: In *pāda* 25b the first four Mahāpīṭhas are mentioned in their short form: O[ḍiyāna], Jā[landhara], Pū[rṇagiri], and Kā[mākhya]. Note that Kāmākhya is here, and elsewhere, abbreviated as Ka and not Kā.

26: In *pāda* 26a the reading of A (*hṛdi sthāne tu rudrāṇāṃ*) does not seem correct: *rudrāṇāṃ* might be wrong for *rudrāṇī*, but the connection with the heart (*hṛdi*) is out of place in the enumeration of places related to the daughters in this Mahāpīṭha, which can all be put under the concept of 'firmness', the characteristic feature of this first Mahāpīṭha. The Ṭ also connects Rudrāṇī with the skin (*tvacā*).

27: Kekarā is located in the 'town of the bones' (27d *asthijāpura*). Although *asthija* means 'marrow', we have translated it with 'bones' (*asthi*) on the authority of the Ṭ (*kekarā asthisthāne hāḍeṣu*).

28: In *pāda* 28b the last daughter of Devī is called Bhaṭṭikā (A: Bahikā). The Ṭ which also reads Bhaṭṭikā at first instance, has an alteration by another hand changing Bhaṭṭikā into Haṭṭikā. Furthermore the Ṭ explains *sthairyakāpura* with *ādhāra* (cf. 24 Notes).

After the enumeration of the daughters the lord of the Mahāpīṭha is mentioned, i.e. Ādhārīśa. From the text it appears that he is also called Māndhātṛ (28c), and in this form has his location in the pores of the skin (28c *romapīṭha*). The Ṭ does not consider *māndhātā* to be a personal name, and explains this half-*śloka* with *ādhārīśaḥ māṃsādidhātuṣu tathā romakūpeṣu*, 'Ādhārīśa [is located] in the *dhātus* flesh etc., and in the pores of the skin'. Evidently the Ṭ divides *māndhātā* into *mān* and *dhātā*, assuming that the author of the Ṭ had the same reading of the text as we have. The form *mān* could be an abbreviation for *māṃsa* or better *mānsa* as it is sometimes written, but *-dhātā* (A: *-dāta*) is difficult to connect with the *dhātu* of the Ṭ. Although the explanation of the Ṭ is not acceptable with regard to the text itself, the author of the Ṭ might have had reason not to consider *māndhātā* in *pāda* 28c as another name for Ādhārīśa. Only in the case of this first Mahāpīṭha this occurs. Moreover, only here the lord of the Mahāpīṭha is connected with a location on the body (cf. 51cd; 78ab; 105cd; 123b).

30: 'The Fifty' (30a) refer to the fifty letters of the Sanskrit alphabet, and at the same time to the fifty manifestations of Mālinī representing these fifty letters. The fifty manifestations of Mālinī are added to the sons as their *śaktis* or female consorts.

The translation of *pāda* 30d is open to some doubt, and depends on how one interprets the word *mālinyā*. Regularly it is the instr. sg. from Mālinī, which renders an acceptable translation: 'by them (e.g. the sons) and by Mālinī this whole [body] is garlanded and related to the [fifty] Śaktis'. On the other side *mālinyā* might stand for *mālinyāḥ*, since the *visarga* is often dropped before a sibilant. In this way *mālinyā*[*ḥ*] represents the gen. sg. of the word Mālinī. There is even a third possibility, which results in the same meaning as the previous one: the form *mālinyā* can be considered to be a nom. sg. besides *mālinī*. In this way one should read *pāda* 30d as one compound: *mālinyāśaktisaṃyutam*, 'related to the Śaktis of Mālinī'. As out of the three possibilities two of them have the same meaning, we have opted for the meaning of these two.

In *pāda* 30c the use of the word *mālitaṃ*, 'garlanded', points very strongly to Mālinī. This is, of course, no sheer accidence. The female consorts of the sons are far more important than the sons themselves, the names of which occur only here. Their female consorts, however, being manifestations of Mālinī, figure in many instances of the text. Moreover, the locations on the human body connected with the sons and their consorts are actually those of the consorts proper (cf. Appendix I).

32: In *pāda* 32a we have translated *nādinyā* with an instr. sg. from *nādinī*; a nom. sg. *nādinya* is also possible. The location of Vāmana and Nādinī is described with *kamūrdhvaja* (32b), 'above Brahma'. With 'Brahma' the Brahmarandhra is here meant. The meaning of *pāda* 32d 'above the voice of Devī' is not clear. It is also possible to read *devyā vā ca kamūrdhvajam*, but this seems only to be a variant of *pāda* 32b. The Ṭ has a slightly different reading for *pāda* 32d: [*devyā*] *pāvakam ūrdhvajam* | *dhūmavartiprānte* (corr: *dhūmra-*), 'above Pāvaka, at the top of the column of smoke'. Pāvaka is best known as another name for Agni, or of 'fire' in general. As we have seen before (1,40b), on top of the head a column of smoke is imagined measuring twelve *aṅgulas*. It seems, therefore, that Vāmana and Nadinī are at the end of this column of smoke twelve *aṅgulas* above the head, at least according to the reading of the Ṭ which make good sense.

33: In *pāda* 33a it is possible to regard either Nivṛtti or Nivṛttyā as the name of the female consort of Harṣaṇa. In *pāda* 33c the reading of A (*divyākhyā*) is a common permutation for *vidyākhyā*.

34: The four sons and their *śaktis* mentioned in the preceding *śloka* constitute the 'garland of skulls' (34b: *muṇḍmālā*) of the goddess Mālinī, or perhaps rather the 'headband'. In chapter 7 of the text in which the fifty Śaktis are enumerated together with their location on the body, the four are connected with the *śiromālā* of Mālinī, 'the headband'. Obviously the *muṇḍamālikā* is on the forehead (34a *bhāla*; Ṭ *lalāṭasiṃhāsana*). The explanation of this *muṇḍamālikā* in the Ṭ is *caturbhāgakapāla*, 'the fourfold skull', which probably means that the head is divided into four parts, each part being dedicated to one of the sons mentioned in *śloka* 33.

In the *pādas* 34cd Ekavaktra and Grasanī are situated in what is called the *kāmaṭhamaṇḍala* (MS A), or the *kamalamaṇḍala* (MSS BC) which seems to be a *lectio facilior*, however, meaning 'the circle of lotuses'. The word *kāmaṭha*, however, is not very clear. It means 'belonging to the tortoise (*kamaṭha*)' — a meaning which hardly seems to be appropriate in the context, as *kāmaṭhamaṇḍala* should refer to a particular part of the body. In chapter 7 of our text (see above) the Śakti Grasanī is related to the 'circle of the head' (*śira-maṇḍala*); the KmT connects Grasanī with the mouth (*vaktra*). Both instances refer at least to the head (ṢaṭSS), or a particular part of the head (KmT). The Ṭ follows the explanation as found in the 7th chapter of the ṢaṭSS, and takes *kāmaṭha* also as a synonym for 'head' (*śiraḥsiṃhāsana*). The meaning 'head' for *kāmaṭha*, however, is not attested in any dictionary, as far as I know, but can perhaps be made plausible. Besides 'tortoise' the word *kamaṭha* may also denote 'a waterjar'. From the globular shape of a jar the meaning 'head' might be derived. It ought to be remarked that the Ṭ in its comment on 34d seems to read *kamaṭha* instead of *kāmaṭha*, but the text of the Ṭ is nearly illegible at this instance. The word *kamaṭha* is found, however, one more time in the text itself (4/5,121d *kamaṭhāpura*). Here the Ṭ gives, however, another explanation of the word: *kamaṭha* = *brahmarandhra-sthāna*. *Kamaṭha* in the sense of the Brahmarandhra can be explained (see: Notes on 121d). Consequently, *kāmaṭha* might be explained with 'belonging to the Brahmarandhra', which has a connection with the head.

36-37: In the *pādas* 36cd; 37ab the *bīja* of Ādhārīśa is given in a concealed way. For the interpretation of these lines we have to rely on the Ṭ, as most of the 'secret' names of the *akṣaras* are not known to me from any other source. Thus *nirāśraya*, 'without support', denotes the letter *ha* according to the author of the Ṭ. The third letter after the *ha* is the *ṣa* when counting backwards and including the *ha* itself. The Ṭ seems to have been in doubt whether to include the *ha* while counting backwards or not: the *ṣa* is twice changed into the *śa*. With regard to the *bījas* of the other Mahāpīṭhas, however, the *ṣa* appears to be correct. The *ṣa* then is 'adorned' (*maṇḍita*) with the *antahīna*, '[the letter] without end'. According to the Ṭ this is the *ā*. Most likely a reference is made to the Bhairava An-anta, which represents this *ā* in the Śabdarāśi-system (cf. ch. 7). The *bīja* of Ādhārīśa is completed with the letter called 'atmosphere' (*antarikṣa*), which can only stand for the *anusvāra* (*aṃ*), as this is the most usual 'ending' of a *bīja*. The Ṭ does not explain the *antarikṣa*. Summarizing, the *bīja* of the lord of the first Mahāpīṭha, Ādhārīśa, is the sacred syllable ṢĀṂ.

There might be some doubt as to the name of the fourth guardian of this Mahāpīṭha: A reads Mahotkaṭā, while BC have Balotkaṭa. The Ṭ corresponds with the reading of A. The KmT (2,45b) also has Mahotkaṭa. The reading of A and the Ṭ seems therefore correct. There is, however, a difficulty here: the seventh guardian of the fourth Mahāpīṭha is unanimously called Mahotkaṭa (116b) in the MSS ABC, while in the KmT (2,99b) he is called Balotkaṭa. Furthermore in the complete list of the guardians the first guardian is called Balotkaṭa (133d), while the latter is named Mahotkaṭa (136d). It follows thus that with regard to the seventh guardian of the fourth Mahāpīṭha all the MSS of the ṢaṭSS agree that his name is Mahotkaṭa. Consequently, one is inclined to opt for the reading as found in the MSS BC, and to read *balotkaṭaḥ* in pāda 37d instead of *mahotkaṭaḥ* (= MS A & Ṭ). Yet we have opted for the reading *mahotkaṭaḥ*, although an evident inconsistency is the result of this choice: two guardians have the same name. A determinant factor in this regard is the fact that all MSS of the KmT read this *mahotkaṭaḥ* in the present instance. Since the KmT is anterior to the ṢaṭSS, the reading of the KmT is followed — a reading which corresponds with the oldest MS of the ṢaṭSS. Consequently, if the list of guardians of the Mahāpīṭhas should be made 'correct', the name of the seventh guardian of the fourth Mahāpīṭha might be changed into Balotkaṭa, although this name is only found in the KmT, of which all the MSS consulted are unanimous in reading Balotkaṭa. The fact, however, that there might be two guardians with the same name, is found once more: both in the second and in the fourth Mahāpīṭha a guardian named Bṛhatkukṣi is found.

38: Note that the names of the six guardians all refer to an elephant, especially Gaṇeśa: Caturbhuja, Gaṇādhyakṣa, Gajavaktra and Vināyakya are all names for Gaṇeśa; Airāvatya refers to the elephant of Indra; Mahotkaṭa should mean 'the one with an abundance of rutting fluid', which can only be applied to elephants. The variant reading Balotkaṭa (see Notes previous *śloka*) has the non-committal meaning 'the one with immense strength', which is not an epithet only applicable to elephants. The epithet *mahotkaṭa* is not found in any of the current dictionaries, but it looks very much like the usual designation of an elephant in rut, *madotkaṭa* (Amarakoṣa, 1538).

Unlike the daughters and the sons, the guardians are not connected here with any location on the body nor with any physical faculty. It is only after the complete enumeration of the guardians (133-137) that they are connected with the human body (139-142). The Ṭ, however, gives their relation with the body as soon as they are mentioned in each Mahāpīṭha. For *pādas* 38cd the reading of the MSS BC has been chosen: ... *saṃyogaḥ* ... *prokto'pi* ..., as in the reading of A (... *saṃyugāḥ* ... *proktāpi* ...) the gender of *saṃyuga* is not correct and double Sandhi is found in *proktāpi*. The meaning of both readings, however, is the same. *Purā* (38d) means 'previously', although the locations of the guardians are not mentioned before by Bhairava, not in the KmT, nor in the ṢaṭSS. One might argue that *purā* is wrong for *purāḥ*, 'towns', thus referring to the localities of the guardians. The designation *pura*, however, appears to be strictly reserved for the locations of the daughters. The locations of the guardians are in the Ṭ always referred to with *sthāna*.

40: After Her visit to Ulaṃbikā/Oḍiyāna Devī goes to the second Mahāpīṭha, Jālandhara, which is identified with the place Karālaṃba. As is said in the *pādas* 40cd, the place immediately becomes 'full of fire'. Since this second Mahāpīṭha is characterized by the concept of 'heat' (*uṣṇa*) or *tejas* (cf. 24 Notes), this condition of the place is understandable.

41: Although the place is blazing with flames all over, it is yet agreeable and cool (*saumya*): the flames are only an illusion (cf. next *śloka*). What precisely is meant with 'fierce word' (*ugra śabda*) is not clear, but probably it refers to the fact that this second Mahāpīṭha represents the faculty of speech (cf. 20b), and to the concept of 'heat' of this place.

42: In the *pādas* 42ab the name Jālandhara is etymologically explained. It is connected with *jvāla*, 'flame' (40cd; 41ab), and with *jāla*, 'illusion; magic' (42a). Besides the obvious meaning 'illusion; magic' for *jāla*, it may also be derived from *jala*, 'water', the only substance which can control (42c *dhṛtaṃ*) fire.

44: The subject of *paśyaty* (44b) is Devī, Who is described as *vicitraracanānekā* (44a; cf. *anekopāyaracanā* (15a)). Before Her She observes an *indrajālaka*. It is not certain what exactly is meant by *indrajālaka* here, but probably it is some kind of delusion conjured up by Her own magic. Apparently the Goddess is amazed at its appearance, and asks after its origin (44c) since She has never seen it here before (44d). The use of *adhvara*, 'sacrifice' (44d) here does not fit too well in the context. Probably it has been confused with the word *adhvan*, 'road', which we have translated here. Possibly we have to do here with another attempt to explain the name Jālandhara: *indra-jāla* + *adhara*.

45: After having asked for the origin of the delusion, it does not answer to the question of Devī, but remains silent as it appears. Devī assumes that the illusion is too startled to speak. When Devī addresses it again, it appears that the illusion has the shape of a female, as can be deduced from *tuṣṭā* (45b) and *tubhyaṃ* (45c). The meaning of *tuṣṭā* in this context is not very clear: perhaps the female illusion is so pleased by

Devī, that it is unable to utter a sound. The reading of the KmT (2,53d: *bhraṣṭā*, 'bereft [of your senses]') seems more to the point.

The fact that the female illusion does not reply to Devī's question is used to explain the name of the local deity in Karālamba, who is identical with the magic illusion mentioned before. Therefore Devī proclaims her to be called 'the one with the terrible mouth' (*karālavadanā*; cf. *ugra śabda* in 41c). In the text the goddess is not mentioned by name, except for this instance. The Ṭ calls her Karālā Devī, while the KmT has Karālī (KmT 2,57d; 63a). Since the goddess can obviously endure Devī's *tejas*, she is also called *māyājālaniyāmikā* (45d). The construction of the *pādas* 45cd is peculiar. We have assumed that *karālavadane* and *māyājālaniyāmike* are both vocatives of a fem. sg. The literal translation of this line then runs: '[Therefore] for you [there will be the invocations] "O Karālavadanā", and "O Māyājālaniyāmikā"'.

46: The lord of Karālā is actually called Śrīkuṇḍalīśa (51d; 58b). Perhaps *pāda* 46d should run: *chrīsiddhaḥ kuṇḍalīyakaḥ*.

47: The epithet *aśeṣārthavida* (47a) for Kuṇḍalīśa means 'omniscient'. In *pāda* 47d both MS A and the KmT (2,56b) read *duhitā*, which is the nom. sg. of *duhitṛ*, while a plural is actually required (*duhitaraḥ*) since there are ten daughters in this second Mahāpīṭha. The MSS B (*duhitās*) and C (*duhitāḥ*) solve this inconsistency by accepting a form *duhitā* besides *duhitṛ*. The ten daughters are called after their mother Karālā, *karālinī* (47c).

49: For *uṣṇatva* (49a) see Notes on *śloka* 24. The fourth daughter, Pāvanī, is connected with the 'realm of colours' (*varṇagocara*). Note that her name is the same as the female consort of the second son in the fourth Mahāpīṭha. It is doubtful to what *varṇagocara* refers. The translation 'letters' for *varṇa* seems out of place here, compared with the other 'towns' in the enumeration which are all related to the concept of 'heat' or 'radiance'. Possibly *varṇa* should be translated in this context with 'colour', or 'lustre'. The reading of the MSS BC (*vartma-gocara*) probably refers to the eyelids. The Ṭ explains *varṇagocara* with 'the eyes' (*netra*) or 'the atmosphere' (*ākāśa*).

50: The daughter called Harṣaṇī is related to what is called *sarvabhakṣāṅga* (50a). In the Ṭ this is explained with *sarvabhakṣā aṅkeṣu*, which is not clear to me. Harṣaṇī might be related to the stomach, where all the food is consumed. In *pāda* 50b Carcikā is mentioned, situated in what is 'both touched and not touched' (*spṛṣṭāspṛṣṭeṣu*). In the KmT this daughter is called Jayā (KmT 2,58c), but three manuscripts (FJK) read Carcā. It is not clear to what particular place she is related, nor what its relation to the concept of *uṣṇa* might be. The Ṭ offers no solution for *spṛṣṭāspṛṣṭeṣu*, which it only repeats from the text.

51: In *pāda* 51a MS A reads Pracaṇḍa (wrong for Pracaṇḍā) instead of Caṇḍā. Both in the KmT (2,58d) and in the Ṭ the name appears as Caṇḍā. Instead of Rugminī (MS A) the MSS BC and the Ṭ read Rukminī. The Ṭ concludes this enumeration of the ten daughters with *iti sākinī* (cf. Notes *śloka* 19). The *pādas* 51cd are not explained in the Ṭ, but it gives another name of Kuṇḍalīśa, namely Kuraṅkośa (*kuraṅkośaḥ nāmāntareṇa kuṇḍalīśaḥ*), which looks very much like the name of the lord of the third Mahāpīṭha, Kuraṅgīśa (78a).

52: In the KmT (2,59a) and in the Ṭ the second son is called Sumati instead of Sumata (*pāda* 52c). The place allotted to Sumata and Vajriṇī is the mouth. The Ṭ did not understand the form *cāsye* (52c), or had a corrupt reading of the text, since it only states ... *vajriṇī vajrasiṃhāsana*: Vajriṇī is located in the Vajrasiṃhāsana, which does not make much sense and seems to be clearly a 'solution' based on the name Vajriṇī.

54: According to the Ṭ the son Meghanirghoṣa and his *śakti* Khirvarā are related to the front teeth (*rājadanta-siṃhāsana*), which corresponds with the 7th chapter of the ṢaṭSS where Khirvarā is said to be *rājadantagā*. The Ṭ has a different reading for the names of the son and his *śakti*, which are respectively Megha and Nirghoṣadhāriṇī or Khikhirvarā.

55: Śikhivaktra and Māyā are located in the *siṃhāsana* of the tongue (55b), which is also stated in the 7th chapter (*rasanā*). The Ṭ defines *jihvā* with *sarasvatīsiṃhāsana*, which is not correct (cf. Notes *śloka* 114).

56: Kālakuṭa and Nārāyaṇī are located on the Suṣumṇā (56c) or Madhyamā, the central one of the three Nāḍīs. In the Ṭ (*karṇa-siṃhāsana*) and in chapter 7 (*śravaṇau dakṣavāmau*) the two ears are mentioned in this respect.

57: The reading of A for the *pāda* 57a corresponds with *śloka* 46a. The MSS BC regard *ete* as referring to the sons. In the *pādas* 57cd & 58ab the name of Kuṇḍalīśa, Lord of this second Mahāpīṭha, is explained. According to the Ṭ the basis in the *pādas* 57cd is described, which is called *kuṇḍala* (Ṭ: *ittham mūlasthāne kuṇḍalābhidhāne*). The basis called *kuṇḍala* (lit. 'circle') consists of a square, a triangle and a hexagon. The description is very much alike the description of the fourth Saṃvartāmaṇḍala, which is located in the Mūlādhāra (2,12cd-14ab).

58: In *pāda* 58a the reading of MS A, which we have followed, differs considerably from the reading of the MSS BC. The Ṭ which reads *kuṇḍo īśānāgniyukto yaḥ* for *pāda* 58a, follows BC. The 'Agni of the Kuṇḍala' (58a *kuṇḍalīyāgni*) is probably Vaḍavānala, who is mentioned in connection with the fourth Saṃvartāmaṇḍala (2,14a). The MSS BC probably did not understand this mention of Agni in connection with the *kuṇḍala*, and changed *kuṇḍala* to *kuṇḍa*, which denotes the circular fire-pit. In this way the mention of Agni was made plausible. The Ṭ explains that Īśa and Agni are identical (Ṭ *ya īśaḥ īśvaraḥ saiva agnir ucyate*). The fact that the Lord of this Mahāpīṭha is identified with Agni is not surprising, as the characteristic of this place is *uṣṇa* or *tejas*.

In the *pādas* 58cd and 59ab the *bīja* of Kuṇḍalīśa is given in a concealed way, as it was done in the case of the first Mahāpīṭha (36cd; 37ab). 'The letter taken previously' was the *akṣara ṣa* (36c); the letter after this one is the *śa*. The *śa* then is 'covered' (*carcita*) with the *viṣamāṅga*. According to the Ṭ with *viṣamāṅga* the vowel *e* is meant. *Viṣama* means 'odd number'. Since the *e* is the eleventh letter, the explanation of the Ṭ seems correct. Moreover, the *e* is written in the Nāgarī-script above the consonant: in this way the term 'covered' is understandable.

59: In *pāda* 59a *vibhāga* can only designate the *anusvāra*, as the Ṭ confirms. Thus the *bīja* of Kuṇḍalīśa is ŚEṂ.

The second guardian of the second Mahāpīṭha is called Bṛhatkukṣi (59c), the namesake of the fifth guardian of the fourth Mahāpīṭha (116a).

60: We have seen that the names of the guardians of the first Mahāpīṭha all point to an 'elephant'. The same appears to be true here: *meghavarṇa*, 'cloud-coloured', refers to the identification of the elephant with a rain-cloud; *bṛhatkukṣi* ('fat-bellied'), *ekadaṃṣṭra*, *gaṇeśvara* and *vighnarāja* are all epithets of Gaṇeśa; *mahānanda*, 'of great bliss', is not known to me as an epithet peculiar to elephants. Perhaps it is a permutation with *mahānāda* ('making a loud noise') which designates an elephant. It should be kept in mind, however, that none of the MSS of the ṢaṭSS or of the KmT (2,61c) have a variant reading of *mahānanda*. The surmise, however, that the six guardians of this Mahāpīṭha should all be considered as a form of Gaṇeśa, is corroborated by the fact that the KmT calls them *gaṇeśvarāḥ*, 'manifestations of Gaṇeśvara' (KmT 2,61d).

62: After Her visit to Jālandhara Devī next turns to the Great Forest of Sahya, where the third Mahāpīṭha Pūrṇagiri is located. The Ṭ reads *pūrṇagiripīṭhe sahyavana-pallikā*: 'In the Pīṭha Pūrṇagiri [there is] a small forest-village [called] Sahya'. In contrast with the places mentioned in connection with the preceding two Mahāpīṭhas Sahya is known: the Sahyādri are the Western Ghats. The goddess usually related to this place, however, is called Ekavīrā (cf. Sircar 1973: 27; 68) and not Caṇḍākṣiṇī, as she is called in this part of the text. Although Sahya is called a forest in *pāda* 62b, it is also a mountain, as becomes clear from 70b (*parvato'yaṃ*) which refers obviously to Pūrṇa-*giri*.

In *pāda* 62c the expression *saṃpūrṇamaṇḍalārcibhiḥ* is not clear to me. The literal translation of *saṃpūrṇamaṇḍala*, i.e. 'the complete circle', does not make much sense here. Most likely *saṃpūrṇamaṇḍala* has a specific, technical meaning. In 72c the lord of this third Mahāpīṭha is called *saṃpūrṇamaṇḍalādhara*. The use of *saṃpūrṇa* in the context of the third Mahāpīṭha called *Pūrṇa*-giri might easily be caused etymologically, but this assumption is not very helpful in understanding the meaning of Saṃpūrṇamaṇḍala. The use of *arci* ('flame') in this context suggests that the Saṃpūrṇamaṇḍala might have a 'fiery' nature. It is rather attractive, therefore, to regard the Saṃpūrṇamaṇḍala as another designation for the Saṃvartāmaṇḍala to which the god of fire, Agni, is very closely related. The use here of Saṃpūrṇamaṇḍala instead of Saṃvartāmaṇḍala might be due to the etymological reasons referred to above.

63: The *śloka* 63 has been inserted by the author of the ṢaṭSS, and is not found in the corresponding passage of the KmT (2,63cd ff.). In *pāda* 63a the word *jagat* as found in *śloka* 62d (*jagat-traya*) is explained with *śarīra* ('body'). Devī Who filled the three worlds or the human body with the 'lustre of the Saṃpūrṇamaṇḍala' (62cd) is identified with the *kalā* situated above the palate (*tālūrdhvasthā*). This identification with this particular *kalā* is unfortunately not explained in the Ṭ. Perhaps it refers to the eighth Chapter of our text in which a *kalā* called *amṛtātmikā* is mentioned, which is located 'at the end of sound' (*nādasyānte*) (= KmT 5,94 ff.). In this way the location 'above the palate' might be understandable. Probably in the same way one should understand KmT 6,65cd (= ṢaṭSS *paṭala* 10): *amṛtākhyāṃ parāyoniṃ bhāvayen mastakopari*, 'one should imagine the *yoni* of Parā which is called *amṛta*, above the head'. *Parā* refers here to the triple graduation of creation: *para*, *sūkṣma*, and *sthūla*. The mention of *amṛta* in this context is furthermore seen in *śloka* 68c of this chapter of the ṢaṭSS, in which it is stated that the local goddess becomes 'filled' with the divine *amṛta* (*divyāmṛtena pūryantīṃ*), as well as in *pāda* 63d.

The fact that the world 'ends and begins with the Rudras' (63c) refers to the concept that both the world and the human body are constituted by the fifty *akṣaras* of the Sanskrit alphabet, which are here called the [fifty] Rudras, the male counterpart of the fifty — female — Mālinīs.

65: Before the *pādas* 65ab the KmT reads one half-*śloka* which is not included in the ṢaṭSS: *tāvac caṇḍākṣī balavat paricāryam anekadhā* (KmT 2,65cd), which is evidently the continuation of 64cd (*yāvat* ... *tāvac*). In the ṢaṭSS *yāvat* in *pāda* 64c is not followed by a corresponding *tāvat* — the occurrence of *tāvac* in *śloka* 68a (note that the first two words of *pāda* 68a are nearly identical with the 'missing' line from the KmT) seems to be at too great a distance to connect it with the *yāvat* of *pāda* 64c.

In the *pādas* 65cd the name of the local goddess, Caṇḍākṣiṇī, is mentioned for the first time, and is at the same time identified with Devī. As we have observed earlier (Notes on 24) the basic idea of the second and the third Mahāpīṭha is irregular: instead of the usual order 'water' (*jala*) and 'fire' (*tejas*) we find the reverse here. Yet, although the third Mahāpīṭha should be connected with *drava/jala* ('water') according to the system of the ṢaṭSS, we find in *pāda* 65c a clear reference to *tejas* (*tejobhābhiḥ pradīpyantī*) in order to explain the name Caṇḍākṣiṇī and its relation to Devī in this Mahāpīṭha. The name Caṇḍākṣiṇī literally means 'She with the burning eyes'. The reading of the MSS BC for *pāda* 65d seems a *lectio facilior*, in which *caṇḍākṣiṇyā* is either a regular instr. sg. fem. from *caṇḍākṣiṇī*, or a nom. sg. fem. ending in *-yā* instead of *-ī*. The MS A reads for *pāda* 65d *caṇḍākṣinyo paṣe (pathe?) smṛtā*, which does not make much sense, however, at first sight. The form *caṇḍākṣiṇyo* before *paṣe* is only possible when one assumes the reading *'paṣe*, or regards the two words as one single compound (*caṇḍākṣiṇyopaṣe*). The latter possibility can be safely ruled out since a word *upaṣa* (perhaps: *upaśa* or *upasa*) does not exist, although one could consider a word *upāsa* (from the verb *upās-* 'to do homage') which is, unfortunately, not attested for in any text. The former possibility, a word *apaṣa* (perhaps *apaśa* or *apasa*), is not very helpful either: no such word is found in any of the current dictionaries. The best change gives perhaps the reading *apasa* as a thematic derivation from Vedic *apás*, 'watery'. With regard to its meaning it would correspond with the concept of *drava/jala* for this third Mahāpīṭha. The word itself, however, is not very likely. Moreover, the word *caṇḍākṣiṇyo*, which precedes it, can only be a nom. or voc. pl. which does not fit in. It seems, therefore, that an emendation is required in *pāda* 65d: *caṇḍākṣiṇyā poṣe smṛtā*, in which *caṇḍākṣiṇyā* is a nom. sg. fem. ending in *-yā* instead of *-ī*; *poṣa* ('thriving') refers to the characteristic quality of Devī in this Mahāpīṭha, i.e. *puṣṭi* (cf. 20c), both words being derived from the same root *puṣ-*.

66: From *pāda* 66a it becomes clear that Devī finds Herself on a mountain (*adrau*), on which slopes the 'Great Forest of Sahya' is located (cf. 62 Notes; 70b). The KmT (2,67a) reads in this instance *yasmin adrau* instead of *tasmin adrau* (MS C). The reading of MS A seems to follow the KmT here: *ya[smin a]drau*. Therefore the reading of the KmT has been followed here, although none of the MSS of the ṢaṭSS actually have this reading.

In *pāda* 66b the epithet *ghanojjvalā* has been translated with 'bright as the lightning', although this meaning for *ghana* is not attested, as far as we know. The word *ghana*, however, can denote a 'cloud'. In this way the epithet *ghanojjvalā* might be understood as 'flaring up from a cloud', which is the lightning, of course. In *śloka* 66 the 'fiery' nature of Devī in this third Mahāpīṭha is stressed again (cf. 24 Notes; 62 Notes; 65 Notes).

68: The reading of the *pādas* 68ab is not correct, assuming that Devī is the subject of the verb *paśyati* (68b), to which the epithet *amitatejasā* (68b) points. Although Devī was already identified in *śloka* 65d with the local goddess Caṇḍākṣiṇī, it appears that She sees this local deity before Her. Consequently one should expect an acc.

caṇḍākṣiṇīm, which is metrically possible. The reading of the ṢaṭSS seems to be a corruption of the text of the KmT: *caṇḍākṣiṇī tv* instead of *caṇḍākṣiṇīty* (KmT 2,69a).

The local goddess is 'filled' by Devī with the Divine Fluid (68c *divyāmṛta*), as a result of which she becomes 'abounding in the qualities of the Divine Hosts' (68d *divyaughaśālinī*). As we have observed earlier (cf. notes on 1,5) there are three *oghas*: *divya*, *mānava* and *siddha*, of which the *divyaugha* is the most eminent one. By means of the Divine Fluid from Devī Herself the local deity is 'promoted' to the highest *ogha* (lit: stream).

69: Again in the *pāda* 69b one finds a reference to the name of this third Mahāpīṭha in the epithet *pūrṇamanorathā*, as well as in the following two *pādas* (69cd) in which twice a form of the root *pṝ-* (to fill) is used.

70: In *pāda* 70b the Mt. Pūrṇagiri is referred to as 'abounding in *tapas*' (*tapotkaṭa*). The KmT (2,71b) reads instead *tavodbhavaḥ*. Although the third Mahāpīṭha is related to *drava/jala* (cf. 24 Notes) its 'fiery' nature was observed already in *śloka* 65cd (cf. Notes). Here again the connection of this Mahāpīṭha with 'fire' is referred to. In this context it should be remembered that from the earliest times onwards fire and water are closely connected (cf. Gonda 1960: 68 ff.). In his commentary on ŚT 1,44 Rāghavabhaṭṭa enumerates the names of the ten bodily fires from three — unknown — sources. In the third series of these ten names we find as the seventh bodily fire one called Drāvaka (*drāvakākhya*), a name which is derived from the same root *dru-* as the word *drava* which is characteristic for this third Mahāpīṭha.

71: In *pāda* 71c all the three MSS read *jīva-*, while the KmT (2,72c) has *teja-* instead. The Ṭ allots the *tejaskandha* to the second Mahāpīṭha. The reading of the KmT points again to the fiery nature of this Mahāpīṭha (see above). This unanimous referring in all three MSS to *jīva* instead of the more appropriate *teja* as found in the KmT might be explained by the *śloka* 63 which is not found in the KmT. Here it is stated that everything subsists (*jīvita*) on the Divine Fluid (*amṛta*). Perhaps the mentioning of *jīva* instead of *teja* or *jala* refers to the fluid *par excellence*, the Amṛta, circuitously. In *pāda* 71d Pūrṇagiri and its Mistress are brought in relation with the third *yuga*, the Dvāpara Yuga. We have not seen that the two preceding Mahāpīṭhas were connected with the first two *yugas* (Kṛtā or Satya, and Tretā respectively), nor is the fourth Mahāpīṭha connected in any way to the fourth *yuga*, the Kali Yuga. The fifth Mahāpīṭha falls, of course, beyond the scope of this series since it is transcendental. Although not explicitly stated, it seems probable that the first four Mahāpīṭhas are connected with the four *yugas* owing to the tendency of the Indian mind to systematize.

72: The lord of this third Mahāpīṭha is called Kuraṅgīśa (72b) in the MSS B & C, while MS A always reads Kuruṅgīśa. In the KmT (2,73b) he is called Cakrānanda. We have chosen for the reading Kuraṅgīśa which is also found in the Ṭ instead of the reading as found in MS A, because it corresponds better with an etymological explanation of the name as found in 85cd; 86ab. Moreover, the Ṭ gave Kuraṅkośa as another name for the Lord of the second Mahāpīṭha (cf. 51 Notes), which sounds very much like Kuraṅgīśa. Thus we see that with regard to the third Mahāpīṭha not only the characteristic feature of the second Mahāpīṭha (fire) shines through, but also that the name of its Lord is very similar to the secondary name of the Lord of the second Mahāpīṭha.

Compared with the names of the previous two Mahāpīṭhas (Ādhārīśa and Kuṇḍalīśa) the name Kuraṅgīśa has the ring of being a more 'real' name, belonging to a particular local deity. The word *kuraṅga* means 'antilope' or 'deer' in general, but it is also the name of a mountain. According to the Bhāgavata Purāṇa (5,16,26) and the Devībhagavata Purāṇa (8,6,30) Mt. Kuraṅga is one of the mountains surrounding the Meru (cf. Kirfel 1967: 104). In this way Kuraṅgīśa should mean 'The Lord of Mt. Kuraṅga'. The reading of MS A, Kuruṅgīśa, could be connected with the name of a king mentioned in the ṚgS 8,4,19. Here we find a *dānastuti* for a certain king named Kuruṅgá (Sāyaṇa: ... *kuruṅganāmno rājño dānaṃ stauti*).

For the word *saṃpūrṇamaṇḍala* (72c) see Notes on *śloka* 62c.

In *pāda* 72d we emended the reading of MS A (*granthadhāro*) to *granthādhāro*, which is actually found in the KmT (2,73d).

73: In *pāda* 73c the form *tebhyas* (masc.) is not correct, since it obviously refers to the twelve daughters mentioned in the *pādas* 73ab. Instead of *tebhyas* one should expect *tābhyas* (fem.), which the KmT reads (KmT 2,74c).

74: In *pāda* 74b the reading of MS A (*pratīhāra*) has been emended to *pratīhārās*, which is grammatically correct. The reading of BC (*praticārās*) corresponds more or. less with the KmT (2,75b).

In the same *pāda* the expression *tadardhataḥ* is used to denote the number of servants in this third Mahāpīṭha. Thus 'half that [number = 12]' makes six, which is indeed the number of servants here. The reading of MS A here (*tad ucyateḥ*) does not make much sense, even when reading *tad ucyate* which is obviously meant.

75: For the location called *drava* (75a) see the Notes on *śloka* 24. The location of the second daughter Sutārā is not clear. The reading of MS A (*sinyakā priye*) does not make much sense. The MSS BC read both *saityakāśraye* which is not clear either; the Ṭ finally locates Sutārā in the *sainyasthāna*, but unfortunately does not explain the location any further. Although B&C have the same reading *saityakāśraye*, it is probably wrong for *sainyakāśraye*: both A and the Ṭ read *-nya-* for *-tya-* (two easily interchangeable ligatures), which at least allows the compound to be translated, 'the resort of the army'. This translation, however, does not make much sense in the context. All the locations of the twelve daughters are in some way or other related to the idea of 'flowing' or 'fluidity', the basic characteristic of this third Mahāpīṭha. The eleventh daughter Viśālākṣī does not seem to follow this pattern, since she is located in the ears, but the reading of the text does not appear to be correct (cf. *śloka* 77 Notes). The meaning of *sainyaka* or perhaps *saityaka* within the concept of 'fluidity' is not known to me. Perhaps one should consider the root *sinv-* (to wet), or *sic-* (to pour out) as the basis for a word *sainyaka*, but in that case *sainyaka* is obviously a wrong reading.

76: The fifth daughter is here called Śubhākṣī (76a), while in the KmT (2,76d) she is named Sulocanā. Both names have more or less the same meaning: 'She with the auspicious eyes', and 'She with the beautiful eyes', respectively.

77: The ninth daughter is called Viśvākṣī in the Ṭ and MS A (Viśvakṣī in A is obviously a slip of the pen). In the KmT (2,77b) she is called Vṛkānanā, 'She with the face of a wolf', a completely different name. Her location is in 'the flow of Viṣṇu' (*viṣṇuvāha*), which the Ṭ explains with *mūtrasthāna*, 'the place of the urine'. A connection of Viṣṇu and urine is not known to me from other sources. Most likely the compound *viṣṇu-vāha* is a wrong reading for *śiśna-vāha*, or rather *śiṣna-vāha*, 'the stream from the penis' (cf. *śloka* 122 Notes).

In *pāda* 77c Viśālākṣī is related to the ear (*śrutau* as the loc. sg. of *śruti*), which is corroborated in the Ṭ (*śrotrasthāna*). The location of Viśālākṣī in the ears does not seem correct when compared with the locations of the other daughters, which all have a relation with the concept of 'fluidity'. Most probable *śrutau* is an incorrect spelling of *srutau*, 'in the stream' (from *sruti*). It remains vague, however, which particular stream of the human body is meant.

78: The first son is here called Vāli (MS C & Ṭ), while the KmT reads Vali.

79: According to the Ṭ Vāli and Mohinī are connected with the ornaments of the right ear, and Nanda and Prajñā with those of the left ear, according to the Ṭ.

80: The Ṭ locates Hayagrīva and Lāmā on the right arm, and Haya with Vināyikī on the left arm.

81: From *pāda* 81b it becomes clear that Devī/Mālinī holds a skull in Her left hand.

83: Since the Goddess holds a skull in Her left hand, it follows that the trident (*triśūla*) is in Her right hand. The eleventh son is here called Śukra (Ṭ: Śuka), while in the KmT (2,79c) his name is Śakra.

84: According to the Ṭ Caṇḍa (KmT 2,79c: Caṇḍādhipa) and Bhīṣaṇī are located on the right shoulder.

85: In the *pādas* 85cd we find the usual etymological explanation of the name of the particular Mahāpīṭha, Kuraṅgīśa. The word *ku-* is regarded as a synonym for earth (*pṛthivī*). It is not clear what exactly is meant with *navāmbu* (85d): 'fresh water', or 'the nine-fold waters'. The latter interpretation might refer to the Nine Seas (*navārṇava*), but the relation with the Lord Kuraṅgīśa is not clear. For the sake of completeness we give the etymological explanation of the name Kuruṅga as proposed by Sāyaṇa in his commentary on ṚgS 8,4,19: *kuruñ jetuṃ gacchati kulaṃ vā gacchatīti vā kuruṅgaḥ*, in which the first part of the compound *kuruñ-* is either identified with the verb 'to conquer' (*jetum*) or with the noun 'family' (*kula*). The explanation by means of *kula* by Sāyaṇa points rather to the name Kuraṅga than Kuruṅga of the text. The postfix *-ga* is explained with *gacchati*, 'he goes'. Sāyaṇa further remarks that besides the form Kuruṅga the name Kuruṇḍa is also found, in which *-ḍa* has the same meaning as *-ga* (*ḍo 'nyatrāpi dṛśyata iti gamer ḍaḥ*). The meaning of the name Kuraṅga or Kuruṅga remains puzzling. Probably the name is of Munda origin. (cf. Kuiper 1948: 76 n.).

86: In *pāda* 86b the author returns to the meaning of *ku-* in the name Kuraṅga by stating explicitly that the meaning 'bad' or 'despicable' for *ku-* is not what is meant by the name Kuraṅga.

In the *pādas* 86cd and 87ab the *bīja* of Kuraṅgīśa is given. According to the Ṭ the letter *śa* is indicated with Kuṇḍalīśa. An argument in favour of this explanation in the Ṭ might be the fact that the *bīja* of the Lord of the previous Mahāpīṭha, Kuṇḍalīśa, is ŚEṂ, in which the basic consonant is the letter *śa*. Subsequently the third letter after the *śa* is the *sa*. This *sa* is above (lit. 'standing on the head of', *śirogata*) the letter called Arghīśa, which stands for the *ū* (cf. Appendix II). Next, the *bīja* is stated to be *svāṅkita*, 'marked by itself' (87a). This remark is rather enigmatic, but can only refer to the *anusvāra* (*aṃ*). Most likely the reading of BC (*khaṅkita*) should be followed here, which should be read as *khāṅkita*, 'marked by the aperture'. The expression *khāṅkita* is identical with *mahābilagata* in *pāda* 115a, which also denotes the *anusvāra*. In this way the *bīja* of Lord Kuraṅgīśa is SŪṂ.

87: In *pāda* 87d the order Durmukha, Sumukha has been chosen for, thus following the MSS BC and the Ṭ. In *śloka* 135cd the same order is found unanimously in the three manuscripts. The reverse order (Sumukha, Durmukha) as found here in MS A, corresponds with the parallel passage in the KmT (2,80d).

88: The fifth and the sixth guardians are called Avighna and Vighnakartṛ, respectively, in the KmT (2,81a).

90: In *pāda* 90a all the manuscripts read *pūrṇaṃ* instead of *śīghraṃ*, which the KmT reads here (KmT 2,82c). Although it is possible to translate *pūrṇaṃ* in such a way that it makes sense, it could also be a wrong reading for *tūrṇaṃ*, which has the same meaning as *śīghraṃ* of the KmT. In the Gorakṣasaṃhitā where the Mahāpīṭhas are also discussed (p. 9) we find exactly the same *pāda* with *tūrṇaṃ* instead of *pūrṇaṃ* or *śīghraṃ*.

After Her visit to the Forest of Sahya where the third Mahāpīṭha Pūrṇagiri was 'founded', Devī/Mālinī continues Her journey to the river Ucchuṣmā, which runs through the forest of Mahocchuṣma (90c). In the first chapter of our text the forest itself was only mentioned (1,37b *ucchuṣmavana*). Obviously the river and the forest are closely related to each other. According to the Ṭ the forest of Mahocchuṣma is to be located in the 'central aperture' (*madhyarandhrasthāna*), a location also mentioned in 1,44c. As 1,46ab states, the location of this forest of Mahocchuṣma is in the Brahmarandhra.

91: In the forest of Mahocchuṣma there are two ponds, called Nīla and Mahāhrada (1,37c: Hrada and Nīlahrada). As the Ṭ already stated in its commentary on 1,44d; 45a, the two ponds are to be identified with the two eyes (91d). The Kmt does not make this identification between the two ponds and the eyes in the corresponding passage, and reads for *pāda* 91d *divyājñāguṇaśālinī* (KmT 2,84d). The identification of the two ponds with the eyes agrees with the particular faculty of Devī in this fourth Mahāpīṭha, e.g. the faculty of 'seeing' (cf. *śloka* 20d).

92: With *aṃbikā* (92b) which literally means 'mother', probably Devī is meant. The local goddess, however, is also called 'mother' (cf. 94a).

It is doubtful what exactly is meant by *viṣvāṅgī* (92c) and *tattvāṅgī* (92d). The Ṭ unfortunately is silent on this point. Possibly the two ponds are meant, or rather two local goddesses dwelling in the ponds.

94: With *mātā* (94a) the local goddess Mahocchuṣmā (cf. 95c) is meant, while *mātā* in *pāda* 94c should refer to Devī Herself.

95: In *pāda* 95c only MS A reads *mahocchuṣmā* as the name for the local deity. The Ṭ also calls her by the same name. The reading of the MSS B & C agrees with the KmT (2,88a): *tāvocchuṣma*, which presumes a word *tāva* besides *tāvat* (cf. 100 Notes).

98: In *pāda* 98a reference is made to a *kalpa*. In the Notes on *śloka* 71 we have assumed that all the four Mahāpīṭhas are related to one of the *yugas*. The fourth Mahāpīṭha consequently belongs to the Kali Yuga. That *kalpa* here most likely refers to the Kali Yuga is corroborated by the KmT (2,90c), where the corresponding *pāda* runs *bhaviṣyati kalau prāpte*.

The name of the Lord of this Mahāpīṭha is Cakrānanda (98b; also 114b; 115b), who in the KmT was the Lord of the previous Mahāpīṭha (cf. 72 Notes). In the KmT the name of the Lord of Kāmarūpa is Candrānanda (KmT 2,90d). In the Ṭ Cakrānanda nor Candrānanda is mentioned, but there the Lord is called Madandhrīśa. The Ṭ explains the name with *ma[da?]n dhrāvayati karoti ca*, 'he arouses ardent passion', an explanation which corresponds with the explanation of the name Cakrānanda as presented in 113cd; 114ab.

99: The meaning of *pāda* 99c is puzzling at first sight. Obviously it is a wordplay on *kāma* in relation with the name Kāmarūpa, but why also *śūnya* (KmT 2,92a *tubhyaṃ*) is mentioned in this context is difficult to understand. In *pāda* 97 the name Kāmarūpa was already explained: the *rūpa* of *kāma* are the visible manifestations of *kāma* on the human body. As the Lord of this fourth Mahāpīṭha, Cakrānanda, arouses carnal desires in the human body (cf. 113; 114), it becomes obvious that the context of *pāda* 99c should be placed in the sphere of carnal love. Therefore it is perhaps more correct to translate *kāmuka* with 'lover' or 'one who is after carnal love' than with a meaningless 'one who wishes'. The translation of *pāda* 99c would then run: 'for the one who is after carnal love he [provides] lustful voidness'. Still the appearing of *śūnya*, 'voidness', in this context does not make much sense. Most likely *śūnyaṃ* in *pāda* 99c is a wrong reading for *śūnaṃ*, 'swollen'. In this way *śūnaṃ* might refer in this context to the swollen male member during carnal love (cf. *śūnagātra*, 'having swollen limbs'; *śūnāṇḍameḍhratā*, 'the swollen condition of the testicles and the penis'). The expression *kāmukaṃ śūn(y)aṃ* might thus be understood as 'the lustful swollenness', or simply 'erection'.

100: The reading of MS A in *pāda* 100d (*tāva* for *tāvat*) might be due to a slip of the pen (*tāva[d] ḍikkarikāḥ*), or indeed presumes a form *tāva* besides *tāvat* as we observed above (cf. 95 Notes). The reading of the KmT (2,93b *tava*) seems better, and is easier to translate.

In the same *pāda* the word *ḍikkarikāḥ* is a variant reading for *dikkarikāḥ*. It should be understood as a female derivation from *dikkara*, 'youthful', and not be connected with the subst. *dikkarika* (= *dikkarin*) meaning an 'elephant of the quarters', as this translation of the word makes little sense in the context.

101: Although the position of the verb *bhaviṣyanti* at the beginning of an odd-numbered *pāda* (101c) might suggest a close relationship with the preceding *pāda* (101b), this is not very likely here. The servants who are mentioned in *pāda* 101b are never given any epithet in their enumeration of the particular Mahāpīṭhas. Therefore the epithets *jagaddīpa* (101c) and *jagadānanda* (101d) most likely refer to the daughters and sons of Devī in the Mahāpīṭha Kāmarūpa.

102: The reading of the MSS B & C in *pāda* 102a *mahādevī* is corroborated, neither in the Ṭ nor in the KmT (2,94c). The first daughter is called Prabhā in all the other MSS.

The 'towns' (*puras*) of the thirteen daughters of Devī in this fourth Mahāpīṭha all have some relation with the concept of 'quickness' or 'sudden motion', as was already suggested by the characteristics of this Mahāpīṭha, e.g. *śīghra* (cf. *śloka* 24 Notes). The third daughter is unanimously called Śaṃsā in the three MSS and in the Ṭ. The KmT, however, mentions Śāntābhā as the third daughter (KmT 2,94c); MS F of the KmT only reads Śāntā at this instance. The *pura* of Śaṃsā is called *ākuñcana* (102c), which usually refers to the bending (of a limb). The meaning of its simplex *kuñcana*, 'sudden contraction (of veins or muscles)', however, seems to be a better translation of this particular *pura* in view of the characteristic of this Mahāpīṭha. The fourth daughter, Bhānumatyā (Ṭ: Bhānumatī), is called Bhānuvatyā in the KmT (2,94d).

103: Śrībalā (Ṭ Śrībālā), the fifth daughter (103a), is situated in a 'town' called *vapana*. The word *vapana* means 'the act of shearing/shaving/cutting off', which does not seem to fit in with the idea of 'quickness' or 'sudden motion'. The Ṭ reads instead of *vapana-grāma pavana-sthāna*, 'the place of the wind/breath', which corresponds better with the other 'towns' in this particular series. A confusion between the two words is certainly acceptable in manuscripts. Another possibility for a better reading of *vapana* could be *vamana*, 'the act of vomiting', which would also fit nicely with the other 'towns'. Confusion in manuscripts between the letters *pa* and *ma* is not seldom found, due to the shape in Nāgarī-script of the two, which resemble each other very much, certainly when not neatly written.

The daughters Hāriṇī (103b) and Hariṇī (103c) are called Hārī and Hāriṇī, respectively, in the KmT (2,95a). Instead of *dhāvana* (103c) the Ṭ reads *pācara-sthāna*, 'the place of fire/wind', which was corrected into *pācana-sthāna*, 'the place for cooking'. Instead of Mālinī (103d) the KmT reads Śālinī (KmT 2,95b).

104: The twelfth daughter, Kauśikī, is related to the 'town' called *śoṣana*, 'drying up', (from the root *śuṣ-*), but this meaning hardly fits in with the context. Most likely one should connect the word *śoṣana* here with the word *śoṣa*, 'breath', or *śūṣa*, 'vital air' (either from the root *śu-* or *śuṣ-*/*śvas-*. In this way we have translated *śoṣana* with 'panting'.

105: The name of the last daughter of Devī is open to some doubt. The KmT (2,96a) has her name as Śākodarī, which is difficult to understand: 'herb-bellied'? Both MS C and the Ṭ read Śukodarī, 'parrot-bellied', while the form Sūkodarī of the MSS A & B is not understandable unless *sūka* is a wrong spelling for *suka*, which in its turn is sometimes written instead of *śuka*, 'parrot'.

Apart from the name of this thirteenth daughter of Devī, her particular *pura* is also a kind of problem. The word *naiḥsvana* (105b; MSS B & C) is not attested for in any dictionary, but might easily be understood as a derivation from *niḥsvana*, 'soundless', a meaning which does not fit with the other 'towns' of this Mahāpīṭha, however. The reading of MS A (*nesvapada*) is probably the same reading as found in the Ṭ (*tesvapada*), since the letters *n* and *t* are easily confused in manuscripts. Moreover the vowel *ai* is often written as an *e* in manuscripts. In this way the manuscripts have either a form *naiḥsvana* (BC) or *naisva* (AṬ). The meaning of these two words is not clear. Perhaps the solution is found by reading *-śva-* instead of *-sva-*. Consequently the word might be connected with the verb *ni-śvas-* (often: *niḥ-śvas-*), 'to draw in the breath', or with *niḥ*-śvas-, 'to sigh'. Both meanings fit with the characteristics of the other twelve 'towns' — a derivation from the verb *niḥ-śvas-* seems to be the most likely. Therefore *naiḥsvanapura* of the text has been translated with 'the town of sighing'.

In *pāda* 105cd the Lord of the particular Mahāpīṭha is mentioned, as usual after the enumeration of the daughters. His name Cakrānanda is not given here, but he is endowed with epithet *svājñānanda* and is called a Mahāsiddha associated with the other constituents (*śeṣabhāva*), viz. the sons with their female consorts and the various parts of the body (cf. 113ab).

106: Bhānu and Vāyuvegā are connected with the 'second shoulder' (106b). Since the last pair of the previous Mahāpīṭha, Caṇḍa and Bhīṣaṇī, were related to the right shoulder (cf. 84 Notes), it follows that here the other or left shoulder is meant, which the Ṭ confirms (*vāmaskandha-siṃhāsana*).

107: The Ṭ has the form Pāvanī for the name of the female consort of Anantahetu instead of Pāvanyā. The name of the son himself is here Anantahetu (MS A), while the MSS B & C seem to read Anantadeha. The KmT (2,96c) has the same as MS A. The Ṭ only gives Ananta as his name.

In *pāda* 107ab the reading of BC differs completely from the reading as found in MS A. The name of the son is beyond doubt: the MSS B & C both read Surāja (= KmT 2,96d), while the Ṭ has the form Surājan (nom. sg.: Surājā). The reading of MS A (Sugajā, from Sugajan) is most probably a slip of the pen for the right Surājā since the *ga* and the *rā* look very much alike in written form.

The name of his *śakti* is completely different in the two readings: A reads Aṃbhikā (obviously wrong for Aṃbikā), while BC read Laṃbikā. A strong objection against the reading of A (Aṃbikā) is the fact that Aṃbikā is mentioned in this same enumeration as the female consort of Antaka (cf. 110a). Moreover, Aṃbikā represents the letter *ha* in the Mālinī-system (Appendix II). Although the 'correct' Mālinī-order of the fifty letters of the Sanskrit alphabet is not completely followed in the case of the five Mahāpīṭhas with regard to the female consorts of the sons, some groups of consorts/letters are always found together. From Appendix III[a] it becomes clear that the letter *ha* is out of place here and that the letter *ṣa* should be expected, which is represented in the Mālinī-system by Laṃbikā or Laṃbodarī, a name which is very much like the name Laṃbikā in our text. Following the reading of MS A would result in the appearance of the letter *ha* twice (*sc.* 107a & 110a), while the letter *ṣa* would have been left out completely. The Ṭ seems to follow the reading of A here, as it reads *surājā ha ambikā prāṇasiṃhāsane rodhane (A: rocane) vā*. Another point concerning the reading of MS A is its mentioning of the letter *ṣa* in the text itself, which we do not find in any other instance in this *paṭala*.

In *pāda* 107d none of the three manuscripts has a correct reading; thus we have emended the *pāda*. We have regarded *mahāmātryā* as the instr. sg. of *mahāmātrī*, which seems to be the name in B & C: *mahāmātry-a[r]jano* (wrong for: *-arjunau*). It is the only occurrence of the fact that a female consort of a son has been enriched with an epithet, since Chagalī (108a) is her personal name. It is not clear why it is only Chagalī who is endowed with the title Mahāmātrī. Most probably however it is the result of a wrong interpretation or reading of KmT 2,97a, where the fifth son is not simply called Arjuna, but Mahāvaktrārjuna.

108: The form *yukte* (108d) is obviously not correct, since a loc. sg. belonging to *stane* and *dvitīyake* does not make sense. Possibly the writer of the text simply forgot to write the small vertical stroke after *-kte*, which should have resulted in the reading *yukto*. We have seen that the sg. can be used in cases like this (107ab *śurājo laṃbikā ... saṃvyavasthitaḥ*). Bhīma and Pūtanā are, of course, connected with the left breast of the Goddess.

109: In *pāda* 109a the reading of MS A is possible (*droṇakaḥ siddha āmoṭī*), but does not seem correct, because nowhere else the sons are given the title *siddha*. The Ṭ reads the name Reṇuka instead of Droṇaka. According to the Ṭ the location of Bhasmaka and Paramātmī is in the *jīvasthāna*.

110: The *pādas* 110cd are omitted in the MSS B & C. Consequently the location of Ketudhvaja and Icchā on the back of the two hands is not mentioned, nor are the buttocks mentioned as the location for Viśālākṣa and Mahākālī. This last omission, however, is made up for by BC in their variant reading of 111b.

111: The reading of MS A for *pāda* 111d has a rather 'primitive' appearance. The whole of the *pādas* 111cd is much better in BC. Nevertheless the reading of MS A has been followed for the lines after *śloka* 110ab, since following BC would result in not mentioning the location of Ketudhvaja and Icchā. Probably something has gone wrong with regard to the *ślokas* 110 and 111 already before the writing of MS A.

112: The last son of Devī in Kāmarūpa is called Caturvaktra (112a), while in the KmT (2,97d) his name is Caturānana, which has, of course, the same meaning. The location of Caturvaktra and Śukrā Devī is in the *śukra-siṃhāsana* (Ṭ). The word *śukra* used in connection with human beings usually denotes the *semen virile*. Here, however, this is not possible, since all the locations of the sons and their female consorts refer to the body of Devī/Mālinī. Consequently, we have translated *śukra* here with 'ovary'.

113: In the *pādas* 113cd and 114ab the name of the Lord of this fourth Mahāpīṭha, Cakrānanda, is explained with 'The one who brings the circle in a state of bliss' (114a *cakram ānandaya-*). With 'circle (*cakra*) is probably meant the group of Yoginīs participating in the rituals (cf. 3,106a: *cakrakrīḍā*). The means to bring about this state of bliss (*ānanda*) is called *madya* (113c), and it is of two kinds: either it originates from knowledge (*jñāna*), or from some drug (*dravya*). *Madya* denotes any intoxicating beverage, to which *dravya* refers in the first place. A very fervent teacher, however, can also bring people in a state of bliss by spiritual means — this kind of *madya* is regarded as 'originating from knowledge' (*jñānasamudbhava*).

114: The *bīja* of Lord Cakrānanda is presented in a secret way in the *pādas* 114cd and 115ab. The consonant of the *bīja* is described as 'the first one after the three *siddhis*' (*trisiddhyādya*). In view of the aforesaid one could argue that the 'three *siddhis*' are the consonants of the three preceding Mahāpīṭhas, namely *ṣa*, *śa*, and *sa*. The first consonant after these three is the letter *va*. The Ṭ in which 114cd and 115ab are quoted reads the compound *trisiddhādyaṃ* instead of *trisiddhyādyaṃ*, but reaches the same conclusion, namely that the letter *va* is meant. The *va* then is 'adorned' (114d *vibhūṣita*) with the letter called Sarasvatī, which stands for the *ī* according to the Ṭ. Finally, the expression *mahābilagatam* can only refer to the *anusvāra* (*aṃ*). The result of the above is the *bīja* VĪṂ for the Lord Cakrānanda.

115: The second guardian is called Ghaṇṭakarṇa (115c) in all three manuscripts.The more usual form Ghaṇṭākarṇa is found in 136a and in the Ṭ. The KmT (2,98c) also reads Ghaṇṭākarṇa.

116: The fifth guardian, Bṛhatkukṣi, has the same name as the second guardian of the Mahāpīṭha Oḍiyāna (*śloka* 59c). Sunanda (116a) is called Surānanda in the KmT

(2,99a). The seventh guardian is called Mahotkaṭa (116b), while the KmT (2,99b) reads Balotkaṭa. His namesake is found in the first Mahāpīṭha (*śloka* 37d; cf. Notes on 37).

118: After Her visit to the Mahāpīṭha called Kāmarūpa, the Goddess proceeds to the fifth Mahāpīṭha, the Mātaṅgapīṭha, which is transcendental and consequently not connected with any geographic location, nor with the human body itself. Actually it is situated above the body. For this reason it was not included in *śloka* 20 of this chapter, in which the first four Mahāpīṭhas were all endowed with the faculties of hearing, speaking, procreation and seeing, respectively. Furthermore, no *bīja* is given belonging to the Lord of this Mahāpīṭha, as it is beyond the sphere of speech or hearing. Noteworthy is that none of the lines before the enumeration of the daughters, sons and guardians are borrowed from the parallel passage in the KmT dealing with the fifth Mahāpīṭha (KmT 2,102-107), contrary to the first four Mahāpīṭhas.

In *pāda* 118a the expression *gātrānte*, 'at the end of the body', refers to the fact that the previous Mahāpīṭha was the last one to be related to the human body proper. The fifth Mahāpīṭha is located above the body (118c *koṣṭhordhvaṃ*), 'at the top' (*cordhve*). This latter description of the Mātaṅgapīṭha refers to the fact that it is situated at the end of 'column of smoke' (*dhūmravartiprānta*) which rises upwards from the top of the head to the so-called Dvādaśānta, and has a length of twelve *aṅgulas* (cf. 1,40 Notes).

119: The fifth Mahāpīṭha is above the Brahmarandhra (119a), and in the centre of the Khecarī-cakra (119b); the Śrīśaila is also located here (119c). The location of the Mātaṅgapīṭha is identical with that of the first, and highest Saṃvartāmaṇḍala (cf. 2,5-6). The Mt. Śrīśaila is identical with the Kaumāraparvata, which is called *anākhya* in 1,49d ('without name'). With regard to the Parāpara Krama see the Notes on 3,103-104.

120: The Goddess is 'without parts' (*niṣkalā*) in this location and has a transcendental form (*abhāvarūpiṇī*). She can only be visualized with the mind. As, for instance, Devī had the faculty of hearing in the first Mahāpīṭha, and without it the state of deafness resulted (cf. *śloka* 21 Notes). As Devī is 'pure thought' (120c *cinmātrā*) in the fifth Mahāpīṭha, the Ṭ explains: *tadā mātaṅgapīṭhaṃ cinmātrasthānaṃ tena vinā sarvaṃ śūnyam*, 'the Mātañgapīṭha is the place of pure thought; without it everything is void'.

121: The first daughter, Hārikā, is connected with the moon (121a *candra*), which is confirmed in the Ṭ (*candramāsthāna*). The moon is no particular part of the human body, to which the daughters of the Mahāpīṭhas are usually related. Probably one has to think that with the moon the crescent-shaped moon is meant, which Śiva wears in His hair. Hārī (KmT 2,108a Hāri) is related to the 'town of seeing', which possibly refers to the third eye on Śiva's forehead. The third daughter Gandhārī, is called Gāndhārī in the KmT (2,108a). Vīrā is located in the 'town of the tortoises' (121d *kamaṭhāpura*), which hardly makes any sense in the context of the other 'towns'. In *śloka* 34d a *kāmaṭha-maṇḍala* was mentioned as the location of one of the sons and his female consort of the first Mahāpīṭha. There we translated it with 'the head' (cf. *śloka* 34 Notes). At the present instance the Ṭ explains *kamaṭha* with *brahmarandhra* (*kamaṭhaḥ brahmarandhrasthāne*). To understand this explanation of the Ṭ one has to regard the word *kamaṭha* as a compound: *ka* + *maṭha*, 'the dwelling place (*maṭha*) of Brahma (*ka*)', which could be a synonym for the word Brahmarandhra. If the explanation of the Ṭ is correct, we find in this fifth Mahāpīṭha the only instance that two daughters are related to the same place on the body: Vīrā is related to the *kamaṭhāpura* (Ṭ = Brahmrandhra), while Sukeśī is also related to the Brahmarandhra (123a).

122: The name of the fifth daughter called Nakhī is attested for both in MS A and the Ṭ; the KmT (2,108b) also has Nakhī. Only the MSS B&C read Narkhī. Piṅgalā (KmT 2,108d Piṅgalī) is described as being located in Viṣṇu (122d: *viṣṇu-r-antagā*), at least according to the MS A. Instead of *viṣṇu-* the MS B and the Ṭ read both *śiṣna-*, which is most likely a mis-spelling for *śiśna*, 'penis', while the reading of C (*sista-*) also seems to point to this direction. We have seen already in *śloka* 77a that Viṣṇu seems to be connected with urine (*mūtra*) according to the Ṭ. Consequently, a connection with the male generative member is not improbable. Whether as early as the Vedic times Viṣṇu had a definite connection with the penis remains problematic (cf. Gonda 1969 *s.v. śipiviṣṭá*; penis; phallos), but here as well as in *śloka* 77a there appears to be some reason to connect Viṣṇu with the penis or the flow of urine, at least the MSS seem to indicate this connection.

Apart from the question whether to read *viṣṇu* or *śiṣna* in *pāda* 122d, the construction of the compound is noteworthy. One is inclined to read *piṅgalā viṣṇur antagā*, or *piṅgalā śiṣnam antagā*, in which case the nominative of *viṣṇu/śiṣna* is grammatically incorrect (N.B. the form *śiṣnam* might be an accusative, as the word is either masculine or neuter). A composite form like *viṣṇvantagā* or *śiṣnāntagā* would have been more appropriate, and the loss of a syllable could easily have been made up for by inserting something like *ca* or *tu* after *piṅgalā*: a correct *pāda* of eight syllables would have been the result. Yet the scribe of MS A chooses for a form which looks like a nominative, and most probably the scribes of B&C did the same. Instead of regarding *viṣṇur* and *śiṣnam* as nominativi, however, one should regard the *-r* and the *-m* as a kind of hiatus-filler between two vowels. This phenomenon is not found very frequently in the text of the ṢaṭSS, but the KmT shows ample evidence of both the *r* and the *m* used in this way.

123: As usual after the enumeration of the daughters of a Mahāpīṭha the 'remaining constituants' (*śeṣabhāva*) are related to the Lord of the particular Mahāpīṭha: in this case Antyaja (123b). The Ṭ here calls him Antyajeśa. Instead of Śrīphala the KmT reads Śrīphāla (2,109a).

124: Kaśmala (KmT 2,109a Kaṣmala) and Jñāna are related to the right knee according to the Ṭ. The female consort of Śrīphala is here called Jñāna (124b), which is definitely not feminine. The Ṭ 'solves' this apparent irregularity by calling her Jñānaśakti, the same name she has in the Mālinī-system described in chapter seven of our text (*vide*: Appendix II). Caṇḍa and Kriyā are connected with the left knee.

125: According to the Ṭ Caṇḍāla and Sāvitrī are located on the left shank, while Ceṭaka and Gāyatrī are on the right shank.

126: The sixth son is called Mātaṅga, who is not the same as the Lord of this fifth Mahāpīṭha, also called Mātaṅga (128b; 129a). Instead of Bāhuja (KmT 2,109c: Bāhuka) the Ṭ reads Vajraka. His female consort, Phetkārī, represents the letter *pha* of the Sanskrit alphabet, and is the last of the fifty Mālinīs, or letters of the alphabet. As we saw with regard to the number of daughters and sons in the previous four Mahāpīṭhas, their number is the same in each particular Mahāpīṭha. Furthermore it was explicitly stated in *śloka* 9d that there are nine sons in the fifth Mahāpīṭha. Nevertheless the enumeration of the sons and their female consorts ends with *śloka* 126 having enumerated only seven sons. Obviously there are two sons left. In the KmT (2,109d) these two are mentioned immediately after the seventh son: Vīra and Avyakta. These same names are found in *śloka* 128a of our text.

128: As announced in the Notes on *śloka* 126, the eighth and ninth son, Vīra and Avyakta, respectively, are mentioned in *pāda* 128a. It seems that they are only added for the sake of reaching the same number as the daughters, i.e. nine. They have no female consorts, because there are no more than fifty Mālinīs who were, all fifty already joined to the preceding fifty sons. The author of the ṢaṭSS identifies both of them with the Lord of the Mahāpīṭha, who is called either Antyaja (123b; 128b) or Mātaṅga (128b). The author of the Ṭ also realized the difficulty concerning the eighth and ninth son, and procures a rather simple solution: the two female consorts last mentioned and their locations are connected with the two last sons. Thus Vīra has for his female consort Dahanī and is located on the right foot, while Antyaja is situated on the left foot together with his *śakti* Phetkārī. The problem which the author of the ṢaṭSS met with in incorporating the eighth and ninth son within the required number of nine sons is perhaps also reflected in the structure of the *pādas* 128ab. Firstly he uses an irregular sandhi (128a: *vīro avyakta-*). The same irregularity with regard to the sandhi is also found in *śloka* 110a, which *śloka* together with the following one also produced some difficulties (cf. Notes on both *ślokas*). In *pāda* 128b there is, again, something definitely wrong with the sandhi. The reading of MS A appears to mean a compound of *mātaṅga* and *antyaja*, in which there is a hiatus within the compound, while the compound itself is obviously plural instead of dual. The reading of BC (*mātaṅgo antyajā*) looks like two nominatives singular with the same irregular sandhi as in *pāda* 128a, while the nom. *antyajā* points to a word *antyajas* which does not exist. It is surprising that the author transgresses the sandhi-rules here so evidently, when a correct reading (*mātaṅgaś cāntyajas*, *mātaṅgas tv antyajas*, etc.) is not very difficult to construct.

In the *pādas* 128cd the name Mātaṅga is etymologically explained. Evidently it is understood as a compound of the words 'mother' (*mātṛ*) and 'body' (*aṅga*). At the same time the word 'mother' is seized upon to indicate a connection with the Mother *par excellence*, namely Devī in Her form of Kuṇḍalinī (128c).

129: The explanation of the other name of the Lord of this Mahāpīṭha, Antyaja, is found in the *pādas* 129cd, but is not very clear to me. Antyaja means, of course, 'born (*-ja*) from the lowest caste (*antya-*)'. Here, however, one should translate *antya* with the meaning 'the number of 1000 billions' on the same line as *koṭi* (a crore) in *pāda* 129d.

130: The first guardian is called Heraṃbha in the MS A and in the Ṭ, while the MSS B&C point to the reading Heraṃba. The KmT (2,110a) also reads Heraṃba, which appears to be the usual spelling of the word. The second guardian is called Dhūlika in the Ṭ.

Note in *pāda* 130d the compound *kubja-vāmanaḥ* (= KmT 2,110b), which should be a dual, or, less correct, a plural form. Probably: *kubja* for *kubjo* (*m.c.*).

133: From *śloka* 133 up to *śloka* 137ab the names of all thirty guardians are repeated. There are some minor differences in the names as compared with their names given in the enumerations on occasion of the five Mahāpīṭhas separately. For Balotkaṭa (*pāda* 133d) see the Notes on *śloka* 37.

134: Note the compound in *pāda* 134a: plural instead of the dual. In *pāda* 134b we find Gaṇeśa for Gaṇeśvara (59d), and Vighnarāj instead of Vighnarāja (60a).

135: In *pāda* 135a Mahoda is given instead of Āmoda (87c). The fifth and sixth guardians of the thirth Mahāpīṭha, Vighnakartṛ and Vighneśa (88a), are enumerated here in reversed order while Vighneśa is now called Vimukha (135c).

136: Instead of Ghaṇṭakarṇa (115c) we find Ghaṇṭākarṇa. For Sthūladanta (115d) the synonym Sthūladaṃṣṭra is used in *pāda* 136a.

137: For the guardian called Dhūli (130c), in *pāda* 137a the name Cūli is used. The irregular compound *kubja-vāmanaḥ* (130d) is repeated here (137b).

138: In the *pādas* 138a-c the number of guardians for each particular Mahāpīṭha is given, while in *pāda* 138d it is announced that their position on the human body will be told in the following lines (139-142ab).

139: As we have remarked previously (*śloka* 38 Notes), the Ṭ connects the guardians with a particular part of the body or with a particular physical function of the body in its commentary on each Mahāpīṭha; the complete list of the thirty guardians and their bodily connections as found after the description of the fifth Mahāpīṭha is not found in the Ṭ.

The connection of the thirty guardians with the human body is not based on their numeral subdivision as they appear in each of the five Mahāpīṭhas (6-6-6-7-5), but on the kind of bodily part or function they are connected with. Thus we find three groups of ten guardians each.

The first ten guardians, from Caturbhuja up to Gaṇeśa, are connected with the ten fingers. Thus Caturbhuja is connected with the little finger of the right hand, Gaṇādhyakṣa with the ringfinger of the right hand, and so on until we reach Gaṇeśa, who is identified with the little finger of the left hand.

140: In the same way as the first ten guardians were connected with the ten fingers, the following ten guardians are connected with the ten toes. Thus Vighnarāja belongs to the little toe of the right foot up to Ghaṇṭākarṇa, who is related to the little toe of the left foot.

141: In this and in the following *śloka* the last group of ten guardians is connected with a particular function of the body. The group begins with Sthūladanta and ends with Vāmana (142b).

The first one of this third group, Sthūladanta, is connected with *meṣa* (141a) which means 'ram'. With regard to following *unmeṣa* and the other bodily functions of the guardians belonging to this last group, the translation 'ram' for *meṣa* is hardly acceptable. The word *meṣa* should be derived here from the root *miṣ-* ('to open the eyes'). As the following *unmeṣa* denotes 'the opening of the eyes', it is almost inevitable that *meṣa* should denote 'the shutting of the eyes'. In this way *meṣa* should be understood as a short form for *nimeṣa*, which has that meaning. The Ṭ confirms this meaning of *meṣa*: *sthūladantaḥ nimeṣasthāne*. Although the word *meṣa*, 'shutting of the eyes', is not found in the current Skt dictionaries, it does not seem to be an invention of our author. In a Kṛtabhāṣā, a kind of Old Javanese Sanskrit dictionary, from Puri Kawan (Singaraja, N. Bali; cf. Schoterman 1981: 425) the following entry is found (F.77B): *meṣā kdap ning netra*, '*meṣā* [means] the blinking of an eye'. The fact that the word is here of the feminine gender, does not imply that one should accept *meṣā* instead of *meṣa* in *pāda* 141a, although the compound *meṣonmeṣe* allows both versions of the word. In Balinese *lontars* the distinction between short and long vowels of Skt words is often quite arbitrary, if such a distinction is made at all. The same *meṣa* is found in the compound *vajrameṣa*, 'flash of lightning', which serves as the Skt synonym for Old Javanese *glap* (Bhāṣā Ekalawya from Griya Kadampal, Krambitan, Bali; F.66B (cf. Schoterman 1981: 430)).

Bṛhatkukṣi and Sunanda are connected with *vyāya* and *āya*, respectively (141a). These two can be translated with 'departing' and 'arriving'. It is plausible that the two words are related to *vyāna* and *apāna* with regard to their meaning. Therefore we have translated *vyāya* with 'exhaling' and *āya* with 'inhaling', which links them nicely with the next one: *nirodha*, 'keeping of the breath' (141b). The Ṭ reads for *vyāya* the form *vyāpa-sthāna*, and for *āya āpa-sthāna* (the *ya* and *pa* are easily interchanged in manuscripts).

The 29th guardian, Kubja, is connected with *untaka* or *ūntaka*, a word not found in any dictionary as far as I know. The Ṭ connects Kubja with the belly (*kubjaḥ udara-sthāne*). We have translated the word with 'belching', a meaning which has a relationship with the belly as proposed in the Ṭ, and which stands on the same line as some of the other bodily connections in this third group (hiccups, coughing). The only Sanskrit word which (vaguely) resembles the word *untaka*, is *uṇḍuka* or *unduka*, 'stomach' (Meulenbeld 1974: 458). In Malayalam the verb *uyantuka* or *uṟantuka*, 'to belch', is found (Burrow & Emeneau 1961: Nr. 547). In Modern Indonesian, finally, there exists a verb *muntah*, 'to vomit; to belch' (Poerwadarminta & Teeuw 1950: *s.v.*). Whether these words have anything to do with *untaka* of our text remains a guess, although their meaning agrees with one another.

The Ṭ situates Vāmana in the *kāma-sthāna*, which is obviously a wrong reading for *kāsa-sthāna*, 'the place of coughing'.

143-150: From *śloka* 143 as far as the lines in prose (150) the five Mahāpīṭhas are brought in connection with the macrocosm, viz. the days, months, and the year, as opposed to their microcosmic connection, i.e. the human body, which we saw in the previous *ślokas*. This shift is already indicated in *śloka* 143ab of the text. Moreover, the Ṭ which quotes the lines 143-149 in full (N.B. 144 and 145ab are omitted in the Ṭ), adds after *śloka* 143ab another half-*śloka*: *bāhye 'pi kālakalanayā rūpeṇa saṃtiṣṭhanti*, thus making clear that the five Mahāpīṭhas are now to be dealt with regard to the macrocosm (*bāhye*), especially in relation with the concept of time (*kāla*). Note that the added half-*śloka* of the Ṭ neglects the *caesura*.

The exact method of connecting the five Mahāpīṭhas with the days etc. does not become completely clear from the text itself. In the first place we have the fact that in Ṭ which quotes the lines 143-149 in full, *śloka* 144 and 145ab are omitted, as we have remarked before. This omission of one and a half *śloka* could be caused by the fact that *śloka* 144a and *śloka* 145c are identical. In this way the copyist of the Ṭ might easily have overlooked the lines after 144a and before 145c.

The real problem starts in *śloka* 143cd with the compound *dinamadhyodayaṃ* (143c). We have translated the compound with 'the appearance (*udaya*) is at noon (*dinamadhya*)', although 'noon' is usually expressed by *madhyadina* or *madhyaṃdina*.

The translation is suggested by the Ṭ which reads *dinamadhye ṣaṭ ṣaṭ ghaṭikā ṣaṭ ṣaṭ varṇāḥ pīṭhasya udayaṃ kurvanti*. Thus *ghaṭikā*, 'part of the day', is identified with the *varṇas*, which in this context denote the consonants, as we will see below. It appears then that the compound *dinamadhyodayaṃ* should be understood as *dinamadhye udayaṃ*, which would result in a *pāda* of nine syllables, however. In *pāda* 143d we are informed that there are twice six *ghaṭikās*: obviously six *ghaṭikās* before noon, and six after it. The Ṭ confirms this explanation: *evaṃ ghaṭikā triṃśat 30 rātrau yathā triṃśat ghaṭi[kāḥ] 30 | ubhau ahorātrau pañca pīṭhānāṃ ghaṭikā 60*. Evidently the Ṭ multiplies the six *ghaṭikās* of a half day with the number five of the five Mahāpīṭhas. It is not clear, however, what one should do with this information. Skipping the lines 144 and 145 which provide only general information, we come to *śloka* 146ab: 'One should discern in every Pīṭha 72 days'. The 360 days of the year (145ab) are divided by five (*sc.* the five Mahāpīṭhas) in order to reach the number 72. Furthermore we are informed that the sacred syllable OṂ precedes and concludes the five *pīṭhabījas* (148cd). In the description of the five Mahāpīṭhas, however, we have seen that only the first four Mahāpīṭhas possessed a particular *bīja*; the fifth Mahāpīṭha did not have a *bīja*, since it was transcendental. Perhaps in the case of the fifth Mahāpīṭha one should repeat the syllable OṂ, or simply not use a special *bīja*. After the syllable OṂ and the particular *Pīṭhabīja*, the *varṇa-nyāsa* (149ab) follows. Next we find an enumeration of the vowels and consonants belonging to each of the five Mahāpīṭhas (150).

From the above description it does not become clear in what way the five Mahāpīṭhas are to be connected exactly with the days, the months, or the year, nor is it clear in what manner the five Mahāpīṭhas are connected with the daily worship which is obviously the practical object of this section (cf. 151 ff.).

The practical use of the information given in the lines 143-150 might be deduced from the table which the Ṭ gives at the end of its commentary on the present chapter. Thus:

O	JĀ	PŪ	KĀ	MĀ
A	Ā	I	Ī	Ṛ
U	Ū	E	AI	Ṝ
O	AU	AṂ	AḤ	Ḷ Ḹ
gha 4	ca 5	kha 2	ka 1	ga 3
ṭa 9	ṭha 10	ja 7	cha 6	jha 8
tha 14	da 15	ḍha 12	ḍa 11	ta 13
pha 19	ba 20	na 17	dha 16	pa 18
ra 24	la 25	ma 22	bha 21	ya 23
sa 29	ha 30	śa 27	va 26	ṣa 28

Fig. 1.

(N.B. the letters O, JĀ, PŪ, KĀ & MĀ on the top row refer to the five Mahāpīṭhas. The Ṭ reads *na* for the 13th consonant, which should obviously be a *ta*; the *ya* is given the number 33 in the Ṭ, which is wrong for 23. Both mistakes have been corrected in the table).

The first thing to notice in the table is the fact that only 30 consonants of the 34 are used, the *ṅa*, *ña*, *ṇa* & *kṣa* having been omitted. The Ṭ notices this peculiarity explicitly: *varjyāḥ ke te ṅa ña ṇa kṣa catur varjanīyāḥ*. The reason why these four are to be omitted is not clear. It is clear, however, that only 30 consonants can be used: the number 30 evidently refers to the 30 days of a month. Furthermore, each group of consonants is connected with three vowels, only the consonants of the fifth group have four vowels. The numbers accompanying the consonants indicate their regular order in the Sanskrit alphabet, and probably the order in which they are to be used in the daily *pūjā*. Thus on the first day of the month the syllable *ka* belonging to the Mahāpīṭha Kāmarūpa is to be used, evidently together with the three vowels listed above it (*ī*, *ai*, *aḥ*). Although the text does not mention it explicitly, it seems plausible to connect this with the daily *trisandhyāpūjā*, viz. at dawn, noon, and sunset. Each day of the month — probably beginning on the first day of the *śukla-pakṣa* — one has to recite one particular consonant of a Mahāpīṭha three times, each time connected with one of the three vowels, and preceded by OṂ and the particular *pīṭhabīja*, while it is concluded again with OṂ (cf. 148cd-149ab). The three *mantras* for the first day of the month should consequently run as follows: OṂ ṢĀṂ KĪṂ OṂ; OṂ ṢĀṂ KAIṂ OṂ; OṂ ṢĀṂ KAḤ OṂ. The fact that with regard to the fifth Mahāpīṭha four vowels are listed instead of the usual three has to do with the fact that a month does not always have exactly 30 days, nor a year always 360 days. To fill up this difference the fourth vowel of the fifth Mahāpīṭha might be used.

The above-sketched use of the vowels and consonants connected with each of the five Mahāpīṭhas seems probable, although neither from the text itself nor from the Ṭ have this application of the 46 letters in daily worship becomes clear. In this view one could suppose that especially in *śloka* 143c another, more original, reading is meant. Instead of *dinamadhyodaya* the reading *līnamadhyodaya* might be suggested, in which *līna*, *madhya* and *udaya* refer to the three phases of the day: sunset, noon, and dawn (= Trisandhyā). The sequence of the three constituants of the day is peculiar, since generally the reversed order is found, beginning with dawn. When the tripartition of the day should be intended in *pāda* 143c, the reading of the MS A for *pāda* 143d (*ṣaṭ ṣaṭ ṣaṭ ghaṭikā smṛtāḥ*) is not unlikely: each of the three parts of the day has six *ghaṭikās*. The reading of A, however, is not found in the Ṭ, which follows MSS B & C.

Finally, it should be mentioned that there does not seem to be any system in the division of the letters among the five Mahāpīṭhas. Only with regard to the vowels it is clear that these are regularly distributed among the first four Mahāpīṭhas, with the exception of the *ṛ*, *ṝ*, *ḷ*, *ḹ* which are allotted to the fifth Mahāpīṭha. The fact that the five Mahāpīṭhas are connected with letters from the Sanskrit alphabet is probably based on the connection between the five Mahāpīṭhas and the five elements (Pañca Bhūta: *pṛthivī*, *tejas*, *jala*, *vāyu*, *ākāśa*). Both the Pañca Bhūta and the letters of the Sanskrit alphabet constitute the basis for everything which exists. A connection of the five elements with the fifty letters is, of course, more logical (cf. Marquès-Rivière 1950:197), but our text has diminished the number of fifty to 46 because of the practical application with regard to the daily worship.

151: The intention of *pādas* 151cd is that one may recite the *mantras* of the Pīṭhapūjā either from a written source (151c) or by heart (151d).

152: With the *vāmadravyas* are most probably meant the five *MA-kāras* from *māṃsa* to *maithuna*). Note that *mandira* (152c) denotes the human body.

157: Besides the 'real' Guru there are several other persons who may act and are to be followed as a Guru (156cd). Moreover, the Śakti, the female companion of the Guru during ritual proceedings, is proclaimed to have the same authority (157d *śaktimukha*, 'the utterances of the Śakti').

159-160: In the *ślokas* 159cd; 160ab we find a reference to the Six Paths (*ṣaḍadhvan*), which are acknowledged by the followers of the Paścimāmnāya. The most important one appears to be the *śāṃbhavī dīkṣā*, which furnishes instant insight in the doctrine (159cd). The six ways as enumerated in the KmT (10,69-71) are *bhūta*, *bhāva*, *śākta*, *māntra*, *raudra*, and *śāṃbhava*. The fourth path is also called *āṇava*. A similar sixfold way is mentioned by Padoux (1975: 261 ff.): *bhuvana*, *pada*, *varṇa*, *mantra*, *kalā*, and *tattva* (cf. KmT 10). The word *vedha* (160a) seems to be used here as a term to denote *dīkṣā* in general, although it might pertain to the highest kind(s) of *dīkṣā* here (cf. Gupta a.o. 1979:86). Most probably in *pāda* 160b the other five *dīkṣās* or paths are mentioned: *śākta* and *āṇava* (= *mantra*) are clear (note the irregular compound *śākta-ca* + *āṇavaiḥ*; the reading of A, *śākta-d-ānnavai*[*ḥ*] seems to insert within the compound a hiatus-filler *-d-*). However irregular the compound may be, its meaning is clear. This leaves us with three other paths, viz. *bhūta*, *bhāva*, and *raudra*. These three can only be 'hidden' in the word *kuñjaka* (160b). The word *kuñjaka* is not found in any dictionary. At first sight it is a derivation from *kuñja*, 'a place overrun with plants', a meaning which does not, however, make any sense within the context. Likewise a word *kuñjikā* can be safely ruled out. In the context of the fact that we 'miss' three paths, the most sensible thing to do is to divide this trisyllabic word into three parts: *kuñ*, *ja*, and *ka*. In this way *kuñ* may refer to *bhūta* or *bhuvana* (*ku* = earth); *ja*, derived from the root *jan-*, refers to *bhāva* or *pada*; *ka* finally refers to *raudra* or *kalā*, being the first syllable of the latter. Consequently all Six Paths are mentioned in these lines.

164: In *pāda* 164c the reading of MS A has been chosen because of the occurrence of this line in the KmT (3,72). The reading of BC (*upacāraṃ*, 'service'; attendance') is also understandable.

APPENDICES I-III

APPENDIX I

PRASTĀRA AND GAHVARA

Both in the KmT and the ṢaṭSS we find that its authors make use of various kind of codes in order to conceal the more important *bījas* and *mantras* from the eyes of outsiders. This practice of making part of a text unintelligible to outsiders is well-known in ancient civilizations. Some fragments of the Dead Sea scrolls, for instance, are written in alphabets invented for the occasion, or sometimes the code consisted of simply a reversed order of the letters. For the Indian Subcontinent this practice is very often found in texts of a Tantric nature. The most simple way of concealing a line or a *mantra* is by writing it in reversed order (*vilomena*, *vyutkrameṇa*), or by interchanging the syllables of a line (*vyākulitākṣara*), as we see it in the Tantrarāja Tantra (8,72-90) for instance. The use of specially invented alphabets is not known to me from the Indian Subcontinent, but perhaps the characters of the *żaṅ-żuṅ* language used by the Bon-pos of Western Tibet answer to a certain extent to the category of 'secret' alphabets (cf. Haarh 1968:8).

As we have pointed out before (Schoterman 1977:933), the Kulākikāmnāya or Paścimāmnāya to which both the KmT and the ṢaṭSS belong, appears to have developed its own system of codes, subdivided in two separate classes: *prastāra* and *gahvara*. Some of these codes are also found in texts not directly belonging to the Kulālikāmnāya-tradition, or codes are used which are very similar to the *prastāra*- and *gahvara*-system. Thus, for instance, we find in the Vīṇāśikha Tantra (F.3A) the rules for drawing a *prastāra* or square subdivided in 49 smaller squares, in which the 49 letters of the Sanskrit alphabet are to be written.

The importance of the *prastāra*- and *gahvara*-system for the followers of the Kulākikāmnāya may be deduced from a text called the Saṃvartārthaprakāśa by Mukundarāja. The first chapter of this text is called in its colophon *gahvara-prastāranirūpaṇa*, 'A Description of the Gahvaras and Prastāras'. This first chapter opens with the lines *atha manthānabhairavatantrasaṃketanirūpaṇam* || *tatra prathamataḥ prastāragahvaravijñānaṃ vinā paścimāmnāyagranthasaṃgatir nāsti tasmād āha* || 'Now [begins] a description of the technical, specialized terminology of the Manthānabhairava Tantra; in this context at first: without knowledge of *prastāra* and *gahvara* there exists no insight into the texts of the Paścimāmnāya; therefore he tells it'. From the above quotation it is evident that a thorough knowledge of the code-system is indispensable for a true understanding of the texts belonging to the tradition of the Paścimāmnāya. After having thus emphasized the importance of the *prastāra*- and *gahvara*-system, Mukundarāja continues with an enumeration of the various types of *prastāras* and *gahvaras*, and furnishes some information regarding the way to draw them. As Mukundarāja honestly admits, 'he only repeats and clarifies the contents of an earlier work (sc. on the same subject)' (*evaṃ prācīnasaṃgrahakāralikhitā*[*ś*] *caite mayā sphuṭatvena prakāśitāḥ*). Despite these pretensions the information given by Mukundarāja is hardly of any use in drawing the various types of *prastāras* and *gahvaras*. For the exact rules to construct the diagrams we have to resort to the texts of the Paścimāmnāya themselves.

The basic principle of both the *prastāras* and the *gahvaras* is constituted by a geometrical figure divided into 49 small squares, in which the 49 letters of the Sanskrit alphabet (from *a* up to *ha*) are to be written. The 50th letter, the *kṣa*, is regarded as a combination of the *ka* and the *ṣa*, and is consequently not represented in the figure as such. Nevertheless its presence in the diagram is real, as Mukundarāja explains: 'There are 49 squares and 49 letters; in order to reach the full number of 50 (sc. squares and letters) [one should imagine] one square [to be] underneath the central square or letter; there the *kṣa* is situated; the letter *kṣa* is inside the 49th [square] it is invisible; by means of combining *ka* and *ṣa* it is raised' (*ekonapañcāśat koṣṭhā ekonapañcāśad varṇāś ca* | *pañcāśatpūraṇe 'rthe koṣṭhe varṇe cādhastān madhyato 'dhaś caikaṃ koṣṭhaṃ tatra kṣaḥ* | *ekone kṣa-kāro nāpekṣ[y]ate* | *ka-ṣa-saṃyogenoddhārāt* ||). Thus underneath the central square of the figure (*prastāra* or *gahvara*) one should visualize an additional 50th square, in which the letter *kṣa* is located. As the central 49th square always contains the letter *ha*, it follows that the *kṣa* should be imagined underneath it.

Having drawn a particular *prastāra* or *gahvara* divided into 49 squares with the 49 letters of the alphabet inscribed on them, a letter of a word is given by referring to its position in the figure in relation to the adjoining letters (for examples see: Schoterman 1977:933 & p. 186 below). The letter *kṣa* is always described in the texts as a combination of *ka* and *ṣa*, and never by referring to its — invisible — position underneath the letter *ha*.

From the texts we have studied so far, information has been obtained with regard to three *gahvaras* and only one *prastāra*: the Mālinī Gahvara (KmT & ṢaṭSS), the Yoni Gahvara (ṢaṭSS), the Vajra Gahvara (ṢaṭSS), and the Candradvīpa Prastāra (Śrīmatatantrasāra). These four will be described in the following pages. Their names are included in the lists of *prastāras* and *gahvaras*, as found in the first chapter of the Saṃvartārthaprakāśa. The complete list by Mukundarāja is as follows (the numbers are from the manuscript itself):

PRASTĀRA:	GAHVARA:
1) Meru Prastāra,	1) Meru Gahvara,
2) Vajra P.	2) Yoni G.
3) Ṣaṭkoṇa P.	3) Vajra G.
4) Triśūla P.	4) Siddhi G.
5) Khaḍga P.	5) Kuja G.
6) Pīṭha P.	6) Chatra G.
7) Chatra P.	7) Mudrāpīṭha G.
8) Candradvīpa P.	8) Mālinī G.
9) Candrarūpa P.	9) Śabdarāśi G.
10) Prabhañjana P.	10) Pañcapraṇava G.
11) Ratnadeva Pa.	11) Vidyānanda G.
12) Sumeru P.	12) Kāyācchatra G.
13) Astradūtī P.	13) Vajrameru G.
13) Cakreśvarī P.	
14) Yoni P.	14) Varṇa G.

Mukundarāja himself says that there are fourteen *prastāras* and fourteen *gahvaras*. In his list of *prastāras*, however, fifteen different names are enumerated: the number thirteen is used twice. Probably the Astradūtī Prastāra and the Cakreśvarī Prastāra are identical in the way that the *astradūtī* is actually called Cakreśvarī. This assumption, however, does not correspond to the fact that the *astradūtī* is called by the name of Guhyakālī or Guhyakubjikā in the texts (Schoterman 1977: 936).

The Saṃvartārthaprakāśa provides some scanty information with regard to the manner of drawing the various diagrams. Actually, only the Meru Prastāra is explained fully. The result, however, is exactly the same as the Mālinī Gahvara (see below). Furthermore, the shape of some of the diagrams is indicated. Thus the Meru Prastāra, for example, has the shape of a *yoni* or triangle, or of a skulldrum (*ḍamaru*) by which the form of a diabolo is probably meant. This part of the first chapter is, however, rather corrupt. The author himself does not seem to know what he is actually describing, or perhaps he presupposes full knowledge on the subject from his readers. For the moment we will deal only with those *prastāras* and *gahvaras* of which we have found a description in the texts (see above); an accurate description of the others will have to wait untill the necessary rules for constructing them are found in the texts.

I. *The Mālinī Gahvara*

The rules for drawing the Mālinī Gahvara are found in the KmT (4,76-80), and in the corresponding passage of the ṢaṭSS (Paṭala 7). The texts are virtually identical here. Below we present the text of the critical edition of the KmT with references to the important variant readings from the MSS A & B of the ṢaṭSS.

76 , gahvaraṃ tu samālikhet |[1]
saptatrayodaśair bhāgaiḥ, ṣaḍ lopyāḥ ṣaṭkrameṇa tu ||[1]
77 yathā caivaikapārśve tu, dvitīyām evam eva hi |[1]
ekaṃ[2] trīṇi tathā pañca, sapta nava tathaiva ca ||
78 ekādaśa tathāpy evaṃ, trayodaśāvasānataḥ[3] |
pañcāśad ūnam ekena, kartavyaṃ[4] tu yathāvidhi ||
79 kāmarūpād a-kārādau, likhed evaṃ krameṇa tu |
svarāḥ sparśā yathāvṛtyā[5], yāvan madhyam[6] upāgatāḥ ||
80 oḍiyānagataṃ devi[7], haṃsākhyaṃ tu[8] mahātmanam |
kaṣākhyaṃ[9] mantrarājānaṃ[10], saṃyogena tu jāyate ||

1. omitted in A & B 2. ekas: B 3. -vasānugaḥ:. A 4. -tavyās: B 5. -pakṣyā: B 6. -ām: A 7. devaṃ: B 8. taṃ: A 9. kapāṭā: A & B 10. -rājādi: A.

Translation:

76 One should draw a *gahvara* with seven times thirteen parts; six [parts] should be elided [from it] in a row of six.
77 Just as [this is done] on one side, exactly the same [is] the other [side]. One three and five, seven and nine,
78 eleven also, and finally thirteen. [Thus] fourty-nine is made according to the rules.
79 One should start writing [the letters] beginning with the *a* from Kāmarūpa onwards, in their usual order; the vowels and the consonants in the way of a circle, until the centre is reached.

80 In Oḍiyāna, O Devī, [one should write] the one which is called *haṃsa*, the supreme. The one called *kṣa*, the king of *mantras*, then comes into existence by means of combining.

At first sight the rules for drawing the Mālinī Gahvara as laid down in the texts appear to be rather cryptic, and seem to require foreknowledge of the subject in order to enable a Sādhaka to draw the correct figure. First, it is said, one should draw a *gahvara* (76b) subdivided into seven times thirteen parts (76c). The word *gahvara* usually denotes a cave or cavern, but this meaning does not seem to fit in the context. Probably *gahvara* denotes a rectangle here, which is subdivided into seven times thirteen (= 91) parts. The word *gahvara* points at the same time to the name of this particular gahvara, the Mālinī Gahvara. The expression 'seven times thirteen' for the number 91 is used deliberately: it indicates the number of squares on the short side and on the long side of the rectangle, e.g. seven and thirteen respectively, thus making 91 squares in total. Next we are informed that 'six parts should be elided in a row of six' (76d). This should be done twice, on two sides (77ab). When one elides twice six parts, the total number of parts to be elided becomes twelve. As the shorter side of the rectangle counts only seven squares, it is evident that the twelve 'parts' are to be elided from the longer side. That leaves only one square on the longer side of the rectangle, namely in its centre. With *pārśva* (77a) the space to the right and the left of the central square on the longer side of the rectangle is consequently meant. This is confirmed in the next two lines (77cd; 78ab). Here we find an enumeration of seven numbers (1-3-5-7-9-11-13) which amount to 49 in total. The number 49 obviously refers to the 49 letters of the alphabet to be inscribed in the 49 squares. There are seven numbers which should refer to the shorter side of the rectangle, which was subdivided into seven squares as we have seen above. The first number in the series of seven is one, which we could locate in the centre of the longer side of the rectangle. The last number is thirteen, which can only refer to the other longer side of the rectangle consisting of thirteen squares. Between the first number (one) and the last (thirteen) we have the numbers 3-5-7-9-11, five numbers which have a difference of two between each other. Assuming that the figure in which the 49 letters are to be inserted has a regular shape, the following figure can be drawn:

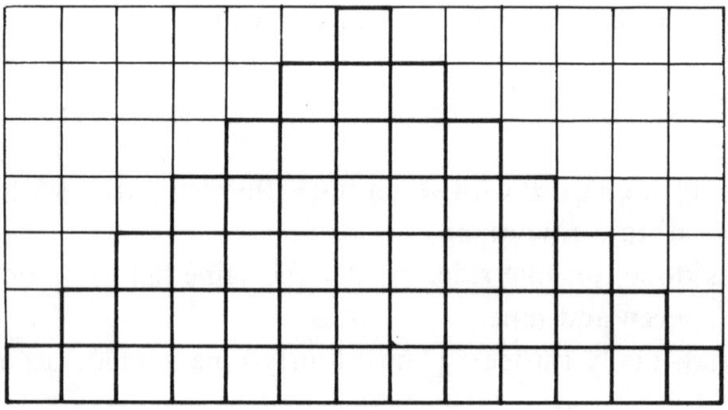

Fig. 2.

Having drawn the figure into which the 49 letters are to be inserted, the next phase is, consequently, the actual filling in of the letters. According to the text one should start with the letter *a* (79a), the first letter of the alphabet. The place where the *a* is located within the diagram, is called Kāmarūpa (79a), one of main Mahāpīṭhas situated in Gauhati (Assam). Probably the one square on the top row of the rectangle is meant with the designation Kāmarūpa. The identification of Kāmarūpa with the letter *a* is confirmed in chapter 34 of the ṢaṭSS. In this chapter the four Mahāpīṭhas Oḍiyāna, Jālandhara, Pūrṇagiri and Kāmarūpa are given a location within the Mālinī Gahvara. The order of the four Mahāpīṭhas is reverse, thus starting with Kāmarūpa. In this way Kāmarūpa is the vowel *a*, Pūrṇagiri the vowel *ṛ*, Jālandhara the consonant *ga*, and finally Oḍiyāna the letter *ha*. In this way the Mahāpīṭhas Kāmarūpa, Pūrṇagiri and Jālandhara are located on the three corners of the Mālinī Gahvara, while Oḍiyāna is situated in its centre (see fig. 3). Note that the fifth Mahāpīṭha, Mātaṅga, is not mentioned in this context. Perhaps this transcendental Mahāpīṭha is identified with the 50th letter, the *kṣa*, which is 'invisible' in the diagram being located underneath the central square (see above). Beginning with the *a* the 49 letters are to be inserted into the 49 squares, one after the other (79b), in the normal order of the alphabet starting with the vowels (*svara*), and next the consonants (*sparśa*). The 49 letters are to be filled in in a circular way (79c *yathāvṛtyā*), but it is not mentioned whether this should be done clockwise or anti-clockwise. With regard to the practical use of the Mālinī Gahvara it makes no difference, however. Possibly both ways are allowed: the clockwise method might then be *anugraha* ('beneficial'), while the anti-clockwise method could be *nigraha* ('maleficent'). Unfortunately the texts are silent on this point. The last letter, the *ha*, is called the *haṃsa* (80b) and is situated in Oḍiyāna (80a). Finally it is stated that the 'King of the Mantras', the letter *kṣa*, is the result of 'combining' (*saṃyoga*), viz. of *ka* and *ṣa* (80cd). Inserting the 49 letters into the 49 squares of the figure, the Mālinī Gahvara is obtained. Thus:

						a						
					ja	jha	ā					
				cha	bha	ma	ña	i				
			ca	ba	sa	ha	ya	ṭa	ī			
		ṅa	pha	ṣa	śa	va	la	ra	ṭha	u		
	gha	pa	na	dha	da	tha	ta	ṇa	ḍha	ḍa	ū	
ga	kha	ka	aḥ	aṃ	au	o	ai	e	ḹ	ḷ	ṝ	ṛ

Fig. 3.

In the figure drawn above of the Mālinī Gahvara the 49 letters are inserted in the clockwise manner. The Mālinī Gahvara presented in fig. 3 is the result of following the rules of the text very closely. It appears, however, that when we find a drawing of the Mālinī Gahvara in a manuscript, it has nearly always a triangular shape. Only incidentally the shape of fig. 3 is found (Ṭ F.79A). This common triangular shape of the Mālinī Gahvara might be induced by the shape of the *yoni*, a triangle, since Mālinī represents the yoni *par excellence* (KmT 4,107cd = ṢaṭSS 7, 39cd: *eṣā hy ekāparā yonir mālinī sarvakāmadā*). The *yoni*-shaped Mālinī Gahvara is drawn as follows (the letters are filled in anti-clockwise):

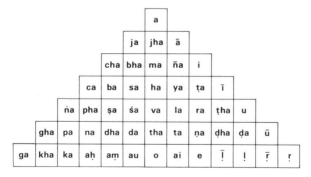

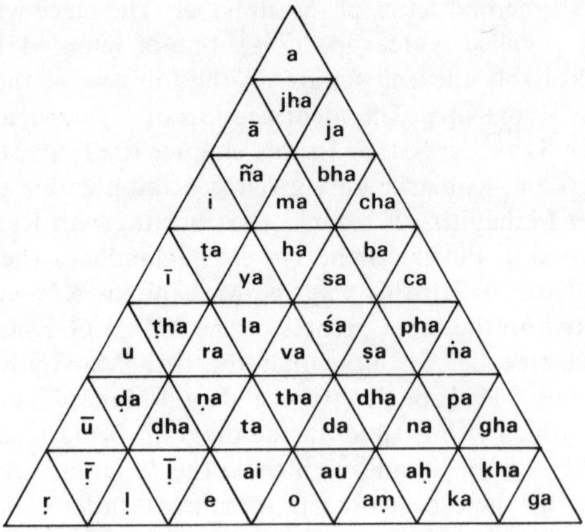

Fig. 4.

Taking the Mālinī Gahvara for example there are various ways to 'hide' a particular letter, depending on its location in the figure. Thus, for instance, there is only one way to indicate the *a* due to its location at the top: *jha-ūrdhva*, '[the letter] above the *jha*'. The same proves to be true for the letters *ṛ* and *ga*, which can only be described with *ṝ-pūrva* and *kha-anta/paścima*, respectively. The other 45 letters have at least three possibilities. The letters on the borders of the figure have only four possibilities, namely: the letter *ka* can be expressed with 1) *aḥ-kha-madhya*, 2) *kha-pūrva*, 3) *aḥ-paścima*, 4) *pa-adhaḥ*. Those letters which are surrounded on all sides by other letters offer most possibilities. Thus there are eight ways to indicate the letter *ha*: 1) *sa-ya-madhya*, 2) *ma-va-madhya*, 3) *śa-ña-randhra-*, 4) *bha-la-randhra*, 5) *ma-adhaḥ*, 6) *ya-paścima*, 7) *va-ūrdhva*, 8) *sa-pūrva*. The use of *randhra* seems to be restricted to those cases in which a letter is referred to in a 'diagonal' way, but in the texts this rule is not always followed and *madhya* is used instead.

II. *The Yoni Gahvara*

A description of the Yoni Gahvara is found in the ṢaṭSS 28,110-129, where it is used to give the *mantra* of Mahantārī Saptavaktrā in a concealed way. Apart from making use of the Yoni Gahvara the *mantra* itself is presented in a reverse order (*vilomena*). Since MS A of the ṢaṭSS is not complete (see Introduction), we give the text of MS B:

śrībhairava uvāca ||
110 kathayāmi varārohe, yathoktaṃ yonigahvare |
uddhāraṃ saptavaktrāyā, mahantāryā bravīmy aham ||
111 susame mandire ramye, nimnonnatavivarjite |
puṣpaprakaraśobhāḍhye, gandhadhūpādhivāsite ||
112 aliphalguṣasampūrṇe, bhakṣyabhojyamanora[me] |
yoginīṃ pūjayet tatra, kumārīṃ samayānvitām ||
113 nirahaṅkāracittas tu, uddhared yonigahvaram |
dakṣiṇottaragaṃ sūtraṃ, pātayed varavarṇini ||

114 vāyupūrve dvitīyaṃ tu, tṛtīyaṃ pūrvanairṛte |
tribhiḥ sūtrair varārohe, ādyā yoni[ḥ] prapadyate ||
115 tasya madhye ca ṣaṭ sūtrā, dakṣinottaragā[ḥ] sthitāḥ |
paścimottaragāḥ ṣaṭ ca, ṣaṭ ca paścimadakṣiṇe ||
116 jāyante 'ṣṭādaśa sūtrā, antyarekhāvivarjitā[ḥ] /
yonayaś caiva pañcāśad, eka ūnā bhavanti tāḥ ||
117 adhordhvakramayogena, samastavyastagāḥ priye |
eka[ṃ] trīṇi|tathā pañca, saptaś caiva tathā nava ||
118 ekādaśaṃ tathāpy eva, trayodaśāvasānagāḥ |
pūrvaśṛṅge bhaved ekā, a-kāraṃ tatra vinyaset ||
119 sṛṣṭiyogā[ḥ] svarās tatra, ekamārge gatāḥ priye |
kuṇḍalīkramayogena, sarve caiva yathākramam ||
120 sasphuṭā[ḥ] kathayiṣyāmi, yathā tanmaṇḍale sthitā[ḥ] |
pūrvaśṛṅge tu yā yoniḥ, śrīkaṇṭhas tatra vinyaset ||
121 tasyādhaś ca varārohe, pracaṇḍo diṇḍir eva ca |
anantaś ca tathaiva syus, tribhī rudrai[r] dvitīyakā ||
122 krodheśaś ca tathāṣādhī, dhātrīśaś ca tathaiva ca |
pañcārtha[ḥ] sūkṣmasaṃyuktas, tṛtīyā paṅktir uttamā ||
123 mahāsena umākānto, bāliḥ śaktibhṛgus tathā |
mīnaḥ śivottamaś caiva, trimūrtiḥ saptamaḥ smṛtaḥ ||
124 saptarudragatā paṅktiś, caturthī yonigahvare |
krūraś ca ardhanārīśo, mahākālaś ca śvetakaḥ ||
125 lākulaś ca bhujaṅgaś ca, meṣaś caivaikarudrakaḥ |
arīśānasamāyuktā, pañcamī navarudragā ||
126 anugrahīśo drārukaś ca, dviraṇḍo 'tha vakas tathā |
chagalaṇḍaś ca khaḍgīśaḥ, śikhīśaś ca pināki[ś] ca ||
127 lohitaḥ kūrmo arghīśaś ca, ṣaṣṭhaikādaśabhiḥ smṛtā |
sadyaś ca lāṅgalīśaś ca, bhauktiḥ someśvaras tathā ||
128 jhaṇṭiḥ sarmā haraś caiva, ajitā sthāṇur eva ca |
caturvaktras tithīśaś ca, ekākṣir bhārabhūtikaḥ ||
129 trayodaśibhir ākhyāta, saptamī yonigahvare |
paṅktir eṣā varārohe, jñātavyā kulayogibhiḥ ||

After announcing that He will tell the *mantra* of Mahantārī Saptavaktrā according to the Yoni Gahvara (110), Bhairava describes the spot where the figure should be drawn by the Sādhaka (111; 112ab). Only when the Sādhaka has worshipped a Yoginī, who is a girl before her *menses* and who is an initiate to the Doctrine (*samayānvitā*), he is allowed to produce the Yoni Gahvara, at least if he is of unselfish mind (112cd; 113ab). Next follow the rules for drawing the Yoni Gahvara (113cd-118ab). The Sādhaka should first draw a line running from South to North (113c *dakṣiṇottara* (AB)), next a line running from the North-West to the East (114a *vāyupūrva* (BC)) and finally a line running from the East to the South-West (114b *pūrvanairṛte* (CA)). These three lines constitute the first *yoni* (114cd (ABC)). As the triangle is subdivided into 49 other triangles or *yonis* later on (cf. 116cd), this first *yoni* is called *ādyā*, 'the first'. Inside the big triangle six lines should be drawn running from South to North (115ab (C^1B^1 up to C^6B^6)), six lines to the North-West (115c (C^1A^o up to C^6A^1)), and six lines running to the South-West (115d (B^1A^1 upto B^6A^6)). In this way there are eighteen lines (116a), not counting the three lines of the triangle itself, the three outer lines (116b: *antyarekhā*). Consequently the figure is now subdivided into 49 small triangles or *yonis* (116cd), which constitute one complete figure but should at the same time be considered as individual units (117b *samasta-vyasta-ga*). The Yoni Gahvara then looks as follows:

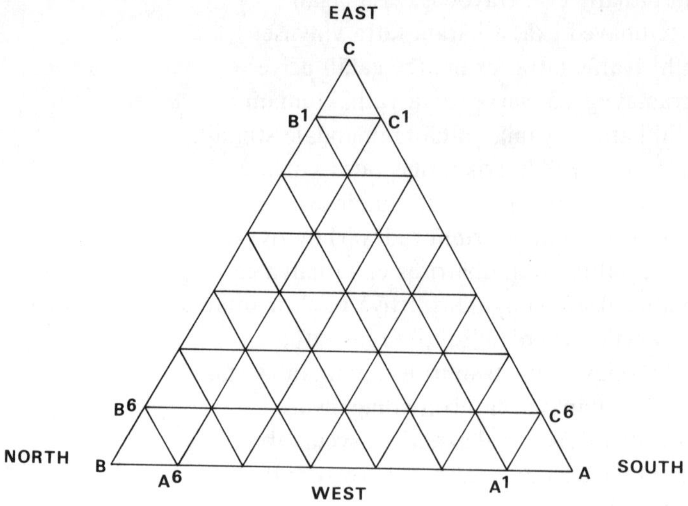

Fig. 5.

In the lines 117cd and 118ab we find the same series of seven numbers (1-3-5-7-9-11-13) which we saw in the description of the Mālinī Gahvara (see above). As will become evident from the following lines, the number refers to the seven rows (*paṅkti*) in the figure of the Yoni Gahvara.

From *śloka* 118cd onwards the 49 letters are enumerated as well as their place in the figure. This is done row by row. On the top row, the eastern summit (118c *pūrvaśṛṅga*), the vowel *a* is placed. From this place onwards the other vowels originate and in their normal order are distributed over the figure in a circular way (119c *kuṇḍalīkramyogena*; cf. Mālinī Gahvara 79c *yathāvṛtyā*). The use of *sṛṣtiyoga* (119a) may point to a clockwise-direction of the letters. Both in the Mālinī Gahvara and in the Yoni Gahvara the 49 letters are filled in in a circular way, which reminds one of the Kuṇḍalinī as She sleeps in the lowest *cakra* having the shape of a coiled snake:  Perhaps the expression *kuṇḍalīkrama* (119c) hints at this connection. The 49 letters are given in the text by referring to the Rudra (122d), which belongs to each of the 49 letters. We have already seen that each of the letters was represented by a manifestation of Mālinī. Here they are represented by a manifestation of Bhairava or Rudra. For a complete list of these manifestations I refer to Appendix II.

Anticipating *śloka* 122cd, the author has already stated that on the eastern summit of the triangle the letter *a* is placed (118cd), which is indeed represented by Śrīkaṇṭha (120d). The second row (121d *dvitīyakā* [*paṅktiḥ*]) has three Rudras: Pracaṇḍa, Diṇḍi and Ananta (*kha, tha, ā*). The third row contains five Rudras: Krodheśa (*ka*), Āṣādhin (*ta*), Dhātrīśa (*da*), Pañcārtha (*ga*), and Sūkṣma (*i*). The fourth row has: Mahāsena (*aḥ*), Umākānta (*ṇa*), Bāli or Vāli (*ya*), Śaktibhṛgu (*sa*), Mīna (*dha*), Śivottama (*gha*), and Trimūrti (*ī*). The fifth row enumerates nine Rudras: Krūra (*aṃ*), Ardhanārīśa (*ḍha*), Mahākāla (*ma*), Śvetaka (*ṣa*), Lākula (*ha*), Bhujaṅga (*ra*), Meṣa (*na*), Ekarudraka (*ṅa*), and Arīśāna (*u*). The sixth row contains eleven Rudras: Anugrahīśa (*au*), Drāruka (*ḍa*), Dviraṇḍa (*bha*), Baka or Vaka (*śa*), Chagalaṇḍa (*ba*), Khaḍgīśa (*va*), Śikhīśa (*pha*), Pināki (*la*), Lohita (*pa*), Kūrma (*ca*), and Arghīśa (*ū*). The seventh and final row has thirteen Rudras: Sadya (*o*), Laṅgalīśa (*ṭha*), Bhaukti (*ai*), Someśvara (*ṭa*), Jhaṇṭi (*e*), Sarman (*ña*), Hara (*ḹ*), Ajitṛ (*ḷ*), Sthāṇu (*ḷ*), Caturvaktra (*ja*), Tithīśa (*ṝ*), Ekākṣi (*cha*), and Bhārabhūtika (*ṛ*).

The names of the 49 Rudras correspond in majority with the names given in Appendix II, which is based on the seventh chapter of our text. There are minor differences such as, for instance, Caturvaktra for Caturānana. Some wrong spelling occurs: Drāruka should be Dāruka; Bhaukti is actually called Bhauti. Only in *śloka* 125c the text of MS B seems definitely wrong. The fifth row enumerates among its members a certain Arīśāna (125c), who should represent the vowel *u*. In Appendix II the *u* is identified with a Rudra called Amarin, which seems to be the right name (cf. ŚT 2,29b: Amareśvara). Consequently the *pāda* should be emended to *a[ma]rīśa-samāyuktā* or *a[ma]rīśāna-saṃyuktā*.

The text for constructing the Yoni Gahvara offers the method of placing the 49 letters in the figure in two ways, which have the same result, of course: 1) starting from the eastern corner with the *a*, in filling in all the other letters clockwise, in a circular way (118cd-120ab), 2) giving the letters for each row (121cd-129cd). The Yoni Gahvara when completed, looks as follows:

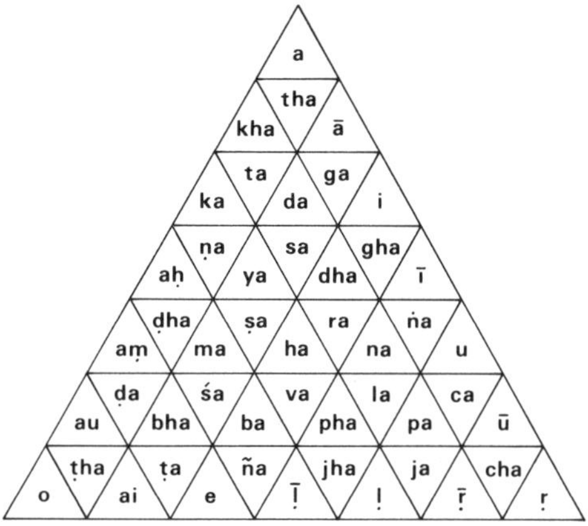

Fig. 6.

III. *The Vajra Gahvara*

The Vajra Gahvara is described in ṢaṭSS 39,49-95, and this particular code is used to conceal the *mantra* of Vajrakubjīśvarī (39,96 ff.). Again MS A misses the relevant pages, thus we give the directions for constructing the Vajra Gahvara as they are found in MS B (MS C follows B very closely, and has only some negligible variants):

śāntacitto gurus tatra, tatra sūtrāṇi pātayet ||
59 pañcaviṃśati sūtrāṇi, pūrvāparāyatāni tu |
daśa dakṣakuberābhyām[1], guruvaktropadeśataḥ ||
60 yāmyāt saumyapadaṃ yāti, caturviṃśati koṣṭhakāḥ |
nava pūrvāparāś[2] caiva, bhavanti hy avicārataḥ ||
61 bhavanti nava paṅktyā[s] tu, yāmyottaragatās tv imāḥ |
pañcamī tatra yā paṅktir, garbhasūtratrayasya vai ||
62 pūrvāparasya pārśve tu, viṃśa sūtrāṇi lopayet |
daśakaṃ daśakaṃ caiva, yaṃ[3] ca[3] vāme ca dakṣiṇe ||
63 jāyate madhyamaḥ koṣṭho, madhyasūtre vilopite |
ādyapaṅktyā[ṃ] sṛjet[4] teṣāṃ, yathā devi tathā śṛṇu ||
64 dvitīyaṃ lopayet sūtraṃ, na tṛtīyaṃ caturthakam |
lopayet pañcamaṃ tyajya, ṣaṭ sūtrāṇi tu lopayet ||
65 agre ekaṃ parityajya, punar ekaṃ vilopayet |
ekaṃ saṃtyajya ṣaḍ lopya, punar ekaṃ na lopayet ||
66 tasyāgre lopayed ekam, eka[ṃ] dhāryam alopitam |
ekaṃ vināśayec cānyam, anyat sūtraṃ na lopayet ||
prathamapaṅktiḥ ||
67 dve sūtre (ty) anu lopyaikaṃ, punar ekaṃ na lopayet |
tasyāgre lopayed ekam, ekaṃ dhāryam alopitam ||
68 agre sūtracatuṣkaṃ tu, lopayed aviśaṅkitaḥ |
ekaṃ cālopitaṃ cānyaṃ, lopayed dhāraye 'grajam ||
69 tasyāgre lopayed ekam, anyam ekaṃ na lopayet |
agre catuṣkaṃ saṃlopya, dhārayel lopitāgrajam ||
70 tasyāgre lopayed ekam, ekaṃ naiva vināśayet |
punar ekaṃ vilopyeta, agre sūtradvayam tyajet ||
dvitīyapaṅktiḥ ||
71 dvitīyaṃ lopayet sūtraṃ, caturthaṃ ṣaṣṭhamaṃ tathā |
lopayet taṃ varārohe, aṣṭamanavamā ubhau ||
72 ekādaśaṃ tathā bhadre, tridaśaṃ daśapañcakam |
saptasaptaṃ ca cāṣṭaṃ ca, viṃśamaṃ ca dviviṃśamam ||
73 caturviṃśaṃ varārohe, lopayen nānyathā kramam |
śeṣaṃ dhārya prayatnena, tṛtīyaiṣā bhavet priye ||
tṛtīyapaṅktiḥ ||
74 dvitīyaṃ lopayet sūtraṃ, caturthaṃ ca tathaiva ca |
ṣaṣṭhamaṃ saptamaṃ caiva, daśamaṃ dvidaśaṃ tathā ||
75 caturdaśaṃ tathā bhadre, ṣoḍaśaṃ ca tathaiva ca |
ekūnaviṃśaṃ viṃśaṃ ca, dvāviṃśaṃ ca tathaiva ca ||
76 caturviṃśaṃ tathā bhadre, lopayen nānyathā kramam |
śeṣa[ṃ] dhārya prayatnena, caturthīti prakīrtitā ||
caturthapaṅktiḥ ||
....

89 asmin mātā parā śaktir, yathā saṃsthā bravīmy aham |
śrīkaṇṭhavācakādyās tu, samastavyastayā[5] nyaset ||
90 uḍḍiyānagataṃ devaṃ, madhyakoṣṭhaṃ ha-saṃjñakam |
samastavyastayogena, anulomavilomagam ||
91 sa-kārādi-ja-kārāntā, guruvaktropadeśataḥ ||
sa a ṣa |3| ā śa i va ī la |6| u ra ū ya ṛ ma ṝ bha ḷ |9| ba ḹ pha e pa ai |6| ha | na o
dha au da aṃ tha aḥ ta ka ṇa kha ḍha ga ḍa gha ṭha ṅa ṭa ña |6| cha jha ja ||

1. lakṣa- instead of dakṣa-: BC 2. -paraś: B 3. paṃca (?): BC 4. mṛjet: BC
5. -vyasta sā: B.

In the *ślokas* 49-58ab some general directions are given before the actual drawing of the Vajra Gahvara is explained. Thus the Sādhaka is warned not to betray the secrets of the Vajra Gahvara to impostors and other people who are not to be trusted. Next the place where the figure is drawn is shortly described. Before starting to draw the Vajra Gahvara the Sādhaka should invite a woman (*strī*) who has to be a Kulajā yoginī (cf. 3,26d) and has to have her periods (*rajo'nvitā*); she should be worshipped with care (*pūjanīyā prayatnena*). After this eight maidens (*kumārī*) or more, or only the Sādhaka's own female consort should be worshipped, and other men and women who are initiated into the Doctrine. The Sādhaka should erect (*samutthāpaya-*) a circle (*maṇḍala*), and mark it with gold. Should he not follow these preliminary directions, the *mantra* (sc. of Vajrakubjīśvarī) will be ineffective. Finally the Sādhaka is ready to draw the Vajra Gahvara, following the instructions of his *guru*.

First he should draw 25 lines running from East to West (59ab); next ten lines from South to North (59c). The result is a rectangle with on its longer side 24 squares (*koṣṭhaka*), and nine squares on its shorter side (60a-d). Thus the figure has nine rows (*paṅktyā*) running from South to North (61ab). The basic figure for drawing the Vajra Gahvara looks as follows:

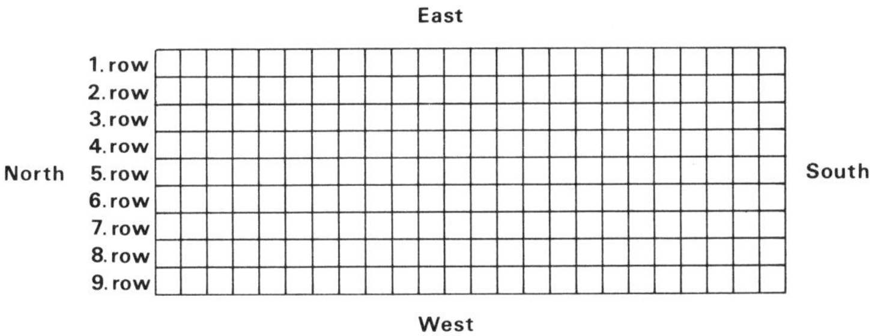

Fig. 7.

The Ṭ has nothing to add, except for the fact that the figure contains 216 squares in total, which is correct but of no particular importance. The first row to be described in the text is the fifth or central row (61cd-63ab), which constitutes only of one square (63a *madhyama koṣṭha*) in the completed figure of the Vajra Gahvara. The method of constructing the figure of the Vajra Gahvara is based on the principle of rubbing out particular lines, while others are maintained. The term used for 'rubbing out' is *lopaya-*, while the verb *tyaj-* is used when a line is maintained in the basic figure. The figure of the Vajra Gahvara is described by telling which lines on a particular row are to be rubbed out, and which not. The sequence is from North to South.

The text is not very clear with regard to the fifth row. Twenty lines are to be rubbed out (62b): ten from the North and ten from the South (62cd). Furthermore, mention is made of 'three kernel lines' (61d *garbhasūtratraya*) at the East and West side (62a). Probably the 12th, 13th, and 14th line running from East to West are meant. It is not clear why the genitive case is used in *pāda* 61d. The Ṭ quotes *pāda* 61d in full (*pañcamī tatra yā paṅktir garbhasūtratrayasyaiva*), and explains: *tatra dīrghatve sthitāḥ paṅktayaḥ nava | tāsāṃ madhye yā sā madhyamī paṅktiḥ tasyāḥ pañcaviṃśati sūtrāṇi vidyanti | tāni sūtrāṇi prāntasūtre dve varjye | tathā madhyasūtratrayaṃ varjyam | ubhābhyāṃ pañca sūtrāṇi varjyāni | śeṣāṇi dakṣiṇottaragatāni | madhyamapañca(rny)āṃ paṅktau lopyāḥ |yathā garbhatrayaṃ varjya | ekabhāge daśa lopyāḥ tathā aparabhāge daśa lopyāḥ pañcamadhyāntakṛte sthātavyāḥ madhyakoṣṭhasyāpi trirekhāmayasya ekā rekhā lopyā | yena madhyakoṣṭhaṃ suśobhanaṃ bhavati | evaṃ madhyamapaṅktau ekaviṃśā rekhā lopyāḥ | tiṣṭhanti catvāro yathā | garbhakoṣṭhakasya dvayaṃ prānte rūpam | ubhau rekhācatuṣkam | yathā*  *iti madhyapaṅktau nirṇayaḥ* |, 'There, on the longer side (e.g. from North to South), are nine rows. The [row] which is in the middle of these, is the central row; this has 25 lines. With regard to these [25] lines: two [lines], the lines on the [two] sides, should remain untouched, and so should the three lines in the centre [of the row]. Together with the two [lines on the borders] five lines should remain untouched. With regard to the remaining lines running from South to North: on the [central]row should be rubbed out .... Thus: leaving aside the three kernel [lines] ten lines sould be rubbed out on the eastern side and ten on the western side; the lines in the centre and on both ends of the fifth [row] should remain. Besides one line should be rubbed out of the central square which consists of three lines, so that the central square becomes splendid (conspicuous?). Thus 21 lines are to be rubbed out in the central row. There remain four [lines]: the shape of the kernel sqare is two at its sides; together [the shape of the kernel square) consists of four lines. Thus: 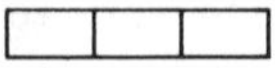 '.

Following the instructions of the Ṭ strictly, one does not succeed in obtaining a central square consisting of three squares, as drawn in the text. The instructions of the Ṭ lead to the following fifth row: the lines on the two sides are not to be rubbed out (1st & 25th), likewise the three central lines (12th, 13th & 14th). Next twice ten lines are to be rubbed out (2nd-11th & 15th-24th). Finally one line of the central three lines should be rubbed out (13th). The result is as follows (the lines not to be rubbed out are drawn in black):

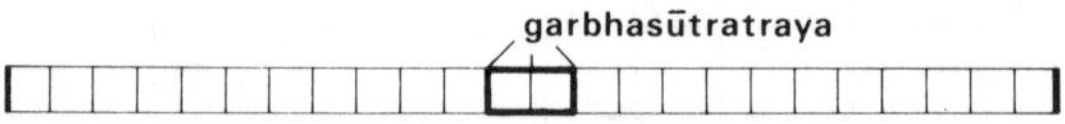

Fig. 8.

Obviously there remain four lines, as the Ṭ states (1st, 12th, 14th & 25th), but the shape of the kernel square does not encompass four lines, nor does it look like the drawing in the text. Moreover, the maintaining of the first and the 25th line is completely senseless. It seems therefore that the Ṭ is wrong when it states that the two lines on the side (*prāntasūtra*) are not to be rubbed out, unless with *prāntasūtre* the two lines to be drawn at both sides of the kernel square are meant (11th & 14th), but in that case one is supposed to know beforehand the outcome of the process of drawing. Assuming that the Ṭ is right in stating that the kernel square consists of four lines, the fifth row is as follows:

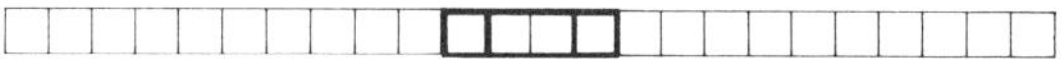

Fig. 9.

Returning to the text of the ṢaṭSS one should perhaps emend *pāda* 61d (*garbha-sūtratrayasya vai*; Ṭ *-sūtratrayasyaiva*) to *garbhasūtratrayasyaikam*, 'One [line] of the three central lines he should rub out (62b *lopayet*)'. The line to be rubbed out is the 13th, as said in *pāda* 63b (*madhyasūtre vilopite*). There remains one problem in the text itself. In *pāda* 62d we have read *yaṃ ca* instead of *paṃca* which the MSS B & C seem to read. The reading *pañca* should refer to the number of lines which are left untouched after rubbing out twice ten lines (62bc) and the central line (61d). That leaves, however, a total number of only four lines which remain in the fifth row, and not five. The reading *pañca* in *pāda* 62d would be correct, when the original reading of *pāda* 61d is maintained (*-trayasya vai*), but then the meaning of the *pādas* 61d; 62a is not clear to me. Moreover, the five lines left untouched are not in the North and the South (62d *vāme ca dakṣiṇe*), but one is in the centre, viz. the 13th line. It seems therefore acceptable to emend *paṃca* to *yaṃ ca* in *pāda* 62d. In this way the author explains that from the twenty lines (62b), ten are to be rubbed out in the North and the other ten in the South. One could raise one objection to *yaṃ ca*: since it refers to *daśakaṃ daśakaṃ* (62c), the reading *yac ca* would be grammatically correct.

The First Row. After having explained the fifth or central row the text continues with a description of the other rows. The first row is described as follows (64-66): 'One should rub out the second line, not the third; the fourth [line] he should rub out; leaving aside the fifth, he should rub out [the following] six lines; having left aside the one in front [of previous one], he should rub out another one; leaving undisturbed another one, and having rubbed out [the following] six, he should not rub out the next one; he should rub out the one in front of this; the next one is to be maintained and is not rubbed out; he should destroy the following one, but he should not rub out the other one'. The construction of the first row is clear from the directions given in the text. Although nothing is said with regard to the first line, we assume that it is not to be rubbed out, just as the last one is not rubbed out. Following the directions sketched above the first row of the Vajra Gahvara is as follows:

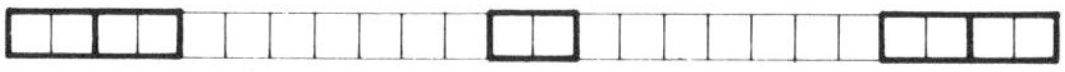

Fig. 10.

Following the rules as given in the Ṭ, the first row of the Vajra Gahvara has a slightly different form:

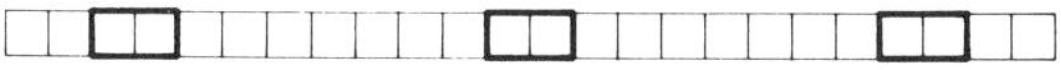

Fig. 11.

The Second Row. Unfortunately the first *pāda* (67a) is doubtful with regard to the reading of two *akṣaras*. Comparing, however, what is said here about the first two lines with what is said with regard to the last two lines (70d: *sūtradvayaṃ tyajet*), we assume that in *pāda* 67a the illegible *akṣaras* have something to do with the verb *tyaj-*. Consequently we propose the reading *dve sūtre tyajya lopyaikaṃ*. The construction of the second row is clear then: two lines (1st & 2nd) should not be rubbed out; the third is rubbed out (67a); the following one (4th) is not rubbed out (67b); the next one (5th) is rubbed out (67c), while the next one (6th) is maintained (67d); the next four lines

(7th-10th) are to be rubbed out (68ab); the next one (11th) is left alone, but the following is rubbed out (68cd); the next one (13th) is kept (68d); the 14th line is not maintained (69a), while the next one (15th) is not rubbed out (69b); the next four lines (16th-19th) are rubbed out (69c); the 20th line is maintained (69d); the next one (21st) is rubbed out (70a); the 22nd is preserved (70b); the 23rd is rubbed out (70c), while the last two lines (24th & 25th) are maintained (70d). According to the directions of the text the second row of the Vajra Gahvara is as follows:

Fig. 12.

Again the Ṭ gives directions which result in a second row of the Vajra Gahvara, slightly different from the ṢaṭSS itself. According to the directions of the Ṭ the second row looks as follows:

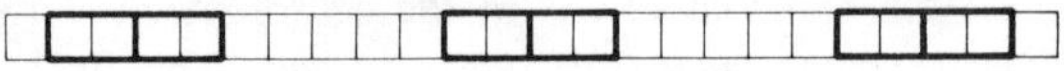

Fig. 13.

The Third Row. With regard to the drawing of the third row the text only indicates which lines are to be rubbed out. These are respectively the 2nd, 4th, 6th, 8th, 9th, 11th, 13th, 15th, 17th, 18th, 20th, 22nd, and 24th. Although *pāda* 73c is obviously corrupt — one should expect *saptadaśaṃ cāṣṭādaśaṃ* —, its meaning stands beyond doubt. The third row as explained in the Ṭ is exactly the same. Thus the third row of the Vajra Gahvara is as follows:

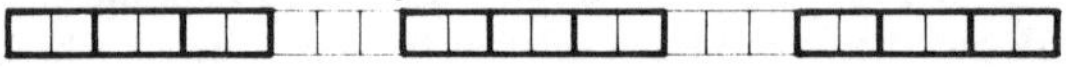

Fig. 14.

The Fourth Row. Again with regard to the fourth row the text only indicates which lines are to be rubbed out. They are respectively the 2nd, 4th, 6th, 7th, 10th, 12th, 14th, 16th, 19th, 20th, 22nd, and 24th. Thus the fourth row of the Vajra Gahvara looks as follows:

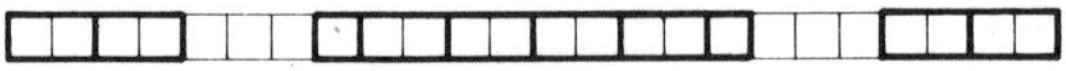

Fig. 15.

The Ṭ has a different conception of the fourth row, at least with regard to the first and the last square. Note that both in the ṢaṭSS and the Ṭ the second and fifth square in this row consist of three smaller squares. The fourth row of the Vajra Gahvara according to the Ṭ is:

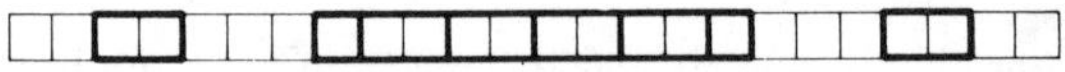

Fig. 16.

With the description of the fourth row (74-76) the texts ends in describing the different rows of the Vajra Gahvara. Consequently the sixth, seventh, eighth, and ninth row are not mentioned specially. The Ṭ, however, states that these four rows are to be repeated for the other rows in the figure of the Vajra Gahvara. In the lines between *śloka* 76 and *śloka* 89 the number of squares on each row is explained symbolically, and the power of the figure and some other items are explained. Since this information has no direct importance for the construction of the Vajra Gahvara proper, we have omitted these lines.

Before going into the actual division of the 49 *akṣaras* within the figure of the Vajra Gahvara, it is pertinent to decide the exact shape of the figure itself. As is obviously clear from the descriptions of the five rows above, the figure of the Vajra Gahvara as described in the ṢaṭSS differs in some details from the Vajra Gahvara as drawn on the basis of the rules given in the Ṭ. The 'two' Vajra Gahavaras are as follows:

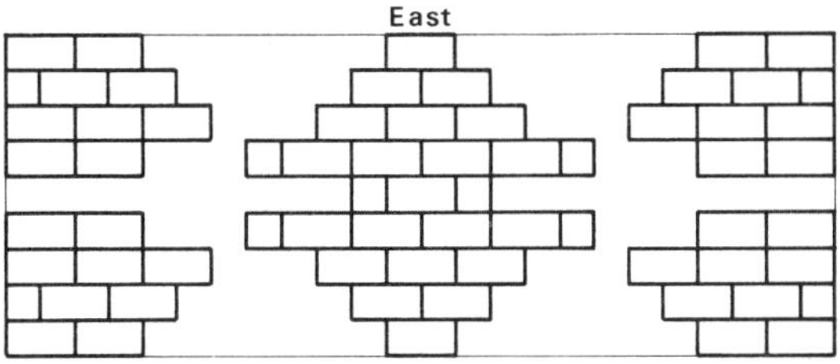

Fig. 17.

Vajra Gahvara according to the ṢaṭSS

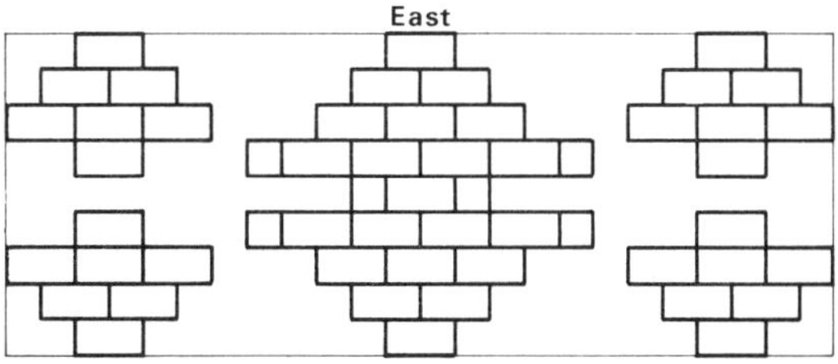

Fig. 18.

Vajra Gahvara according to the Ṭ

At first sight the shape of the Vajra Gahvara as described in the Ṭ is the most appealing, but this can hardly be a decisive factor in choosing between the two figures. Yet, the Vajra Gahvara as described in the Ṭ is most probably the right one on purely practical grounds. In the ṢaṭSS as well as in the Ṭ the order of the 49 *akṣaras* is given in which way they are to be inserted in the figure (ṢaṭSS after *śloka* 91). From this it becomes clear that in the first row three *akṣaras* are to be inserted, in the second six, in the third nine, in the fourth six again, and in the fifth or central row only one. The first row of the Vajra Gahvara according to the Ṭ has indeed three squares, but the first row of the Vajra Gahvara according to the ṢaṭSS itself has five squares! The same proves to be true with regard to the fourth row. There are six *akṣaras* allotted to this row, but the figure of the ṢaṭSS shows eight squares, while the figure of the Ṭ has the right number of squares for this row. Another point in favour of the Ṭ figure is found with regard to the second row. For this row six *akṣaras* are allotted. The figure of the Ṭ has these six squares. The figure of the ṢaṭSS has also six squares in the second row, but the first and last square both consist of three smaller squares instead of the usual two. It seems that author of the ṢaṭSS has tried to maintain the square contours of the basic figure (Fig. 7) by filling up the 'empty' spots at the sides of the rectangular. This may explain the added squares at the beginning and end of the first, second, and third row. In the same context one should consider Fig. 8, in which the first and final lines of the fifth row are not rubbed out according to the ṢaṭSS.

Having thus decided to choose for the Vajra Gahvara of the Ṭ, there remains one peculiarity in the figure which seems superfluous. The second and fifth square of the fourth row both consist of the usual two smaller squares plus another, third, square which creates an evident irregularity in the shape of the figure. As both the ṢaṭSS and the Ṭ have these two additional squares, there might be a specific reason for their occurrence in the fourth row. The enlargement of these two squares in the fourth row could serve the purpose of simplifying the junction of the three separate parts of the figure. The texts themselves, however, give no direction whatsoever that this should be done, nor did I find a drawing of the Vajra Gahvara in any manuscript with its three parts united. This hypothetical figure of the Vajra Gahvara would look as follows (the method of describing a particular *akṣara* by means of referring to its neighbouring *akṣaras* becomes less complicated in the 'united' Vajra Gahvara):

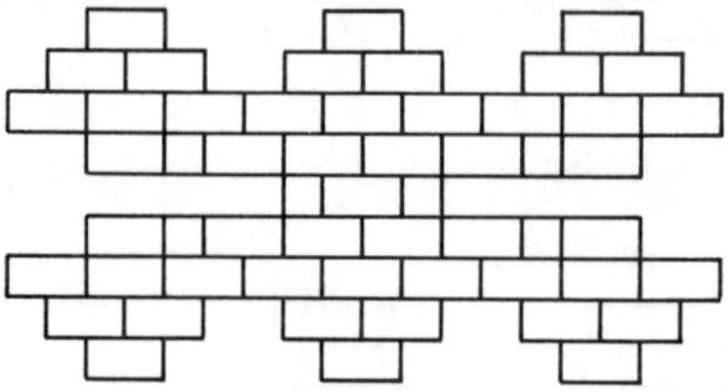

Fig. 19.

Finally the 49 *akṣaras* can be inserted into the figure. Śrīkaṇṭha, who represents the vowel *a* (see Appendix II), is the first to be written in the figure. Further it is said that the *akṣara ha* is in the central square called Oḍiyāna (90ab), the same place it occupies in the Mālinī Gahvara (cf. p. 185). The text gives the order of the 49 *akṣaras* row by row. Thus on the first row *sa*, *a*, *ṣa*; on the second *ā*, *śa*, *i*, *va*, *ī*, *la*, and so on from the *sa* upto the *ja* in the third square of the ninth row (91a). The vowel *a* is consequently placed in the middle square of the first row. Obviously the order of the *akṣaras* is not accidental. Beginning with the *a* in the *pūrvaśṛṅga* (cf. Mālinī Gahvara), the letters are inserted into the figure clockwise, every time skipping one square until one reaches the north-eastern corner of the figure, in which the *sa* is inserted. The 49th *akṣara*, the *ha*, is then placed in the centre of the figure. From the enumeration of the 49 *akṣaras* as given after *śloka* 91 the order of the *akṣaras* becomes clear: the last one (*sa*), the first one (*a*), the 48th (*ṣa*), the 2nd (*ā*), etc. The *mantra* of Vajrakubjīśvarī, for which the Vajra Gahvara is used, is presented in a similar way: the *mantra* consists of a

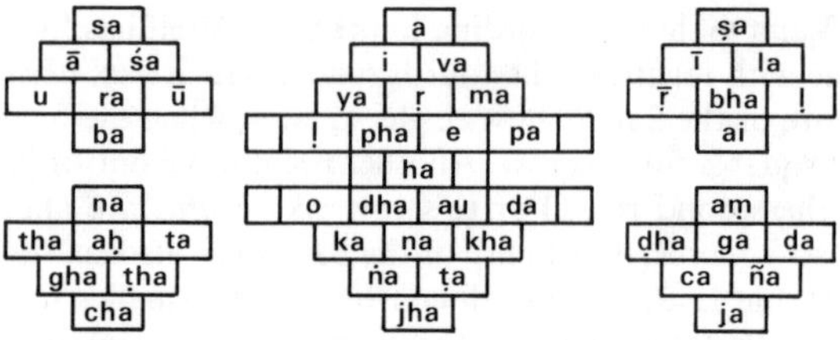

Fig. 20.

combination of two separate *mantras*. One of these is given in its normal order (*anuloma*), the other starting at the end (*viloma*). Thus the order is 1) 1st syllable of the one *mantra*, 2) last syllable of the other *mantra*, 3) 2nd syllable of the one *mantra*, 4) penultimate syllable of the other *mantra*, etc. The Vajra Gahvara with all the 49 *akṣaras* is shown in Fig. 20.

The Candradvīpa Prastāra

The directions to draw the Candradvīpa Prastāra are found in the Śrīmatatantrasāra (F.2A), where it is used to give the names of the Nāthas, Siddhas etc. of the Kulākikāmnāya. After the usual description of the spot suitable for the drawing of the figure, the Sādhaka is obliged to worship a maiden (*kumārī*) and a boy (*kumāra*), and next eigth Yoginīs and eigth Vīras with food and liquor. Then he should draw the Candradvīpa Prastāra:

14 uddharec caturasraṃ tu, aṣṭarekhopalakṣitam |
pūrvapaścimarekhaṃ tu, dakṣiṇottarataḥ sthitam ||
15 candradvīpaṃ tu nāmedaṃ, caturviṃśaṃ navādhikam |
īśānādikramāl likhya, mātṛkāṃ kulanāyikām ||
16 kādimāntaṃ caturviṃśad, bāhyapaṅktau nyased budhaḥ |
svara ṣoḍaśa dve paṅktau, mādihāntaṃ tṛtīyake ||

The text is rather concise, and for that reason not very clear. The Sādhaka should draw a square with eigth lines (14ab): eight from East to West, and eigth running from South to North (14cd). This figure is called the Candradvīpa (15a). Thus:

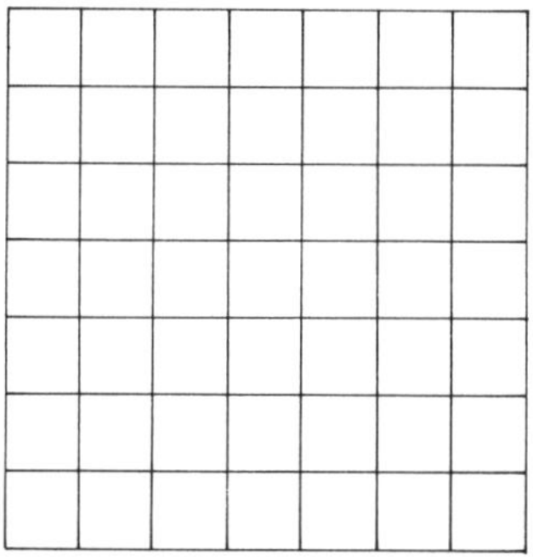

Fig. 21.

Next the numbers 24 and nine are mentioned (15b). Since these make 33 together, it is most likely that the 33 consonants of the Sanskrit alphabet are meant. These should be written (sc. in the diagram) in their proper order (15c *krama*) beginning from the north-east (15c *īśāna*). Next the (sixteen) vowels (*mātṛkās*) are to be inserted into the diagram. The form *mātṛkāṃ* is acc. sg. instead of the correct acc. pl. (*mātṛkāḥ*). The sixteen vowels are called 'The Ladies of the Kula System' (*kulanāyikā*). The 24 consonants are the letters from *ka* to *ma* (16a *kādimānta*), which is not correct as they number 25! Obviously one should take the consonants from the *ka* onwards up to the *bha*, which do number 24. These are to be inserted by the wise in the outer row (16b). The sixteen vowels are to be inserted in the second row (16c), and the nine remaining consonants from *ma* up to *ha* are to be written in the third row (16d). Note the incorrect gender of *tṛtīyake* which should be feminine, and the form *dve* which ought to be *dvitīyakāyām*. Both irregularities are probably *metri causa*. The diagram of the Candradvīpa Prastāra as drawn above (fig. 21) has seven rows, when we count them in the same manner as in the case of the Mālinī Gahvara and the Vajra Gahvara. Obviously this method is not valid for the drawing of the Candradvīpa Prastāra, where only three rows are mentioned. To reach the number of three rows, one has to count them from the central square to the rim of the diagram. In this way there are three rows at all four sides of the central square. This way of counting the rows, however, contradicts the contents of *pāda* 16d where it is said that the *ha* is also in the third row. Obviously something is wrong in the text. Inserting the 49 *akṣaras* into the figure following the method of the three rows, and placing the *ha* in the central square, results in a drawing of the Candradvīpa Prastāra which is effective:

North-East

dha	na	pa	pha	ba	bha	ka
da	o	au	aṃ	aḥ	a	kha
tha	ai	ṣa	sa	ma	ā	ga
ta	e	śa	ha	ya	i	gha
ṇa	ḹ	va	la	ra	ī	ṅa
ḍha	ḷ	ṝ	ṛ	ū	u	ca
ḍa	ṭha	ṭa	ña	jha	ja	cha

Fig. 22.

To demonstrate the validity of the Candradvīpa Prastāra as drawn above (Fig. 22), we will give the name of the Ādinātha as it is given in the Śrīmatatantrasāra:

ṇa-tha-madhyagataṃ gṛhya, ṛ-u-madhyoparisthitam |
au-śa-madhyaṃ tadante ca, ta-ḍha-madhyā(ruhaṅ) ||
ra-ṅa-madhyaśirobhinnam, e-ha-madhyaṃ tadagrataḥ |
ādyanāthasya nāṁedaṃ, tavādya prakaṭīkṛtam ||

When read according to Fig. 22 the name Tūṣṇīśa is the result, who is probably identical with Matsyendranātha or Mīnanātha (cf. Schoterman 1977: 934).

SUPPLEMENT

Just after putting the final touches to the present study I came across eight photos of an illustrated paper manuscript from Nepal, which were taken by a tourist in Kathmandu. It became immediately clear to me that the manuscript contained several drawings of *prastāras* and *gahvaras* which were very similar to the ones discussed in the preceding pages. Although time was too short for a profound study of the manuscript and its illustrations, incorporation of the relevant drawings into the present study seemed important to me. Therefore I present those drawings here with only a few short explanatory remarks.

The photographies show thirty-two pages of the manuscript which might be longer. Among these thirty-two pages there are nine pages which contain text parts written in Sanskrit and Newari. The text parts give particulars with regard to a *pūjā*: *bījas*, *mantras* and ingredients are summed up. Several deities are mentioned by name, among which we find Kubjeśī and Kubjīnātha. The major part of the manuscript, 23 pages, is filled with a great number of drawings of *prastāras*, *gahvaras*, *maṇḍalas* and other figures with a ritual purpose. The leaves of the manuscript which were photographed, provide no indication with regard to the name of the text, but the date of its composition is given: *saṃvat* 802 in the month of Caitra (1681 A.D.). The manuscript appears to be of Newari provenance, but the Newari texts are full of Skt words which have been 'Newarized' by means of Newari case-endings and auxiliary verbs — a common feature in these kind of Newari texts.

The drawings of the *prastāras* and *gahvaras* are provided in most instances with a proper name which is included in the list of *prastāras* and *gahvaras* from the Saṃvartārthaprakāśa (cf. p. 182). Only a few names are not found in the list. More important perhaps is the fact that besides the proper name of a particular *prastāra* or *gahvara* the text also gives in some instances the name of the text in which the *prastāra* or *gahvara* can be found. The names of various texts are mentioned in the legends to the drawings, most of which belong to the School of Kubjikā (see below). It appears then that the present manuscript was compiled from several texts of the Kubjikā School mainly, in order to facilitate the reading of those parts which are written in some kind of code. As becomes apparent from the list below, the legends to the drawings are written in a language which is Newari only because of the Newari case-ending *-yā* which has a genitive connotation, the Newari demonstrative pronoun *thva*, 'this', and the verbal form *juro* (Fig. 40; *juro* is the 1st form of the verbal stem *ju-l*, 'to become', which is used as a finite verb here; *thva* and *thva juro* correspond to Skt *iti*). Twice (Figs. 31 & 36) we find *ehi* after the legend instead of *thva*/*thva juro*. Probably it has the same meaning as the latter two, but I do not know it from Newari.

Legends to the drawings

Fig. 23: *tripurayā yoginīhṛda[ya]yā jonigahora.*
Fig. 24: *aheṭasatrikāvinirgatā prastāracakra thva.*
Fig. 25: *sumerugahvara.*
Fig. 26: (legend outside the photo?).
Fig. 27: *matsārayā praśtāraṃ candrarūpanāma.*
Fig. 28: *ratnadevayā prastāra thva.*
Fig. 29: *prabhaṃjādi.*
Fig. 30: *candradvīpāvatārayā prastāra thva.*
Fig. 31: *mattottara(masasta) prastāra ehi.*
Fig. 32: *tripurayā vidyānandayā varṇṇagarvaraprastāra thva.*
Fig. 33: *caturvviṃśatisāhasreyā sumerugahvara thva.*
Fig. 34: *sumerugahvara.*
Fig. 35: *matottarayā pīṭhaprastāra thva.*
Fig. 36: *uttarayā jayadrathayāmalayā tṛtīyakhaṇḍa[yā] vajraprastāra ehi.*
Fig. 37: *vajragahvaraprastāra.*
Fig. 38: *vajrakubjisiddhikubjimantroddhāra anulomavilomena vajraprastāra.*

Fig. 39: *matottarayā vajraprastāra thva.*
Fig. 40: *ugracaṇḍi khaḍgaprastāra thva juro.*
Fig. 41: *śrīmattayā tilakaprastāra thva.*
Fig. 42: *padmaprastāra thva.*
Fig. 43: *utta[ra]yā siddhilakṣmī paṃcācalaprastāra thva.*
Fig. 44: *jayadrathajāmalayā dvitīyakhaṇḍayā mantracakreśvarīprastāra thva.*
Fig. 45: *matottarayā cchatraprastāra thva.*

Besides these drawings which are reproduced on the following pages, the manuscript contains two drawings from the Ṣaṭsāhasra Saṃhitā. Since these drawings agree almost completely (cf. No. 1 below) with the parallel drawings from the Ṣaṭsāhasra Saṃhitā, I have not included these drawings here. The two drawings are the following:

No. 1: the Vajra Gahvara which is identical with Fig. 20. The only difference is the confusion of *śa* and *sa*. The legend to the drawing reads: *ṣaṭsāhasrayā vajragahvara-prastāra thva.*

No. 2: the Yoni Gahvara which is identical with Fig. 6. The legend runs: *ṣaṭsāhasra[yā] yonigahvala.*

As it appears all the drawings are provided with a legend except Fig. 26, but most likely its legend was not photographed as half of the upper row of the figure has fallen outside the photography at my disposal. The legend to Fig. 26 was probably written above the upper row of the figure. Comparing the names of the figures with those in the list from the Saṃvartārthaprakāśa (p. 182) we find that the majority of the names is contained in the list. It does not become clear, however, whether the author of the present manuscript makes a distinction between the terms *prastāra* and *gahvara*, as is obviously the case in the Saṃvartārthaprakāśa. Twice (Figs. 32 & 37) the two terms are combined into *gahvara-prastāra*. It is therefore doubtful in some instances whether a name refers to the *prastāra*- or to the *gahvara*-list in the Saṃvarthaprakāśa. Thus the Sumeru Gahvara (Figs. 33 & 34) may be identical with the Meru Gahvara, the Meru Prastāra or the Sumeru Prastāra in the list of the Saṃvartārthaprakāśa. In three instances the names found in both texts differ slightly: the Prabhañjādi (Prastāra?; Fig. 29) is most likely identical with the Prabhañjana Prastāra from the Saṃvartārthaprakāśa; the Candradvīpāvatāra Prastāra (Fig. 30) should correspond with the Candradvīpa Prastāra; the Mantracakreśvarī Prastāra (Fig. 44) is probably the Cakreśvarī Prastāra. Three names do not occur in the enumeration of the Saṃvartārthaprakāśa: the Tilaka Prastāra (Fig. 41), the Padma Prastāra (Fig. 42) and the Pañcācala Prastāra (Fig. 43). The latter, 'the Prastāra of the Five Mountains', has the number 'five' in common with the Pañcapraṇava Gahvara of the Saṃvartārthaprakāśa, but probably another figure is meant. In the text around this figure the five mountains are mentioned by name: Mt. Udaya, the 'Sun-rise' mountain (E.), the Malaya mountain range (S.), the Lokāloka mountains (N.), Mt. Kailāsa (Centre?) and Mt. Meru (cf. p. 202).

The texts which are mentioned in relation with the various drawings are the following: Tripurā(-rahasya or -rṇava?; Figs. 23 & 32), Yoginīhṛdaya (Fig. 23), Śrīmatta (Fig. 41), Mat[a]sāra (Fig. 27), Matottara (Figs. 31; 35; 39; 45), Caturviṃśatisāhasra (Fig. 33), Uttara (Figs. 25; 36; 43), Jayadrathayāmala (Figs. 36 & 44) and the Ṣaṭsāhasra Saṃhitā (see above). The Śrīmatta, Matasāra, Matottara, Caturviṃśatisāhasra and Ṣaṭsāhasra Saṃhitā are all texts belonging to the School of Kubjikā. The text called Uttara might be identical with the Matottara. The other three texts are well-known from Tantric literature.

From the legend to Fig. 38 it becomes clear that the figures are used to present the *mantras* of various deities in a twofold way: either in the 'normal' order of the *akṣaras* (*anuloma*), or in the reversed order (*viloma*). The names of four deities are given in connection with a particular figure: Vajrakubjī and Siddhikubjī (Fig. 38), Ugracaṇḍī (Fig. 40), Siddhilakṣmī (Fig. 43).

The legends of two figures are not clear to me. Below Fig. 31 is clearly written *mattottara masasta prastāra ehi*, of which only *mattottara* (wr. f. *matottara*[*yā*]) and *prastāra* are understandable. The legend to Fig. 24 reads *ahetasatrikāvinirgatā* ..., which is not clear to me. Perhaps *ahetasatrikā* should be understood as a compound ('the Trikā of Ahetasa'?), but it remains puzzling. Furthermore, the use of the female gender seems peculiar in comparison with the other legends. Finally it should be noticed that in the legend to Fig. 33 we find both a Skt (loc. sg.) and a Newari case-ending (*-sāhasre-yā*).

Before presenting the drawings themselves a few might be said about these figures. The figures of the *prastāras* and *gahvaras* are very neatly drawn by the author of the manuscript, and show only a few imperfections with regard to the inserted *akṣaras*. Due to the character of the script used, a Newari variant of the *nāgarī*-alphabet, no distinction is made between *ba* and *va*: both have the same sign व. This is, of course, a very common feature, and is usually not the cause of much misunderstanding in a regular text. In an enumeration of the letters of the alphabet, however, it is imperative to make a distinction between the two letters. In some instances it is difficult to decide which of the two is actually intended, in particular in those figures where the regular order of the letters seems to have been changed without any apparent system (see below). Although there are different signs for the ṛ and the ṝ (ऋ&ॠ), in most instances the ऋ is used for both. Unfortunately the same sign is used for the *jha*. There is no other way in checking the correctness of the various figures in the manuscript than by 'using' the codes in connection with the particular texts as mentioned. Since time was too short to do this, the figures with the inserted letters have been accepted at face value. There is not much doubt about the correctness of the triangular and square figures in my opinion: the manner in which the letters are inserted, appears to be systematical. The order of the letters in the Figs. 35-39 seems much less systematical. A 'regular' way of inserting the letters of Fig. 35 is shown in Fig. 35′. With regard to Fig. 41 there is no doubt that the drawing is wrong with regard to the inserted letters: several are lacking, and the *ḍha* is written twice (see below).

A curious aspect in some of the drawings is the fact that the 50th syllable, the *kṣa*, is included. As we have seen before (p. 182) the *kṣa* is regarded as a combination of the *ka* and the *ṣa*, and is not written but is invisibly present in the figure beneath the central letter of the figure. In the present manuscript, however, there are seven drawings which include the *kṣa*, and allot to it a place of its own. In one instance (Fig. 23) the *kṣa* is simply written besides the *ha*, outside the proper figure. In Fig. 25 the *kṣa* is also placed outside the drawing, but in its own small triangle. In the Figs. 33; 44; 45 the *kṣa* is placed in a square which seems to complete the shape of the drawing. For this purpose the sacred syllable OṂ is also added to a drawing in one instance (Fig. 36). There is only one figure in which the *kṣa* constitutes an integral part of the drawing, and cannot be omitted (Fig. 42). Because the *kṣa* is provided with the *visarga* (*aḥ*) in four instances (Figs. 25; 33; 36; 44), it rather looks like a *bīja* (i.e. *kṣaḥ*) than a syllable actually.

Apart from the proper name of the figure, the text from which it originates and sometimes the name of a particular goddess the drawings provide little additional information. Only in two drawings (Figs. 40 & 43) indications are found with regard to the 'direction' of the figure. Thus in Fig. 40 the North (*vāma*) and the South (*dakṣa*) are indicated. Fig. 43 gives also the regions of the sky together with the names of the mountains located there (cf. p. 200): East *udayādisthitaṃ pūrve*; South *yāmya malaya-parvvata*; West [ ] *sthitaṃ pāśabhṛto diśi* (lit. 'in the region of the one who holds the noose (i.e. Varuṇa)'); North *lokālokaṃ sthitaṃ saumyaṃ*; Centre (?) *saidhy(e) kailāsaparvvataḥ*. No mountain is mentioned in connection with the western region; perhaps Mt. Meru which is mentioned in the southern region (*merudharadeveśi*), is located there. The seven horizontal rows of Fig. 29 are connected with seven of the Eight Mothers (Mahālakṣmī is omitted), and with the series Unmanā, Samanā etc. (cf. Padoux 1975: table opp. p. 346).

The order of the figures as presented below does not follow the sequence of their appearance in the manuscript. I have 'arranged' the figures according to their outward shape. Finally, I have not indicated the few corrections which were necessary. In most of the instances it regards the letter *ḍha* which is written instead of the correct letter (see above).

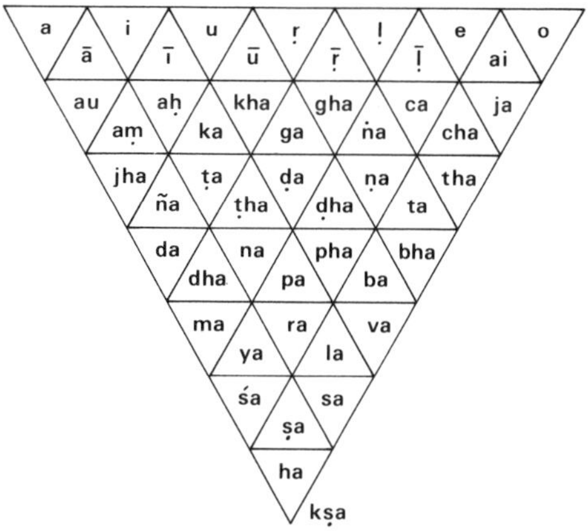

Fig. 23. Yoni Gahvara.

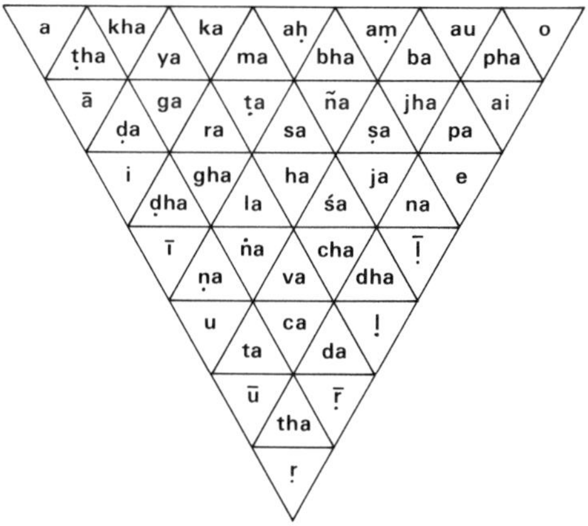

Fig. 24.

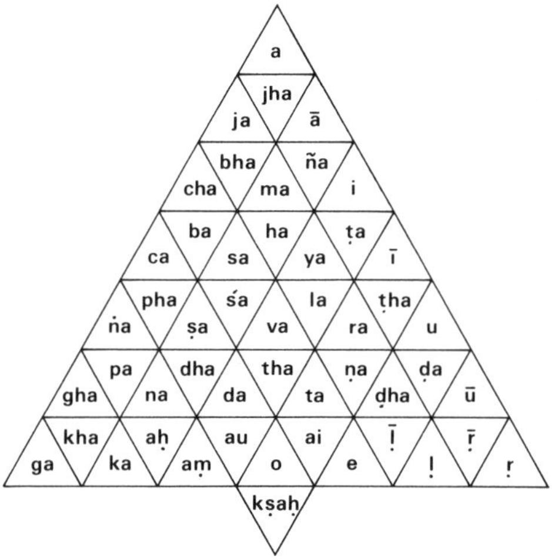

Fig. 25. Yoni Gahvara.

a	ā	i	ī	u	ū	ṛ
ta	tha	da	dha	na	pa	ṝ
ṇa	sa	ṅa	o	kha	pha	ḷ
ḍha	ṣa	au	ha	aṃ	ba	ḹ
ḍa	śa	gha	aḥ	ga	bha	e
ṭha	va	la	ra	ya	ma	ai
ṭa	ña	jha	ja	cha	ca	ka

Fig. 26.

ka	kha	ga	gha	ṅa	ca	cha
bha	a	ā	i	ī	u	ja
ba	aḥ	ma	ya	ra	ū	jha
pha	aṃ	sa	ha	la	ṛ	ña
pa	au	ṣa	śa	va	ṝ	ṭa
na	o	ai	e	ḹ	ḷ	ṭha
dha	da	tha	ta	ṇa	ḍha	ḍa

Fig. 27. Candrarūpa Prastāra.

a	ā	i	ī	u	ū	ṛ
ja	jha	ña	ṭa	ṭha	ḍa	ṝ
cha	bha	ma	ya	ra	ḍha	ḷ
ca	ba	sa	ha	la	ṇa	ḹ
ṅa	pha	ṣa	śa	va	ta	e
gha	pa	na	dha	da	tha	ai
ga	kha	ka	aḥ	aṃ	au	o

Fig. 28. Ratnadeva Prastāra.

cāmuṇḍā	ṛ	ṝ	ḷ	ḹ	e	ai	o	unmanā
aindrāṇī	ū	ḍa	ḍha	ṇa	ta	tha	au	samanā
vārāhī	u	ṭha	ra	la	va	da	aṃ	vyāpinī
vaiṣṇavī	ī	ṭa	ya	ha	śa	dha	aḥ	śakti
kaumārī	i	ña	ma	sa	ṣa	na	ka	nādāntam
maheśva[rī]	ā	jha	bha	ba	pha	pa	kha	nāda
brahmāṇī	a	ja	cha	ca	ṅa	gha	ga	nirodhikā

Fig. 29. Prabhañjādi Prastāra.

ka	kha	ga	gha	ṅa	ca	cha
bha	a	u	o	ū	ā	ja
ba	ai	ma	ya	ra	ṛ	jha
pha	aḥ	sa	ha	la	au	ña
pa	e	ṣa	śa	va	ṝ	ṭa
na	ī	ḹ	aṃ	ḷ	i	ṭha
dha	da	tha	ta	ṇa	ḍha	ḍa

Fig. 30. Candradvīpāvatāra Prastāra.

a	ā	i	ī	u	ū	ṛ
ta	tha	da	o	kha	dha	ṝ
ṇa	ṅa	na	ya	ra	pa	ḷ
ḍha	au	sa	ha	la	aṃ	ḹ
ḍa	ma	ṣa	śa	va	gha	e
ṭha	bha	ba	aḥ	ga	pha	ai
ṭa	ña	jha	ja	cha	ca	ka

Fig. 31.

ḹ	gha	va	dha	jha
ḷ	ga	śa	na	ña
ṝ	kha	ṣa	pa	ṭa
ṛ	ka	sa	pha	ṭha
ū	aḥ	HA	ba	ḍa
u	aṃ		bha	ḍha
ī	au	ja	ma	ṇa
i	o	cha	ya	ta
ā	ai	ca	ra	tha
a	e	ṅa	la	da

Fig. 32. Vidyānanda Varṇagahvara Prastāra.

						a						
					ā	jha	ja					
				i	ña	ma	bha	cha				
			ī	ṭa	ya	ha	sa	ba	ca			
		u	ṭha	ra	la	va	śa	ṣa	pha	ṅa		
	ū	ḍa	ḍha	ṇa	ta	tha	da	dha	na	pa	gha	
ṛ	ṝ	ḷ	ḹ	e	ai	o	au	aṃ	aḥ	ka	kha	ga
						kṣaḥ						

Fig. 33. Sumeru Gahvara.

						ha						
					sa	ṣa	śa					
				va	la	ra	ya	ma				
			bha	ba	pha	pa	na	dha	da			
		tha	ta	ṇa	ḍha	ḍa	ṭha	ṭa	ña	jha		
	ja	cha	ca	ṅa	gha	ga	kha	ka	aḥ	aṃ	au	
o	ai	e	ḹ	ḷ	ṝ	ṛ	ū	u	ī	i	ā	a

Fig. 34. Sumeru Gahvara.

a	ka	ṅa	jha	ma	ña	ca	kha	ā
	u	ḍa	pa	ra	pha	ḍha	ū	
		ḷ	dha	va	da	ḹ		
			o	ṣa	au			
				ha				
			aṃ	sa	aḥ			
		e	ṭa	śa	ba	ai		
	ṛ	cha	tha	la	na	ja	ṝ	
i	ga	ṇa	ṭha	ya	bha	ta	gha	ī

Fig. 35. Pīṭha Prastāra.

a	ka	ḍa	pa	ma	pha	ḍha	kha	ā
	u	ṅa	tha	ra	da	ca	ū	
		ḷ	jha	va	ña	ḹ		
			o	ṣa	au			
				ha				
			aṃ	sa	aḥ			
		e	ṭa	śa	ṭha	ai		
	ṛ	cha	dha	la	na	ja	ṝ	
i	ga	ṇa	ba	ya	bha	ta	gha	ī

Fig. 35′.

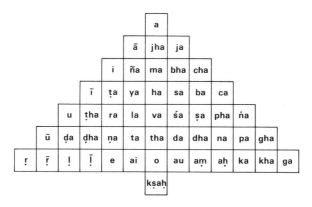

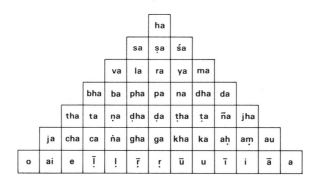

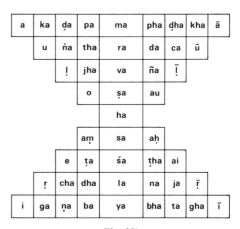

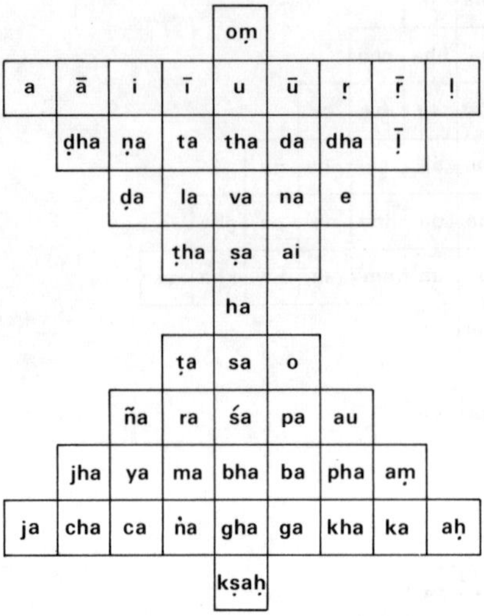

Fig. 36. Vajra Prastāra.

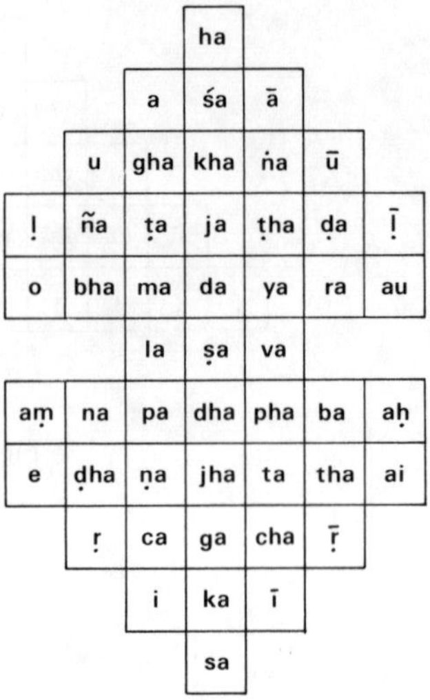

Fig. 37. Vajra Gahvara-prastāra.

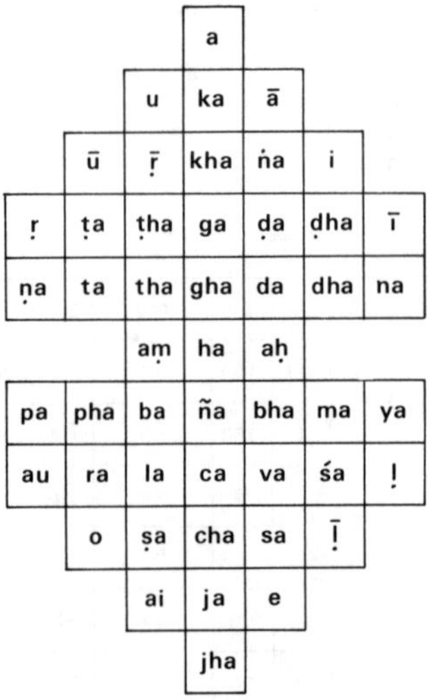

Fig. 38. Vajra Prastāra.

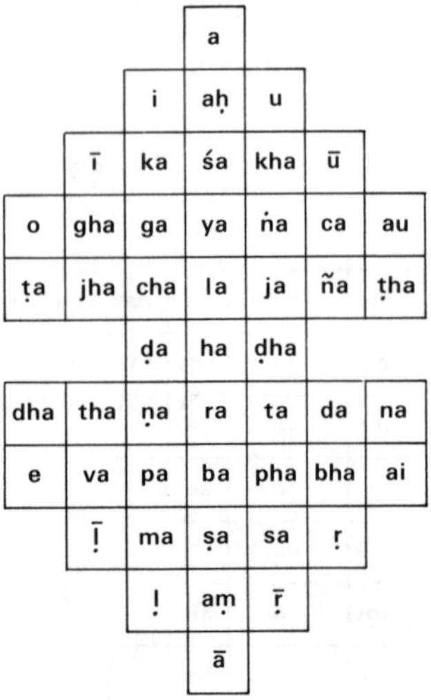

Fig. 39. Vajra Prastāra.

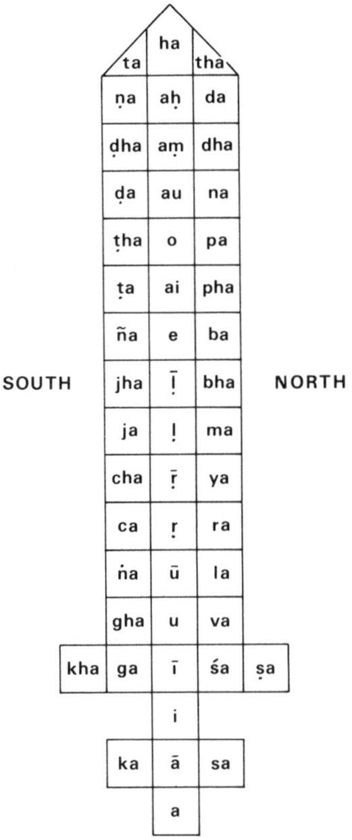

Fig. 40. Khaḍga Prastāra.

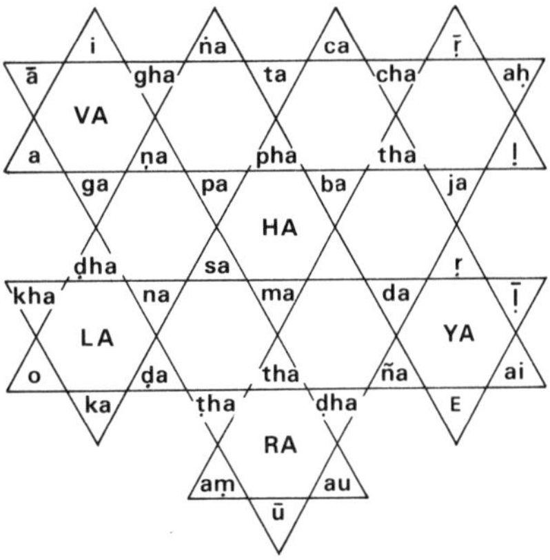

Fig. 41. Tilaka Prastāra.

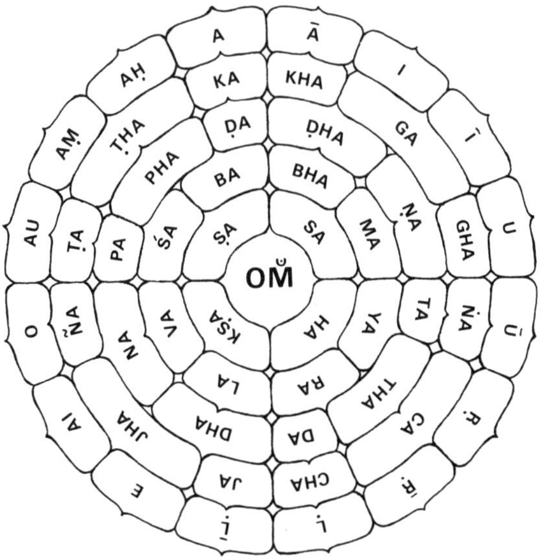

Fig. 42. Padma Prastāra.

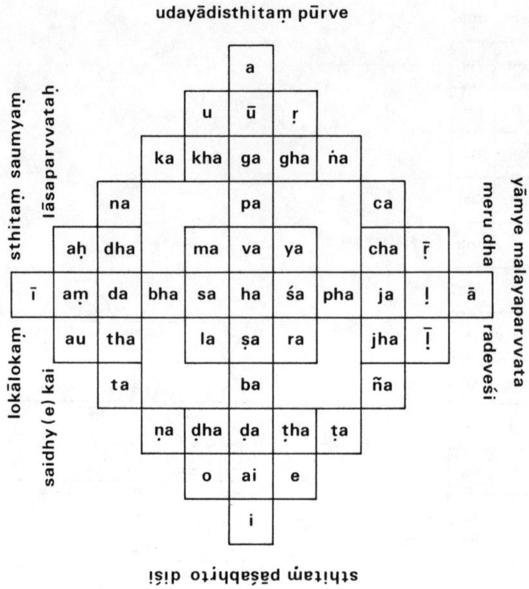

Fig. 43. Pañcācala Prastāra.

					kṣaḥ						
sa	ṣa	śa	va	la	ra	ya	ma	bha	ba	pha	pa
na	dha	da	tha	ta	ṇa	ḍha	ḍa	ṭha	ṭa	ña	jha
ja	cha	ca	ṅa	gha	ga	kha	ka	aḥ	aṃ	au	o
ai	e	ḹ	ḷ	ṝ	ṛ	ū	u	ī	i	ā	a
					ha						

Fig. 44. Mantracakreśvarī Prastāra.

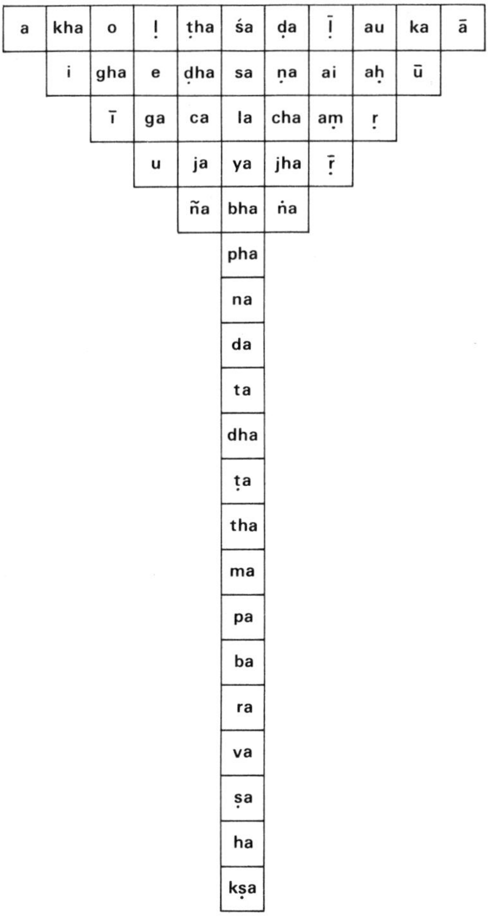

Fig. 45. Chatra Prastāra.

APPENDIX II

MĀLINĪ AND ŚABDARĀŚI

I. *Mālinī*

As we have observed earlier (Schoterman 1977: 935-936) Devī in Her manifestation of Mālinī plays an important role in the KmT and the ṢaṭSS. In this second Appendix we will restrict ourselves to the presentation of a list of the fifty *śaktis* of Mālinī, their location on the body of Mālinī, and the particular *akṣaras* of the Sanskrit alphabet they represent. With regard to the theoretical background of Mālinī in the process of creation we refer to Padoux (1975: 254-260).

The most striking feature of the fifty Mālinīs as representations of the fifty *akṣaras* is their actual order. The Mālinī-order of the fifty *akṣaras* does not run from *a* to *kṣa*, but from *na* to *pha*. Therefore Mālinī is called *nādiphāntarūpā*, 'having the shape from *na* to *pha*'. Both in the KmT and in the ṢaṭSS the *nādiphāntakrama* of the Sanskrit alphabet occurs several times (Schoterman 1977: note 63) in various contexts. The first time, however, when Mālinī is explained in both texts, She is presented by means of the Mālinī Gahvara (KmT 4,82-106; ṢaṭSS 7,6-38). The KmT gives in a concealed way the fifty *akṣaras* and their location on the body of Mālinī; the ṢaṭSS does the same, but also furnishes the names of the fifty *śaktis* (in the KmT these names are found in the 17th and 24th Chapter). For this reason we shall give the text of the *nādiphāntakrama* as it is found in the seventh *paṭala* of the ṢaṭSS, based on the MSS A & B (C follows B almost to the letter).

5 evaṃ nyāse kṛte devi, uddharen[1] mālinīṃ[1] śubhām[1] | (= KmT 4,81ab)
nādiphāntakrameṇaiva, yathā bhavati tac chṛṇu ||
6 pa-dha-madhye[2] śikhā jñeyā, nādinī tatra saṃsthitā |
ta-da-madhye tu[3] grasanī, sthitā ca śiramaṇḍale ||
7 e-pūrvākṣaracatuṣkaṃ[4] tu[4], śiromālā nigadyate |
nivṛttiś ca pratiṣṭhā ca, vidyā śāntis tathaiva ca ||
8 anantaśaktir[5] vijñeyā, brahmāṇḍasya tu vyāpikā[6] |[7]
tṛtīyaṃ nayanaṃ devyā, ṅa-cha-madhyagataṃ tathā ||
9 cāmuṇḍayā[8] samopetaṃ[9], jñātavyaṃ varavarṇini |
na-da-madhyagatau jñeyau, dvidhābhūtau tu locanau ||
10 priyadarśanī[10] deveśi[11], sūryasomātmikā[12] smṛtā |
cakṣuryugme varārohe, dakṣavāmakrameṇa tu ||
11 ṭa-pūrvā[13] nāsikā jñeyā, guhyaśaktisamanvitā |
ḍha-ta-madhyagataṃ gṛhya, dvirabhyāsapade sthitam ||
12 nārāyaṇī tathā devī, śaṅkaranārāyaṇī[14] tathā |
śravaṇau dakṣavāmau tu, jñātavyau varavarṇini ||
13 ṭha-ḍa-pūrvayutau varṇau, mohanīprajñayā yutau |
adhastāt[15] karṇayor devi, bhūṣaṇau dakṣavāmakau ||

14 sa-ca-madhyagataṃ vaktraṃ[16], vajriṇīsahitaṃ priye |
kha-visargasya madhyasthaṃ, karālinyāsamanvitam ||
15 dakṣadaṃṣṭrā adhobhāge, tava devi prakīrtitā[ḥ] |
ka-ga-madhyagataṃ varṇaṃ[17], kapālinyāsamanvitam ||
16 adhovāme tu daṃṣṭrā[s] tu, vijñeyā[s] tu kulāṃbike |
kha-ante tu śivā jñeyā, dakṣa ūrdhve tu daṃṣṭragā ||
17 kha-ūrdhve[17a] ghoraghoṣā ca, vāma[18] ūrdhve[18] tu[18] daṃṣṭragā[18] |
gha-ca-madhyāt samuddhṛtya, khirvarā[19] rājadantagā[20] ||
18 ña-pūrvā[21] rasanā devyā, māyā devī virājate |
jha-ūrdhve[22] vāgeśvarī[22] devī, vācāyāṃ[23] saṃsthitā[23] sadā[23] ||
19 śa-la-madhye[24] gatā[24] kaṇṭhe, devī ca śikhivāhinī |
ma-cha-madhyagataṃ[25] caiva, ra-ma-randhragataṃ[25] tathā ||
20 vāyuvegā ca bhīmā ca, skandhau tu dakṣavāmagau |
ḍa-ṇa-madhyagataṃ[26] gṛhya, ū-ḍha-madhye[27] dvitīyakam ||
21 vināyakī ca lāmā ca, bāhū[28] dakṣiṇavāmakau |
u-ra-madhyagataṃ caiva, dvidhābhūtaṃ tu kārayet ||
22 pūrṇimāsahitā[29] devyā, hastamadhye[30] varānane[30] |
ja-ma-pūrvasthitau[31] varṇau, jhaṅkārīkurdanīyutau ||
23 aṅgulyau dakṣavāmau[32] ca, devyāyāḥ parikīrtitau |
aṃ-ka-madhye[33] karapṛṣṭhau, saṃjīvanyādibhiḥ sthitau[34] ||
24 ña-ṭha-randhragataṃ gṛhya, kapālinyāsamanvitam |
vāmahastordhvavaktraṃ[35] tu, amṛtākhyena pūritam[36] ||
25 dakṣiṇe tu kare jñeyaṃ, ṭa-ṇa-randhraṃ[37] tu daṇḍakam[38] |
dīpanyayā[39] samopetaṃ, śūlasya kathitaṃ mayā ||
26 a-cha-randhragataṃ śūlam, uttānam[40] ūrdhvavaktragam |
jayantyayā[40a] samopetaṃ, yathā lakṣaṇalakṣitam ||
27 gha-ṇa-madhye[41] tu hṛdayaṃ, pāvanyayā samanvitam |
(ṭa)-tha-randhragataṃ gṛhya, paramātmāsamanvitam |[42]
ātmasthāne varārohe, visargasahitaṃ smṛtam ||
28 ya-sa-madhyagataṃ prāṇam, aṃbikayā[43] samanvitam |
ja-ca-randhragataṃ gṛhya, ra-va-madhyagataṃ[44] punaḥ ||
29 chagalī[45] pūtanā[46] devī, stanobhau[47] dakṣavāmagau |
jha-pūrve[48] caiva amoṭī, stanamadhye payaḥ[49] smṛtaḥ ||
30 na-sa-randhragataṃ gṛhya, laṃbodaryāsamanvitam[50] |
udaraṃ caiva deveśi, ka-ṣākhyaṃ tattvanāyakam[51] ||
31 saṃhāryayā[52] samopetaṃ[53], nābhideśe virājate |
bha-ña-madhyagataṃ gṛhya, mahākālīsamanvitam[54] ||
32 nitaṃbaṃ[55] kathitaṃ devyā, va-ṣa-madhyagataṃ tathā |
kusumāyudhāsamopetam[56], guhyaṃ devyā virājate ||
33 au-aḥ-madhyagataṃ bījaṃ, krūrādevīsamanvitam |
śukraṃ tu kathitaṃ devyā, jñātavyaṃ muktidāyakam ||
34 ṇa-tha-madhyagataṃ[57] bījaṃ, dvidhābhūtaṃ tu kārayet |
tārā devīti[58] saṃyuktā, ūrū dakṣe tu vāmake[59] ||

35 ṇa-tādhaḥsaṃsthitau[60] bījau, jñānaśaktikriyānvitau |
dakṣavāmakrameṇaiva, jānuyugmaṃ prakalpayet ||
36 tha-dādhaḥsaṃsthitau varṇau, gāyatrīsāvitrikānvitau |
jaṅghobhau[61] dakṣavāmau[62] tu, jñātavyau[63] varavarṇini ||
37 tha-dha-madhyagataṃ varṇaṃ[64], dahanyayā[65] samanvitam |
dakṣapādagataṃ devi, na-ca-madhyagataṃ[66] punaḥ ||
38 phetkāryayā[67] samopetaṃ[68], vāmapāde virājate |
evaṃ samyagvidhānena, uddhṛtā mālinī priye || (= KmT 4,106cd)

1. mālinī tu pari(t): A 2. pa-tha-: A, e-va-: B 3. -ṣu: B 4. -kṣaraṃ ( ): A 5. anantā sānta: A 6. vyāpakā: A 7. after *śloka* 8ab A inserts locane dakṣavāme tu, na-tha-madhyagataṃ priye 8. cāmuṇḍāyā: A 9. samopītā: A 10. -darśane: B 11. tu deveśe: B 12. somasūryāgnikā: A 13. ña-pūrvaṃ: A 14. śaṅkaraṃ nāyanī: A 15. adhasthī: A 16. vaktre: B 17. karṇaṃ: B 17[a]. ga-ṅa-madhyā: A 18. ūrdhvā( ) dantage: B 19. khervarā: B 20. gha(cakraghā): A 21. ṭa-: A 22. (raudra) vāgīśvarī: A 23. saṃsthitā śabdadarśane: A 24. -madhyasthitaṃ: A 25. -gataś(-s): B 26. ū-ra-: A 27. ḍa-ṇa-: A 28. bāhu: A 29. -sahitau: B 30. hastaumadhye virājate: B 31. ja-pūrve tu sthitau: A 32. -vāme: A 33. a-ka-: A 34. sthitaḥ: A 35. -hastaurdhva-: B 36. pūritaḥ: A 37. ya-pha-: A 38. -kaḥ: A 39. dīpanyāyā: A, dīpanyāyāḥ: B 40. uttanam: B 40[a]. jayantyāyā: AB 41. -madhyaṃ: A 42. omitted in B 43. ambikāyā: A 44. ra-ma-randhragataṃ: A 45. chāgalī: B 46. pūtalā: A 47. stanau tau: B 48. a-pūrve: B 49. paya: A 50. -taḥ: A 51. -kaḥ: A 52. saṃhāryāyā: A 53. -tā: A 54. mahākālasamanvitaḥ: A 55. nitambaḥ: A 56. -[sa]mopītāṃ: A 57. na-tha-: A 58. devī tu: B 59. vāmage: A 61. jaṅghau tau: B 62. -vāme: B 63. jñātau tau: A 64. varṇau: A 65. dahanyāyā: B 66. (ṅa)-ṣa-: A 67. -karyāyā: AB 68. -ta: A.

As a minute translation of the above lines would be a rather tedious affair, we shall present the contents of these lines in the framework of a clearly arranged table (p. 216). Before doing so, however, some remarks should be made.

7: The four *śaktis* representing the 'headgarland' (*śiromālā*) of Mālinī are Nivṛtti, Pratiṣthā, Vidyā, and Śānti. These four are identified with the 'four *akṣaras* before the vowel *e*' (7a), which are *ṛ*, *ṝ*, *ḷ*, and *ḹ*, respectively. Thus Nivṛtti represents the *ṛ*, Pratiṣṭhā the *ṝ*, Vidyā the *ḷ*, and Śānti the *ḹ*. That Śānti is identified with the *ḹ*, and not with the *ṛ*, can be inferred from KmT 23,34c (*ḹ ḷ ṛ ṝ tu śāntyādyā*).

8. These four *śaktis* together are evidently called the 'Śakti of Ananta', who is inherent to the Brahmāṇḍa (8b). This reference is not clear to me. After the *pādas* 8ab the MS A inserts a half-*śloka*, which states that the letter (singular!) between *na* & *tha* is located in the right and the left eye. This line cannot be correct for various reasons. Between the *na* and the *tha* there are two letters (*dha* & *da*) according to the Mālinī Gahvara, while the MS has a singular (*na-tha-madhyagataṃ*); in those instances where two different letters are intended, the text always uses the dual (cf. 13a; 35a; 36a). Moreover the two eyes are to be identified both with the same letter, the *dha*, which is to be taken twice (9d *dvidhābhūtau*) and comes after the letter *ca* in the Mālinī-order of the alphabet (cf. 9cd; 10ab). The letter *da* is the penultimate letter, before the *pha*, and is identified with the right foot (cf. 37a-c). Finally, no *śakti* is mentioned here representing the two eyes.

9: In *pāda* 9a we have opted for the reading of MS B with regard to the proper name Cāmuṇḍā, viz. an instrumental sg. The MS A appears to read instead a genitive (*cāmuṇḍāyā[ḥ]*) which is less correct in connection with the following *samopeta* than an instrumental. In four other instances we find a similar form of the genitive case lacking the *visarga* of a femine proper noun in connection with *samopeta*: 25c (MS B has the *visarga*), 26c (MSS AB), 31a (MS A), and 38a. Only once we find a compound ending in *-samopeta* with a feminine proper noun for its first member (32c *kusumāyudhā-samopeta*). In all the instances we have opted for an instrumental sg. instead of the genitive case. The same confusion between the genitive and the instrumental is found thrice in connection with a proper feminine noun and *samanvita* (cf. Notes on *śloka* 14).

12: Both ears are identified with the letter *ṇa* (11c) which should be repeated twice consequently (11d). It seems that two *śaktis* are connected with this letter: Nārāyaṇī and Śaṅkara Nārāyaṇī (12ab), at least according to MS B. It is doubtful, however, whether this is actually the case. Usually, when two parts of the body are represented by two *śaktis*, two different letters are also given. Thus, for instance, the two arms are identified with the *ḍha* and the *ḍa*, and represented by the two *śaktis* Vināyakī and Lāmā (20cd; 21ab). The other way round, when two parts of the body are identified with the same letter, only one *śakti* is mentioned. Thus both eyes are to be connected with the letter *dha*, and identified with the *śakti* Priyadarśanī (9cd-10cd). Here we would have a combination of the two: two parts of the body (both ears), one letter (*ṇa*), and two *śaktis* (Nārayaṇī & Śaṅkara Nārāyaṇī). That something is wrong here, is already indicated by the fact that *pāda* 12b, in which the second *śakti* is mentioned, consists of nine syllables instead of the regular eight. Moreover it is only the *śakti* Nārāyaṇī who represents both ears (KmT 24,33ab *nārāyaṇī ṇa karṇau tu, vāmadakṣi-ṇayor ubhau*). MS A has the required eight syllables for *pāda* 12b, reading *śaṅkaraṃ nāyanī* instead of *śaṅkaranārāyaṇī*, but this does not make much sense and might rather be a corrupt reading for the text of MS B. That two *śaktis* could be meant by the author of the text, however irregular in the context this may be, could be inferred by the use of *tathā* in both *pādas*.

14: In *pāda* 14d there is the problem whether to read *karālinyā samanvitam* or to consider the two words as one compound: *karālinyāsamanvitam*. In the first case the proper name of the *śakti* is Karālinī, in the latter Karālinyā. The change of a feminine noun ending in *-ī* to *-yā* is not unusual, especially with regard to proper names. There are three other instances in the text where it is difficult to decide whether to read two separate words or a compound ending in *-samanvita* (15d; 24b; 30b). In three instances *samanvita* is connected definitely with a feminine proper noun in the instrumental case (27b; 28b; 37b), although twice one of the MSS used seems to point to a genitive instead of an instrumental (28b (MS A); 37b (MS B)) — a similar confusion between the genitive and the instrumental we have seen with regard to *samopeta* (see Notes on *śloka* 9). The use of *samanvita* as the final member of a compound with a feminine proper noun for its first member is attested three times (11a; 31d; 33b). Thus we find three instances of a compound ending in *-samanvita* with a feminine proper noun for its first member, three instances of *samanvita* connected with the instrumental of a feminine proper noun or at least no compound ending in *-samanvita*, and four instances where it is doubtful to choose between a compound with a feminine proper noun ending in *-yā* instead of *-ī* for its first member, or two words of which the first is a feminine proper noun ending in *-ī* declined in the instrumental case. As there are various readings in case *samanvita* is connected with a noun (instrumental or genitive), and no various readings when *samanvita* constitutes the final member of a compound, with regard to its first member, we have opted for the reading of a compound ending in *-samanvita* with as its first member a feminine proper noun ending in *-yā* instead of *-ī*, instead of two separate words of which the first is the instrumental of a feminine ending in *-ī*, since no various readings are found with regard to the first word. The fact that when reading two separate words the first word should be an instrumental rather than a genitive, is corroborated by the use of *yuta* in this context: there is no doubt that in 22d *yuta* functions as the last member of a compound with a feminine proper noun for its first member, while in *pāda* 13b *yuta* is connected with the instrumental case of two feminine proper nouns, although the dual would be more appropriate than the singular here.

Besides the problem connected with the correct reading of *pāda* 14d, there is still another difficulty. The *śakti* Karālinyā is related to the letter *ka* (14c), but in the enumeration of the sons and their female consorts of the second Mahāpīṭha (*Paṭala* 4/5), this particular *śakti* is called Kaṅkaṭa (see: Appendix III), which corresponds to the KmT (chapter 24). In the same way the next *śakti* Kapālinyā (15d) does not correspond either with the KmT or with the enumeration of the second Mahāpīṭha, where the *śakti* representing the letter *kha* is called Kālī or Kālikā.

15: As we have observed above (Notes on *śloka* 14), the *śakti* representing the letter *kha* (15c) is here called Kapālinyā (15d), while in the KmT and in Chapter 4/5 of the ṢaṭSS she is called Kālī or Kālikā, respectively. Both Karālinyā and Kapālinyā belong to the fixed group of five *śaktis* representing the letters *ka*, *kha*, *ga*, *gha*, and *ṅa*, which are identified with the teeth of Mālinī (KmT 24,30cd *khirvirā ghoraghoṣā ca, śivā kālī ca kaṅkaṭā*). In the *nādiphānta*-order of the Sankrit alphabet these five are always enumerated one after the other as they constitute the five gutturals (KmT 24,31ab *ka-varge daśanās tīkṣṇā evaṃ devyā virājate*). The last three *śaktis* — Śivā, Ghoraghoṣā and Khirvarā — of the enumeration in this seventh chapter of the ṢaṭSS correspond with both the KmT and chapter 4/5 of the ṢaṭSS; the first and second not. Karālinyā (14cd the letter *ka*), however, might correspond with Kālī/Kālikā, who represents the letter *kha*. Kapālinyā representing the letter *kha*, seems to be out of place. The *śakti* Kapālinyā or Kapālinī (KmT 24,26cd) represents the letter *ṭa*, and is identified with the skull in the left hand of Mālinī (*śloka* 24). Note that the *pāda* 15d in which Kapālinyā is mentioned, is exactly identical with *pāda* 24b, in which the other Kapālinyā representing the letter *ṭa* is recorded.

18: *pāda* 18c consists of nine syllables in both manuscripts.

23: The letter between *aṃ* and *ka*, the *aḥ*, has to be taken twice and identified with the back of both hands (*karapṛṣṭha*). The *śakti* representing this letter is called Icchā Śakti in the KmT (KmT 24,27ab: *icchāśaktir visargākhyā, karapṛṣṭhāv ubhāv api*), and in the enumeration of the fourth Mahāpīṭha simply Icchā (4/5,110b). Here we find that the letter *aḥ* is represented by Sañjīvanī or Sañjīvanyā etc. (23d). Which other *śaktis* besides Sañjīvanī there could be is not clear to me. Moreover it is not very likely that one letter (*aḥ*) should be represented by more than one *śakti* (cf. Notes on *śloka* 12).

24: The letter *ṭa* is represented by Kapālinyā (24ab), and identified with the *ūrdhvavaktra* of the left hand (24c) which is filled by 'what is called Amṛta' (24d). In the KmT the *śakti* Kapālinī is located in the left hand (KmT 24, 26cd: *kapālinī vāmakare, ṭa-varṇaḥ parikīrtitaḥ*) without any reference to *ūrdhvavaktra*. In the fourth chapter of the KmT, however, there is a reference to this *ūrdhvavaktra*: *ña-ṭha-madhyagataṃ gṛhya vāmahaste pradāpayet || ūrdhvavaktrakapālaṃ tu amṛtākhyena pūritaṃ* (KmT 4,94cd; 95ab). Thus it appears that Mālinī holds a skull (*kapāla*) in Her left hand with the opening upwards (*ūrdhvavaktra*) because it is filled with Amṛta, of course.

26: In Her right hand Mālinī holds a *triśūla*, the shaft (*daṇḍaka*) of which is identified with the letter *ra*, and represented by the *śakti* Dīpanyā (25a-d). The next letter, the *ja*, is represented by Jayantyā (26c). The exact location of this *śakti* in relation with the body of Mālinī is not very clear from the text itself. In the KmT the *śakti* Jayantyā is identified only with the *triśūla* (KmT 24,25d *jayantyā śūlaṃ ja smṛtā*), but from the *pādas* 26ab (= KmT 4,96cd) it seems that she is identified, more precisely, with the point of the *triśūla*, which is directed to the skull filled with Amṛta in the other hand of Mālinī.

27: After *śloka* 27ab in which the letter *pa* is identified with the heart (*hṛdaya*) and connected with the *śakti* Pāvanyā, the MS A contains a half-*śloka* which is omitted in MS B. According to MS A it deals with the letter between *ṭa* (?) and *tha*, which is the *la*. This cannot be correct, since the letter *la* is mentioned in *śloka* 28d, being represented by the *śakti* Pūtanā (29a). The letter referred to with (*ṭa*)-*tha-randhragata*, should be the letter *sa* which is not mentioned elsewhere in the text otherwise. In the KmT the letter *sa* is represented by the *śakti* Parāparā (KmT 24,24b *sa-kāre ca parāparā*), while the ṢaṭSS names her Paramātmā (better: Paramātmī?). Her place is in the *ātmasthāna*, 'the place of the Self' (27e). Furthermore the letter *sa* is connected with the *visarga* (27f). Obviously the text of MS A is not correct, as it points to the letter *la* probably. The *tha* of MS A is most likely a corrupt reading for the *ṣa*, which is often confused with the *tha* in manuscripts as they have a similar shape. In order to 'obtain' the letter *sa* in the Mālinī Gahvara one consequently can only read *ma-ṣa-randhragata*, which fits in with the use of *randhra* (cf. p. 186). That this correction of the text is probably correct, might be inferred from the KmT where the letter *sa* is described with *ma-ṣa-madhyagata* (KmT 4,98a). In this fourth chapter of the KmT the letter *sa* is called the *ātmabīja*, 'the *bīja* of the Self' (KmT 4,98b), which corresponds with the *ātmasthāna* of our text. Furthermore the letter *sa* is said to be 'of Śiva's nature' (KmT 4,98b *śivātmaka*). The letter *sa* is the only letter which is connected with another letter, e.g. the *aḥ* (27d) *visargasahita* (= KmT 4,98c). Thus the letter connected with the Self of Mālinī is not merely the *sa*, but rather *saḥ*. This *saḥ* obviously looks very similar to a *bīja* or *mantra*. That this is probably the case can be inferred from the designation *ātmabīja* (KmT 4,98b). Moreover it is stated explicitly in the KmT that the letter *sa* together with the *visarga* is the 'most excellent *mantra*' (KmT 4,98d *uddhṛtaṃ mantram uttamam*). In this way the designation *ātmabīja* (KmT 4,98b), and its location in the *ātmasthāna* (27e) becomes understandable. According to the 15th chapter of the ṢaṭSS there are two types of *mantras*: female and male, the first actually being called *vidyā*. The difference between the two is formed by the fact that a female *mantra* has for its first letter the *s*, while a masculine *mantra* begins with the *h*. Inevitably these two are connected with Śiva and His Śakti in a Tantric context. Thus it is not surprising that the letter *sa* is located in the Self of Mālinī. The mention of its being connected with the *visarga* (*aḥ*) perhaps points to Śiva (KmT 4,98b *śivātmaka*), although Śiva is represented by the *ha* rather than the *aḥ*. Yet this line of thought combining the *sa* with the *aḥ*/*ha* as a representation of the union between Śiva and His

Śakti can be made plausible in the order of the *nādiphānta*-alphabet itself. In the MVT we find a slightly different order of the fifty letters: after the letter *pa* (ṢaṭSS 7,27ab) the letters *cha*, *la*, and *ā* follow (MVT 3,39c). Next the MVT enumerates the *sa*, *aḥ*, and *ha* (MVT 3,39d; 40a *sa jīvo visargayuk* (!) ||*tatparaḥ kathitaḥ prāṇaḥ*). In the ṢaṭSS the order of these letters is: *pa*, *sa*, *ha*, *cha*, *la*, *ā*. Thus the triplet *sa*, *aḥ*, *ha* of the MVT is reduced to *sa*, *ha* in the ṢaṭSS, the *aḥ* being mentioned earlier (after the *ña*: *śloka* 23cd), but a reference to the *visarga* is seen in the compound *visargasahita*.

Having thus discussed the various problems connected with the presentation of the Mālinī-order of the Sanskrit alphabet in the seventh chapter of the ṢaṭSS, we can summarize its contents in the following table:

Letter:	*Śakti:*	*Location on the body of Mālinī:*
na	Nādinī	crest
tha	Grasanī	head
ṛ	Nivṛtti	headband
ṝ	Pratiṣṭhā	headband
ḷ	Vidyā	headband
ḹ	Śanti	headband
ca	Cāmuṇḍā	third eye
dha	Priyadarśanī	eyes
ī	Guhyaśakti	nose
ṇa	Nārāyaṇī (Śaṅkara N.)	ears
u	Mohanī	ornaments of the right ear
ū	Prajñā	ornaments of the left ear
ba	Vajriṇī	mouth
ka	Karālinyā	lower right teeth
kha	(Kapālinyā)	lower left teeth
ga	Śivā	upper right teeth
gha	Ghoraghoṣā	upper left teeth
ṅa	Khirvarā	front teeth
i	Māyā Devī	tongue
a	Vāgeśvarī	speech
va	Śikhivāhinī	throat
bha	Bhīmā	right shoulder
ya	Vāyuvegā	left shoulder
ḍha	Lāmā	right arm
ḍa	Vināyakī	left arm
ṭha	Pūrṇimā	palms
jha	Jhaṅkārī	fingers of the right hand
ña	Kurdanī	fingers of the left hand
aḥ	Sañjīvanī	back of the hands
ṭa	Kapālinyā	skull in the left hand
ra	Dīpanyā	shaft of the *triśūla* in the right hand
ja	Jayantyā	point of the *triśūla*
pa	Pāvanyā	heart
sa	Paramātmā	the Self
ha	Aṃbikā	breath
cha	Chagalī	right breast
la	Pūtanā	left breast

Letter:	*Śakti:*	*Location on the body of Mālinī:*
ā	Amoṭī	milk
ṣa	Lambodaryā	belly
kṣa	Saṃhāryā	navel
ma	Mahākālī	buttocks
śa	Kusumāyudhā	private parts
aṃ	Krūrā Devī	ovarian fluid
ta	Tārā Devī	tights
e	Jñānaśakti	right knees
ai	Kriyā	left knees
o	Gāyatrī	right shanks
au	Sāvitrī	left shanks
da	Dahanyā	right foot
pha	Phetkāryā	left foot

As we have remarked earlier (Schoterman 1977: note 63), the *nādiphānta*-order of the alphabet occurs eight times in the KmT and the ṢaṭSS. The order of the fifty letters is more or less the same each time with one striking exception, however: the place of the letter *tha* (cf. Schoterman 1977: note 64). In the KmT three out of the four places place the *tha* between the *ḹ* and the *ca*, while in the ṢaṭSS only in two instances out of the four the *tha* comes immediately after the *na*. In the MVT the *tha* is located between the *ḹ* and the *ca* (MVT 3,37b). In other texts in which the *nādiphānta*-alphabet is given, the letter *tha* is placed after the *na*: KnT (F.36A), Agnipurāṇa (145,6c). Both these texts are related more directly to the ṢaṭSS than to the KmT — with regard to the Agnipurāṇa this concerns only the five chapters dealing with Kubjikā (Agnipurāaṇa 143-147) (Schoterman 1980: 346). Apart from these two texts we find the *nādiphānta*-order of the alphabet in the Gorakṣasaṃhitā (Chapter seven), a text which seems to be closely related to the texts of the Kulālikāmnāya. In the seventh chapter of this text, which is unfortunately far from complete, we find a description of the fifty *śaktis* in the *nādiphānta*-order. In the text as edited by Janārdana Pāṇḍeya the opening of the seventh chapter is lacking. On page 30 of the edition a description of the fifty *śaktis* is given with regard to their outward appearance (*mūrti*). Since the text is incomplete the first *mūrti* is that of the *śakti* Pratiṣṭhā (= the letter *ṝ*); next follow Vidyā, Śānti, Cāmuṇḍā, Priyadarśinī, and the other *śaktis*. In the missing pages of the manuscript, before the description of the *śakti* Pratiṣṭhā, most probably Nādinī, Grasanī, and Nivṛtti are described. Consequently in the Gorakṣasaṃhitā the letter *tha* (= the *śakti* Grasanī) is also placed immediately after the *na*, the first letter in the *nādiphānta*-order of the alphabet. Although it is rather hazardous to draw any conclusions at this phase of research, it seems that the letter *tha* was originally located between the *ḹ* and the *ca*, while in later texts its position was shifted forwards, following immediately after the *na*. In this way the two initial letters of the *nādiphānta*-order correspond with the two final letters: *na*, *tha*, ..., *da*, *pha* compared to the usual order of the Sanskrit alphabet. Before proceeding with Śabdarāśi, the male counterpart of Mālinī, some remarks should be made regarding the application of the Mālinī-system in ritual. As in the MVT (cf. Padoux 1975: 255) the main application of the *nādiphānta*-order of the fifty letters seems to lie in the practical side of worship, instead of the philosophical. The identification of the fifty letters and *śaktis* with various parts of the body of Mālinī points unmistakanbly to the practice of *nyāsa*. As the KmT (17,84cd; 85ab) says: *mālinī śabdarāśiś ca, trividyāghorikāṣṭakam* || *dvādaśāṅgaṣa-ḍaṅgena, etad dehaṃ kulātmakam* |, 'a body characteristic of the Kula-doctrine [is consecrated by *nyāsa* of] Mālinī, Śabdarāśi, Trividyā, Aghorikāṣṭaka, Dvādaśāṅga, and Ṣaḍaṅga' (cf. Agnipurāṇa 145,1-5; Schoterman 1977: 936). The principal *nyāsa* for the followers of the Kula-doctrine is thus sixfold (cf KnT F.33A: *nyāsaḥ ṣoḍhā pravikhyātaḥ, paścimānvayasevinām*). As the KnT is mainly concerned with the practical side of worship, it gives the Mālinī-*nyāsa* in full (KnT FF.34A ff.). It appears that Mālinī is of three kinds: 1) *bhavā*, 2) *sthairyā*, and 3) *saṃhārī* — the threefold cycle of existence (creation, maintenance, absorption), The Mālinī-*nyāsa* in its creative aspect is composed of *nyāsa* of all fifty letters and their *śaktis* in the usual order from *a* to *kṣa*. Thus: '*a vāgeśvarī*' on the crest; '*ā amoṭī*' on the head; etc. The *nyāsa* of Mālinī in Her aspect of maintenance is composed of the fifty letters and their *śaktis* in the *nādiphānta*-order, and the third *nyāsa* (absorption) begins with the *kṣa* and its *śakti* up to the *a* with Vāgeśvarī. It is significant that the order of the various parts of the body is always the same (from the crest to the left foot) in all the three *nyāsas*: only the order of the letters with the accompanying *śaktis* is changed. In the *mantra* accompanying the actual *nyāsa* a distinction is made between the three kinds of *nyāsa* as well. In the *nyāsa* of creation the name of the *śakti* is always in the vocative singular ('*a vāgeśvari*'); in the *nyāsa* of maintenance the name of the *śakti* is in the fourth, or dative singular case ('*na nādinyai*'); in the *nyāsa* of absorption the name of the *śakti* is in the first, or nominative singular case provided with the *visarga* ('*kṣa saṃhāryāḥ*'), as the KnT explicitly states (*prathamāntā visargayuktā*).

II. *Śabdarāśi*

Śabdarāśi, or rather Śabdarāśibhairava (cf. Padoux 1975: 244), is the name of Śiva representing the fifty letters of the Sanskrit alphabet in their usual order from *a* to *kṣa*. As in the case of Mālinī, each of the fifty letters is identified with a particular part of the body, and represented by a manifestation of Śiva. These fifty manifestations are called Bhairavas (ṢaṭSS 7,45c), Rudras (ŚT 2,35c), *lipīśvara*, 'Lords of the letters' (Agnipurāṇa 293,40d), or simply *devatā*, 'deities' (KnT F.40A). In the seventh chapter of the ṢaṭSS these fifty Bhairavas are enumerated immediately after the enumeration of the fifty *śaktis* of Mālinī (7,45-66). Their location on the body is mentioned, as well as the letters with which they are identified. The fifty letters are not given by means of the Mālinī Gahvara, but appear 'without cover' in the text. Thus the first letter and accompanying Bhairava is described as follows: *a-kāras tu śikhāntasthaḥ, śrīkaṇṭhas tatra saṃsthitaḥ*. The names and the locations of the fifty Bhairavas correspond with similar lists elsewhere (Agnipurāṇa 145,28-30; 293,41-47; ŚT 2,29-35; KmT 24,4-20 (reversed order!)), although minor differences do occur. In this second appendix we restrict ourselves to a simple enumeration of the fifty letters, the fifty Bhairavas and their locations, as they are presented in the seventh chapter of the ṢaṭSS.

Letter:	*Bhairava:*	*Location on the body of Bhairava:*
a	Śrīkaṇṭha	crest
ā	Ananta	mouth
i	Sūkṣma	right eye
ī	Trimūrti	left eye
u	Amarin	right ear
ū	Arghin	left ear
ṛ	Bhārabhūti	right nostril
ṝ	Atithi	left nostril
ḷ	Sthāṇu	right cheek

Letter:	*Bhairava:*	*Location on the body of Bhairava:*
Ḷ	Hara	left cheek
e	Jhaṇṭhīśa	lower teeth
ai	Bhautin	upper teeth
o	Sadyojāta	lower lips
au	Anugraha	upper lips
aṃ	Krūra	uvula
aḥ	Mahāsena	tongue
ka	Krodha	right shoulder
kha	Caṇḍa (B: Pracaṇḍa)	right arm (A & B: *bāhumadhya*)
ga	Pracaṇḍa (B: Pañcārtha)	(right) elbow (KnT: right hand)
gha	Śiva	(right) wrist (? *kaṅkaṇa*; KnT: fingers)
ṅa	Ekarudra	fingers of the right hand (KnT: nails)
ca	Kūrma	left shoulder
cha	Ekanetra	left arm (A & B: *bāhuka*)
ja	Caturānana	(left) elbow (KnT: left hand)
jha	Ajita	(left) wrist (? *kaṅkaṇa*; KnT: fingers)
ña	Śarman (A: Ṣarma)	fingers of the left hand (KnT: nails)
ṭa	Someśvara	right buttock (KnT: right thigh)
ṭha	Lāṅgulin (A: Lāṅgalin)	right thigh (KnT: right shank)
ḍa	Ḍāru	right knee (KnT: right foot)
ḍha	Ardhanārin	right shank (KnT: toes of the right foot)
ṇa	Umākānta	toes of the right foot (KnT: nails)
ta	Āṣāḍhin	left buttock (KnT: left thigh)
tha	Diṇḍi (B: Daṇḍi)	left thigh (KnT: left shank)
da	Dhātrin	left knee (KnT: left foot)
dha	Mīna	left shank (KnT: toes of the left foot)
na	Meṣa	toes of the left foot (KnT: nails)
pa	Lohita	right part of the diaphragm (*dakṣakukṣi*)
pha	Śikhin	left part of the diaphragm (*vāmakukṣi*)
ba	Chagalaṇḍa	spine
bha	Dviraṇḍa	navel
ma	Mahākāla	heart
ya	Vālīśa or Bālīśa	skin (KnT: *liṅgāgra*)
ra	Bhujaṅga	blood
la	Pinākin	flesh
va	Khaḍgin	sinews
śa	Vakīśa (A: Dhakīśa)	bones
ṣa	Śveta	marrow
sa	Bhṛgu	semen
ha	Lakulīśa (B: Lakulin)	breath
kṣa	Saṃvartaka	anger (*krodha*)

In the ṢaṭSS the fifty letters and their Bhairavas are connected with the Eight Mothers, or better the 49 letters as the *kṣa* seems to be regarded separately. The division of the 49 letters follows the classification of the letters in the alphabet, and their various locations on the body of Bhairava keep pace with that classification. Thus:

1) a-aḥ: Brahmāṇī; the locations have all some relation with the head (51a: *śirojāta*).
2) ka-ṅa: Māheśvarī; the locations are all related to the right arm.
3) ca-ña: Kaumārī; the locations are all related to the left arm.
4) ṭa-ṇa: Vaiṣṇavī: the locations are all related to the right foot.
5) ta-na: Vārāhī: the locations are all related to the left foot.
6) pa-ma: Aindrāṇī: the locations are all related to the torso (61c: *śarīra*).
7) ya-va: Cāmuṇḍā.
8) śa-ha: Mahālakṣmī.

The seventh and eighth group should be taken together, at least with regard to the locations. Thus skin (*tvac*), blood (*rakta*), flesh (*māṃsa*), sinews (*snāyu*), bones (*asthi*), marrow (*majjan*), and semen (*śukra*) are probably identical with the seven Dhātus, although instead of *snāyu medas* ('fat, marrow') is more usual (cf. ŚT 1,33). Perhaps because *majjan* is already mentioned in the list, the author has changed the original *medas* for *snāyu*, as *majjan* and *medas* are very much alike in meaning. Another possible reason for the occurrence of *snāyu* in this series might be found in a confusion or blend between the seven Dhātus and the six Kośas. The six Kośas are basic elements of the human body, which is called consequently *ṣāṭkauśika*. The six Kośas are *snāyu*, *asthi*, *majjan*, *tvac*, *māṃsa*, and *asra* (blood); the first three originate from the father, the other three from the mother (cf. ŚT 1,47). Together with the series of seven 'breath' (*prāṇa*), is mentioned which stands apart from the other seven by its very nature. This is corroborated by the fact that in the text the letter *ha* is mentioned again after the eighth group (*śa-ha*) has been discussed, and connected with Mahālakṣmī. Now the letter *ha* and the *kṣa* are taken together: *ha paramaśivaḥ prāṇe, kṣa krodhe saṃvartakah. smṛtaḥ*. The letter *ha* is here identified with Parama Śiva instead of the Bhairava Lakulīśa as before. It seems that this second identification of the letter *ha* is at a higher level — the concept of *prāṇa* which the *ha* represents, is far more important than the locations of the other letters. Its connection with Saṃvartaka might also point in this direction, as Saṃvartaka appears to be very important for the Kula-doctrine (cf. *saṃvartāmaṇḍala*). It is therefore surprising that Saṃvartaka, the letter *kṣa*, is identified with the concept of 'anger' (*krodha*) which does not fit in with the eminent position of Saṃvartaka, nor with the locations of the other letters. Yet the three MSS of the ṢaṭSS, the KmT (24,4a *kṣa saṃvartaḥ sthitaḥ krodhe*), and the KnT (F.40A) all read *krodha*. Only in the Agnipurāṇa we find a different location of the letter *kṣa* and Saṃvarta[ka]: *kṣa saṃvartaś ca koṣagaḥ* (Agnipurāṇa 145,30d). Instead of *krodha* the text reads *koṣa*, which should mean 'body' here (cf. 4/5,118c *koṣṭha*, 'body', which is derived most likely from the same root as *koṣa* or *kośa*). The identification of Saṃvartaka with the human body is more satisfactory than its identification with the concept of 'anger'. Moreover it reminds one strongly of the denomination *ṣāṭkauśika* for the human body (see above). Thus two letters, the *ha* and the *kṣa*, are singled out from the other letters. The letter *ha* is singled out because of its location ('breath; vital air'), and is subsequently given a more prominent representative (Parama Śiva instead of Lakulīśa); the letter *kṣa* has a different position from the other letters due to its very nature (the combination of *ka* and *ṣa*), its representative (Saṃvartaka), and its location (the human body) which encompasses all the other locations from *a* to *ha*.

The *nyāsa* of Śabdarāśi as explained in the KnT (FF.39A ff.) is of three different kinds, like the *nyāsa* of Mālinī (creation, maintenance, and absorption). The sequence of the fifty letters is always from *a* to *kṣa*, and the locations are always the same (from the crest upto the complete body). The difference between the three kinds of *nyāsa* is found in the accompanying *mantras*, particularly with regard to the declination of the proper name of the Bhairava. Thus in the *nyāsa* of the creative aspect of Bhairava (*bhava*) the vocative singular is used ('*a śrīkaṇṭha*' on the crest, etc.); in the *nyāsa* of maintenance (*sthairya*) the dative singular case is used ('*a śrīkaṇṭhāya*' on the crest, etc.); in the *nyāsa* of absorption (*saṃhāra*) the nominative singular case provided with the *visarga* is used ('*a śrīkaṇṭhaḥ*' on the crest, etc.). Obviously the *nyāsa* of Mālinī and Śabdarāśi follow the same pattern with regard to the accompanying *mantras*, but the three *nyāsas* of Mālinī have a different order of the fifty letters and *śaktis* each time.

Finally something should be said with regard to the third type of *nyāsa* which is related to the absorption of the existing world. The name of the *śakti* or *bhairava* in the *mantras* is declined in the nominative singular case provided with the *visarga*, as the KnT states. The result of this may look like a nominative singular, or a nominative/accusative/vocative plural, depending on the gender and stem of the name declined. Yet the KnT is most likely right in stating that a nominative singular provided with the *visarga* is actually meant: the use of the plural in the *mantras* does not seem likely. The nominative singular is not unusual in a *mantra*, and the addition of the *visarga* is very appropriate in connection with the nature of this third type of *nyāsa*: besides denoting the vowel *aḥ*, the word *visarga* also denotes the destruction or absorption of the world at the end of a Yuga. In this way the explicit mention of the *visarga* in connection with the proper name of a *śakti* or *bhairava* in the *mantra* becomes understandable.

APPENDIX III

I. **Oḍiyāna** (*devī*: Raktā (śrotukāmā); *pati*: Ādhārīśa; *bhūta*: pṛthivī; *yuga*: Satya; *bīja*: ṢĀṂ).

Daughters:	Location (*pura*):
1 Rudrāṇī	skin
2 Rudraśākī	hair of the head
3 Govaktrā	hands & feet
4 Sumukhī	beard
5 Vānarī	teeth
6 Kekarā	bones
7 Kālarātri	sinews
8 Bhaṭṭikā	'firmness'

Sons:	Śakti:	Location (*siṃhāsana*):	Letter:
1 Vāmana	Nādinyā	above the Brahmarandhra	na
2 Harṣaṇa	Nivṛtti	headband	ṛ
3 Siṃhavaktra	Pratiṣṭhikā	headband	ṝ
4 Mahābala	Vidyā	headband	ḷ
5 Mahākāla	Śānti	headband	ḹ
6 Ekavaktra	Grasanī	head	tha
7 Bhairava	Priyadarśanī	eyes	dha
8 Pracaṇḍa	Guhyaśakti	nose	ī

Guardians:	Location:	
1 Caturbhuja	little finger	(right hand)
2 Gaṇādhyakṣa	ring-finger	(right hand)
3 Gajavaktra	middle finger	(right hand)
4 Mahotkaṭa	forefinger	(right hand)
5 Airāvatya	thumb	(right hand)
6 Vināyakya	thumb	(left hand)

II. **Jālandhara** (*devī*: Karālinī (vaktukāmā); *pati*: Kuṇḍalīśa; *bhūta*: tejas; *yuga*: Tretā; *bīja*: ŚEṂ).

Daughters:	Location (*pura*):
1 Mālā	heat
2 Śivā	burning
3 Durgā	cooking
4 Pāvanī	lustre
5 Harṣaṇī	digestion
6 Carcikā	'touched and not touched'
7 Suprabhā	splendour
8 Prabhā	brightness
9 Caṇḍā	brilliancy
10 Rugminī	light

Sons:	Śakti:	Location (*siṃhāsana*):	letter:
1 Śakuni	Cāmuṇḍā	third eye	ca
2 Sumata	Vajriṇī	mouth	ba
3 Nanda	Kaṅkaṭā	upper teeth	ka
4 Gopāla	Kālikā		kha
5 Pitāmaha	Śivā	lower teeth	ga
6 Pallava	Ghoraghoṣikā		gha
7 Meghanirghoṣa	Khirvarā	front teeth	ṅa
8 Śikhivaktra	Māyā	tongue	i
9 Mahādhvaja	Vāgeśī	voice	a
10 Kālakūṭa	Nārāyaṇī	suṣumṇā	ṇa

Guardians:	Location:	
1 Meghavarṇa	forefinger	(left hand)
2 Bṛhatkukṣi	middle finger	
3 Ekadaṃṣṭra	ring-finger	
4 Gaṇeśvara	little finger	
5 Vighnarāja	little toe	(right foot)
6 Mahānanda	*anāmikā*	

III. **Pūrṇagiri** (*devī*: Caṇḍākṣiṇī (puṣṭyarthe); *pati*: Kuraṅgīśa; *bhūta*: jala; *yuga*: Dvāpara; *bīja*: SŪṂ).

Daughters:	Location (*pura*):
1 Haṃsāvalī	motion
2 Sutārā	*sainyaka*
3 Harṣā	phlegm
4 Vāṇī	tears
5 Śubhākṣī	semen
6 Mahānandā	marrow
7 Sunandā	fat
8 Koṭarākṣī	blood
9 Viśvākṣī	urine
10 Yaśovatī	perspiration
11 Viśālākṣī	'stream'
12 Sundarī	*amṛta*

Sons:	Śakti:	Location (*siṃhāsana*):	letter:
1 Vāli	Mohinī	ear-ornaments	u
2 Nanda	Prajñā		ū
3 Daśagrīva	Śikhivāhinī	throat	va
4 Hayagrīva	Lāmā	arms	ḍha
5 Haya	Vināyakī		ḍa
6 Sugrīva	Kapālinyā	skull (left hand)	ṭa
7 Gopati	Pūrṇimā	hands	ṭha
8 Bhīṣmaka	Jhaṅkarī	fingers (right hand)	jha
9 Śikhaṇḍin	Kurdanī	fingers (left hand)	ña
10 Khaṇḍala	Dīpanī	shaft of the trident	ra
11 Śukra	Jayantī	trident	ja
12 Caṇḍa	Bhīṣaṇī	right shoulder	bha

Guarduans:	Location:	
1 Āmoda	*madhyamikā*	(right foot)
2 Pramoda	*tarjanī*	(right foot)
3 Durmukha	big toe	(right foot)
4 Sumukha	big toe	(left foot)
5 Vighnakartṛ	*tarjanī*	(left foot)
6 Vighneśa	*madhyamikā*	(left foot)

IV. **Kāmarūpa** (*devi*: Kāmeśvarī (īkṣaṇecchayā); *pati*: Cakrānanda; *bhūta*: vāyu; *yuga*: Kali; *bīja*: VĪṂ).

Daughters:	Location (*pura*):
1 Prabhā	quivering
2 Prasūti	turning around
3 Śaṃsā	contraction
4 Bhānumatyā	stretching out
5 Śrībalā	cutting off
6 Hāriṇī	jumping
7 Hariṇī	running
8 Mālinī	yawning
9 Kandukī	laughing
10 Muktāvalī	chattering
11 Gautamī	shaking
12 Kauśikī	panting
13 Śukodarī	sighing

Sons:	Śakti:	Location (*siṃhāsana*):	letter:
1 Bhānu	Vāyuvegā	left shoulder	ya
2 Anantahetu	Pāvanyā	heart	pa
3 Surāja	Laṃbikā	belly	ṣa
4 Sundara	Saṃhārī	navel	kṣa
5 Arjuna	Chagalī	right breast	la
6 Bhīma	Pūtanā	left breast	cha
7 Droṇaka	Āmoṭī	milk	ā
8 Bhaṣmaka	Paramātmī	*paramātma*	sa
9 Antaka	Aṃbikā	breath	ha
10 Ketudhvaja	Icchā	back of the hands	aḥ
11 Viśālākṣa	Mahākālī	buttocks	ma
12 Kalyāna	Kusumāyudhā	private parts	śa
13 Caturvaktra	Śukrā	ovarian fluid	aṃ

Guardians:	Location:	
1 Laṃpaṭa	*anāmikā*	(left foot)
2 Ghaṇṭakarṇa	little toe	(left foot)
3 Sthūladanta	shutting of the eyes	
4 Gajānana	opening of the eyes	
5 Bṛhatkuksi	exhaling	
6 Sunanda	inhaling	
7 Mahotkaṭa	keeping the breath	

V. **Mātaṅga** (*devī*: Kuṇḍalinī; *pati*: Mātaṅga/Antyaja; *bhūta*: ākāśa).

Daughters:	Location (*pura*):
1 Hārikā	moon
2 Hārī	seeing
3 Gandhārī	smell
4 Vīrā	Brahmarandhra
5 Nakhī	heart
6 Jvālinī	crest
7 Sumukhī	navel
8 Piṅgalā	penis
9 Sukeśī	Brahmarandhra

Sons:	Śakti:	Location (*siṃhāsana*):	letter:
1 Śrīphala	Tārā	thighs	ta
2 Kaśmala	Jñānaśakti	knees	e
3 Caṇḍa	Kriyā		ai
4 Caṇḍāla	Sāvitrī	shanks	au
5 Ceṭaka	Gāyatrī		o
6 Mātaṅga	Dahanī	right foot	da
7 Bāhuja	Phetkārī	left foot	pha
8 Vīra	(Dahanī)	(right foot)	(da)
9 Avyakta	(Phetkārī)	(left foot)	(pha)

Guardians:	Location:
1 Herambha	yawning
2 Dhūli	hiccups
3 Piśāca	sneezing
4 Kubja	belching
5 Vāmana	coughing

APPENDIX III[a]

The order of the fifty *akṣaras* according to the Mālinī-system (Appendix II) compared with the order of the *akṣaras*, as they are found in connection with the five Pīṭhas:

Mālinī: na, tha, ṛ, ṝ, ḷ, ḹ, ca, dha, ī, ṇa, u, ū, ba, ka, kha, ga, gha,
Pīṭhas: na, ṛ, ṝ, ḷ, ḹ, tha, dha, ī, ca, ba, ka, kha, ga, gha,

Mālinī: ṅa, i, a, va, bha, ya, ḍha, ḍa, ṭha, jha, ña, aḥ, ṭa, ra,
Pīṭhas: ṅa, i, a, ṇa, u, ū, va, ḍha, ḍa, ṭa, ṭha, jha, ña, ra,

Mālinī: ja, pa, sa, ha, cha, la, ā, ṣa, kṣa, ma,
Pīṭhas: ja, bha, ya, pa, ṣa, kṣa, la, cha, ā, sa, ha, aḥ, ma,

Mālinī: śa, aṃ, ta, e, ai, o, au, da, pha.
Pīṭhas: śa, aṃ, ta, e, ai, au, o, da, pha.

BIBLIOGRAPHY

A. *Primary Sources*

Agnipurāṇa, ed. by Āchārya Baladeva Upādhyāya (Benares, 1966).
Atharvaveda-Pariśiṣṭa: see Kohlbrugge, D. J.
Amarakośa, ed. by the Nirṇaya Sāgara Prakāśana (Bombay, 1969).
Ṛgvedasaṃhitā with the commentary of Sāyaṇa, ed, by F. M. Müller in 4 vol. (Benares, 1966).
Kathāsaritsāgara, ed, by Jagadīśalāla Śāstri (New Delhi, 1970).
Kālikāpurāṇa, ed. by Śrī Biśwanārāyaṇa Śāstri (Benares, 1972).
Kubjikānityāhnikatilaka, NAK No. 1-239/201[k]; NAK No. 5-8541/101 (unless stated otherwise references to the KnT pertain MS 1-239/201[k]).
Kubjikāmatatantra, MS A NAK No. 5-875/55; MS B NAK No. 1-1473/33; MS D NAK No. 1-1633/32; MS F NAK No. 1-118/305; MS G ASB No. 4733/5805; MS H NAK No. 1-285/28; MS J NAK No. 5-896/56; MS K NAK No. 1-113/303 (references to particular *ślokas* of the KmT pertain to the critical edition of the text which is in preparation; when no particular MS is mentioned the other references pertain to MS G).
Kulamūlaratnapañcakāvatāra, NAK No. 1-1552/120.
Kauṭilīya Arthaśāstra, ed, by R. P. Kangle in 3 parts (Bombay, 1965-1973).
Kaulajñānanirṇaya, ed, by P. C. Bagchi (Calcutta, 1934).
Gorakṣasaṃhitā, ed. by J. Pāṇḍeya (Part I) (Vārāṇasī, 1976).
Tantrarājatantra (Part I), ed. by Lakṣmaṇa Śāstri (London, 1918).
(*idem*) (Part II), ed. by Sadāshiva Mishra (Calcutta/London, 1926).
Tantrasārasaṅgraha, ed. by M. Duraiswami Aiyangar (Madras, 1950).
Ṭippanī, NAK No. 5-4775/209.
Tantrāloka, ed. by M. K. Śāstri (Srinagar, 1921-1938).
Devy-upaniṣad, ed. by J. Varenne (Paris, 1971).
Praśna-upaniṣad: see Jacob, G. A.
Buddhacarita, ed. by E. S. Johnston (New Delhi, 1972).
Bhagavadgītā, ed. and trans, by Radhakrishnan (London, 1967).
Bhāgavatapurāṇa, ed. by the Nirṇaya Sāgara Prakāśana (Bombay, 1950).
Manthānabhairavatantra, NAK No. 5-1928/1009.
Mahānirvāṇatantra, ed. by A. Avalon (New Delhi, 1977).
Mahābhārata, ed. by The Bhandarkar Oriental Research Institute (5 vol.) (Poona, 1971-1976).
Mātṛkābhedatantra, ed. by Chintamani Bhattacharya (Calcutta, 1933).
Mānavadharmaśāstra: see Bühler, G.
Mālinīvijayottaratantra, ed. by M. K. Śāstri (Srinagar, 1922).
Meghadūta, ed, by M. R. Kale (New Delhi, 1969).
Vājasaneyisaṃhitā, ed. by Paṇḍit Jagadīśalāla Śāstri (New Delhi, 1971).
Vīṇāśikhatantra, NAK No. 1-1076/171.
Śāradātilakatantra, ed. by A. Avalon (2 parts) (Calcutta, 1933).
Śāradātilakatantra, ed. by M. J. Bakshi (Benares, 1963).
Śrīmatatantrasāra, NAK No. 5-4849/1538.
Śrīmatasāra, NAK No. 5-5849/1538.
Śvetāśvatara-upaniṣad: see Jacob, G. A.
Ṣaṭsāhasrasaṃhitā, MS A ASB No. 8329/5804; MS B NAK No. 5-428/54; MS C NAK No.5-4775/209.
Saṃvarodayatantra, ed, by S. Tsuda (selected chapters) (Tokyo, 1974).
Saṃvartāmaṇḍalasūtravyākhyā, NAK No. 5-879/199.
Saṃvartārthaprakāśa, NAK No. 4-1060/1622.
Sādhanamālā, ed. by B. Bhattacharyya (Baroda, 1925; 1928).
Svacchandatantra, ed. by M. K. Śāstri (7 vol.) (Srinagar, 1921-1935).
Haṭhayogapradīpikā, ed. by Pancham Singh (New York, 1974).

B. *Secondary Sources*

Bagchi, P.C.
1926 On Some Tantrik Texts Studied In Ancient Cambodia, in: IHQ Vol. V.
1930 idem, in: IHQ Vol. VI.
Bharati, A.
1965 The Tantric Tradition, London.
Bhattacharya, B.
1968 The Indian Buddhist Iconography, Calcutta.
Bhattacharya, D.C.
1974 Tantric Buddhist Iconographic Sources, New Delhi.
Bhattasali, N.N.
1972 Iconography of Buddhist and Brahmanical Sculptures in the Dacca Museum, Benares.
Bodewitz, H.W.
1973 Jaiminīya Brāhmaṇa I, 1-65, Leiden.
Briggs, G.W.
1973 Goraknāth and the Kānphaṭa Yogīs, New Delhi.
Brinkhaus, H.
1978 Die altindischen Mischkastensysteme, Wiesbaden.
Brunner, H.
1974 Un Tantra du Nord: Le "Netra Tantra", in: BEFEO Tome LXI, Paris.
Bühler, G.
1969 The Laws of Manu, New York.
Burrow, T, & Emenau, M.B.
1970 A Dravidian Etymological Dictionary, Oxford.
Cchabra, B.Ch.
1965 Expansion of Indo-Aryan Culture, New Delhi.
Coedès, G.
1964 Les États Hindouisés d'Indochine et d'Indonésie, Paris.
Damais, L.-Ch.
1962 Études Javanais II: Le Nom de la Déité Tantrique de 1214 Śaka, in: BEFEO Tome L, Paris.
Dey, N.L.
1971 The Geographical Dictionary of Ancient and Mediaeval India, New Delhi.
Dowson, J.
1968 Hindu Mythology, London.
Edgerton, F.
1953 Buddhist Hybrid Sanskrit Grammar and Dictionary (two volumes), New Haven.
Farquhar, J.N.
1920 Outline of the Religious Literature of India, Oxford.
Gonda, J.
1938 Altind. *anta-*, *antara-*, usw., in: BKI 97, The Hague.
1947 Skt. *Utsava-* "festival", in: India Antiqua, a Volume of Oriental Studies presented to J.Ph. Vogel, Leiden.
1960 Die Religionen Indiens I, Stuttgart.
1963 Die Religionen Indiens II, Stuttgart.
1969 Aspects of Early Viṣṇuism, New Delhi.
Goudriaan, T.
1981 Two Stanzas of Balinese Sanskrit Located in an Indian Tantra, in: BKI 137-4, The Hague.
Goudriaan, T. & Gupta, S.
1981 Hindu Tantric and Śākta Literature, Wiesbaden.
Goudriaan, T. & Hooykaas, Ch.
1971 Stuti and Stava, Amsterdam.
Gulik, R.H. van
1961 Sexual Life in Ancient China, a preliminary survey of Chinese sex and society from c. 1500 B.C. till 1644 A.D., Leiden.

Gupta, S., Hoens, D. J. & Goudriaan, T.
1979 Hindu Tantrism, Leiden/Köln.
Haarh, E.
1968 The Zhang-Zhung Language, København.
Hazra, R. C.
1963 Studies in the Upapurānas, Vol. II, Calcutta.
Jacob, G. A.
1971 A Concordance to the Principal Upaniṣads and Bhagavadgītā, New Delhi.
Johnston, E. S.
1930 Some Sāṃkhya and Yoga Conceptions of the Śvetāśvatara Upaniṣad, in: JRAS.
Kane, P. V.
1968-'77 History of Dharmaśāstra (five volumes), Poona.
Kavirāj, J. G.
1972 Tāntrika Sāhitya (in Hindi), Lucknow.
Khanna, M.
1979 Yantra, the Tantric symbol of cosmic unity, London.
Kirfel, W.
1967 Die Kosmographie der Inder, Hildesheim.
Kohlbrugge, D. J.
1938 Atharvaveda-Pariśiṣṭa über Omina, Wageningen.
Kooy, K. R. van
1972 Worship of the Goddess according to the Kālikāpurāṇa (Vol. I), Leiden.
1973 A Critical Edition of the Kubjikāmatatantra, in: BSOAS Vol. XXVI-3, London.
1977 Die sogenannte Guptahandschrift des Kubjikāmatatantra, in: ZDMG Suppl. III-2, Wiesbaden.
Kosambi, D. D.
1977 The Culture and Civilisation of Ancient India in Historical Outline, New Delhi.
Kramrisch, S.
1964 The Art of Nepal, Vienna.
Kuiper, F. B. J.
1948 Proto-Munda Words in Sanskrit, Amsterdam.
Lorenzen, D. N.
1972 The Kāpālikas and Kālāmukhas, two lost Śaivite sects, New Delhi.
Mallmann, M.-Th. de
1963 Les Enseignements Iconographiques de l'Agni-Purana, Paris.
1975 Introduction à l'Iconographie du Tantrisme Bouddhique, Paris.
Marqués-Rivière, J.
1950 Amulets, Talismans & Pantacles, Paris.
Meulenbeld, G. J.
1974 The Mādhavanidhāna and its chief commentaries, Leiden.
Mitra, R. L.
1971 The Sanskrit Buddhist Literature of Nepal, Calcutta.
Mookerjee, A. & Khanna, M.
1977 The Tantric Way, London.
Monier-Williams, M.
1951 Hinduism, Calcutta.
1964 A Sanskrit-English Dictionary, Oxford.
Negelein, J. von
1912 Der Traumschlüssel des Jagaddeva, Giessen.
Neumann, E.
1974 The Great Mother, Princeton.
Padoux, A.
1975 Recherches sur la Symbolique et l'Énergie de la Parole dans certains textes Tantriques, Paris.
Pandey, L. P.
1971 Sun Worship in Ancient India, New Delhi.

Pāṇḍeya, J.
1976 The Gorakṣasaṃhitā (Part I), Benares.
Pāṇini, see: Renou.
Poerwadarminta, W.J.S. & Teeuw, H.
1950 Indonesisch-Nederlands Woordenboek, Groningen.
Przyluski, J.
1950 La Grande Déesse, Paris.
Rau, W.
1972 Töpferei und Tongeschirr im vedischen Indien, Wiesbaden.
Rawson, Ph.
1971 Tantra, catalogue of the Tantra Exhibition at the Hayword Gallery, London.
1973 Tantra, the Indian Cult of Ecstasy, London.
1978 The Art of Tantra, London.
Regmi, D.R.
1965 Medieval Nepal (Part I), Calcutta.
1966 Medieval Nepal (Part II & III), Calcutta.
Renou, L.
1966 La Grammaire de Pāṇini (two vol.), Paris.
Ruben, W.
1939 Eisenschmiede und Dämonen in Indien, Leiden.
Sahai, Bh.
1975 Iconography of Minor Hindu and Buddhist Deities. New Delhi.
Śāstri, H.P.
1905 A Catalogue of Palm-leaf & Selected Paper MSS belonging to the Durbar Library, Nepal (Vol. I), Calcutta.
1915 idem Vol. II, Calcutta.
Schoterman, J.A.
1977 Some Remarks on the Kubjikāmatatantra, in: ZDMG Suppl. III-2, Wiesbaden.
1979 A Note on Balinese Sanskrit, in: BKI 135-2/3, The Hague.
1980 A Link between Purāṇa and Tantra: Agnipurāṇa 143-147, in: ZDMG Suppl. IV, Wiesbaden.
1981 An Introduction to Old Javanese Sanskrit Dictionaries and Grammars, in: BKI 137-4, The Hague.
Sharan, M.K.
1974 Studies in Sanskrit Inscriptions of Ancient Cambodia, New Delhi.
Sircar, D.C.
1965 Select Inscriptions bearing on Indian History and Civilisation, New Delhi.
1973 The Śākta Pīṭhas, New Delhi.
Sprockhoff, J.F.
1979 Die Alten im alten Indien, ein Versuch nach brahmanischen Quellen, in: Saeculum XXX-4, Freiburg/München.
Tucci, G. & Heissig, W.
1970 Die Religionen Tibets und der Mongolei, Stuttgart.
Whitehead, H.
1921 The Village Gods of South India, London.
Woodroffe, J.
1975 Śakti and Śākta, Madras.
1978 Principles of Tantra (two vol.), Madras.

INDEX

(References to specific lines of the text also include the accompanying Notes)